American Gothic Literature

ALSO OF INTEREST AND FROM MCFARLAND

Property and Power in English Gothic Literature
by Ruth Bienstock Anolik (2016)

*Demons of the Body and Mind: Essays on Disability
in Gothic Literature* edited by Ruth Bienstock Anolik (2010)

*Horrifying Sex: Essays on Sexual Difference
in Gothic Literature* edited by Ruth Bienstock Anolik (2007)

*The Gothic Other: Racial and Social Constructions
in the Literary Imagination* edited by Ruth Bienstock Anolik
and Douglas L. Howard (2004)

American Gothic Literature

*A Thematic Study
from Mary Rowlandson
to Colson Whitehead*

RUTH BIENSTOCK ANOLIK

McFarland & Company, Inc., Publishers
Jefferson, North Carolina

LIBRARY OF CONGRESS CATALOGUING-IN-PUBLICATION DATA

Names: Anolik, Ruth Bienstock, 1952– author.
Title: American gothic literature : a thematic study from Mary Rowlandson to Colson Whitehead / Ruth Bienstock Anolik.
Description: Jefferson, North Carolina : McFarland & Company, Inc., 2019 | Includes bibliographical references and index.
Identifiers: LCCN 2018042894 | ISBN 9780786498512 (softcover : acid free paper) ∞
Subjects: LCSH: Gothic revival (Literature)—United States—History.
Classification: LCC PS374.G68 A85 2019 | DDC 813/.0872909—dc23
LC record available at https://lccn.loc.gov/2018042894

BRITISH LIBRARY CATALOGUING DATA ARE AVAILABLE

ISBN (print) 978-0-7864-9851-2
ISBN (ebook) 978-1-4766-3340-4

© 2019 Ruth Bienstock Anolik. All rights reserved

No part of this book may be reproduced or transmitted in any form or by any means, electronic or mechanical, including photocopying or recording, or by any information storage and retrieval system, without permission in writing from the publisher.

Front cover image by Shaun Lowe (iStock)

Printed in the United States of America

McFarland & Company, Inc., Publishers
  Box 611, Jefferson, North Carolina 28640
  www.mcfarlandpub.com

To the memories of my loved ones:

Vince Hausmann: Maybe you were right.
But thanks for the ongoing inspiration.

Dorene Hirsch and Clara Schneider:
For always being there in Bayside.

Herbert and June Bienstock:
I continue to stand on your shoulders.

Acknowledgments

Thanks to everyone who patiently waited for me to emerge into the land of the living.

To Bob: Thank you for the decades of patience with the Gothic chaos, and for your ongoing technical support.

To Jonathan and Rachel Anolik, and Sarah Anolik Katz (and your loved ones): for making my life more interesting and complicated than any Gothic novel. Thanks for the inspiration.

To Josh and Linda: I'm glad you're still here.

To the Carel family. David: Thanks for your interest and research help. Warren and Cecily: Thanks for bringing David, and Lauren, into my life, for your support and patience, and for everything else! Lauren: Thank you for perfectly completing the set.

To Frieda Lefeber: Thank you for your friendship and wisdom, with gratitude to you for generously sharing your artwork.

To Mary Garvin: Thanks for the gifts of time and your kindness.

To Peter Vari: Thanks for your last-minute contribution.

To Barbie Zelizer: Thanks for your interest and for your brilliant suggestion.

For Carol Bernstein, Sandra Berwind, Peter Briggs, Susan Dean, and Katrin Burlin: "She had been working at [the manuscript] for close on three hundred years now. It was time to make an end" (Virginia Woolf, *Orlando*). Thanks for the decades of challenge and support.

Table of Contents

Acknowledgments vi

Introduction: Power and Possession in American Gothic Literature 1

Part I. Possessed and Dispossessed

1. The American Woman: Still Possessed 18
2. A New Possession: Slavery and Beyond 34
3. Return of the Dead: The Rebirth of the Dispossessed Native American 55

Part II. Possessing and Dispossessed

4. Dispossessed Possessor: The Displaced Patriarch 78
5. Masterless: The Anxieties of Freedom 104
6. Return of the Master: The New Patriarch 143

Part III. Gothic Conversations: Transgressing the Boundaries of American Cultures; Crossing the Atlantic

7. Textual (Dis)Possessions: Hannah Crafts a Textual Labyrinth 178
8. Intertextual Voices in Gloria Naylor's *Mama Day*: Shakespeare, the Bible and the Dispossession of the Reader 221
9. Among Women: Convergences and Divergences in Gothic Space 234

Conclusion: Toward a Fourth Century of American Gothic 271

Chapter Notes 281

Works Cited 294

Index 303

Introduction
Power and Possession in American Gothic Literature

American fiction begins with Charles Brockden Brown, the first citizen of the United States of America to write novels (in the 1790s); that is to say American literature begins with the Gothic novel with all its recurrent trappings, including a central preoccupation with issues of possession and power of all kinds. The dominance of the Gothic mode in Brown's writing stands to reason since the Gothic was a dominant form in England during the 1790s, the decade that saw the blossoming of Ann Radcliffe, the mother of the English Gothic, and the explosion of Matthew Lewis' *The Monk* in 1796. The influence may have been working both ways. Recent scholarship suggests that the roots of the English Gothic are to be found in two earlier related forms of American literature: the providence tale, which identifies the Puritan belief in the spiritual and supernatural presence within everyday life; and the captivity narrative, which tells the horrifying stories of Europeans, mainly women, captured by "inhuman" Native Americans. Nancy Armstrong and Leonard Tennenhouse make a compelling case in *The Imaginary Puritan* that the American captivity narrative influenced the rise of the British novel, as in Samuel Richardson's English captivity tales, *Pamela* (1740) and *Clarissa* (1748). James Hartman develops this insight in *Providence Tales and the Birth of American Literature*, asserting that the prevalence of the supernatural in the Gothic mode derives from the writing of the American Puritans—the providence tale and the captivity narrative—which provides the central trope of confinement as well as the struggle between inhuman, supernatural, absolute Evil and the innocent subject: "Gothic action and setting constitute a ... major convention common to all these tales. Violence and torture fill Cotton Mather's Indian stories" (Hartman 27). Thus the Puritan contribution to American culture includes the literary tendency toward the lurid and supernatural, in addition to the affinity for rigidity in religion, law, and culture. Bridget Marshall also makes a case for the interrelatedness of the English and the American Gothic in *The Transatlantic Gothic Novel and the Law*. She notes that Brown was actually a transatlantic figure, who "enjoyed a better reputation in England and France than in America" (91). Thus, from its origins, the American Gothic has conversed with the British versions of this transgressive mode, which resists all boundaries including generic boundaries, and boundaries between national literatures.

Yet synchronization and influence are not enough to account for the affinity of the new American literature for the English form. As Siân Silyn Roberts notes in "A Transnational Perspective on American Gothic Criticism": "Clearly something about the Gothic form spoke to American interests, something that goes well beyond the repudiation of British themes or its ability to articulate an indigenous culture" (22). Mark Edmundson observes, as do many other writers, that the Gothic mode becomes a safe way to contain and anchor social fears: "the anxiety is displaced and brought under temporary, tenuous control" (12) in the Gothic, allowing for the safe exploration of real fears. The new American writers, beginning with Brown, were thus attracted to the tropology of the English form because it was well suited to articulate their anxious and dark experience and world view. Inhabitants of new America found themselves, like the English Gothic subject, in constant encounter with the dangerous unknown, the dark uncharted frontier, and the mysterious, seemingly spectral Other, the Native American. Thanks to Cotton Mather and other pre–Revolutionary Puritan writers like Mary Rowlandson, author of a captivity narrative, the American enterprise had already been set up as a blood-curdling Gothic struggle between supernatural forces for Good and Evil. Americans in their new home were already haunted by a dark past and present: the parricide of the Revolutionary War, and the ongoing genocide of African Americans and Native Americans.

Other writers have explored similar themes. In *The Transatlantic Gothic Novel and the Law, 1790–1860*, Marshall identifies realistically grounded anxieties shared by the two countries, and expressed in the Gothic literature of each: "Along with the extreme and sometimes laughable horrors that Gothic novels portrayed, they also quite often … reflected concerns about very real horrors of their readers' contemporary world, especially in the realm of the legal system…. In both England and America, the legal system was the subject of concern and plans for reform" (154–155). As Marshall suggests, the law only appeared to be sane and rational; below the surface it was an insane and cruel system. The Gothic highlights this reality for its readers, Marshall argues, as it opposes the irrationally cruel law with humane "morality, justice and even reason" (160). Karen Weyler also points to "the historical association of the gothic with political criticism" (*Intricate Relations* 4). In *Nightmare on Main Street*, Mark Edmundson adds that the particular affinity for the Gothic in recent American culture derives from the pervasiveness of fin-de-siècle anxiety. This insight also roots the American Gothic tradition to the English Gothic: the moment of origin of the English Gothic was the decade preceding the turn of the nineteenth century. In my book on the English Gothic, I develop this notion, pointing to moments where the true source of Gothic horror is neither supernatural nor inhuman, but is instead the monstrous human tyrant and the legal or religious system that sustains him. I also argue that the English Gothic, developing in the late eighteenth century, was working to oppose the new forms of containment and control that were also developing in the eighteenth century, as observed by Michel Foucault.

Thus, as Brown asserts in the often-quoted passage in his note "To the Public" in *Edgar Huntly* (1799), all that was necessary to create a new American Gothic from the English form was a simple exchange of old images for new: "Puerile superstitions and exploded manners; Gothic castles and chimera, are the materials usually employed for this end [engaging the reader]. The incidents of Indian hostility, and the perils of the western wilderness are far more suitable [for] a native of America" (3-4). As Brown suggests, the English Gothic presents a welcoming and familiar space for the American writer. As he also suggests, the American Gothic must revise the English so that it can reflect American settings and anxieties.

* * *

The American writer also found in the English Gothic a mode already predisposed to contemplate another set of issues with which Americans were grappling: questions of power and property, of great interest to a country that was exploring new ways of taking ownership, including appropriating Native American and English property, and taking possession of the lives and bodies of African Americans. In *Property and Power in English Gothic Literature*, I argue that an anxious preoccupation with all matters of possession and power is the link between the disparate texts that bear the English Gothic label. Anxieties regarding the powers of property inheritance and possession may be teased out of a variety of Gothic tropes: the dark, labyrinthine property; the usurped property; the possessing ghost. Anxieties about self-possession, the power of self-control, are expressed in the trope of slippery identities that can easily be lost and restored, in the motif of the confined or fleeing woman and the dangerously evil man, and in the ghostly possession of human beings, and the recurrences of madness and other altered states. Anxieties of authorial power and possession appear in the tropes of the lost or fragmented manuscript. As the material contexts of possession and power change in America, the Gothic conventions evolve to reflect this.[1] In the conclusion of *Property and Power in English Gothic Literature*, I propose an examination of how changing conditions of possession and power in America result in American transformations of Gothic literature, the project of the current book.

Transatlantic Gothic

Despite the shared concerns and cultural connections between the English and American Gothic, surprisingly little critical attention has been focused on the convergence and divergence of the two. Bridget M. Marshall has done much work to focus attention on this lacuna and to replace it with scholarship. In *The Transatlantic Gothic Novel and the Law, 1790–1860*, Marshall notes that transatlantic studies of the Gothic are unusual: "Most scholars of the Gothic are clearly rooted in either the British or American tradition" (2). Marshall adds that "establishing a stark line between British and American Gothic seems specious" (3) since "transatlantic exchange was particularly important to the genre of the Gothic novel" (3). In the Introduction to *Transnational Gothic: Literary and Social Exchanges in the Long Nineteenth Century*, Marshall and her co-editor Monika Elbert address the need for a critical "perspective that eschews national borders in order to explore the central role that cross-cultural exchange played in the development of the Gothic" (1). They propose the "English-language Gothic" (6) as a term to encompass all literatures that have a deep interrelated connection, to encourage awareness of "the way the Gothic transgresses national borders and is reinterpreted as it crosses cultures" (6). This stance might appear problematic in that it suggests erasing literary differences that deserve critical attention; however, it is tempered by an essay in Elbert and Marshall's collection. In "A Transnational Perspective on American Gothic Criticism," Siân Silyn Roberts notes "the Gothic's remarkable formal adaptability," adding that "the majority of critics tend to agree" that the American version is "an altogether new incarnation of the form, with wholly 'American' preoccupations … chiefly race, frontier expansion and revolution" (22).

American Gothic Revisions

Despite the usefulness of recognizing the relationship of the English and American Gothic, it is essential to note the unique qualities of the American

Gothic. Since the anxieties of power and possession are generated by tensions evoked by actual legal and cultural contexts, which vary among nations, the American Gothic evolves as the material contexts of law and culture change, indicating the continuing flexibility of the Gothic mode. Thus, while both English and American forms align in meaningful ways, ultimately the American Gothic transforms the mode to address the unique anxieties of the new world, and in doing so establishes a new form.

The American Gothic creates or recreates a variety of Gothic patterns. One American revision is the locus of horror. In the English form, fear is usually found in a distant exotic location, far from rational England. The American Gothic model presents horror much closer to home—in the invasion of the foreign into a home-like sanctuary. This new American paradigm somewhat jarringly suggests the experience of the Other, the Native American in America, and appears throughout the American Gothic canon, as early as Brown's *Wieland* (1798) and as recently as Colson Whitehead's *Zone One* (2011). The American Gothic responds to other uniquely American concerns: the anxieties evoked by participating in the parricidal American Revolution, the explosive convergence of the Romantic notions of selfhood and Enlightenment fears of authority in American political ideologies. As in the English Gothic, the horrifying events of the French Revolution posed new challenges to Romantic ideologies of liberation, resulting in uniquely American doubts about its foundational principles. American anxieties about deviating from rational non-revolutionary Enlightenment principles lead to images of the mad and possessed American patriarch, as in Brown's *Wieland* (1798).

Before moving to the variety of ways in which the American Gothic revises the terms of the English Gothic, Part I of this book, "Possessed and Dispossessed," begins with a chapter focused on the static situation of the American woman as reflected in the American Gothic. As the title of Chapter 1, "The American Woman: Still Possessed," suggests, the situation of women did not change much after the Revolution because English common law, governing women's rights, continued to limit the freedom of American women, largely through the systems of *coverture* and primogeniture. Thus the American Female Gothic, written by and for women, presents a close approximation of the English Female Gothic. Writers of the nineteenth century, like Louisa May Alcott, Charlotte Perkins Gilman, and Elizabeth Stoddard, and more recent writers, like Edith Wharton and Gloria Naylor, turn to the English Gothic forms to articulate the still-horrifying situation of American women.

The other chapters in Part I move toward Gothic texts that address more uniquely American problems of personal power and possession. Chapter 2,

"A New Possession: Slavery and Beyond," addresses the anxieties that developed in response to the "peculiar institution" of chattel slavery. These anxieties are to be found in the nineteenth-century work of white writers, like Edgar Allan Poe, and African American writers like Frederick Douglass and Harriet Jacobs (writers of slave narratives), and Charles Chesnutt. Indeed, Toni Morrison (whose fiction and theory demonstrate the uses of the Gothic in the representation of American anxieties) asserts that the darkness at the root of the American Gothic represents the discomfort of white America with the black Other: "a resident population, already black, upon which the imagination could play; through which historical, moral, metaphysical, and social fears, problems, and dichotomies could be articulated. The slave population, it could be and was assumed, offered itself up as surrogate selves for meditation on problems of human freedom, its lure and its elusiveness" ("Romancing the Shadow" 37).

Teresa Goddu also argues that anxieties and guilt generated by those dispossessed by American history result in the persistence of the Gothic in American literature: "the gothic infiltrates and informs the canon of American literature" (8), "specific sites of historical haunting, most notably slavery" (10), but also "the violent origins of the nation in Indian massacre" (*Gothic America* 11). Arnold Krupat argues even more forcefully for the inclusion of Native Americans within the paradigm of American Gothic literature, arguing, with some justice, that Morrison's reading is competitive and exclusionary. As Krupat says of Morrison, "despite her admirable desire to map a new geographical 'space for discovery, intellectual adventure, and close exploration'... she does not find a place within that space for the literature of 'the indigenous American'" ("Review: Red Matters" 657). Chapter 3, "Return of the Dead: The Rebirth of the Dispossessed Native American," moves to American Gothic representations of this shameful American particularity, the dispossession and dislocation of the powerless Native Americans, starting with the pre–Revolutionary demonization of the Native American in the writing of Puritan writers like Cotton Mather and Mary Rowlandson. The anxieties evoked by the mistreatment of Native Americans are also addressed by post–Revolutionary white American writers like Charles Brockden Brown and Edgar Allan Poe, and by contemporary Native American writers like Sherman Alexie and Louise Erdrich. Much of this fiction imagines (with varying degrees of horror and triumph) the return of the repressed Native American as does D.H. Lawrence in his idiosyncratic but incisive *Studies in Classic American Literature* (1923). Lawrence anticipates an America haunted by the returning ghosts of the repressed and unknown Native American:

The Red Man died hating the white man. What remnant of him lives, lives hating the white man.... He is dispossessed in life, and unforgiving. He doesn't believe in us and our civilization, and so is our mystic enemy, for we pushed him off the face of the earth.... The Red Man is dead, disbelieving in us.

He is dead and unappeased. Do not imagine him happy in his happy Hunting Ground. No. Only those that die in belief die happy. Those that are pushed out of life in chagrin come back unappeased for revenge ["Fenimore Cooper's White Novels" 35].

* * *

While Part I of this book concentrates on the marginalized and dispossessed in Gothic America, Part II, "Possessing and Dispossessed," focuses on a more dominant and powerful figure, the white patriarch, and also on his counterpart, the young powerless white man. This pair of male figures appear with regularity in the English Gothic (including Walpole's *Otranto*; Radcliffe's *Sicilian Romance*, *Mysteries of Udolpho*, *The Italian*; and Lewis' *The Monk*) and are transformed in the American Gothic. In the English Gothic the powerful and tyrannical aristocratic patriarch is the central source of fear; he fully possesses his wife and children, his castle and his wealth—much of which he has acquired through illegal or immoral means. The anxious representation of this figure reflects the real dangers posed by patriarchal tyranny. The good young man—sometimes the patriarch's son, or the lover of the patriarch's daughter—has little independent power or wealth by virtue of age and social standing. Yet he frequently counters the immoral powers of the patriarch. Often the Gothic novel moves toward a reversal of positions: the corrupt patriarch is unmasked and dispossessed, and the good young man replaces him, often through inheritance, or by marrying the patriarch's daughter. The smooth maneuvering of the young man into a position of wealth and power reflects the social realities for a young man in England; he might begin life in a weak position, but he was destined to inherit his father's position, whether in the aristocracy or in trade. His path was clear and he merely had to weather the storms of youth to arrive at his designated situation. The fantasy of the English Gothic is that the young man will remain morally superior to the patriarch, even when he attains power and possession. Part II focuses on a different aspect of the Gothic narrative—picking up where the English Gothic ends: the fall and later rise of the patriarch, and the troubling impact of this counter-revoluion on the young American man in Gothic literature. Chapter 4, "Dispossessed Possessor: The Displaced Patriarch," tells a story unique to American history, only imagined in the English Gothic: the decline and fall of the monarchic and aristocratic patriarchy after the Revolutionary War. The new vacuum of leadership is emblematized by the headless horseman in Washington Irving's "The Legend of Sleepy Hollow," and the failed patriarch in Irving's "Rip Van Winkle" (1820). We also see examples of other unstable and deposed patriarchs in Harriet Beecher Stowe's *Uncle Tom's Cabin* (1852), Melville's *Beneto Cereno* (1856), and Mark Twain's *Pudd'nhead Wilson* (1894). Significantly the deposed men of Irving's stories literally and figuratively lose their heads as a consequence of the Revolutionary War; in the works of other writers, powerful patriarchs or their scions fail because of the destabilization of patriarchal identity in the wake of the Revolution, and, paradoxically, as a consequence of slavery.

Whereas the English Gothic fears the usurping peasant as much as the grasping aristocrat, the American Gothic presents a country populated by white male usurpers who fear the consequences of their deeds. American culture and history are founded upon the dispossession by white Europeans of property, self, and narrative of others: the property stolen from the English king, and from the Native Americans; the appropriated selves of African Americans. Indeed, Americans had to wrest their own selves and identities from the English,[2] and to appropriate the literature of England, reinventing it as American literature. The American Gothic thus expresses a sort of *horror vacui* (a fear of emptiness, to borrow a design term) regarding the recent absence of the master, and a fear of what will rush in to fill the vacuum left by the abjected English. In Chapter 5, "Masterless: The Anxieties of Freedom," we encounter a new American type—reflecting this new American reality: the young man who has become independent of his ruler and guide, and who stands to possess whatever he sees. This grasping young man often appears literally ravenous with hunger, like Brown's young Edgar Huntly, Irving's Ichabod Crane, and young Ned, the voracious customer who appears in Nathaniel Hawthorne's *The House of the Seven Gables* (1851). Rather than reveling in their freedom, many of these young men flounder, grappling with what Lawrence identifies in his essay "The Spirit of Place" as the fear of freedom, of being "masterless" (*Studies in Classic American Literature* 9). These texts are also concerned that American youth, lacking paternal guidance, will go astray in the uncharted wilds of America. Charles Brockden Brown's young anti-heroes, Edgar Huntly and Wieland, experience the dangers of masterlessness, as does Washington Irving's Ichabod Crane, though the fate of Brown's characters is tragic while Irving provides a comical solution for his young man. The last generation in Poe's "The Fall of the House of Usher" (1839) also illustrates the tragic aspects of orphan-hood, the vacuum left by the absent parent. Louisa May Alcott's potboiler, "Perilous Play" (1869), reacts to new freedoms for young people in her time by providing an example of young unguided women, as well as men, losing their path; her method is perhaps even more lurid than that of her male colleagues. Alcott's young protagonists ingest hashish to enhance their explorative wandering leading to dire consequences. Chapter 6, "Return of the Master: The New Patriarch," focuses on the return of that long-absent and repressed figure, the powerful and tyrannical patriarch, who emerged through the booming American economy after the Civil War, in the person of the robber baron. This chapter considers the endurance of the patriarch as he re-appears in F. Scott Fitzgerald's "The Diamond as Big as the Ritz" (1922), William Faulkner's *Absalom, Absalom!* (1936), Shirley Jackson's *The Haunting of Hill House* (1959), and Toni Morrison's *A Mercy* (2009).

The new American models of land acquisition, maintenance, and transmission are at the root of a number of the texts discussed in parts I and II. In England, concentrated patriarchal power was a consequence of the finite amount of land on that small island, resulting in competition and usurpation within the pool of heirs, at least in Gothic literature. In eighteenth-century America, the supply of land was virtually unlimited because of the "continuing expropriation of Native American populations" (Charles Post "Agrarian Class Structure and Economic Development in Colonial British North America" 465) allowing the young man who did not inherit land the alternate possibility of participating in the "continuous migration to lands made available through 'Indian removal'" (463). The diluted and diminished power of the American patriarchal landowner was thus also a consequence of readily available land. David Mogen, Scott P. Sanders and JoAnne Karpinski locate an additional set of anxieties resulting from the ongoing westward move. In their introduction to *Frontier Gothic* (1993), they locate the dark, mysterious Gothic space in the unknown landscape (cultural and geographic) that lies beyond the American frontier. The American Gothic, like the English Gothic, is preoccupied with boundaries, borders and walls; however, the different geographies result in different boundaries. In England the landscape is fully mapped and enclosed; to borrow Foucault's model, the land is fully contained within the structures of eighteenth-century political and epistemological power. In the American paradigm, the internal border demarcating the frontier separates the regions already under social and cultural control from those wild and unknown regions that are beyond the control of the systems of power, and that are occupied by mysterious dark Others, the Native Americans. The English Gothic protagonist has to journey to the foreign European continent to discover dark mystery,[3] Catholic Italy being a favorite. However, the American Gothic frequently takes place on American soil; American Gothic characters discover mystery in the country that they call home, right over the border of the frontier. As the American land becomes settled and mapped, Mogen et al. argue that a new frontier emerges, the cultural line between different peoples in America, the line separating the known Self from the mysterious Other. In this, they also indicate the cultural line that divides the American writer from any precursors, including but not limited to the English. This boundary results in a sense of belatedness and discomfort on the part of the American writer: first experienced by the early writers who felt excluded from the English tradition, and later, by Americans alienated from the "foreign" cultures of other Americans.

Leslie Fiedler sums up the array of American anxieties that culminate with the cultural anxiety of the American writer: "Through these gothic images are projected certain obsessive concerns of our national life: the ambiguity of our relationship with Indian and Negro, the ambiguity of our encounter with nature, the guilt of the revolutionist who feels himself a parricide—and, not least of all, the uneasiness of the writer who cannot help believing that the very act of composing a book is Satanic revolt" (*Love and Death in the American Novel* xxii). In a nation founded on Puritan principles, the idea that writing as an American is an act of revolt against the preceding English culture is potent indeed.

* * *

Thus American writers are haunted by feelings of inadequacy, and of guilt, as American literature finds itself haunted by the looming ghost of its predecessor, English literature. An accounting for the relationship between these two literatures may be found in Sigmund Freud's early twentieth-century model of the uncanny. Significantly, Freud deploys a metaphor of property and appropriation when describing the psychological state that "arouses dread and horror" ("The Uncanny" 193): "It does occasionally happen that he [the psychoanalyst] has to interest himself in some particular province of that subject [aesthetics]; and this province usually proves to be a rather remote one.... The subject of the 'uncanny' is a province of this kind" (193). Freud's notion of the uncanny is also rooted in the space of the home, which is often the central space of the Gothic. The word Freud uses for uncanny, "unheimlich," literally means un-homelike, meaning, as Freud indicates, "the opposite of what is familiar" (195). In this vocabulary, we may see the alignment of the Gothic with the uncanny: the Gothic is always the place of the "unheimlich": the uncomfortable home that is not at all homey; the dysfunctional family that occupies the dangerous and mysterious domicile. Freud points to the linguistic association of the Gothic and the uncanny: "some languages in use to-day can only render the German expression 'an *unheimlich* house' by 'a haunted house'" (218). Freud's formulation of the uncanny also indicates a useful application to the special situation of the

American Gothic. Freud states that the uncanny "occurs either when infantile complexes which have been repressed are once more revived by some impression, or when primitive beliefs which have been surmounted seem once more to be confirmed" (226). Thus the uncanny is "nothing new or alien, but something which is familiar and old-established in the mind and which has become alienated from it only through the process of repression ... something which ought to have remained hidden but has come to light" (217). Freud's model works well as an explanation of the relationship between the late-arriving American literature, and the long-established English literature, the earlier "infantile" form, or, to use Brown's term, the "puerile" stage that American literature seeks to repress. Thus the American Gothic may be understood as the uncanny returning double of its precursor, the English Gothic.

However, the imperatives of an enlightened and supposedly innocent young America dictate that our fictions be sunny and rational. In fact, to use Freud's terminology, American culture and literature attempt to repress any tendencies toward the dark haunted literature of the English past, as illustrated by an early critical tendency to deny the Gothic presence in American literature.[4] As Mogen et al. note, "the early American literary commentator James Kirke Paulding urged writers to create 'rational fictions' consistent with the enlightened spirit of the eighteenth century" (13). Brown's statement in the Preface to *Edgar Huntly*, quoted above, quite clearly indicates his plan to repress English forms and "superstitions." Hawthorne, a possibly more disingenuous—or more anxious—critic than Paulding (in light of his own authorship of *The House of the Seven Gables* [1851] and *The Scarlet Letter* [1850] as well as other similarly Gothic shorter works), writes in his preface to *The Marble Faun* (1860), a Gothic novel conventionally set in foreign Italy, "No author, without a trial, can conceive of the difficulty of writing a romance about a country where there is no shadow, no antiquity, no mystery, no picturesque and gloomy wrong, nor anything but a commonplace prosperity, in broad and simple daylight, as is happily the case with my dear native land" (vi). By 1860 this was patently untrue, as America already had many dark wrongs in its short past, with clearly more to come in the near future. Irving, too, paradoxically denies the Gothic mode while engaging it. In his ghost story "The Legend of Sleepy Hollow" (1820), he presents a disclaimer of the possibilities of haunting in new, busy America:

> Local tales and superstitions thrive best in these sheltered long-settled retreats; but are trampled underfoot by the shifting throng that forms the population of most of our country places. Besides, there is no encouragement for ghosts in most of our villages, for they have scarcely had time to finish their first nap, and turn themselves in their graves, before their surviving friends have traveled away from the neighborhood;

> so that when they turn out at night to walk their rounds, they have no acquaintance left to call up. This is perhaps the reason why we so seldom hear of ghosts. [Irving *The Legend of Sleepy Hollow and Other Stories* 289].

Fiedler accounts for the American discomfort with the Gothic, and for the need to dissociate America and American literature from the Gothic shadows of Europe: "By the time our own first attempts [at the Gothic] were being made, there was everywhere in the United States (aware of itself as a product of the Enlightenment) an uneasiness with darkness of all kinds.... Certainly the generation of Jefferson was pledged to be done with ghosts and shadows, committed to live a life of yea-saying in a sunlit, neo-classical world" (128). Thus the Gothic mode, with its dark evocations of revolution and social disorder, simply does not fit comfortably with early representations of a bright national myth of origins.

Yet the realities of American history and culture demand that the darkness of the past culture that we seek to repress, the English Gothic, reappear in a new and unrecognizable form, the American Gothic. American writers cannot refuse the repressed that returns, finding in the dark recesses of the Gothic a literature resonant with the repressed dark history, and tormented irrational reality of American culture. Indeed, the Gothic mode makes an early appearance in American literature in the work of Brown, Irving, and Hawthorne and endures persistently in the centuries that follow.[5] As Chris Baldick asserts, the Gothic mode "has remained defiantly undead as a significant presence in Western literature ever since [the end of the high Gothic period in the late 1820s]" (Introduction *Melmoth* ix). The American text is thus haunted by this uncanny and undead literature, the literature that recalls the past culture that America seeks to repress, evoking the uncanny realization that Freud articulates: "'So the dead *do* live on'" (224). There are, of course, moments when the repressed returns unmediated, in its original form; for example, in one passage of *Huntly*, Brown slips just a little. Writing of his entrapment in the wilderness Huntly narrates, "It was of little moment whether the scene of my imprisonment was a dungeon not to be broken, or a summit from which descent was impossible" (216). Thus the very landscape of America is itself *unheimlich*: like the English home—or dungeon—yet uncannily unlike the English space. The *unheimlich* quality of the American landscape is yet another explanation for the American location of the Gothic narrative in an American setting; for Americans, the uncanny is to be found right at home.

* * *

Harold Bloom's characterization of American literature as belated and nostalgic aligns with Freud's notion that the uncanny refers back to earlier repressed experiences. In *The Western Canon* Bloom asserts that American writers are acutely aware of arriving late to the Western tradition (32). Bloom's insight also works to explain the dedication of American literature to the Gothic tradition, which is also nostalgic and belated, always yearning for a return to the ideal pre-narrative, pre-adult state, England in the American case. The awareness of the vast looming tradition haunts the imagination of the belated and excluded American writer. Susan Manning, the writer of the introduction to *The Sketch Book* by Washington Irving quotes from Irving's sketch of his attempt to visit the Reading Room of the British Museum: "The librarian now stepped up to me and demanded whether I had a card of admission.... I soon found that the library was a kind of literary 'preserve,' subject to game laws, and that no one must presume to hunt there without special license and permission." Manning explains that the sketch "presents the problem for all aspirant American authors in the century following the Declaration of Independence. How was an American—in rebellion from and in thrall to a parent literature, coming belatedly into a field pre-possessed by august forebears—to gain legitimate access to a chosen profession on new terms?" (Introduction, *The Sketch Book* vi). Harold Bloom adds, "Cultural belatedness ... has a particular poignance in the United States of America. We are the final inheritors of the Western tradition" (*The Western Canon* 32).

While the first American writers sensed that they were belated to the tradition, the writers who followed them had additional reasons to experience the poignancy of belatedness. Previously excluded writers—immigrants, women, African Americans, and Native Americans—who had not partaken of the American canon from the outset, each experienced a new moment of belatedness to the developing American tradition. These newly-arrived writers turned to the Gothic not to create something new, as Kathleen Brogan suggests in *Cultural Haunting*, but to stake out their own territory, as their American precursors had done before them. Like their precursors, the new American writers discovered in the Gothic an inclusive, welcoming canon, with a longstanding preoccupation with dispossession and displacement. Additionally the Gothic tradition presented the opportunity to translate the superstitions of the old country into an acceptable American form. In the essay "American Stories of Cultural Haunting" and the subsequent monograph *Cultural Haunting*, Kathleen Brogan persuasively argues for the presence of a particular strain of ethnic Gothic writing: tales of "cultural haunting" that make use of the familiar Gothic trappings—haunted houses, family secrets, endangered inheritances, imprisonment and escape, and encounters with the unspeakable and the supernatural ("American Stories" 149)—to explore the collective history and memory that ghosts emblematize. In Brogan's formulation, the ghost stories of marginalized writers are the alternative to official history and the figure of the ghost is a response to a troubled and disrupted past.[6] As Brogan's study and the books discussed in Part III—"Gothic Conversations: Transgressing the Boundaries of American Cultures; Crossing the Atlantic"—suggest, the Gothic mode, traditionally associated with women, and other marginalized people, holds a particular appeal for ethnic women writers. As members of an ethnic group, these women are alienated from the dominant culture because they are belated to the tradition. As women, they are alienated from their own culture as the result of gendered cultural constraints. Indeed, female ethnic writers are doubly dispossessed as women because the dominant culture to which they aspire is often also informed by a tradition of displacing women.

* * *

Teresa Goddu's observation about African American writers may be usefully applied to other newly-emerging groups: "African-American authors' appropriation and revision of gothic conventions shows that the gothic is not a transhistorical, static category but a dynamic mode that undergoes historical change when specific agents adopt and transform its conventions" (*Gothic America* 152). Mogen et al. reframe this discussion in their terms, that of the "frontier gothic"; in multi-cultural America, as the geographic frontier is replaced by the social, cultural frontier, the line that divides different groups, beyond which other unknown and mysterious American cultures beckon. They write:

> Gothicism must abide on a frontier—whether physical or psychical.... American frontier gothic literature explores frontiers in social, racial, and gender politics as well.... The immanence of the gothic otherness makes the frontier gothic mode especially attractive to those who write from the margins of the traditional canon, whose work expresses the experience of those who have been displaced ... the literature of American frontier gothic reveals that positive and negative forces are entwined in the pluralism that is at the heart of the American experience, in the parallel realities lived by the myriad groups of individuals who together are America. The revelation of not just dissonances, but of fundamental differences in our varied experiences of the structure of reality is cause for wonder and for terror, for hope and for anxiety [26].

The Gothic transgressions of social and cultural boundaries appear in the intertextual conversations covered in Part III. Building on the discussions of African American, Native American and female American writers in Part I, Part III considers what happens when these American writers come together (or bring others together) for discussion in the common space of Gothic literature. Chapter 7, "Textual (Dis)Possession: Hannah Crafts a Textual Labyrinth," attempts to untangle a web of texts that Hannah Crafts weaves in *The Bondswoman's Narrative* (1853–1860). These texts include Charles Dickens' *Bleak House* (1852–1853) and Hawthorne's *The House of the Seven Gables* (1851). Chapter 8, "Intertextual Voices in Gloria Naylor's *Mama Day*: Shakespeare, the Bible and the Dispossession of the Reader," considers what happens when a female African American writer brings Shakespeare's magical *The Tempest* and the Bible—both packed with magical images of slavery, of liberation, of salvation, and of resurrection—into her story of the descendants of slaves. The final chapter, Chapter 9, "Among Women: Convergences and Divergences in Gothic Space," examines a slightly more contentious intertextual conversation between a group of Jewish American writers—Cynthia Ozick, Marge Piercy, Judith Katz and Ellen Galford—as they each re-create a supernatural folk figure in order to carve out their own space within the Jewish patriarchal tradition. The maternal anxieties that appear in these texts open up the conversation to additional texts: Cynthia Ozick's *The Shawl*; *Beloved* by the African American writer Toni Morrison; "The Shawl" by the Native American writer Louise Erdrich. Part III of this book thus reveals the uses that contemporary American writers continue to make of the permeable, multi-vocal Gothic text.

A key argument of this book is that the flexible and constantly evolving Gothic mode remains both popular and culturally important, as the terms of power and possession that haunt Western culture continue to evolve. The Conclusion, "Toward a Fourth Century of American Gothic," considers the ongoing evolution of the American Gothic, focusing on the meanings of our two most recent monsters: the vampire and the zombie.

Part I

Possessed and Dispossessed

1

The American Woman
Still Possessed

Despite the transformations of the Revolutionary War, the conditions of the married woman under American law remained almost identical to the situation of the English wife under English common law. In 1854, the English reformer Barbara Bodichon observed, "The laws in the United States are generally much the same as ours" (132). Linda K. Kerber notes this as a paradox of American revolutionary ideology:

> The revolutionary generation of men who so radically transgressed inherited understandings of the relationship between kings and men, fathers and sons, nevertheless refused to revise inherited understandings of the relationship between men and women, husbands and wives, mothers and children. They continued to assert patriarchal privilege as heads of households and as civic actors.... When American revolutionaries challenged laws governing the relations between male subjects and the king, reconstituting men as individuals free of patriarchal constraint, they left intact the system of the old English law of domestic relations [*No Constitutional Right to Be Ladies* 9, 11].

In *The Transatlantic Gothic Novel and the Law, 1790–1860*, Bridget Marshall notes the struggle of the new American legal system: "During and after the American Revolution, Americans wrestled with whether (and how) to import and interpret British law for the American scene.... English Common Law was eventually accepted" (3). Thus the Revolution that destabilized the old order and re-inscribed the identity of the American male citizen made little impact upon the identity of the post–Revolutionary American woman who found herself in the same situation as her pre–Revolutionary self and her English counterpart. Winston Langley and Vivian Fox also note the continuing influence of English common law on the American legal system: "English settlers brought with them to the American colonies the common law system ... the *Commentaries* of William Blackstone ... became the ... primary reference on women's position throughout the nineteenth century"

(*Women's Rights in the United States* 6–7). Langley and Fox further observe: "Colonization and revolution in America did not fundamentally alter the English common law tradition of the legal identity of a husband and wife [*coverture*]. Although each colony and then state enacted its own laws on property and inheritance rights, in principle, the position of married women fit Blackstone's description that 'husband and wife are one in law'" (80). Kerber reminds us that the concept of *coverture* determines the rights of the husband over the body of the wife as well: "the old law of domestic relations began from the principle that at marriage the husband controlled the physical body of the wife.... There followed from this premise the elaborate system of *coverture* ... treating married women as 'covered' by their husbands' civic identity, ... placing sharp constraints on the extent to which married women controlled their bodies and their property" (xxiii). Donna Dickenson provides a useful context for the operation of the old system in America. "Coverture can be seen as a form of backlash: not only against old corruption, but also against the threatening freedoms of Native American women.... Native American marriage customs were frequently matrilocal and matrilineal" (*Property, Women's Rights and Politics* 89). The uses of *coverture* in America resulted in the situation described by Amy Erickson: "The peculiar English system of *coverture* was taken to extremes in the American colonies, particularly the northern colonies" (*Women and Property in Early Modern England* 233).

Not until the 1830s and 1840s did "the legal fiction of marital unity [begin] to undergo modification through the enactment of married women's property acts, which allowed married women to keep their property in their own name" (Langley and Fox 80–81). This pattern of change in America echoes the process in England, where women's property rights were also restored in the late nineteenth century. In America, the nineteenth-century changes in the status of women included "greater control over their inheritances from their fathers and husbands ... new rights to manage what was now stipulated as their property" (Gillian Brown "Hawthorne, Inheritance and Women's Property" 108); the New York Married Women's Property Acts (1848 and 1860) were significant milestones in this process. However, vestiges of *coverture* continued into the twentieth century (Langley and Fox 237).

Not Entirely American: The Displaced American Woman Writer

The identity of the American woman was further complicated by her exclusion from the definition of "American" being developed in eighteenth-

and nineteenth-century America. In "Romancing the Shadow," Toni Morrison asserts that early American identity was forged through a series of negations. Americans were not English; they were also not "savages," like the Native and African Americans. Only a short leap from these negations leads to the assertion that Americans were also not female. We see the dismissal of female American identity in Herman Melville's implicitly gendered definition of the American writer in "Hawthorne and His Mosses" (1850): "let him write like a man, for then he will be sure to write like an American" (*Heath* 1:2621). Thus in Melville's equation, American equals male.

Indeed Melville's statement, which clearly defines the American writer as male, is not the only influential dismissal of the female American writer. Nathaniel Hawthorne, too, begrudges women a place in the canon and in the marketplace, complaining famously of the "damned mob of scribbling women."[1] In "Not in the Least American" Judith Fetterley argues that this approach works to define women writers as essentially un–American, categorically unable to locate themselves within the American canon. As Fetterley suggests, the solution of female American writers was to carve out a new place for themselves in the American canon. Since the realm of the supernatural was already colonized by the major American canonical writers who saw no place in their territory for women, women staked their separate territory in the American canon by moving toward the unappropriated domain of realism and declaring it their own.[2] Fetterley identifies and explains the resulting affinity of the woman writer for the tradition of realism in the nineteenth century: "describing things as they are, not as popular myth, self-serving delusion, or cultural romance would have them, serves as the primary, if not the only, way to change the reality they describe" (*Provisions* 11).

The Realism of the Female Gothic

But the turn to realism was not a turn from Gothic terror and horror. The strategies of American women writers echo the strategies of English female writers, most notably Ann Radcliffe, the late eighteenth-century "mother of the Gothic." Radcliffe famously invented the technique of the "explained supernatural" to tease her readers with hints of the supernatural only to realistically explain all at the end, thus protecting her credentials as a proper and sensible woman. Radcliffe's returns to reality do not undermine her indictment of the patriarchy; in fact her realism stresses that the demonically cruel father and husband, rather than the supernatural, is the actual source of danger for her female protagonists. Like Radcliffe, American women authors validate their sensible, proper, and realistic credentials to create terrifying situations that are engendered not by a ghost, but by a system of laws that allows the patriarch full power over his women. American writers of the Female Gothic echo Radcliffe's insight that in a social and economic system that subjugates women, Gothic horror is a realistic reflection of female life, and the Gothic text a re-enactment of the material world. Although there are a number of ghost stories in the canon of the American female Gothic, including some of the ghost stories of Edith Wharton, many of the female narratives, including some of the stories in Wharton's collection, actually lack a ghost.[3] Such stories as Louisa May Alcott's "A Nurse's Story," Elizabeth Stoddard's *The Morgesons* (1862) and "LeMorne Versus Huell" (1863), Charlotte Perkins Gilman's "The Yellow Wallpaper" (1892) and "The Giant Wistaria" (1891), Shirley Jackson's *We Have Always Lived in the Castle* (1962), and Gloria Naylor's *Linden Hills* (1985) derive their horror from non-supernatural, human sources, often men who try to appropriate the bodies and property of the female protagonists. As in the case of Louise, the missing mother in Radcliffe's *A Sicilian Romance* (1790), and the imprisoned wives in Gilman's "The Yellow Wallpaper," and Naylor's *Linden Hills*, the ghost of the Female Gothic is often the woman herself, invisible and confined. Both the American and English canons portray the spectralized woman, reflecting the system of *coverture* that reduced a married woman to an invisible possession of her husband. In this, the American Female Gothic text reflects the English Gothic tradition, responding to gendered distribution of power that was unchanged by the American Revolution.

The American Wife

Charlotte Perkins Gilman's *The Yellow Wallpaper* (1892) contains many features that mark it as an American text. Gilman's story is a response to the infamous "rest cure" imposed by the American physician, S. Weir Mitchell, upon his female patients. The female narrator of the story is confined by her husband and brother, rational scientists and physicians, following the protocol of the "rest cure," thus providing a reasonable explanation for her imprisonment. The tone of American rationality continues in the total absence of any supernatural force. This story deploys a variety of tropes borrowed from the English Gothic, displaying the dominant theme of the English Female Gothic: the dangers of the legally-empowered husband. Gilman illustrates that the social dangers faced by married American women were similar to those of their English counterparts. The husband, who invokes his own authority, and that of his physician brother-in-law, to impute mental instability to his wife, thereby justifying her incarceration, evokes Mr. Rochester in Charlotte Brontë's *Jane Eyre* (1847), and the husband in Mary Wollstonecraft's *The Wrongs of Women* (1798), as well as the inhumanly cruel husband Sir Percival Glyde, who threatens the social, psychological and physical existence of his wife in Wilkie Collins' *The Woman in White* (1859). These three husbands all villainously call upon the authority of the medical profession, working to amplify their legal powers by diagnosing their wives as mad.

Indeed, the ghost of the possessive Edward Rochester (and Bertha Rochester as well) hovers over the text of Gilman's "The Yellow Wallpaper." The narrator's description of her abode invites us to recall English ghosts and prisons: it is an "ancestral hall.... A colonial mansion, a hereditary estate, I would say a haunted house.... It makes me think of English places that you read about, for there are hedges and walls and gates that lock" (165–166). Like Mr. Rochester, the husband in "The Yellow Wallpaper" recasts his wife as a madwoman and a ghost, locking her in a room at the top of the house; as in the English Female Gothic, the invisibility and anonymity of the female protagonist emblematize and literalize the conditions of *coverture*. The mother's loss of her child under *coverture* is also emblematized by the plight of Gilman's new mother, deprived of her child, as in Wollstonecraft's *Wrongs of Women* in which the villainous husband separates his supposedly mad wife from her infant.[4]

As "Wallpaper" indicates, the scientifically endorsed rest cure did more harm than good in repressing female agency and creativity.[5] The narrator recognizes this: "Personally, I disagree with their ideas. Personally, I believe that congenial work, with excitement and change, would do me good" (165–166). The means of the narrator's opposition is the writing that results in the text of "The Yellow Wallpaper," and the imagination that constructs a trapped uncanny double, whom the narrator ultimately frees. The narrator describes the wallpaper behind which she imagines her double trapped: "sprawling, flamboyant patterns committing every artistic sin" (167). The pattern is "dull enough to confuse the eye in following, pronounced enough constantly to irritate and provoke study, and when you follow the lame uncertain curves for a little distance they suddenly commit suicide—plunge off at outrageous angles, destroy themselves in unheard-of contradictions." This description of the yellow wallpaper accurately depicts the outlines of the convoluted, confusing and artistically transgressive Gothic narrative. In this description Gilman, or her narrator, invites the reader to discover beneath the surface of the realistic short story the "flamboyant" and "extravagant" narrative pattern of the Gothic novel, the mode that does indeed "provoke study" with its indeterminacy as it commits "every artistic sin." The wallpaper thus becomes a reflexive emblem for Gilman's story: beneath the realistic surface of confining social conventions lurks the possibility for imaginative and fantastic escape.

Within this story of personal dispossession of the wife, then, we find a subtext of narrative possession and dispossession. The woman, dispossessed of her freedom, her child and her writing, works to reclaim herself by "reading" the text of the wallpaper and appropriating the narrative that lies beneath the lines of the wallpaper: the familiar Gothic story of the enclosed woman who escapes the walls that enclose her. In this, we can see that the yellow wallpaper functions as a palimpsest and that upon close "study" the narrator discovers the primary text that lies beneath, the Gothic text that gives her an admittedly fantastic promise of freedom: "At night ... it becomes bars! The outside pattern, I mean, and the woman behind it is plain as can be" (174). The subtext of the wallpaper evokes female tales of imprisonment and escape in the English Gothic and suggests that American women writers like Gilman, who are haunted by their English precursors, and share their limitations, welcome this influence because it provides them with models of escape. In fact, the triumph of the narrator occurs primarily on the imaginative level; the woman whom she sees behind the bars of the wallpaper escapes—"I can see her out of every one of my windows" (177). But on the literal realistic level the triumph of Gilman's narrator, her resistance to the possession of her husband, is qualified. Although the door is unlocked, her husband prostrated by horror at the story's conclusion, the narrator pays the price of her sanity. The American Female Gothic, then, like the English Gothic, re-enacts the legal metaphors of marital possession in its literary tropes. Like its English predecessors, the American Female Gothic works to demystify the ideology of romantic love, to reveal the horrifying consequences of its economic subtext, and to indulge in fantasies of escape that have little hope of being realized in the actual world. Writers of the American Female Gothic, themselves in a paradoxically pre–Revolutionary state, not yet entitled to the full rights of American citizenship, embrace the literary forbears who provide them with paradigms and responses that resonate with the condition of the American woman.

Yet, despite the similarities in contexts and paradigms, the American Female Gothic does diverge from the English form, transforming the trope of Gothic closure in one significant way. In the English model, the dark, demonic male is typically vanquished or subdued by the end of the text, forced to relinquish his possession of both woman and property; the dangerous male is disposed of and replaced by a good husband, as in *Sicilian Romance, Udolpho,* and *The Woman in White,* or weakened and thereby rendered less threatening, as in *Jane Eyre*. The conventional English Female Gothic closure thus enacts a utopian fantasy of female resistance to the legal claim for female possession. This resistance is qualified in the American Female Gothic. "The Yellow Wallpaper" concludes with the incoherent insanity of the wife; the husband seems to have fainted only temporarily, and his wife's heightened insanity is likely to provide him with additional justification for further restrictions upon his wife in the future. Ultimately the realism of the American text refutes the imagination of the English text.

Elizabeth Stoddard's "Lemorne Versus Huell" (1863) also emphasizes that the ongoing danger for women lies in the contemporary set of laws dominated by men, and also cedes to legal and narrative realism. Even the surprising end, evoking a moment of Gothic recognition and horror, is firmly set within realism. After her courtship, the narrator, Margaret Huell, learns that her marriage to Mr. Uxbridge, the lawyer for the LeMorne family, has been contracted by her aunt as a solution to a dispute between the two families over "a tract of ground [which was] very valuable." Margaret realizes that, like the property, she is a possession: "I was not allowed to give myself—I was taken" (*Heath* 1:2670). A poor girl, she has been used as a commodity in trade by her own aunt and husband; the equation of the woman and the land, both property, is made painfully clear. Margaret's revelation re-enacts the movement of the English Gothic toward demystifying the cultural secret that romantic courtship is actuality a serious economic game. Margaret has been led to believe that Edward Uxbridge, the lawyer for the side opposing her aunt, courts her out of love. When they meet, she reports that "his eyes were fixed upon me," the conventional penetrating eyes of the Gothic hero-villain. Even during the courtship, Uxbridge reveals his potential power; he is "a pale, stern-looking man." His "domineering disposition" is revealed in the way that "he controlled his horse." When Margaret and Uxbridge become engaged at a ball, she narrates, "When we emerged into the blaze and glitter of the supper-room I sought refuge in the shadow of Mrs. Bliss' companion, for it seemed to me that I had lost my own"—an astute metaphor for the woman's loss of substance and identity in marriage under *coverture*. That same evening, the lawyer Uxbridge tells her, "I know you Margaret; you are mine!" As he discusses the transaction with the aunt, he kisses Margaret with a kiss of "appropriation." We later learn that in exchange for Margaret, Uxbridge purposely loses the case for the land, so Margaret is in effect a bribe. The encounter of the innocent and independent Margaret with the legal immorality of the marriage market presents the demystification of the terms of marriage, a common theme of the Female Gothic. However, Stoddard's story does not re-enact the fantastic rescue of the English heroine, typical of all of Radcliffe's endings. Stoddard's story ends only with a belated recognition of the actual, realistically grounded truth, which is nonetheless blood-curdling: "As [the clock] struck I said, '*My husband is a scoundrel*,' and woke with a start" (2672). Margaret's Cinderella fantasy is over and her realistic nightmare marriage is only beginning.

A strategy that Stoddard adopts directly from the English Female Gothic is the conflation of the language of women's rights and anti-slavery discourse, a rhetorical tendency to erase the boundaries between women's sufferings and the horrors of slavery that presents itself most spectacularly in Charlotte Dacre's English Gothic novel, *Zofloya or the Moor* (1806). Before Margaret becomes enmeshed in the courtship, the impoverished young girl briefly enjoys a respite from bondage to her rich, difficult aunt: "free and alone," she savors a "sense of liberty" and "a taste of freedom." When Margaret is discovered out alone by Uxbridge, she says to him, "'I am a runaway. What do you think of the Fugitive Slave Bill?'" His response prefigures Margaret's future as chattel-wife: "'I approve of returning property to its owners'" (*Heath* 1:2666).

Louisa May Alcott also presents an American re-enactment of the English theme of the dangers of the powerful male, without resorting to the supernatural. "A Nurse's Story" is one of Alcott's many sensation stories that were rescued from the oblivion of nineteenth-century story magazines by Madeleine Stern in the late twentieth century. This story features all the prerequisites of the English Gothic text, including madness, suicide, family secrets, inherited sins or curses, the noble (American) family, the weak (though benevolent) Catholic clergyman, his equally weak, and good, young brother, and, of course, the dangerous male, who replaces the supernatural as the source of terror. Rather than present any actually supernatural moments, Alcott applies the language of the supernatural to describe realistic human psychological conditions, including the "horror" (298) of madness. Characters are "haunt[ed]" (299) by fear of recurring madness. Curses are not supernatural, but genetic; "the sins of the parents shall be visited upon the children" (299)—a curse that blasts a number of Gothic families—describes a familial tendency to a condition that sounds much like manic-depression. For this unhappy family, "the curse of insanity" is the "awful inheritance [bequeathed to the] descendants" (304). Kate seems to practice paranormal mesmerism to put people to sleep, displaying her uncanny "powers" (301). But, as a nurse, she actually draws more from the world of science and healing than from the paranormal world. In Alcott's story, evil power also comes from the real, material world: the aptly named Robert Steele. Steele is a human "villain" (314), who holds a secret that threatens the social standing of the Carruth family, the kindly employers of (the also aptly named), Kate Snow.

The realistic approach to the supernatural is evident throughout the story. Alcott resorts to supernatural terms to describe Steele's villainy. When he first appears to Kate, she sees "a tall, dark figure that glided by me as noiseless as a shadow" (306); ghostlike, he "haunted the house" (313). His villainy appears to transcend the human. Kate's patient Elinor warns her that he is "the evil genius of the family, beware of him or he will take possession of you as he has of us" (306). He is himself "possessed of a devil" (315); repeatedly he is referred to as "the enemy" (317), a euphemism for the devil. To Kate he seems "all-powerful" (313), "possessed" by "a fierce spirit" (327). To achieve his full power, Steele deploys quasi-supernatural powers of surveillance. He spies on Elinor, Kate and Harry from a window high above Elinor's private conservatory. He spies on Kate as she dances late at night, thinking she is alone. When Kate secretly conveys a letter for Elinor, she "looks up to see Steele at the window … for a moment I sat looking at him as if he were a ghost" (324). At end of the story, this human devil becomes a fallen angel. Authentically in love with Kate, he is found years later in a state of decline, having long cherished her "nosegay of white and purple heath" (321). Even at the peak of his deviltry, Kate has recognized the human core of his goodness, assuring the Carruths that he has a conscience "in spite of the evil spirit that possesses him" (315). Early on in his interchange with her she sees a "wonderfully soft and sweet expression" (316) pass over his face. Even Steele recognizes that he could be saved by human love. He tells Kate, "I think you could cast out my devil if you tried" (317). Certainly Steele's threat is social rather than supernatural. His supposed mother, an evil old woman at the center of the plot, reveals that she is the first wife of Mr. Carruth and that therefore Mrs. Carruth's marriage is bigamous and her children illegitimate. The first Mrs. Carruth threatens to bring social scandal to the Carruths, almost worse than death to an upper class nineteenth-century American family. Steele causes other real harm to the family. His looming presence exacerbates Elinor's madness; he ruins Harry, leading the younger son of the family, to follow his dangerous inclinations to debauchery, almost causing Harry's death. As Harry says about Steele's sordid associates, "they know where to find me and how to tempt me" (319). Steele also tempts Kate with his seductive allure.

As Steele is the conventional hero-villain to be found at the center of most English Gothic texts, Kate Snow is the plucky heroine. Taking on the English role of peasant as secret aristocrat, she is secretly a "gentleman's daughter" (295). Despite being a servant Kate immediately receives her own space; she is led to an apartment that "looked a perfect nest of comfort" and is informed that it is "mine." In her reduced role as a poor servant, Kate's power paradoxically is the silence imposed upon her as a servant and as a woman, the silent power of the subaltern, described in "Can the Subaltern Speak?" by Gayatri Chakravorty Spivak. Kate's silent observation of the events in the house allows her to truthfully tell Steele: "'I understand you better than you think'" (325). Kate, the yielding Snow, accomplishes more with submission than she would with challenge, as she silently resists Steele's prying questions. Her cold impassive approach ultimately succeeds in opposing the metal of Steele, who has warned her that it is "dangerous to oppose me" because he is "master of the house" (316). Following in the tradition of Ann Radcliffe, the mother of the English Female Gothic, the end result of Alcott's narrative is the demystification of marriage. We see the rotten foundation of the Carruths' seemingly happy marriage. We learn that marriage is often based upon material concerns rather than romance. The marriage of Amy, Elinor's sister, is clearly based on economic choices. Having lost his fortune, Amy's fiancé "was ready to sell himself for another.... Amy ... seemed quite satisfied with her purchase" (321). Like Radcliffe, Alcott realistically warns her young, impressionable, and romantic readers about entering into a legal institution that might trap them

* * *

The uncanny correspondence between the American Female Gothic and its English counterpart—based on a shared response to the similar legal situation of married women in both countries—continues in recent American literature. A somewhat surprising example of this doubled literary relationship is well illustrated by Gloria Naylor's *Linden Hills* (1985), the story of a doomed African American family, and the outsiders who witness their fate. Naylor's novel is a text that appropriates a space for itself in the American tradition by bearing signs of being haunted by the English tradition. The setting of the novel is the eponymous community where the old orders of hierarchy hold sway: social prominence is determined by geographic proximity to the home of the ruling family, the Nedeeds. Buried within the center of this community, locked in the cellar of the Nedeed house on the bottom crescent of Linden Hills, is the last of the Nedeed wives, whose fate faithfully mirrors that of so many other Gothic wives. The narrative structure of *Linden Hills*, whose intricacy is familiar from the English tradition, presents the primary narrative of two good and powerless young men who work at odd jobs as they make their way down the winding drives of the community, the embedded narratives of various community residents whom they encounter, and the buried story of the buried wife.

Naylor's carefully constructed setting is clearly situated within a literary European—rather than a realistically American—landscape. The first sentence of Naylor's novel identifies Linden Hills as a place that is established within the landscape of the Gothic, rather than in the legally defined borders of the United States: "There had been a dispute for years over the exact location of Linden Hills" (2). Like the settings of Walpole's *The Castle of Otranto*, Radcliffe's *Mysteries of Udolpho* and *The Italian*—all taking place in an unreal and distant Italy, the setting of *Linden Hills* is mysteriously detached from the real world, an oddity in the canon of American Gothic literature, which usually occurs in a recognizably American setting. In her representation of the Nedeed house as the central locus of her Gothic narrative, Naylor pointedly resists the American Male Gothic revision of the English Gothic, the move from the haunted castle to the haunted wilderness, as described by Brown in *Edgar Huntly*. The manor that the Nedeeds inhabit on their property pointedly recalls the castles of the English Gothic lord; it is surrounded by "an artificial lake (really a moat)" (6). And most importantly, the Nedeed house directly evokes the gloomy castles of the English Gothic in that it contains a locked cellar in which the latest Nedeed wife is imprisoned by her husband with her dying child, to punish her for producing a light-skinned child who fails to fulfill the racial dynastic imperatives of the African American Nedeed family.

The erasure of the wife and the mother through imprisonment or death is a staple of the Gothic mode, an indication of female dispensability to the patriarchy (and a reflection of *coverture* and primogeniture); the most common causes for female absence are imprisonment or death. All the Nedeed women undergo this Gothic fate; in a re-enactment of *coverture* and primogeniture each gradually disappears, fading "against the whitewashed boards of the Nedeed home after conceiving and giving over a son to the stamp and will of the father" (18). Willa,[6] whose absence is barely noticed by the community of Linden Hills, imprisoned with her dead child, pointedly echoes the story of Agnes (in Lewis' *The Monk*), who is locked up in the dungeons of the Inquisition with the body of her dead baby. In her intermittently heard cries, Willa also recalls the mother in Radcliffe's *A Sicilian Romance* who, although believed by her children to be dead, is discovered imprisoned in the dungeons of her husband; she has been the source of the ghostly noises heard in the castle. Willa's cries also recall Bertha Rochester of Brontë's *Jane Eyre*, also imprisoned by her husband. Willa re-enacts Bertha Rochester's fate. Like Bertha—and like Bertha's precursor, the insane Saxon princess in Walter Scott's *Ivanhoe*, imprisoned by the conquering Normans, who dies in the fire she sets in her father's conquered castle—Willa dies burning down the patriarchal house that imprisons her.

The embedded story of the Nedeeds, Naylor's Gothic narrative, thus reveals how little the Nedeed family saga revises, resists or subverts the pre-existing paradigm of the English Gothic within which it operates. The story of the rise and fall of the Nedeed dynasty manifests all the conventional motifs that have informed the Gothic since the mode was concretized in eighteenth-century Europe: the demonic dynastic patriarch; the imprisoned and powerless wife; the unstable family and family dwelling; the discovered and fragmented manuscript. The progression of the Nedeed family also follows the conventional narrative course of the Gothic: the current patriarch, inheritor of a sordid legacy, fails to perpetuate his dynasty, and the dynasty falls. The strategy of replication and re-enactment that Naylor deploys is itself typical of the Gothic, a genre defined by convention and re-enactment rather than by originality. As Robert Kiely notes in writing of Radcliffe's successors, the conventions Radcliffe employed were "produced by other writers so quickly and on such a large scale that they were clichés before they had time to become conventions" (*The Romantic Novel in England* 65). Despite the seeming revision of the Gothic villain as African American businessman, Naylor's Nedeed fits quite neatly into the pre-existing paradigms of the English Gothic. Like his tyrannical precursors, he is the richest and most powerful man in his society, exerting complete control over his wife and his property as he pursues his prime imperatives: to perpetuate his dynastic line and to sustain the possessions of the dynasty.[7] Nor is Luther's racial darkness—an essential element of his dynasty that emblematizes his moral darkness—a new Gothic trope forged in America. In fact, Luther's physical darkness links him to the dark line of villains who have long dominated the Gothic. The darkly complected Italians—Manfred (*Otranto*), Montoni (*Udolpho*), Ambrosio (*The Monk*)—and their dark English counterparts, including Mr. Rochester, all display their villainy in their dusky countenances. In fact, H.L. Malchow argues for a racial reading of threatening, swarthy characters as Frankenstein's monster and Heathcliff of Emily Brontë's *Wuthering Heights*; Malchow perceptively argues that "the Other, the outsider, the racially foreign is probably buried in the whole genre of gothic horror" (*Gothic Images of Race in Nineteenth-Century Britain* 38).

Naylor confronts the conventional Gothic conflation of evil and racial blackness, by presenting two good young African American men in her novel. Willie and Lester represent a stock type found in many English Gothic novels, including Horace Walpole's *The Castle of Otranto*, and most of Ann Radcliffe's work: the good but powerless young man whose kind and gentle masculinity counters the power and danger of the evil, tyrannical patriarch. Almost invariably the young man outlasts the patriarch, frequently finding himself in possession of the tyrant's property, and married to a woman who was formerly in the patriarch's possession. As Naylor's young men wend their way down Linden Hills from the outer First Crescent, where Lester lives with his family, they witness (but do not partake of) various episodes that reinstate the Gothic terms of patriarchal domination and usurpation in middle-class American life, a situation that is simultaneously playing out within the Nedeed house.

Like Walpole's and Radcliffe's moral young men, Willie and Lester suggest alternatives to the cruel and despotic patriarch, and gesture to possible transformations of the evil structures of power that haunt the Gothic text. Both men are marginal, outside the patriarchy: Lester lives on the outskirts of Linden Hills; Willie lives outside its boundaries. They possess no steady jobs or professional credentials and no ambitions, other than Willie's vague dream about emulating the poet whose name he bears by becoming a "'black Shakespeare'" (283).[8] Yet Willie and Lester, like their Gothic predecessors insistently defy the cruel terms of the patriarchy in which they live, ultimately succeeding in subverting the powerful institutions and rigid hierarchy of their society. They resist the Linden Hills model of success that is based on selling one's soul to the devilish Nedeeds, and thereby disrupt the Nedeed narrative of success. The doubling of the character into two good young men, who share a close homosocial bond, directly defies the heterosexual imperative of the Nedeed patriarchy, with its insistence on perpetuating the dynastic line; their names echo and parody the names of the last Nedeed heterosexual dyad, Willa and Luther.

Willie and Lester directly subvert the plot of Luther Nedeed, the last in the line of patriarchal tyrants. When Luther tells the community that his wife Willa has gone to visit relatives, no one questions her absence except Lester and Willie. Only they hear "the long thin howl," the cry of the imprisoned Willa mourning the death of her son (42). The two appropriate Luther's narrative of normative middle-class American marriage, and inadvertently reveal its gothicism. They joke between themselves that Luther must have his wife chained to a bed (153); in actuality, Luther does have Willa imprisoned in the basement. In fact, their stance as powerless young men, allows them the perspective of the subaltern and privileges them to recognize the nightmare lurking within a seeming representation of the American Dream. Since they have no place within the structure and are invisible wanderers through Linden Hills, they, like the reader, see each Gothic fragment and are able to identify the Gothic patterns that develop. Willie and Lester thus oppose the norms of Linden Hills by identifying and naming the gothicism of the community. To Willie, entering the Nedeed home is "'like walking into a movie set for

*Wuthering Heights'" (290). When Willie asks Lester if Nedeed always speaks in a stilted, artificial manner, Lester replies, "'Yup, straight out of a gothic novel'" (86).

Naylor's Gothic, like its English predecessors, manifests a preoccupation with questions of possession and power: possession of property, of the body of the wife, and of the narrative. As in the conventional Gothic, the central problem of Naylor's narrative is whether the aristocrat, the demonic lord of the realm, can perpetuate his dynasty and sustain his possession. Walpole's castle, for example, has been usurped by the ancestor of the present patriarch Manfred, who in turn obsessively attempts to perpetuate his dynasty and sustain his control over the property, even as his attempts lead him to bigamy, incest, and finally to the murder of his own child. Linden Hills is also held in the grip of a powerful, demonic and murderous dynast, who also threatens even his own wife and child. The driving force of the Nedeeds and of the anachronistically feudal community of Linden Hills "is simply the *will* to possess" (17); Naylor thus reveals the direct line between the Gothic villain and the ambitious, grasping American patriarch. The original Luther Nedeed came from Tupelo, Mississippi, "where it was rumored that he'd actually sold his octoroon wife and six children for the money that he used to come North" (2). He acquires the land, develops it as a community of houses for successful African Americans and begins a dynasty. One of his descendants works out a feudal arrangement with the inhabitants of Linden Hills; he gives them "a-thousand-year-and-a-day lease—provided only that they passed their property on to their children. And if they wanted to sell it, they had to sell it to another black family or the rights would revert back to the Nedeeds" (7).

The closure of Naylor's novel exactly re-enacts the conventional Gothic closure: the destruction of the dynasty and its structures. The Nedeed dynasty, like Manfred's in *Otranto*, ends with the death of the dynast's only child. Luther's child is physically incapable of perpetuating the dynasty as is Manfred's sickly son, Conrad, who is crushed to death on his wedding day. The Nedeed son and heir is too light-skinned to carry on the family tradition despite Luther's recreation of family rituals guaranteed to produce a dark clone-like Nedeed male from a light mother—thereby effacing the genetic influence of the female line and echoing the effacement of the mother within primogeniture, in which material property moves directly from father to son. Like Manfred, who mistakenly kills his own daughter at the end of *Otranto*, Luther in his insane quest for dynasty kills his own son. Thus Naylor recapitulates the conventional destruction of the Gothic dynasty in showing the death of the Nedeed heir and the burning of the Nedeed house. As Michelle Massé writes, "In destroying Luther along with herself, Willa aggressively brings a local structure of oppression to an end: there will be no new Luther to rule this house or Linden Hills" (*In the Name of Love* 249). Yet, given the intertextual web of Gothic texts in which *Linden Hills* exists, it is likely that, although there will be no more Luther Nedeeds, as there are no more Manfreds, the supply of oppressing men and oppressed women is limitless; the structures of oppression will, in fact, endure and recur in the Gothic, as they have for hundreds of years. *Linden Hills*, in its uncanny re-enactment of the Gothic, confirms and perpetuates the patterns of power and possession, suggesting that they are still relevant even in late twentieth-century America.

As Naylor's examination of the darkness of the English Gothic villain indicates, her textual appropriation points to surprising connections. The story of the Nedeeds, accumulating power as they promote the dispossession and effacement of the cultural heritage of the black community, is appropriately told in a narrative set within the English literary tradition, effectively effacing any black literary influence. The American Gothic narrative of the deracinated husband and wife is thus a reflexive text in which narrating and narrative are congruent; the African influence is erased from both. Naylor's replication of the English Gothic in twentieth-century America also works to amplify sad affinities between England of the eighteenth and nineteenth centuries and twentieth-century America: the conflicts within the conventional Gothic—between male and female, rich and poor; the tendency to racialize the conflict between good and evil as between white and black—remain unresolved, as available to Gothic rendering today as when Walpole first developed a blood-curdling genre to capture their horror. Naylor's repetition thus becomes itself a source of claustrophobic horror, an indication that the social horror of inequity is unending and inescapable. The repetition in Naylor's text thus exemplifies Eugenia DeLamotte's observation that Gothic repetition in itself is horrifying: "In Gothic romances ... devices and images of repetition suggest a double horror of boundedness and boundlessness in both spatial and temporal terms. The same events seem to recur again and again, trapping the protagonist in a single instant of time yet simultaneously evoking the nightmare of eternity" (*The Perils of the Night* 95). Naylor's repetition of the oppressive structures of the English Gothic suggest that the structures of patriarchal oppression are eternal, and that women and members of other marginalized groups are doomed to remain imprisoned within history. Thus, instead of providing the positive catharsis the English writers like Radcliffe fantastically anticipate, the repetition of Naylor's American novel sadly and realistically accepts that the cycles of social and gender oppression will endure. If the American Revolution did not effect a substantial change in the status of women, what hope is there for the future?

This repetition of the cycle of gender oppression might seem to be an overreaction to gender relations in America at a time when the principles of *coverture* and primogeniture seemingly are long gone. Is Naylor's recapitulation merely nostalgia for the bad old days and the archaic literary response that they generated? Actually, no; for while the basics of *coverture* and primogeniture were overturned long before 1985, the publication date of Naylor's novel, one brick of that structure still remained, a living reminder of the abuses of the earlier systems. Not until 1992 "did the Supreme Court specifically announce that it would no longer recognize the power of husbands over the bodies of their wives. That is the moment when *coverture*, as a living legal principle, died" (Kerber 307). And so, Naylor, like her English predecessors works to demystify and highlight a continuing abuse of marriage law. No less than Radcliffe in the late eighteenth century, Naylor, like her English precursors, warns her female readers of the actual danger that still loomed for them within modern marriage in modern America.

2

A New Possession
Slavery and Beyond

Although married women in England and America were metaphorically and legally property, giving early feminists the opportunity to compare the civil death of marriage to the civil death of slavery, the horrible situation of the chattel slave in the United States far exceeded the limitations placed upon married women, and presented a new, uniquely American form of possession and power. While the cruel husband *could* control the wife's property, children and body, the brutal possession of the American slave was the norm. Slaves had no legal right to own property, including their own bodies, children or the fruits of their labors. Consequently, masters were free to brutalize their slaves physically and mentally; slave women had no legal protection against rape; and slave children were routinely stolen from their families. And so issues of power, possession, and dispossession that preoccupied English Gothic literature from its origins took on new form and urgency in the literature by and about African Americans during and after slavery.

The system of slavery, the institution that commodified the bodies of human beings, turning them into the building blocks of American structures, presented a daunting challenge to a number of core American ideals, including the principle of freedom based on self-possession and individual integrity. As Toni Morrison points out, a daunting challenge to American ideology was "the presence of the unfree within the heart of the democratic experiment" ("Romancing the Shadow" 48). In the nineteenth century especially, the idea of personal mobility was connected to the notion of selfhood, or manhood, which was usually synonymous. The right of personal mobility was at the root of the idea that it was the Manifest Destiny of the United States to expand the frontier into the West, as articulated in a quotation attributed to Horace Greeley in 1865: "Go west, young man,"[1] addressed directly to the young (white) American male who possessed the mobility to obey.[2]

Immurement

The unique constrictions of American slavery appear in the American reconstruction of the Gothic tropes of enclosure and confinement, motifs that emblematize the loss of self-possession in both the English and American traditions.[3] In response to the system of chattel slavery, the American Gothic transforms and intensifies the trope of confinement, re-presenting enclosure as *immurement*, in which the body is not only enclosed *within* the structure, surrounded by the walls of an attic or a dungeon, it is *incorporated into* the structure. The immured body, like the body of the slave, becomes part of the edifice; the freedom and identity of the slave are sacrificed to the physical and ideological structures of power

The Jim Crow cookie episode in Hawthorne's *House of the Seven Gables* presents a biological metaphor for the immurement of the slave's body. The "First Customer" in Hepzibah's little shop, her sad attempt at business, is "a little urchin" (49), who is the embodiment of hungry American capitalism. His first purchase is a "Jim Crow" (50) cookie, emblematizing the commodified body of the slave in America. The cookie is bought and then swallowed by the little white boy in a "cannibal-feast" (50). This voracious little boy repeatedly returns to consume increasingly exotic types of cookies. In digesting the Jim Crow cookie and incorporating it into his body, the boy literalizes the process whereby the body of the commodified slave becomes the building material for the structures of slavery. In devouring a variety of creature-shaped cookies, he emblematizes the voraciousness of American capitalism, engulfing everything in its wake.

* * *

Responding to the seeming paradox of the darkness of early American literature, including Hawthorne's works, Toni Morrison notes that "for a people who made much of their newness ... it is striking how dour how troubled, how frightened and haunted our early and founding literature truly is." Morrison argues that this darkness results from the paradoxical presence of a dark and enslaved "resident population" (37). Morrison additionally points to the usefulness of the "Africanist" (45) figure in the struggle for a new, distinct national identity. The new American knew what he was *not*: he was not English; he was not female; in addition, Morrison adds he also was not black, not "savage" and not enslaved, as was the quintessential "racial other" (46), the black, enslaved "not-me" ("Romancing the Shadow" 38).[4]

Morrison focuses on the contrast between darkness and whiteness, in the works of Edgar Allan Poe, especially in his novel *The Narrative of Arthur*

Gordon Pym (1838).⁵ Certainly Poe's preoccupation with darkness is well explained by Morrison's argument. However, there is another dominant trope in Poe's fiction that addresses another aspect of slavery, the powerless, multifaceted immobility of the slave, emblematized by Poe's revision of the trope of confinement into an image of immurement, as in "The Fall of the House of Usher" (1839; discussed in Chapter 5) and "The Black Cat" (1843). Following the path delineated by Morrison, Lesley Ginsberg makes a persuasive case for the veiled presence of slavery in the latter story, connecting the imagery of "The Black Cat" with depictions of domesticity, including the treatment of slaves and pets, found in management manuals for antebellum plantation owners. Ginsberg asserts that Poe's reference to the iconography of the plantation manuals "deconstructs the sentimental strategies of repression so common to antebellum rhetoric" ("Slavery and the Gothic Horror of Poe's 'The Black Cat'" 99) and reveals that at "the core of proslavery ideology was the equating of slaves with animals" (103). Thus the torture endured by the two black cats of the story echoes the abuse of the body of the American African slave. Poe's story reveals a guilty horror of the havoc that can be wreaked when power is concentrated in a single figure as it was on the patriarchal plantation.

"The Black Cat" also illustrates the usefulness of the Gothic text in the discourse of slavery, which was an experience of daily horror. Ostensibly a story of madness, alcoholism and murder, "The Black Cat" presents a narrator who is possessed in a psychological sense. Drunk, or perhaps drunk with power, he is insanely driven to kill the beings that he possesses, even though he ostensibly loves them: his two cats and his wife. The moral and psychological devolution of the narrator reveals white anxiety about the corrupting effect slavery exerts on the possessor of such power, the slave owner—a common theme expressed in slave narratives that were addressed to the sensibilities of the potentially sympathetic and helpful white Northern audience. The transformation of Poe's narrator follows the same arc. He describes his prelapsarian self as benevolent: "From my infancy I was noted for the docility and humanity of my disposition.... I was especially fond of animals" (254). Whereas in the slave narratives the institution of slavery is the corrupting force, in Poe's story alcoholism ostensibly leads to moral decline: "Fiend Intemperance" (255) corrupts the narrator and he becomes cruel to his animals. The graphic description of torture and mistreatment—the narrator cuts out the eye of his "remarkably large and beautiful ... entirely black, and sagacious cat" (254–255) and then hangs him from a tree—recalls the graphic descriptions of the brutal treatment of slaves to be found in slave narratives.

Even more pointedly, after killing his wife, the narrator, exhibiting no remorse, calmly decides that the roughly plastered walls in the cellar of his house allow him to implement his plot to immure her. He plans to "displace the bricks ... insert the corpse, and wall the whole up as before" (258). The immurement of the murdered wife certainly highlights her status as the possession of her husband and illustrates the temptation for women to equate their situation with slavery. If we see the narrator as emblematizing the unbridled power of the plantation master, we can see in his wife's abject situation a reflection of the situation of the wife of the plantation owner, who had no power in her own home.[6] However, the title creature, representing the black slave, is the focal point of the story. The inadvertent walling up of the black cat, whose mistreatment has already aligned him with the figure of the black slave, illustrates the position of the slave body within the system of slavery. The motif of immurement destabilizes the relationship between the body and the self, as does the system of slavery. The immured body is not fully possessed by the self, which cannot fully direct the movement of the body through space, thus reflecting the powerlessness of the slave to control his own body. In fact, Poe repeats the image of the immured cat, creating a second cat, an uncanny double, that further disturbs the narrator and unsettles the reader. The narrator initially hangs his first black cat, even though he recognizes as he is engaged in the act that he is performing a "sin." Soon after, his house is unaccountably destroyed by fire. This staple of Gothic fiction, the burning of the building that represents the center of power, reflects the anxieties aroused by the sin of slavery. When the narrator visits the ruins on the following day, he discovers that, despite the destruction of the entire house, an inner wall, an "exception," still stands. The narrator and a small "eager" crowd see on the remaining wall, "as if graven in *bas relief* upon the white surface, the figure of a gigantic *cat*.... There was a rope around the animal's neck" (256), recalling the lynching of slaves. White guilt for these crimes and anxieties of justice or revenge are evident in the closure of the story. As the police search his home for clues to his wife's disappearance, the narrator arrogantly taps on the wall within which lies the body of his wife; he hears the cat's screams and realizes that "I had walled the monster up within the tomb!" (259). Ironically, but not atypically for the Gothic, the all-powerful white man encounters the fate he has imposed upon others. He narrates the story on the eve of his execution for murder, presumably from within the confinement of prison, thus revealing the anxiety of the text about the possibilities of retribution for the sins of slavery. The narrative articulates the fear that slavery will bury not just the commodified slaves, but the perpetuators of the system as well.

* * *

The lingering effects of slavery are painfully visible in Charles Chesnutt's seeming ghost story, "Po' Sandy" (1888). Writing in the American South, only decades after Emancipation, Chesnutt, an African American, was born into freedom and well-educated; he put his education to use teaching former slaves. Chesnutt's story of slavery presents all the physical and emotional horror of the slave narratives, including the trope of immurement.[7] Writing when he does, Chesnutt imagines a future more comic than tragic, in which former slaves exert power to appropriate property from the master.

The embedded story of the slave Sandy is told by a former slave, Uncle Julius, to John and Annie, white Northern property owners. Julius obligingly provides all the horrifying and supernatural tropes necessary to gain the attention of his auditors. He tells of Sandy, a slave whose master, "'Mars Marrabo McSwayne'" (46), controls his body completely; the master often sends Sandy far away to work "'fer a mont' er so'" (46) until poor Sandy "'didn't hardly knowed whar he wuz gwine ter stay fum one week's een' ter de yuther'"(46). After the master cruelly sells Sandy's wife while he is away, swapping her to a speculator for "'a noo 'oman,'" Sandy, realizes that he will never see his wife again, and "'tuk up'" with the new woman, Tenie, a conjure woman who moves the story toward the supernatural. Since Sandy prefers to stay at home, Tenie turns him into a tree; her spell is meant to protect Sandy from having to travel far from home to work on other plantations. Ironically, Tenie's spell further limits Sandy's mobility and humanity. And in fact, Tenie's plan backfires, as Sandy terribly moves from temporary immurement in a tree to permanent immurement. The slave master unknowingly uses the tree for lumber to build a new kitchen, thus incorporating the commodified body of the slave into his structure. In this story, then, as in Hawthorne's Jim Crow cookie episode, the American Gothic trope of immurement unveils the horrors of the system of slavery, founded upon the commodified body of the slave, reduced to building material. Uncle Julius carefully leads his audience back to the unnatural and bloody world of slavery. The men who cut down the tree that is Sandy encounter great difficulties: "'all de creakin,' en shakin,' en wobblin' you ever see'" (50). Even more horrifying, when the workers take the tree trunk to the sawmill, they encounter further difficulties: "'all de seekin,' and moanin,' en groanin'" (51). Tenie, on discovering what has occurred, runs to the sawmill; she knows Sandy will die, but she wants a chance to apologize. The story has a tragic and ghostly ending. Tenie goes mad and the wood from Sandy is used to construct the master's new kitchen. Of course, the structure is haunted by Sandy's ghost, and so the master is forced to relinquish his property. The kitchen is dismantled, and the lumber is used to make a schoolhouse—even in death poor Sandy is on the move.

Ultimately the property on which the schoolhouse rests is bought by John and Annie, Uncle Julius' auditors.

Moreover, the story of Sandy is immured within Julius' narrative, which is itself immured within the frame narrative of the white man, John, whose meta-narrative explains the situation as Julius tells the story to his curious and sympathetic listeners. It thus appears that John is fully in control: he possesses the property; he possesses the narrative. Poor Uncle Julius is merely an old, powerless former slave with little mastery of the English language. And yet, the frame narrative and the embedded story combine to tell a very different story, an American story of freedom, subversion, and revolution, as Julius uses his embedded narrative to master his audience. From the outset, we see Julius exhibiting his narrative control. Rather than marginalizing him, his dialect provides him with narrative authority as his auditors, John and Annie, and the reader who is John's audience, find themselves mystified, struggling for meaning. This confusion suggests that Julius' dialect is an American form of the antique Gothic document, fragmented and difficult to comprehend. His narrative also recalls the occasional subversive moment in the English Gothic when the obscure narrative of the servant impedes the purpose of the master. In the English Gothic, the obstacle to the master's control is temporary. In Charles Chesnutt's American Gothic, the subversion of the servant endures beyond the final frame.

Not only does Julius' narrative resist the apprehension and control of the white listener, he uses his confusing narrative to appropriate property from his confused auditors. As John suspects, there is a subtext to Julius' story, which is told to promote his own purposes. Julius' story works to discourage John from tearing down a building that is needed by the members of Julius' church. Julius' appropriation of narrative and property is abetted by the powerful effect of his story on Annie who provides the empathetic female perspective. When she hears Julius' story, Annie responds, "'Poor Tenie'" (53). This response appears to be a contestation of Julius' narrative: Annie's statement feminizes the title of the story and translates it into normative "white" English, thereby transforming the story from a narrative of slavery and its horrors into a tragic love story. And yet Annie's response indicates Julius' power over his narrative rather than his dispossession. For by moving and engaging Annie with his story, he accomplishes his goal: she decides that she cannot use the lumber from the old structure for her new kitchen and soon after convinces her husband to donate the building to Julius' church.

The name of the church in need of a new building, "the Sandy Run Colored Baptist Church" (54), provides a comical indication that Sandy and Tenie exist only in the world of fiction, and that the name of the slave has been inspired by the name of the church in whose cause he has been invented. In this story, as in the American Female Gothic narratives, the absence of any actual ghost suggests that the real horror of American life is derived not from the supernatural but from the material world. Annie recognizes this when, after hearing the story, she says, "'What a system it was ... under which such things were possible'" (53). Annie responds to the actual meaning of the story, the reality of loving spouses being separated, and bodies being crushed under slavery. But John, increasingly hapless, simply does not recognize this level of meaning; he asks, "'What things?... Are you seriously considering the possibility of a man's being turned into a tree?'" (349). And so the embedded (and fictional) narrative that relates the dispossession of the slave's body is ironically deployed at the narrative level to dispossess the white landowner of both property and meaning, as John's inability to interpret Julius' story leads to his loss of property. Even Annie—kindred spirit that she is—is dispossessed by Uncle Julius' narrative power. Annie does not fully understand the economic subtext of Julius' story, although her apprehension of the emotional subtext suggests that she understands the horror of slavery, because she too is marginalized and dispossessed. (Indeed, Chesnutt does suggest similarities between the subjugation of the woman and of the slave.) The concluding speech of the story belongs not to John the narrator, nor to Annie who is speaking to John. As the story ends, Annie quotes the words of Julius, addressing John's final objections to the transaction: "'Uncle Julius says that ghosts never disturb religious worship'" (349). And so this story ends with Julius in control of narrative and property. And John? He is buried within the layers of the narrative, his narrative immurement a reflection of Sandy's fate.

The Real Horrors of Slavery: Gothic Strategies in Slave Narratives

While Chesnutt's story of immurement quite consciously operates at the level of the fictional Gothic, the slave narrators, who were intent on presenting a realistic, factual account of slavery also, somewhat paradoxically, deployed Gothic tropes to tell their true histories. Like Uncle Julius, their stories also have a direct goal: to elicit sympathy for a cause that was to them a matter of life and death. Frederick Douglass' *Narrative of the Life of Frederick Douglass, an American Slave* (1845) plunges the reader into the world of the Gothic almost immediately. The first extended memory from Douglass' childhood is the detailed story of the horrifying physical and sexual abuse endured by his aunt. She is tortured by an overseer, "a savage monster" who ties her "up to a joist" (3), and as she dangles, whips "her naked back till she was literally covered with blood" (4). Douglass thus turns to a literary motif to describe the true horror of his situation: the image of the upright bloody woman is the stuff of nightmares and of horror fiction.[8] Indeed Douglass ends the story of his aunt's whipping with a full-throated echo of the excesses of Gothic rhetoric (quite accurate in this instance): "It was the blood-stained gate, the entrance to the hell of slavery" through which his childhood self "was about to pass." He ends with the conventional Romantic iteration of the failure of language in the face of horror: "I wish I could commit to paper the feelings with which I beheld" the "terrible spectacle" (4). Given his upbringing, it is not surprising that when he later discusses leaving his first place of servitude, Great House Farm, Douglass writes, "my home was charmless; it was not home to me" (17). Douglass uncannily anticipates Freud's definition of the *"unheimlich"* (unhomelike) in "The Uncanny," and thus sets the tone for the future events of his story: they take place in a natural world that is uncannily twisted and deformed, with no place of sanctuary for the enslaved.

Indeed, Douglass' life as a slave has more in common with the Gothic text than with a conventional domestic history; he and his fellow slaves live against an everyday backdrop of "atrocious cruelty" (21), "bloody transactions" (5), a system in which a slave may be "literally cut to pieces" (21)—again the language of horror necessary to depict a life of horror. He suffers under a cruel patriarchal system, reflecting the evil patriarchies of the English Gothic: the Church and the State. The patriarchs who head the patriarchy of slavery are as cruel as any tyrants in horror literature. Douglass compares his master to a "grim-visaged pirate" (59), a pillaging character seemingly more suited to the explosive English Gothic text than to an account of the supposedly genteel South. But the comparison is apt. Douglass' master is "a cruel man, hardened by a long life of slaveholding" (3). The overseer Mr. Plummer is a "savage monster" (3). The allegorically named Mr. Severe is "a cruel man … enough to chill the blood and stiffen the hair" (7). The story Douglass tells about the also allegorically named Mr. Gore leaves little doubt as to the monstrosity of the whites who control this inhuman and unnatural system. Douglass introduces the episode with a description of Mr. Gore: "his savage barbarity was equaled only by the consummate coolness with which he committed the grossest and most savage deed" (13). And certainly these words hardly do justice to the action Douglass narrates. A slave named Demby runs into a creek to escape a whipping and refuses to come out. Mr. Gore gives him three chances and then, "without consultation or deliberation with any one, not even giving Demby an additional call, raised his musket to his face, taking deadly aim at his standing victim, and in an instant poor Demby was no more." Demby is reduced to the gore that is the name of his murderer; his mangled body sinks out of sight and "blood and brains marked the water where he had stood." Every spectator except Mr. Gore experiences "a thrill of horror" (14). In this passage Douglass makes it clear that despite the dehumanizing labels imposed upon the slaves, the supposed African savages, Mr. Gore is the barbarous savage in this scene. Slavery may be "dehumanizing" (9)—but it is the whites who become the animals in this system.

Douglass also amplifies the horror of plantation life by comparing the plantation to the Gothic space of hell, inverting the American myth of the new Eden to show the American hell of the American slave, as Joseph Bodziock observes in his reading of Douglass' *My Bondage and My Freedom*. This inversion also appears in the *Narrative*. Douglass sets the stage: "Colonel Lloyd kept a large and finely cultivated garden…. It abounded in fruits of almost every description," including "the hardy apple of the north" (9). This garden is set up as "a temptation to the hungry swarms of boys," but any slave who succumbs to the temptation has "to take the lash" (9). As Bodziock notes, the master of the plantation himself is indeed "not God, but Satan" ("The Cage of Obscene Birds" 258). There are other moments in which Douglass equates the system of slavery with the evil supernatural of the Christian tradition. He condemns "the darkest, foulest, grossest and most infernal deed of slaveholders," as well as condemning the hypocrisy of their Christianity, calling one master "a merciless *religious* wretch" (46). When Douglass is jailed after an aborted escape attempt, he describes the "swarm of slave traders, and agents" who come to the jail to assess the value of the slaves; he compares these whites to "fiends of perdition," looking like "their father, the devil" (54). Similarly Douglass describes the moral decline of a formerly kind mistress ruined by "the fatal poison of irresponsible power" in religious and supernatural terms: "that angelic face gave place to that of a demon" (19). The introduction of the figure of Satan, the image, in the Gothic as well as in the Bible, of absolute supernatural Evil, is a clear gesture to the supernatural forms of the Gothic, in which Satan himself is a recurring nemesis. Douglass also draws on the Gothic and Christian trope of the return from the dead; when he resists a master, he says, "It was a glorious resurrection from the tomb of slavery" (43).[9]

Ultimately, though, Douglass (like the writers of the Female Gothic) adopts the realistic focus upon human evil, rather than depending upon a supernatural explanation for evil in this world. In this vein, Douglass deploys the Gothic tropes of human evil: sexual abuse and the related trauma; family dysfunction, including incest. In the opening sentences of his book Douglass tells us that his mother was a "dark" slave and "my father was a white man" (1). Without actually connecting the dots, he thus suggests the possibility that his conception was the result of rape. Douglass' mother is absent from his early childhood, reflecting the situation of many slaves, and of the typical Gothic narrative in which the mother is erased by repressive social conditions.[10] The aunt, whose beating the young Douglass witnesses, is the target of abuse because of sexual jealousy. A slave owner buys a woman to serve as a "breeder" (37), forcing her to have sex with a slave who happens to be married to someone else. When this forced sex results in twins, "the children were regarded as being quite an addition to his wealth" (37). Douglass thus deploys Gothic strategies to emphasize that the political system of slavery is like the old evil systems described in the English Gothic, the aristocratic patriarchy and the hierarchal church—all are the evil products of human society. There is no protection for slaves within the legal system of the United States, as the system of slavery is impervious to the law, or actually is the law, like the Church and State in the English Gothic. As in the claustrophobic English Gothic text, no space or haven exists outside of the system. The narrative form thus echoes the situation described by William Lloyd Garrison: "There is no legal protection, in fact ... for the slave population, and any amount of cruelty maybe inflicted on them with impunity" (Douglass Introduction xiii). The trope of confinement reflects this claustrophobic situation in both the English Gothic and in Douglass' narrative. He describes his fellow slaves as "shut up in mental darkness" (49), and repeatedly finds himself physically enclosed. During his failed escape he describes the escape route: there was a watchman at every gate, a guard at every ferry; a sentinel on every bridge; a patrol in every wood: "We were hemmed in upon every side" (50). When he is captured, he finds himself "within the walls of a stone prison" (55).

The slave narrative had a very clear and direct purpose: to convince Northern readers to recognize the humanity and rationality of the slave, in order to gain support for the cause of abolition. Given this serious purpose it might seem counterproductive for a clearly intelligent and dignified writer to turn to tropes associated with irrelevant and outlandish fiction. Yet, Douglass' choice of the mode of his text ultimately reveals the choices of a thinking writer. As William Lloyd Garrison writes, Douglass' narrative is addressed to readers who "do not deny that the slaves are held as property," but who are unaware of "cruel scourgings, of mutilations and brandings, or scenes of pollution and blood, of the banishment of all light and knowledge ... concubinage, adultery, and incest" (xii). This is the stuff of the Gothic, not of history, and so Douglass turns to the form that will best convey the urgency of the situation to his innocent readers. In turning to Gothic tropes, Douglass uses a code for horror that is readily accessible to white readers in his time. This code allows him to access established metaphors to convey hellish horror, metaphors which, as he shows, were better suited to describing the situation of the slave than the motifs of other, more respectable genres. Douglass also thus establishes himself as an heir to the Western literary tradition, like his fellow American writers and readers.[11]

* * *

Like Douglass, Harriet Jacobs turns to the Gothic in her slave narrative *Incidents in the Life of a Slave Girl* (1861), to appeal to her readers and to set herself up as a literate, human being, and writer. Like Douglass, Jacobs confronts the odd necessity of proving herself a person with an inner life; she reminds her "reader" that in the world she comes from she is an object: "a slave *being* property, can *hold* no property" (9). Jacobs draws on the full panoply of Gothic tropes in her narrative. She compares slavery to the "Inquisition" (32) and to "hell" (37), two staples of Gothic horror. Invoking the conventional supernatural curse, Jacobs describes "slavery [as] a curse to the whites as well as to the blacks," leading to "the widespread moral ruin occasioned by this wicked system" (46). She points to the warping of the family structure that is a result of slavery, evoking the twisted patriarchy that is the foundation of the Gothic text: "it makes the white fathers cruel and sexual; the sons violent and licentious; it contaminates the daughters and makes the wives wretched" (46). Jacobs also returns to the essential Gothic trope of confinement: escaped slaves are hunted and returned to their "den of bones" (33). One escaped slave is confined to a "cell" (21), in "chains" (22), and "covered with vermin" (23). The horrified reader also encounters many instances of slaves being brutally whipped and tortured. In fact, Jacobs devotes an entire chapter, "Sketches of Neighboring Slaveholders," to vivid and horrifying descriptions of the varied "punishments" (41) endured by slaves. This innocently titled chapter is unremitting in its infliction of painful details upon the white reader, forcing the reader to imagine the terrifying reality of slavery.

Jacobs amplifies this horror by reminding us that, as in Douglass' narrative, as in the Gothic, there is no escape from the all-encompassing system. She lives confined in a claustrophobic world governed by "tyranny," where there was "no shadow of law" for protection (26). Of the array of tropes, the Gothic trope of the female victim of sexual abuse is the central motif of Jacobs' slave narrative. Jacobs emphasizes that women were particularly endangered by slavery, as potential victims of sexual assault, and constantly vulnerable to the loss of their own children. Jacobs works to align herself with the innocent Gothic heroine. She explains that her mother died "when I was six years old" (9). This detail is not a matter of Gothic fiction; it reflects the historical reality of many slave children who were deprived of their parents. Yet is also aligns with the Gothic trope of the motherless and vulnerable young woman. Similarly Jacobs details her exchanges with the predatory patriarch, allegorically called Dr. Flint. From the time of her "fifteenth-year ... [he began] to whisper foul words in my ear" (26). His coarse attempts at seduction suggest that they will lead to rape and worse: "I began to be fearful for my life" (31). To protect herself from this fate and to exert some control over her own body and destiny, Jacobs chooses to begin a sexual relationship with another white man, the also allegorically-named, undependable, Mr. Sands. Eventually, in her continued attempt to escape the power of Dr. Flint, who is still her owner, Jacobs plans a ruse to convince him that she has safely fled to the North. She actually escapes to "a very small garret" (95) in her grandmother's house, afflicted by darkness and "hundreds of little red insects" (97), burning in summer and freezing in winter. Jacobs endures this "virtual entombment" (note vi) for seven years in order to protect her children, all the while sending messages to Dr. Flint that purport to be her letters from the North. Jean Fagan Yellin connects Jacobs with "the metaphor of 'the madwoman in the attic,' the aberrant alter-ego of 'the angel in the house' who inhabits the parlor in popular nineteenth-century fiction" (Introduction xxxi). However, Harryette Mullen makes an equally compelling case for a competing reading in "The Runaway Tongue"; in escaping *into* the house rather than from the house Jacobs figures herself as the typical Gothic heroine, helpless and innocent.

Mullen's insight is important, for it suggests the Jacobs aligns herself with the young innocent Gothic woman to solve a problem that is personal as well as rhetorical. In acknowledging her status as an unwed mother, Jacobs risks losing her self-respect, and the confidence of her readers. Jacobs has been raised by a strict grandmother, so proper that Harriet feels "shamefaced about telling her such impure things" (27)—meaning Dr. Flint's attempts a seduction. In fact, when Jacobs reveals her pregnancy to her grandmother, she does initially reject her: "'Go away ... and never come to my house again'" (50), only becoming reconciled when Jacobs explains that "I saw no [other] way of escape" (51). The rhetorical problem presents itself as Jacobs directly addresses her narrative to the nineteenth-century Northern woman, to whom she turns in an attempt to evoke empathy as a fellow woman and mother. She describes what she imagines as the white women's happy celebration of New

Year's and then turns to the miseries of the slave mother who also "has a mother's instincts, and is capable of feeling a mother's agonies" (17). By revealing her sexual activity, Jacobs risks estranging these readers who are driven by notions of propriety and purity, the female imperatives of their world. By amplifying her similarities to the innocent and chaste Gothic heroine, Jacobs emphasizes her own innocence.

The Gothic serves another rhetorical function for Jacobs, as a mode that appeals to the emotions, rather than to reason. A prefatory "Note" to the Dover edition quotes from a "northern editor": "'Argument provokes argument, reason is met with sophistry, but narratives of slaves go right to the heart'" (v). Thus Jacobs knowingly adopts the strategy of the emotional and irrational Gothic to appeal to her sentimental nineteenth-century Northern female reader. Although Jacobs adopts the romantic tone, she resists the romantic narrative structure of the English Gothic. Unlike the typical Gothic heroine, she never finds romantic love. The young suitor who is cast off by Dr. Flint never does return to win Jacobs' heart. Jacobs is quite clear in distancing herself from the happy ending which awaits the typical heroine of the English Gothic. Her last address to her reader emphasizes her unique fate: "Reader, my story ends with freedom; not in the usual way with marriage" (164). Jacobs thus revises the famous words of Jane Eyre: "Reader I married him." Jacobs discards the happy ending of the English heroine, to discover an American happy ending, as a free and independent woman.

Revenants in Contemporary American Literature: Fears of the White American Mob

Contemporary African American literature continues the turn toward the haunted Gothic as a means to express the horrors of slavery, and of African American life. Natasha Deón's *Grace* (2016) carves out a space in the genre in casting the narrator of the story of a young slave as her ghost mother. At the end of the novel, once the mother has seen her daughter safely settled in freedom, she allows herself to move from her limbo to the next stage of existence where she expects to rejoin her own dead mother. The last word of Deón's novel is "Loved" (402); she thus invokes Toni Morrison's ghost and links herself to a continuing tradition as she acknowledges the "women and writers of color who came before me" (406).

Toni Morrison's *Beloved* (1987) famously turns to the supernatural figure of the ghost, and to many other Gothic tropes to consider the repressions required to survive slavery and its aftermath. Like her precursors, the writers of the slave narratives, Morrison inverts the conventional linkage of the African figure with monstrosity, emphasizing the savage inhumanity of the whites. Seen through the eyes of a slave child, white men are the monsters, "men without skin" (215); they are compared to the four horsemen of the apocalypse (149). Baby Suggs calls them "white things" (89), hardly human. As Baby Suggs tells Denver about "whitepeople ... even when they thought they were behaving, it was a far cry from what real humans did" (244). Morrison also turns to a trope that recurs in the Gothic, the trope of the crowd, the mob. In Morrison's novel the group represents community but also communal jealousy. The extraordinary plenitude of the feast Baby Suggs holds to celebrate her family's reunion "made them mad.... Loaves and fishes were His [Jesus'] powers—they did not belong to an ex-slave.... It made them furious" (137). And the day after the feast, "the scent of their [collective] disapproval lay heavy in the air" (137). The crowd turns away from Baby Suggs when the family encounters the crisis of the death of Beloved, but the community resurfaces to help Sethe's family in their time of need. Denver, Sethe's daughter, finds contributions of food from the community; "Every now and then, all through the spring, names appeared near or in gifts of food" (249). The crowd reappears in the climactic scene of the novel, when thirty women gather at Sethe's house because they sense that "rescue was in order" (256); they plan to save Sethe from the possession of Beloved. Thirty women, each with her own memories of trauma, approach Sethe's house; some pray, but then in unison, they become a sort of benevolent mob: "they stopped praying and took a step back to the beginning" (259). The crowd of women do rescue Sethe, but from a fate different than what they had anticipated. Sethe, driven mad by her troubles, sees "the loving faces before her [and then] sees him" (262), a white man approaching her house. Returning to her past trauma, she believes that once again a white man is coming for her child: "She flies. The ice pick is not in her hand; it is her hand"; she is about to kill this white man (who is actually benevolent), which would seal her doom, when the crowd saves her. Sethe "is running.... Now she is running into the faces of the people out there, joining them ... to the pile of people out there. They make a hill ... of black people falling" (262), preventing Sethe from killing the white man and destroying herself.

Toni Morrison's notion of the crowd thus disputes the picture developed by Gustave le Bon in his classic study *The Crowd: A Study of the Popular Mind* (1895). Le Bon expresses a clearly condemnatory opinion of the crowd, the manifestation of the democratic will of the people, and of communal thinking. He highlights the dangers of the mob, noting that crowds are "always intellectually inferior to the isolated individual" (914). Le Bon wrote in response to various movements toward democracy occurring in the late nineteenth century, and expressed concern that "the voice of the masses has become preponderant. It is this voice that dictates their conduct to kings" (xv), adding that "civilisations as yet have only been created by a small intellectual aristocracy, never by crowds.... Crowds are only powerful for destruction" (xviii). The dangerous, destructive, revolutionary mob appears periodically in the English Gothic, most notably as the mob which destroys the church at the end of Matthew Lewis' *The Monk* (1796), tearing apart the body of an abbess in the process. The Marquis de Sade, among others, observes that the mobs of late eighteenth-century fiction recall the recent mobs of the French Revolution tearing down the center of power, the Bastille.

* * *

The crowd, the destructive mob that emblematizes conservative antidemocratic fears of a populace gone amok in the English Gothic, resurfaces in the post–Revolutionary American Gothic. Like the crowd of neighbors in *Beloved*, the motif of neighbors turned mob appears in Shirley Jackson's *We Have Always Lived in the Castle* (1962). In Jackson's novel, the crowd is more antagonistic and subversive. Recalling the French mob, they attack the home of the last two descendants of the American aristocratic family, the Blackwoods. When the patriarchal home is set afire, in classic Gothic style, the townspeople initially gather to put out the fire, although there are dissenters in the unruly mob: "'Why not let it burn?'" (152), they call; "'Let it burn'" (152). The fire is brought under control by the town's firefighters, but once they have fulfilled their civic duty, chaos erupts. The fire chief himself "took of his hat saying CHIEF ... and ... while everyone watched, he took up a rock" (154). The entire mob follows his lead, throwing rocks at the patriarchal house. When they see the fleeing sisters, they call, "put them back in the house and start the fire all over again" (157), and surround the girls threateningly. All that remains after the pillaging of the house are ruins of the old building. It "ended above the kitchen doorway in a nightmare of black and twisted wood" (167). Everything is "ugliness and ruin and shame" (167). Inside all their possessions are damaged and destroyed. Merricat, the younger sister, inspired by the remaining fragments of burnt wood that appear to her as spires, concludes, "Our house was a castle, turreted and open to the sky" (177). Jackson thus returns her American Gothic to its English forms. As in Radcliffe's novel, *A Sicilian Romance*, the patriarchal home ends as a ruined castle and the last of the dynastic line becomes a temporary matriarchy. Even when the townspeople, prefiguring Morrison's community, apologetically deliver food to the recluses after the fire, they do so more out of fear than neighborliness. When a boy comes close to the house and teases the reclusive sisters, they immediately receive "a basket of fresh eggs, and a note reading, 'He didn't mean it, please'" (214). Sadly, Jackson cannot imagine a happier ending for her female protagonists.

* * *

The image of the American mob explodes in the form of the zombie mob in many narratives of the twenty-first century, including Colson Whitehead's *Zone One* (2011). The zombie echoes Nathaniel Hawthorne's young Ned, the "little devourer of Jim Crow and the elephant" (67), who voraciously eats his way through a variety of cookies in *The House of the Seven Gables*, as well as his other hungry American brothers. The American zombie mob multiplies the single devouring American, now expanded to the voracious, irrational crowd, eternally hungry for human flesh.

The fiction of the African American writer, Colson Whitehead, is immersed in the genre of horror, frequently invoking the figure of the zombie. In his autobiographical novel *Sag Harbor* (2009), about a boyhood summer in an African American beach community, Whitehead inserts horror imagery in a way that initially seems jarring and inexplicable. Zombie images proliferate throughout the novel. Benji, the adolescent narrator, describes his misguided attempt to impress his high school peers with his learned allusions to "Master of Horror, George Romero" (31), who in his film *Night of the Living Dead* (1968) brought the figure of the zombie to the forefront of popular culture. Benji compares the increasing beach population to the "Hampton Undead … disgorged from … their crypts" (66). When besieged by customers at the popular ice cream shop where he works, Benji thinks wistfully of a "Zombie Hideout" (132) where he can escape. He adds, "I know that when the living dead come, it will not be at the mall that they gather, but at the ice cream shop" (133), returning to their favorite haunts, like the "stragglers" in *Zone One* (2011). Benji vividly describes the hordes of customers descending on the shop (134). Most tellingly, for mystified readers of *Zone One*, Whitehead reveals the explanation of the particular horror associated with the reviled Connecticut of that later zombie novel. In *Sag Harbor*, Connecticut is the source of the largest invasion of ice cream customers: "They boarded a ferry for an outing to the Hamptons.... They raided the curio shops, stopped traffic as the slow herd of them meandered across the street, dawdled in glassy-eyed pleasure at the kitschy whaling paraphernalia." Then, when they finish rampaging through the rest of the town, they pour "stampeding into Jonni Waffle with their tongues hanging over their lips" (248). Behind the rampaging, the glassy eyes, and the hanging tongues lurks the image of the rampaging, mindless zombie mob. Even when Benji sneaks into his former house with a girl, he recalls his younger days when he would imagine "jumping off the porch to escape ... a mass of zombies" (304).

Whitehead's fond nostalgia for zombies erupts in *Zone One*, an unsettling story of a group of soldiers trying to clear lower Manhattan of a worldwide zombie invasion. In this novel, Whitehead amplifies the American Gothic trope of invasion; he also invokes the uncanniness of America by setting his horror story in a world that is, on the material level, remarkably unchanged. Throughout the novel, the point of view character, known as "Mark Spitz," returns to the old haunts of his youth, bewildered to find that after the zombie apocalypse, they still look the same. To Mark Spitz, "New York City in death was very much like New York City in life" (80). Whitehead thus presents a clear example of Freud's uncanny: New York City is the past home that is familiar, yet no longer completely recognizable, no longer homey. One of the many oddities of this strange novel is that Whitehead, an African American writer who frequently explores issues of race in his fiction, seems to suppress racial issues here. George Romero's first film is founded upon American racial anxiety; the surviving African American male protagonist is eventually shot by a local militia who mistake him for a zombie, leaving behind the frequent question of the American Gothic: who exactly is the monster and who is the human? Yet, Whitehead's novel seems devoid of racial themes until the end of the novel when we discover that the source of the name Mark Spitz is a racial stereotype. The original Mark Spitz had "been an Olympic swimmer in the previous century" (287), and the sobriquet is an ironic commentary on the character's unwillingness or inability to swim. As Mark explains this name to his dying friend, he adds, "'Plus the black-people-can't-swim thing, [a] stereotype'" (287). Only then does the reader realize the racial identity of the central character; he is one more in the long line of African American men running from a bloodthirsty mob. Even then, Mark, or Whitehead, represses matters of race. "Mark Spitz" thinks, "There was a single Us now, reviling a single Them" (288), all the living against all the monstrous Others. Mark's words suggest an erasure of the older categories of the human, including race. Yet "Mark" remains skeptical: "They could certainly reanimate prejudice." Connecting racism to the zombies, he thinks: "There were plenty of things in the world that deserved to stay dead, yet they walked" (288). The swimming stereotype returns at the end of the book, when the attempt to clear lower Manhattan fails, and the zombies stream into the city with renewed force. Once again in this novel a sanctuary has fallen, and "Mark Spitz" finds himself alone, surrounded by zombies who stream down the street as he watches from his hiding place. Realizing that no one will be coming to rescue him, he makes a decision: "The river was closer. Maybe he should swim for it.... Fuck it, he thought. You have to learn to swim sometime. He opened the door and walked into the sea of the dead" (322). What eventually happens to Mark—whether he manages to "pass" in the crowd, swim with the tide of the dead to attain freedom, or is overcome by the mob—is as ambiguous as the ultimate meaning of the zombie. This monster, like other Gothic monsters, is available for a multitude of interpretations. The zombies can be seen as embodying a number of fears of invasion: by plagues, tourists, consumers, or by gentrification and urbanization. They could symbolize the desire to return to moral clarity where good is visibly distinguishable from evil, where the reader might be able to indulge in the fantasy of shooting the neighbor next door. At times the book seems like a call for appreciating our present time, fraught as it is: his characters reiterate their nostalgia for the pre-zombie days, our current moment. Just as Whitehead leaves open the question of his main character's fate, he leaves open the question of what exactly the zombies mean.

As *Sag Harbor* clarifies the Connecticut mystery of *Zone One*, Whitehead's most recent book, *Underground Railroad* (2016), offers a compelling interpretation of his zombies. Though less unrealistic and supernatural than *Zone One*, *Underground Railroad* does turn to fantasy, deploying the Gothic strategy of literalization, taking a metaphor (often a legal fiction, like *coverture*) and presenting a literal image of the metaphor (like the imprisonment of the wife). In his book, Whitehead literalizes the metaphor of the underground railroad, imagining the materialization of a physical railroad, with cars, conductors and stations; it is this railroad that whisks Cora, the main character, toward freedom. Furthermore, Whitehead creates a correspondence between *Railroad* to *Zone One* in the imagery of the books and the pattern of the plots. Just as "Mark Spitz" has to move from place to place, finding only temporary sanctuary from the mob, so Cora must constantly pick up and flee as she is repeatedly endangered by the white mob—as irrational, inhuman and bloodthirsty as any zombie crowd—invading her sanctuary. The book begins with the escape of Cora, a young African American slave, who is harried and pursued throughout the novel, which follows the stages of her journey as she repeatedly finds a haven at one of the stops on the underground railroad, until is it invaded by a white mob out to destroy her. When we meet Ridgeway, the unremitting stalker of Cora (recalling Mr. Trappe in Crafts' *The Bondswoman's Narrative*), he is a boy being initiated into a crowd of "patrollers" who terrorize the African American slaves in Georgia; we learn from his point of view of "the excitement of the hunt" (75). As he grows into manhood, "Ridgeway fell in with a circle of slave catchers, gorillas stuffed into black suits" (79) who chase "lost property" (79), escaped slaves. Ridgeway gains "renown for ensuring that property remained property." In the course of the hunt, Ridgeway's mob occasionally goes after whites who abet the Underground Railroad. Ridgeway calls upon one such "man after midnight." We hear only indirectly of the attack: Ridgeway's "fists swelled for two days from beating the man's face in. He permitted his men to dishonor the man's wife in ways he had never let them use a nigger gal" (81). Clearly we are in the natural, realistic Gothic world, like the world of the Female Gothic, in which the actual source of horror is the white human male. The "slave mothers" recognize this as they warn their children: "'Mind yourself or Mr. Ridgeway will come for you'" (81); he is far more threatening than any imaginary hobgoblin. Ridgway the slave catcher is the leader of each invasion of Cora's sanctuary. He expresses his almost supernatural omnipresence when he finally catches up to Cora: "'I go here, I go there. I've been after this one for a long time'" (186).

However, Ridgeway never acts alone. He is always supported by the white racist population, and by the laws of that other hidden mob, the governments of the Southern states, which enable the popular mob to do its work. As in the claustrophobic English Gothic, the real horror is that the entire system is evil, with no way out. However, in the English Gothic, the system is run by individual aristocrats; in Whitehead's America, the system of the masses, the mob, is the font of evil. In South Carolina, Ridgweay gathers "a posse" (130) of "many men" that thunders above Cora's hiding place in a station of the railroad. They ransack "the house and shouted, knocking over cabinets and unending furniture. The noise was loud and violent." When they finally leave, Cora hears "the glass shatter and the pop and crackle of the wood. The house was on fire" (131). This mob thus re-enacts the actions of Shirley Jackson's mob, but they have a new American identity. They are no longer Jackson's revolutionary peasants, destroying the patriarchal home; they are the new American crowd, engulfing and destroying the human beings that they possess. They are zombies. When Cora reaches Whitehead's imaginary North Carolina, she finds an extreme version of the evil state: "In North Carolina, the Negro race did not exist except at the end of ropes" (156). African Americans are denied entry to the state, and are doomed by their very identity. If they are discovered, they are immediately killed (making a fair connection between the American South and Nazi Germany). As Cora peers out from her new sanctuary, "her latest cage" (160), another white mob gathers. A speaker "caught the crowd up" (158), reminding them in a reversal of logic and reality that they, the whites, are threatened by a "black horde" (160); "a colored girl [is dragged] onstage" and hanged, or lynched, with a "rope [thrown] over a thick sturdy branch" (160). Finally, Cora herself is captured by the mob as she hides under a bed, "where they found her, snatching her ankles like irons and dragging her out. They tossed her down the stairs" (184). This mob also enacts vengeance on the white Americans who defy its systems and laws. Before the mob surrounds Cora—"the town moved in and then Cora couldn't see them anymore" (188)—she witnesses the hanging and stoning of her white protectors. Cora does attain one more temporary sanctuary. She is rescued from Ridgway by Royal, "the first freeborn man Cora had ever met" (260), and brought to "the Valentine farm," an African American utopia in Indiana, where she finds a community that welcomes people from the "dispossessed tribe" (264), and romantic love with the appropriately named Royal.

Yet, as Whitehead observes in *Zone One*, for the besieged African American all sanctuaries eventually fail. At a community meeting, a speaker exposes the fantasy of security, reminding the community that in white America, their sanctuary is a "delusion" because "'America too, is a delusion,'" founded for the goal of satisfying the insatiable white hunger: "The white race believes ... that it is their right to take the land. To kill Indians. Make war. Enslave their brothers.... This nation shouldn't exist. Yet here we are'" (285). The words of the speaker regarding the illusory nature of the sanctuary are fulfilled. Like the final sanctuary of "Mark Spitz" in *Zone One*, Cora's sanctuary falls to a horde of invaders. The meeting is interrupted by an inhumanly murderous white mob, with Ridgway at its head; like predatory animals (as inhuman as zombies), "the white men outside whooped and howled over the carnage ... the white posse dragged men and women into the dark, their hideous faces awash with delight" (287). As in *Zone One*, after the sanctuary falls, "each person [is] on their own, as they ever had been" (*Underground Railroad* 288). After one last escape on the underground railroad, pumping a handcar by herself down the tracks, Cora, like "Mark Spitz" at the conclusion of his narrative, emerges into a crowd. Re-enacting a rebirth, Cora exits from the tunnel of the railroad to discover herself on a wagon trail, watching a line of wagons headed west. Cora avoids the two white wagon drivers but manages to mingle into the crowd (like "Mark") by climbing into a wagon ridden by "an older negro man" with kind eyes and "a horseshoe brand on his neck" (306). Thus, although the fate of "Mark Spitz" remains unclear at the end of his narrative, as he plunges into the mob, "the sea of the dead" (*Zone One* 322), we have a clearer sense about the promise of Cora's future at the end of her journey. She has managed to join the American mob journeying to California, and there is a possibility that she may actually discover an American sanctuary that endures.

Thus Whitehead creates a Gothic intertextuality within his own *oeuvre*, with its ever-recurring tropes, as he introduces, develops, and explains his understanding of the figure of the zombie as the white American mob from the perspective of the African American: mindless, barely human, bloodthirsty, eternally voracious, and eternally eager to entrap and drain the black body of its life forces and of its humanity. Like his precursors, Whitehead turns to the genre of horror to fully encompass the horror of African American history, and to remind his audience that, for African Americans, American history has been the claustrophobic site of recurring and inescapable Gothic horror.

3

Return of the Dead
The Rebirth of the Dispossessed Native American

Long before there was an American country, or an American literature, indeed before the emergence of the Gothic in England, the themes of the Gothic infiltrated the American sensibility through accounts of encounters with Native Americans. The captivity narratives of New England, an "important expression of Puritan theological and social thought" (T. Vaughan and Edward Clark *Puritans Among the Indians* vii), which "fused the prominent features of spiritual autobiography, lay sermon, and jeremaid with those of the secular adventure story" (10), anticipated the great theme of the Gothic novel, the encounter of the innocent subject with the unknowable, inhumanly evil Other.[1]

In *Providence Tales and the Birth of American Literature*, James Hartman finds in "Increase and Cotton Mather's witchcraft narratives an unusual blend of the gothic and the domestic" (93). Cotton Mather associated the captivity tale with the providence tale, "the story of God's activity on earth" (Hartman 18), and combined the two genres in the *Magnalia Christi Americana* (1702). Hartman notes that both types of narrative feature "Gothic action and settings" (27). Hartman adds that Mather wrote numerous tales of "bodily possession," including "instances of ventriloquism ... which was considered a preternatural occurrence in the seventeenth century" (27). (Mather thus prefigures Brown's semi-demonic Carwin in *Wieland*.)

David Mogen actually argues that the American Gothic was a conscious artistic response to this first literature, "as native frontier materials were self-consciously adapted to fit gothic conventions" illustrating "how close the two traditions are thematically" ("Wilderness, Metamorphosis, and Millennium" 97). The Gothic also served a useful purpose in that it was a mode ready-made to address issues of possession and dispossession, spectrality and horror, and the naturalization of such experiences in the new savage country, as expressed by Edgar Huntly when he stumbles upon yet another instance of Native American "savagery" and says, "Custom ... had inured me to spectacles of horror" (222). When the world is Gothic, the Gothic is the genre best suited to describe it.

The Demonic, Spectralized and Displaced Indian

From the first, Native Americans were figured as inhumanly evil, supernaturally aligned with Satan. Mary Rowlandson's *A True History of the Captivity and Restoration of Mrs. Mary Rowlandson* (1682), in which the narrator essentially dies and then returns from the dead, sets the tone for the literature that follows. Rowlandson describes the Native American captors, with whom she lives intimately, as "Infidels" (9), "Pagans" (10), "Heathen" (19, 35). Only a short leap from the picture of the Native Americans as non–Christians leads to the alignment of the Native American with Satan, a featured nemesis in a number of English Gothic novels. Rowlandson describes her captors as "hell-hounds" (10). Her first night of captivity is recounted in explicitly infernal terms, as she endures "the roaring, and singing, and dancing and yelling of those black creatures in the night, which made the place a lively resemblance of hell!" (10). Rowlandson seems inspired by her own excessive rhetoric; there are other moments when her narrative takes a delightfully Gothic turn. The Native Americans are not only demonic, they also take on the trappings of that Gothic staple, the lunatic: they are "unstable and like madmen" (38), and toward the end of the narrative, her Native American Master begins "to rant as if he had been mad" (41). At one point, in an anticipation of Brown's American revision of the site of horror, Rowlandson writes that the swamp "in which we lay was, as it were, a deep Dungeon" (20).

Rowlandson's demonization of the Native Americans, as well as the overwrought Gothic excess of her prose, reflects the theology and tone of her Puritan culture. As David Mogen argues in his essay "Wilderness, Metamorphosis, and Millennium," "for most of the first two centuries of colonization Satan's influence was to Puritan settlers as much a fact of life as the New England winter" (95). In his forward to *Puritans, Indians, and Manifest Destiny*, Sacvan Bercovitch elaborates. The Puritans saw the Native American as "the antagonists to the new chosen people ... villains in a sacred drama ... children of the Devil who tempted Christ in the desert.... There were two parties in the new world, God's and the Devil's.... Satan's party is dark-skinned, heathen, and doomed" (17). In the formulation of Cotton Mather, the influential Puritan leader, Native Americans had indeed been created by

God, descending from Adam and Eve, but they had been enticed to the New World by Satan.

In "From Imitating Language to a Language of Imitation," Richard Pointer presents a theory for the demonization of the Native American that is less about theology than about nation building, or identity consolidation. He argues that the Puritan fear of the Native America Other, reveals a fear of losing Puritan Christian identity in the wild New World, and of becoming like the savage inhabitants of that strange place. Thus, the figure of the demonized Native American as absolute Other worked to stabilize Puritan identity during an unsettling time and place (similar to the way the African Other stabilized American identity in Morrison's formulation). Ironically, the early white American narratives do show the permeability of the border between English Christian identity and Native American identity. Rowlandson loses hold of her self-possession and self-definition as a civilized Christian woman in a moment when she describes her own horrifying (and voracious) action: she eats a half-cooked horse's liver "with the blood about my mouth" (21). The scene is later echoed by Brown's Edgar Huntly as he hungrily devours a recently killed panther.

Not only were Native Americans dispossessed of their humanity through demonization, their land was appropriated from them in the forced movement of the clearances. Renée Bergland explains, "the age of Indian Removal is often demarcated as the period between 1820–1850. However, the United States was actively engaged in Indian Removal and Indian war almost continuously from its inception" (*National Uncanny* 50). Additionally, in *The Other Slavery*, Andrés Reséndez documents the Native American experience of the civil death of slavery. He notes that in the middle of the nineteenth century, "the buying and selling of Indians was a common practice" in California (2). In Utah, the Mormon settlers engaged in the practice of buying Native Americans in order to save them, not just spiritually, but also as an investment; for the slavers would torture children "to call attention to their trade and elicit sympathy from potential buyers" (3). Of particular importance is the "clandestine and invisible nature of Indian slavery" (5); the guarantee that everything about the Native American was defined by silence and obscurity.

The American Hell: Appropriations of Native American Lands

Charles Post asserts that the theological imperative of the Puritans and their successors, worked to successfully veil economic expediency in religious obfuscation: the real need for the disappearance of the Indian was the desire to possess the land. Post points to "the continuous reproduction of the frontier through the expropriation of Native American populations" (455), and adds that the "Decimation of Native American populations through force and disease made large swathes of fertile land available for English settlement" (Post 462).

Yet, although the land was desirable to European Americans the demonization (or gothicization) of the Native American extended to the land itself. Hartman notes that "along with the physical devils comes a physical hell, the wilderness these devils inhabit" (Hartman 29). The land, as David Mogen notes, is a "gothic domain" (95) in the Puritan imagination. Charles Segal and David Stineback add that, in the Puritan world-view, fields and cities (the spaces of the European) were safe and civilized. Nature on the other hand, "the wilderness," was the domain of Satan and his minions, the Native Americans: "the territorial domain he [Satan] needed to oppose God in centuries to come" (*Puritans, Indians and Manifest Destiny* 33). Mogen adds that the wilderness could also serve as a locus of Gothic enclosure; he presents "the journey into the wilderness not as a quest but as a captivity, the ordeal of the first American heroes, usually female, struggling to keep the light of faith aglow in heathen darkness" (96).

This view of the land clearly sets the tone for *Edgar Huntly* (1799), in which Charles Brockden Brown depicts the wilderness as the site of Gothic mayhem. It also sets the tone for the representations of the Frontier by the writers who are discussed in the collection *Frontier Gothic: Terror and Wonder at the Frontier in American Literature*. As articulated by David Mogen, Scott Sanders, and JoAnne Karpinski, the editors of this collection, "the frontier is an intrinsically gothic symbol in American literature, evoking supernatural terror" (15), in that the unknown lies beyond the frontier.

Cultural Dispossession: The Erasure of Native American Culture

Since the Native Americans in their pre–Christian state were doomed, they faced two choices as far as the Puritans were concerned: actual death or cultural extinction, loss of cultural, linguistic, and religious identity through assimilation and conversion. Charles Segal and David Stineback note, "Both ways were a victory for God's people over Satan, since the Indian would be conceding, in violence or submission, his cultural nonexistence" (3). Thus the necessary endpoint of the Indian, the ally of Satan, was his death, physical or spiritual. As Segal and Stineback note, this was the same "ultimatum" (37) offered to the Native Americans during the westward movement of the nineteenth century. The final plan for the Native American was articulated in the philosophy of Richard Pratt, the founder of the infamous Indian School in Carlisle Pennsylvania in the late nineteenth century. His express goal for his charges was to fully assimilate them. The students were removed from their families, through force or trickery, and relocated to Carlisle. Once there, the students were forbidden to speak their native languages or dress in their native clothes. The project of the school as stated by Pratt, was to "kill the Indian and save the man." Zitkala-Ša, a Native American writer, who was herself a teacher at Carlisle in the late nineteenth century, wrote a memoir in the early twentieth century, in which she spoke of her own experience at an Indian School in the 1880s. When she arrived at the school, she was forced to allow the cutting of her long hair, a sign of pride and cultural identity. When she hid under a bed, she remembers "being dragged out.... I felt the cold blades of the scissors against my neck.... Then I lost my spirit.... Now I was one of many little animals driven by a herder" (437–438). Later she calls the school a "civilizing machine" (442). Zitkala-Ša's words offer witness to the process of dehumanization; the killing of the Native American spirit, leaving behind an empty and conflicted child.

The Spectralized Indian

As a consequence of the multiple displacements of the Native Americans, dehumanized and exiled from land, culture, and self, all that remained in the white imagination was a dead ghostly entity. Almost from the first encounters with the European, the Native American was written off as dead, ghostly, absent and invisible. As Renée L. Bergland, whose *The National Uncanny* focuses "on the figure of the Indian ghost" (3) asserts, "When European Americans speak of Native Americans, they always use the language of ghostliness" (1). By concentrating almost exclusively on those who perished, early American writers enacted a "literary Indian removal that reinforced and at times even helped to construct the political Indian Removal.... Motifs of dispossession recur again and again in early American descriptions of Native Americans" (3). In *Removals*, Lucy Maddox adds, "the removal of the native population from American territory was paralleled by their exile from nineteenth-century American literature" (144). Maddox explains that "the one significant blind spot in *most* readings of nineteenth-century American literature has been the failure to take seriously the presence of the American Indians as a factor in the shaping of the literature" (173). Bergland adds, "First and foremost, the ghosting of

Indians is a technique of removal. By writing about Indians as ghosts, white writers effectively remove them from American lands" (4). Here was another use of the Gothic mode for American writers, as it offered a pre-existing literary context for ghostliness, as well as for narratives of appropriation.

As early as 1819, Washington Irving was bemoaning the sad fate of the dying Native American in "Traits of Indian Character." Irving is far more sympathetic than his demonizing Puritan forbears toward "The Indians on our frontiers, mere wrecks and remnants of once powerful tribes" (226). Echoing Gothic language of dispossession and usurpation, Irving notes the wrongs done to the Native Americans who were "doubly wronged by the white men. They have been dispossessed of their hereditary possessions ... and their characters have been traduced by bigoted and interested writers" (225). Irving further indicts the "white men [who] are the usurpers of their ancient dominion" (229); the Indians "were invaded, corrupted, despoiled" (233), and subject to treatment that was quite savage: "wigwams were wrapped in flames and the miserable inhabitants shot down and slain in attempting to escape" (231). Despite his sympathy, though, Irving cannot envision a future for the Native Americans: "They will vanish like a vapour from the face of the earth" (233), disappearing into a ghostly mist. Indeed Irving quotes an old warrior who agrees with the white assessment of the future of his people: "'the white man will cease to persecute us—for we shall cease to exist!'" (233).

Edgar Huntly: The Dispossessed and Spectralized Native American

Although the Native American is a significant presence in Charles Brockden Brown's *Edgar Huntly* (1799), he is far more spectral than human. Brown reflects the dehumanization and disappearance of the Indian in his representation of these unknowable, silent and dangerous figures. The Native Americans in *Huntly* emblematize the ghostly, absent Indian, dispossessed of land, identity and existence. The European repression of the presence of the Native American in the North American continent is reflected in Edgar's announcement when he finds himself in the wilderness that "since the birth of this continent, I was probably the first who had deviated thus remotely from the customary paths of men." He claims that "the aboriginal inhabitants had no motives to lead them into caves like this." He also claims that "their successors were still less likely to have wandered hither." Moments later Huntly is surprised by "a human countenance!" (99), the face of the European friend he has been seeking. Clearly Huntly is wrong about the human presence in that wild place, and is probably wrong in denying the possibility of an Indian presence there.

The otherness of the Native American figures renders them unknowable and inhumanly spectral even when they are seemingly present in the novel. Except for some brief passages about Mab, a mysterious—and certainly not entirely human—Native American, and an aside in which Huntly acknowledges "that a long course of injuries and encroachments had lately exasperated the Indian tribes" (166), the Indians are viewed from the outside, without empathy, as murderous, inhuman and silent. They are "strange and uncouth," "brawny and terrific figures," "Red-men" who "made ... frequent and destructive inroads into the heart of the English settlement" (165). This ironic inversion represses the humanity of the Indian, as it also represses the inhumanity of the English who were invading the Indian lands. The inhumanly irrational savagery of the Indians ultimately provides the somewhat random solution for the central mystery of the novel: who killed Huntly's friend Waldegrave? It is discovered that the "hostile" intentions of "a troop" of Native Americans were thwarted and "one of them ... more sanguinary and audacious than the rest would not depart, without some gratification of his vengeance" (270–271)—the unhappy result being the murder of Waldegrave.

The belated revelation that Edgar's family was also brutalized by Native Americans highlights the savagery of the Indians, while also illustrating the psychological repression of the Native American presence and agency. Only belatedly in the novel does Edgar acknowledge that his absent parents and baby sibling were attacked and killed by Native American "assassins," who "assailed" his "father's house ... at the dead of night.... My parents and an infant child were murdered in their beds; the house was pillaged and then burnt to the ground" (166). In an instance of reversal, the white Europeans are dispossessed by the Indians. Huntly frames the lasting psychological impact of this trauma in terms of spectrality, anticipating the terms of the Freudian uncanny (the return of the repressed): "Most men are haunted by some species of terror or antipathy, which they are, for the most part, able to trace to some incident which befell them in their early years. You will not be surprised that the fate of my parents ... should produce lasting and terrific images in my fancy. I never looked upon, or called up the image of a savage without shuddering" (166).

* * *

Edgar Huntly clearly indicates that the motive behind the erasure of the Native American presence, the spectralization of these humans, was to justify the possession of Indian lands. In his Introduction to *Huntly,* Norman S. Grabo notes that the novel responds to a reality of Brown's time and place. The novel is set in 1787 following "the displacement of the Delawares" (xv) in Easton, Pennsylvania, 1756–1758. As Grabo recounts, "the government of Pennsylvania entered into a peace treaty with the Delaware or Lenni-Lenape Indians.... With the defeat of the French ... in 1758, the Indians had to ... accept ultimate English victory and the inevitable settlement of Europeans. Through the 'Walking Purchase of 1737'... the Delaware were outfoxed into surrendering more than twice the territory they had in mind to the Pennsylvania Proprietaries" (xii). Grabo notes that the book is haunted by the displacement of the Delawares, especially in the episode of the dispossession of the Native American woman, "Queen Mab." The events in Pennsylvania are "the origin of the displacement of Queen Mab's cohort, and the source of their bitter resentment against the white invaders ... nobody doubted that the land grab of 1737 weighed heavily on the minds of both whites and Indians" (xii-xiii). To this Bergland adds her insight about the convergence of ghostly possession, psychological possession and land possession in Brown's narrative of Queen Mab: "notably the discussion of her emotions and her thoughts is framed in terms of 'possession.' At the same time, the root of the conflict is contested possession of the land itself" ("Diseased States, Public Minds: Native American Ghosts in Early National Literature" 96). Brown's Queen Mab, originally "know among her neighbors by the name of Old Deb,"[2] is from the tribes of the "Delawares or Lennilennapee" (Brown 197). "All these districts were once comprised within the dominions of that nation," however, "in consequence of the perpetual encroachments of the English colonists, they abandoned their ancient seats," all except for one old woman who resisted this dispossession and stayed to "maintain possession of the land" (197–198). Queen Mab lives with three dogs, her supernatural familiars and the guardians of her property: "they were her servants and protectors" of the space, "That sacred asylum they would not suffer to be violated, and no stranger could enter it but at the imminent hazard of his life" (198).

In the Mab narrative Brown sympathetically emphasizes that there are two sides to the story of possession and dispossession. Mab's clan's suffered the "perpetual encroachments" of the English (198), and, indeed their appropriated village had been on land that became the site of the "barn yard and orchard" (198) of Edgar's uncle. Huntly states: "To the rest of mankind they [Mab and her dogs] were aliens or enemies" (198) but then immediately tells us that to Mab, "the English were aliens and sojourners" (199). From Mab's perspective the invading English, whom she tries to deny and repress in "retain[ing] possession of all this region" (199), resurface as the uncanny and alien presence. When Mab is again displaced, she takes "possession" of an abandoned, unowned hut (201), built by a settler too poor to buy land, who "cleared a field in the unappropriated wilderness" (200) and then disappeared.

Dispossessed, Mab thus takes possession of land that had been appropriated by a white settler, perpetuating a seemingly unending and entangled chain of possession and dispossession. In the narrative of Mab, American property takes on a variety of aspects, some unknown to the English Gothic: the American wilderness and the hut; the building and the land; property inherited, or appropriated. Brown thus works to expand the limited terms of English property possession, as presented in the English Gothic. The conventional English Gothic model of the ultimate inheritor is the noble, aristocratic, displaced and reinstated, young male property owner, who appears in the groundbreaking English Gothic novels, Walpole's Castle of *Otranto* (1764) and Clara Reeve's *Old English Baron* (1777). Brown resurrects this figure as the uncanny, ancient, Native American woman. The name Huntly bestows upon her indicates his awareness of her supernatural power, and also of her lineage as an American "aristocrat": the original Queen Mab, the namesake of the Indian woman, is the Queen of the fairies in English legend. Brown's disposal of Mab is appropriately framed in terms of property possession, and in terms of repression. After Mab's confession of her culpability in the murder of Waldegrave, she "boldly defie[s] her oppressors [and] remain[s] in her ancient dwelling and prepare[s] to meet the consequences" (271). The result of those consequences is hidden from the reader. When Mab is next mentioned, she has already been effaced; we learn in a letter from Huntly to Sarsefield that "Deb's hut has found a new tenant" (275). In his text, then, Brown anticipates and effects the process of repression of the uncanny Native American as well as working to repress the English presence that haunts his novel.

In *Huntly* the conventional problem of possession of the Gothic space—dark, haunted and unknown—the problem that preoccupies American history and literature, echoes the old English questions of property possession and appropriation. The process of the repression of past trauma, and its return in anxious new forms is the transformation that Brown notes in his Preface: "the western wilderness" taking on the tense role of the disputed "Gothic castles" (3) of English literature. As Freud asserts in "The Uncanny" (which seems to be as much about literature as about the science of human psychology), the reappearance of "the frightening element repressed which *recurs*"[3] takes on uncanny forms in later manifestations (217). *Huntly* revisits the questions of possession of real estate that preoccupy the English Gothic but Brown revises the terms, thus creating an American uncanny. The problems of the old world recur in unrecognizable new forms to display the anxieties of his new time and place. While Brown does revisit some old problems of power and possession in *Huntly*, he pointedly refuses to dwell on others. At one point Huntly comes upon a farmstead where he discovers a mother and baby in a barn, while a drunken man lies on a bed inside the house. Huntly deduces that this is the old familiar European scene; he recognizes in the figure a former acquaintance, a "debauched husband or father" (219), "who resided several years in Europe" (219) and had recently returned. The woman in the barn is his abused wife, who "to shun outrage and violence ... had fled, with her helpless infant, to the barn" (220). Huntly concludes that "to suggest a remedy for this distress was not in my power" (220) and makes a rapid departure. Brown thus chooses to identify the abuse of women as an old European problem, originating in England, and of no concern to the new American man, thereby repressing the situation of women in America.

Brown illustrates the point of his Preface as he replaces the disputed and haunted castle with the dark, unknowable wilderness. Brown repeatedly stresses the wild and unknowable nature of the land. A sleepwalker, Huntly suddenly wakes to find himself lost and displaced in a "darkness that environed me.... I was wrapt in the murkiest and most impenetrable gloom" (152). At first Huntly reverts to the old models: "Methought I was the victim of some tyrant who had thrust me into a dungeon of his fortress" (154), and imagines himself "buried alive," prematurely "consigned ... to the tomb" (155), after having "fallen into seeming death" (155)—live burial being a popular motif in the Gothic. Finally, after much exertion and thought, he realizes that he has fallen into a natural space, but no less mysterious and deadly: "a pit" (156), from which there seems to be no escape. Managing to get out of the cave, Huntly begins a nightmarish journey through the wilderness where he is transformed into a new kind of American, a killer and an adventurer, unknown to his previous civilized self. The dangerous wilderness is thus capable of taking possession, as well as of being possessed. Of this new self Huntly says, "I was not governed by the soul which usually regulates my conduct" (184), and admits that anyone who knew him would "scarcely allow credit to my story" (185). In fact (like Mary Rowlandson) Huntly comes dangerously close to being as savage as his nemeses. Using a "Tom-hawk" (158) that he found in the cave, he savagely kills a panther: "The animal fell, struggling and shrieking, on the ground" (159). Huntly extends his savagery by eating the barely dead animal: "I review this scene with loathing and horror.... I did not turn from the yet warm blood and reeking fibres of a brute" (160). Who exactly is the brute here? Later after killing an Indian he leaves the dead "savage ... but made prize of his tom-hawk" (194), having lost the one from the cave. Huntly seems to consolidate his own European identity with the identity he has appropriated from his Native American victim, like Rowlandson transgressing the seemingly impermeable border between the two identities. Thus begins Huntly's nightmarish journey through an Indian-ridden, bitterly cold, and often dark landscape where he is transformed into an adventurer as well as a killer. His heroic deeds take on the physical and violent trappings of the "savages." He rescues a white girl from Indians, carrying her "over a most rugged path," emerging into a "wild and desolate" scene (174), a "wilderness" (175). When the girl's abductors return, he shoots them, waiting in his hiding place until "a tawny and terrific visage" appears (183), leaving behind a "scene of carnage and blood" (186). A typical adventure finds him fleeing from Indians by jumping into a river, only to emerge "from the gulf to encounter new perils" (212), "the bullets [of the Native Americans] that continued incessantly to strike the water at arms' length from my body" (213). Only after wandering in the wilderness for approximately one third of the novel does Huntly manage to stumble back to civilization, suddenly finding himself in the house of Sarsefield, his benefactor. The end of his journey represents a salvation from obliteration, either through physical death or a total loss of his English identity; the land is dangerous indeed.

In fact, over and over again Huntly illustrates the Gothic return from the dead, coming close to symbolic or literal death, then escaping into life. His escape from the cave, in the beginning of his journey, is described explicitly in language of death and birth. Although he believes that "in that grave should I linger out a few days ... and then perish forever" (156), he finds himself at the mouth of the cave, "delivered from my prison and restored to the enjoyment of the air and the light" (164). The tomblike, womblike cave and the double meaning of the word "delivered" highlight the imagery. Saved from death, the English Huntly is reborn as a new, uncannily unfamiliar American. Later in his adventures, Huntly encounters potential rescuers, a rescue party searching for the girl he has saved. When he faints, the "swoon into which I now sunk, was no doubt, mistaken by the spectators, for death" (188). He wakes to find that he has fallen onto one of the Indians he has murdered; his own "disheveled locks were matted and steeped in that gore" (189)— he is aligned with the dead Indian as well as with the savage native. Huntly is thus consigned to the situation of the dead savage until the end of his journey. Upon returning to civilization, he appears as a "spectre," complete with uncouth "garb ... wild and weather-worn appearance ... fusil and tom-hawk" (196). Edgar achieves one last resurrection when he encounters his mentor, Sarsefield, who does not immediately recognize the transformed Edgar, gazing at him "as on one whom he has never before seen" (233). Sarsefield admits that he was among the party that left Edgar for dead. Soon regretting his decision, he had returned to the site, to discover Edgar vanished, seemingly resurrected: "'You had risen from the dead,'" managed to defeat the enemy with "'bullet and dagger ... both of which you could only be supplied by supernatural means, and had disappeared'" (246). Sarsefield later repeats:

"'you were dead.... Now, in a blissful hour, you have risen'" (251). At Sarsefield's home, Huntly also facilitates the revival of Clithero, whom he had sought as part of his investigations into Waldegrave's death. However this rebirth ends in a series of final deaths, Clithero kills the brother of Mrs. Lorimer, the wife of Sarsefield, which also results in the death of their prematurely-born child. As a consequence, Sarsefield cuts off his relationship with Edgar Huntly, essentially killing him socially and economically. The last word of the book—that is mostly framed as a series of letters, mostly from Edgar to his fiancée—is the last word in a final letter from Sarsefield: "'Farewell'" (285). Edgar is reduced to social death, and to silence. Yet he is still a young man; another rebirth may lie ahead.

The Native Americans, however, remain as dead specters, never experiencing any life or moment of rebirth in the novel. Brown provides the reader with little expectation for future resurrection. In fact, Brown advocates death as the proper state of the Native American; only in their death does Huntly appreciate their humanity. On first contemplating a dead Native American, Huntly hesitates, reluctant to "imbrue my hands in the blood of my fellow men" who is, nevertheless, "savage" (171)—here Huntly seems more concerned with his white hands and white soul than the actual death of his "fellow man." When he eventually kills an Indian, Huntly pleads self-defense, adding another reminder of the humanity of his now-dead victim: "Never before had I taken the life of an human creature" (172). Indeed the Native Americans seem to achieve their apotheosis in death. After killing the kidnapping Indians, Huntly gazes at their dead bodies and considers them: "three beings, full of energy and heroism, endowed with minds strenuous and lofty" (185–6). Yet in killing an Indian whom he has wounded, Huntly calls the murder a "cruel leniency" (1993), the mercy-killing of a creature who is ultimately better off dead. Or, in the judgment that D.H. Lawrence later attributes to Ben Franklin, the idea "that a wise Providence no doubt intended the extirpation of these savages." Lawrence aptly observes: "The desire to extirpate the Indian. And the contradictory desire to glorify him" (*Studies in Classic American Literature* 36), as long as he remains dead.

The Return of the Dead: Horror and Glory

In *Studies in Classic American Literature*, published in 1923 when he was living in the Midwest and thinking about American culture as an outsider and a pessimistic modernist, D.H. Lawrence envisioned a future unimaginable to Brown and Huntly: the rebirth of the dead Native American. According the Lawrence's cosmology, the Native American is "dispossessed in life and unforgiving. He doesn't believe in us and our civilization, and so is our mystic enemy, for we pushed him off the face of the earth" (35); once fully erased, and repressed, the Native American will return reinvigorated and re-empowered. In alignment with his contemporary, Freud, Lawrence thus predicted the explosive return of the repressed Native American from the dead: "Then the Daimon of America will work overtly, and we shall see real changes" (36). Only when all Native Americans are dead, can they consolidate into a single vengeful specter and return to repossess their land and its conquerors.[4]

While Lawrence imagines this apocalypse from the perspective of the gloomy twentieth century, Edgar Allan Poe, ever-anxious and ever-vigilant, envisioned this occurrence almost a century earlier in his story, "The Masque of the Red Death" (1842). As I have previously argued,[5] one compelling reading of this story is to see the figure of Red Death as symbolizing both the Native American "red" man, and the disease that was ravaging the Native American population at the time: smallpox, whose symptoms include the red spots that splatter the shrouds that Red Death wears. However, despite the havoc caused by Red Death outside the abbey, where Prince Prospero and his courtiers hide out, and despite the ultimate catastrophe that befalls the court, Red Death is far from the most monstrous creature of the story. In fact, Prince Prospero, the uncaring aristocrat, bears almost the full force of Poe's condemnation, thus recalling the cruel European aristocrat of the English Gothic. The Prince's people are dying, "but the Prince Prospero was happy and dauntless and sagacious" (461). He devotes his energy to saving himself and the other aristocrats, holding fabulous parties in an abbey with "gates of iron" that are welded shut with "furnaces and massy hammers" (461). After the first paragraph, once we are in the abbey with the court, the narrator is silent about Red Death and his victims. The very thought of the plague is repressed; in fact the Red Death seems to be the only taboo topic in the carefree abbey. When the Red Death does appear, the courtiers first think that he is one of their own in costume—they are, after all, "an assembly of phantasms," already spectralized themselves. They are shocked by his transgression since "the masquerade license of the night was nearly unlimited, but the figure [had] gone beyond the bounds of even the prince's indefinite decorum" (463). This figure presents a scandal because he reveals the very image the masqueraders are trying to repress. Bergland emphasizes this meaning: "The entire dynamic of ghosts and hauntings, as we understand it today, is a dynamic of unsuccessful repression. Ghosts are the things that we try to bury, but that refuse to stay buried" (*National Uncanny* 5). Rather than mask reality as the others do, the new arrival brings the horrible truth to everyone's attention, and in doing so transgresses one of their few prohibitions. The revelers recognize that the costume, representing Red Death is, like the chiming of the ebony clock in the black room, a *memento mori*, symbolizing the reality that the courtiers try to repress, as white America was working to repress the calamity they were inflicting upon the Native Americans.

Poe further illustrates Lawrence's prophecy at the end of the story when the invader (yet another intruder within the American Gothic) is unmasked. For, he is not a visible spectacular monster at all. The skeleton mask "besprinkled with the scarlet horror," the shroud "dabbled in *blood*," are merely an empty costume; the Red Death is revealed as an invisible specter. When the panicked courtiers rip the costume away, they find it "untenanted by any tangible form" (464). And so Poe's Red Man, like Lawrence's, has been seemingly reduced by repression, although he retains his dangerous power as an invisible and deadly ghost. Ironically, his spectral state empowers him to penetrate the bolted iron gate. Poe's story suggests the white guilt and anxiety about the ultimate consequence of the repression of the Native American that Lawrence also anticipates. As Renée Bergland asserts, "Native American ghosts function ... as representations of national guilt" (*National Uncanny* 4). Seemingly, at some level Poe recognizes the callousness of white Americans who like Prospero's court, dehumanize others and allow them to suffer. A number of Poe's stories seem to express anxiety about a new oppressive aristocracy appearing in America, including "The Fall of the House of Usher," discussed in Chapter 5. An editor's note to "Masque" indicates that "resentment against aristocratic 'privilege' of all kinds reached a peak [in Poe's times]. For all his fear of [the] 'mob' and for all his Southern-aristocratic pretensions, Poe at times revealed the same healthy democratic bias against the prerogatives of aristocrats" (Preface to "Anti-Aristocratic Tales" *The Short Fiction of Edgar Allan Poe* eds. Stuart Levine and Susan Levine 454). In fact, Poe reconfigures the irrational and destructive populist mob as the irrational and unthinking group of aristocrats in his story. As Gustave Le Bon asserts in his study of the crowd, this group distills and expresses the worst qualities of each individual. The only identifiable individual in the abbey is Prospero; all his followers seem mere copies; they all agree that "it was folly to grieve or to think," and so collectively the courtiers decide to distract themselves with "all the appliances of pleasure," to repress the reality of the people abandoned outside. They are unanimous in this repression; Poe speaks from the perspective of the group when he says "the external world could take care of itself" (461). Poe thus reveals the perspective of the American democrat in this story, as he aligns the aristocrats with the irrational and cruel mob.

The Rebirth of the Dead Native American: Insurrections and Resurrections in Sherman Alexie's Indian Killer

Brown's eighteenth-century novel, *Edgar Huntly* begins with the mystery of who killed Huntly's white friend. *Indian Killer* (1996), by the Native American writer Sherman Alexie, begins with a similar crime: the serial murder of a number of white men. *Indian Killer*, like *Edgar Huntly* rapidly devolves from mystery into nightmare, verging upon the supernatural. Alexie initially presents his novel as a twentieth-century murder mystery in the model invented by Edgar Allan Poe, whose detectives use science and reason to arrive upon a logically satisfying conclusion. Yet Alexie's narrative lacks any significant detective or police force to scientifically solve the case. In fact, *Killer* quickly moves from the form of Poe's modern detective story to the more archaic literary form favored by Poe, the supernatural Gothic. The novel also closely aligns with Lawrence's mystical version of history. Indeed, familiarity with Poe and Lawrence is especially helpful to the reader who expects a scientific solution, and ends up in the confused world of the supernatural.

The novel starts out prosaically enough with a string of murders in the city of Seattle. Eventually the pool of murder victims (all white) includes a racist young man, and a middle-aged family man who watches pornography featuring the subjugation of Native American women. The killer also kidnaps (and returns) Mark Jones, a little white boy, whom the killer observes playing in the park. The killer almost sympathetically thinks that Mark is a "perfect child who, through no fault of his own, might grow up into a monster" (150), that is, a white patriarch, "a powerful man" (151). In each of these crimes, the killer leaves a calling card: two owl feathers. We are repeatedly informed that a number of Native American tribes associate the owl with death. Additionally, both murder victims are stabbed, and the killer scalps the first victim and then eats his eyeballs; later, he "feasted on [the] heart" (328) of the second. The evidence seems sufficient to support the suspicions of the police and the populace (yet another American mob), that the killer is a Native American, and the unidentified murderer becomes known as "the Indian Killer." The illogic of this sobriquet (illustrating the irrationality of the mob) is elucidated by Marie, a young Native American community activist and college student: "'calling him the Indian Killer doesn't make any sense, does it? If it was an Indian doing the killing, then wouldn't he be called the Killer Indian?'" (247). She correctly adds that the name Indian Killer would more logically apply to a white who kills Indians.

As panic pervades the city of Seattle, it is clear that the Indian Killer is also a terrorist, that is, his mission is to spread universal terror through a discreet number of visibly horrifying acts. In fact, when the killer is stalking Mark in the park, he thinks, "the next victim would have to be perfect and beautiful. The killer would have to send a message that would terrify the world" (150). We see the terrorizing effect of the killer in two episodes involving two potential victims. A rabidly racist right-wing radio commentator is frightened out of his wits when he merely imagines that the killer is stalking him in a driveway. Similarly, when a professor who misrepresents and appropriates the stories of Native Americans visits a dark deserted college library, he senses a presence. He imagines that he "hears a strange rattling"; he thinks of "the Indian remains in that basement"; he feels something "brush against his face" (140), and he panics. Running into a "low overhang," he knocks "himself unconscious." The killer thus accomplishes his goal: efficiently creating universal terror without needing to be present everywhere.

Alexie deploys the conventions of the detective story to provide the reader with plausible motives for a Native American to seek out white male victims. Alexie presents vivid profiles of a number of deplorable racist white male characters who do actually seem deserving candidates for the role of murder victim. The most abhorrent of this group is Truck Schultz, who has the most power to spread his vicious beliefs as "host of the most popular talk-radio show in the city" (54). A character who seems to be inspired by real-world models, Truck, with unconscious irony, calls himself "'the Voice of Reason'" (116). Yet he is delighted to stir up fear and violence when the killings begin; and quick to rush to judgment. He exhorts his audience: "'Haven't I told you [listeners] that our current political climate, with its constant vilification of white males would prove to be disastrous?'" (207); "'This country exists because of the constant vigilance and ingenuity of white males ... an Indian savage is killing white men'" (208); "'We have coddled Indians too long and we've created a monster'" (209). True to form, he ends his diatribe with a flourish: "'to paraphrase one of our great military leaders, Philip Sheridan, the only good Indian Killer is a dead Indian Killer'" (209). Later Truck reminds his audience: "'The Indians were Godless people. They were savages'" (344). Truck is thrilled when there is another killing because it is good for his ratings. When he hears the news, he whoops: "'Folks ... the Indian Killer has struck again'" (336). Not surprisingly, his rabble-rousing results in a "race war" (338) in Seattle, with members of the white mob quite stupidly shouting as they beat homeless Native Americans: "'Go back to where you belong, man! Get the fuck out of our country, Man'" (215). One of Truck's listeners suggests a solution: "'to put all Indians in jail'" (335).

Some of the racists in the novel are more subtle but possibly do more harm than Truck, in that they covertly appropriate Native American stories and identities. Professor Clarence Mather (perhaps recalling Cotton), the hapless professor who panics in the library, is described jokingly by Native Americans as "a Wannabe Indian, a white man who wanted to be an Indian" (58). His Native American student, Marie, challenges his choice of reading material in his class, noting that the list is dominated by white male writers claiming to speak for Native Americans. We learn that Mather has discovered old tapes made by anthropologists who interviewed Native Americans in the early twentieth century. When Mather is informed that the tapes violate the Native American tradition of direct orality, instead of destroying the tapes he hides them, appropriating the narratives for himself: "He'd come to see those stories as his possessions, as *his* stories" (138). Jack Wilson's appropriation is even more egregious. Although he is white, he identifies as a Native American, and writes about Native Americans for a largely white audience. In an act of meta-appropriation, Wilson writes a novel called *"Indian Killer,* in which he hopes to have the mystery solved by his popular character, Aristotle Little Hawk, practicing medicine man and private detective" (162). Part of Wilson's problem then, is that he, unlike Sherman Alexie, seems to believe that all Native American issues have a neat clear-cut solution.

Alexie remains true to the detective story form in providing the reader, and the police, with a number of potential suspects, all Native Americans with every reason to hate white men. The most likely of these is John Smith, born Native American, but raised by white adoptive parents. Deracinated, he dreams of being a "real Indian" (130). Alexie suggests that his split identity leads to a schizophrenic split. He has visions and hears voices (23) and "the noise of the crowd in his head" (133). Like most of the Native American characters in the book, John is a recipient of everyday racism. A young man on the street casually calls him "chief" (41), although he seems to lack any actually hostility. We see John "carefully and silently" (42), following the young man, whom we next see as the first victim of the Indian Killer. The narrator shares with the reader the killer's point of view during the first murder: "the killer saw the fear in the white man's blue eyes" (52). This detail uncannily echoes a previous view we have had from inside John's mind, when he imagines killing his boss, seeing "fear in the blue eyes…. John needed to kill a white man" (25). John experiences his anger as not just personal, but communal; he harbors a deep resentment in response to the repression of Native Americans, lamenting at one point that Whites no longer feared Indians: "Somehow, near the end of the twentieth century, Indians had become invisible, docile" (30). In fact, John's anger and pain is the closest he comes to being a "real Indian." Immediately before committing suicide, John says to the appropriating Jack Wilson, as he lightly, symbolically, stabs Wilson: "'Please.... Let me, let us have our own pain'" (412). Despite stacking the evidence against John, Alexie also provides compelling clues that John is not a killer. A police officer, observing John, thinks, "Probably a schizophrenic [he] knew that most schizophrenics rarely hurt anybody except themselves" (363). After John commits suicide, Marie, his friend, tells the police with great certainty: "'He wasn't the Indian killer'" (416).

Marie, too, presents ample evidence for guilt. Like John, she has an unstable identity; she was born to Native American parents, but "her parents, who did speak Spokane, had refused to teach Marie because they felt it would be of no use to her in the world outside the reservation" (33). She is a community activist and student, devoted to the Native American people. Yet her zeal sometimes takes her to extremes. She fights with Mather in class, angrily challenging his promotion of texts that appropriate Native American culture: "'If the real Pocahontas came back you think she'd be happy about being a [Disney] cartoon?'" (314). She wonders if her impressive academic success is not mostly a way to get "revenge" (147) and recognizes that she hates "powerful white men" (147). When she organizes the homeless Native Americans to fight back against white bullies, Marie is actually "shocked by her anger" (375). In fact Boo, "a nice white guy" (331), who volunteers with Marie jokingly asks her "'You're not the Indian Killer, are you?'"; Marie's response is to feel "the anger in her belly and hands" (331). Reggie, Marie's cousin, also presents an unstable split identity and the angry potential to kill; he is the son of a Native American mother and a white father with a "hatred of 'hostile' Indians" (92). He beats his son to make him a subservient Indian, and calls Reggie a "stupid, dirty Indian" (94). Reggie thus learns to hate the Indian side of himself. As a consequence, he is filled with rage. His mother tells the police: "'He said he dreamed about killing people'" (394). When the racial tensions begin in Seattle, Reggie and his friends go around in masks, terrorizing and beating white men. They tell one victim the collective history of Native Americans suffering, beginning with the story of a Native American soldier who was at Iwo Jima. Reduced to homelessness after returning to America, he froze to death. Adopting the soldier's voice, Reggie says: "'Why'd you let me freeze?'" (256). Reggie recounts the collective Native American pain caused by collective white America: "'You killed me on the Washita River.... You shot us before we even spoke. Do you remember?'" (357).

Reggie's diatribe points to a logically impossible yet irrationally probable "solution" to Alexie's murder mystery. As the story unfolds, the reader comes to understand that the "Indian Killer" is not the kind of individual human killer who can be identified by a rational detective. He is, in fact, the mystical supernatural embodiment of the collective rage of the Native American people, as identified by D.H. Lawrence. Maria assures Professor Mather: "'An Indian man is not doing these killings'" (248). And she is quite correct. Alexie has laid the clues for this supernatural solution to his mystery throughout his novel. He insistently reminds us of the shared rage of the Native American people. All the Native American people are appropriately offended by the presence of whites. An old woman says to John "I ain't homeless. I'm Duwamish Indian.... All of this, the city, the water, the mountains, it's all Duwamish lands.... I belong here, cousin. I'm the landlady.... They're the homeless ones. Those white people are a long way from home, don't you think? Long way from E-u-r-o-p-e" (251–252). She continues to John: "But we'll get back at them" (253). Another Native American character explicates: "'Lots of real Indian men out there have plenty enough reasons to kill a white man'" (184).

Ironically, Truck Schultz's racist rhetoric comes close to the reality: "'The Indian Killer is the distillation of their rage'" (346). Truck's followers spread rumors "'that Indians are organizing. They're looking to get revenge'" (188). This is exactly true, in the Lawrentian sense. The anger of individual Native Americans is coalescing to create a single entity: the Indian Killer. When Marie organizes a motley crew of Native American street people to fight back against the white bullies, the narrator tells us, "Although weak with malnutrition and various diseases, they kicked, scratched, and slapped with a collective rage" (374). A Native American says, "'I know who killed those white people.... He's got Crazy Horse's magic. He's got Chief Joseph's brains. He's got Geronimo's heart. He's got Wovoka's vision. He's all those badass Indians rolled up into one'" (219). Some Native Americans, hearing of the killer feel "a strange combination of relief and fear, as if the apocalyptic prophecy was just beginning to come true" (185). Alexie's Indian killer is thus the ghostly specter repressed since the nineteenth century, whose return was predicted by Lawrence. The killer, the reader finally recognizes, is a collective ghost, a nameless "shadow" (70), singing an "invisibility song" as he hunts (152).

Indeed, Alexie provides enough information about Native American ritual to lead the reader to the supernatural conclusion. Ironically, Jack Wilson teaches Reggie the significance of the Ghost Dance, "'thought to be an act of warfare against white people'" (185). Marie tells her department chair, "'Wovoka said if all Indians Ghost danced, then all the Europeans would disappear.... So maybe this Indian Killer is a product of the Ghost Dance.... Maybe this is how the Ghost Dance works'" (313). At the end of the novel, with the serial murders still unsolved, Marie says to the police: "'Indians are dancing now, and I don't think they're going to stop'" (418). In the last chapter of the novel, "A Creation Story," we get our most direct look at the "killer," alone in a "cemetery on an Indian reservation ... the killer carries ... two bloody scalps in a plastic bag. Beneath the killer's jacket, the beautiful knife" (419). As the killer sings and dances, he is joined by "A dozen Indians, then hundreds, and more, all learning the same song, the exact dance ... the killer can dance forever" (420). Alexie thus ends his novel in the territory beyond reason and the rule of law. We are back to the supernatural realm of Lawrence, the world of the Gothic.

And so, this recent Native American murder mystery ends as does *Edgar Huntly*, the first. As in *Huntly*, the solution to the murder mystery is the spectral Native American. Yet in *Huntly* the crimes are committed by living Indians, who are only metaphorically dead. Alexie's Native American killer is the reborn spectral Native American spirit that Lawrence anticipates: "not that the Red Indian will ever possess the broad lands of America. At least I presume not. But his ghost will. The Red Man died hating the white man. Go near the Indians and you just feel it" (41). Alexie's twentieth-century re-incarnation of the "Red Indian" is as filled with hatred and rage as Lawrence anticipates, and also as threatening. Like his predecessors, Poe and Brown, Alexie recognizes that the genre best suited to tell the history of the Native American is horror.

Return of the Human Native American

In *Tracks* (1988), Louise Erdrich transforms the return of the Native American to a more human narrative, and allows her story of rebirth to end with a nonviolent, non-supernatural, and hopeful ending. Not that Erdrich discounts the supernatural traditions of Native American folklore; we hear often enough of conventional ghosts. When Fleur is the only member of her family to be left alive after illness has swept through her tribe, one of the rescuers is afraid to enter the family cabin, "fearing the unburied Pillager spirits might seize him by the throat" (3). Those who remain avoid speaking the names of the dead, to prevent "letting the names loose in the wind that would reach their ears" (5). The living offer a sacrifice to the dead of Fleur's family to deter them from "pester[ing] their daughter just because she had survived." The villagers tell a story of a Land Agent scouting for Native American land who is bedeviled by ghosts out in the woods, spending "a whole night following the moving lights and lamps of people who would not answer him." When they let him go at dawn he has gone mad, "Living in the woods and eating roots, gambling with ghosts" (9).

Although *Tracks* is set in 1912–1924, the time when Lawrence was conjuring up supernatural vengeance and wrath, the first rebirth in the novel presents a perfectly explicable story of metaphorical resurrection. Nanapush, an old Native American man, who also speaks as the voice of the community, and who narrates much of the story, tells of the epidemic (Poe's smallpox) when "'we started dying [of] spotted sickness.'" Nanapush reminds his primary audience Lulu, the daughter of Fleur, that she was born to a dying people: "'Granddaughter, you are the child of the invisible, the ones who disappeared'" (2). Erdrich thus develops a materially realistic metaphor for Fleur's rebirth. Nanapush finds her alone: "'out in your family's cabin'"; by that time Fleur is "the last Pillager" (2), surrounded by the bodies and spirits of her dead family. Her rescue and revival is wondrous but natural. Fleur's multiple escapes from death by drowning are presented in a more ambiguous way, illustrating the tendency for coincidence to appear as magic to a believing audience. Nanapush tells Lulu, "'The first time she drowned in the cold and glassy waters of Matchimanito, Fleur Pillager was only a child'" (10). Her boat tips over and she falls into the water. Two man jump in to rescue her, but oddly they both die soon after. The community attributes it to some sort of supernatural exchange, "By saving Fleur Pillager, those two had lost themselves" (10). The pattern continues: "The next time she fell in the lake ... no one touched her" (11), fearing the consequences. Indeed, when she washes up on shore and a man comes to look, he sees her chest "move ... her eyes spun open, clear black agate, and she looked at him. 'You take my place, she hissed'" (11). And sure enough, this man drowns in his bathtub. Again, possibly coincidence presenting as magic; or possibly Fleur does possess the malignant supernatural power that the villagers fear. Fleur's last near-drowning is no less terrible. Facing the loss of her family land, she "walks into the water ... the water closed over her head" (212); "'This is the third time she has drowned'" (212), says Nanapush.

Fleur's next drastic move results in a more natural and more hopeful rebirth for her child: "'She sent you to the government school.'" Although as Nanapush explains to Lulu, this is to keep her safe, as we know, sending an Indian child to Indian School is tantamount to death, physical, spiritual, or both. Thus Fleur, part human, part supernatural spirit—another Native American with a split identity—passes her last years in sadness. Dispossessed of land, child and community, she disappears forever. But her child Lulu, does reappear, like her mother rescued from a metaphorical death by Nanapush, who himself learns a new, realistic power: the power of writing. Nanapush "'becomes a bureaucrat myself'" (225) to rescue this child, "'to draw you home'" (225). The perfectly natural yet magical event does come to fruition. Erdrich re-presents Lulu returned from school in an image of non-supernatural, non-violent (re)birth. As Nanapush waits outside the school, he sees children coming out: "'you were the last to emerge'" (226). The old Lulu is dead; this reborn Lulu has short hair and an ugly dress. But her grin is "'as bold as your mother's.'" So Lulu also re-enacts the rebirth of her mother, Fleur. The novel ends with this joyous image of humanly (non-supernatural) realized rebirth, as Nanapush and Lulu turn toward home, toward the future.

It would reductionist to attribute the contrast in tone and topic between Alexie's and Erdrich's novels solely to gender. Yet gender does seem to be at play here, especially if we remember the Gothic distinction between Male and Female Gothic that arose in eighteenth-century England. The male tradition of spectacular horror exemplified by Walpole with his smashed son and crushed castle, and Lewis with his nightmare of Catholic atrocity and evil, culminates in the horror and gore of Alexie's novel. Similarly the gentler traditions of female terror, beginning with Radcliffe, in which threats are rarely realized, and the supernatural is explained away, culminate in the naturalistic rescue of the child at the end of Erdrich's narrative. Erdrich seems to suggest a possibility for a future in which the spectral Native American returns from the realm of rage and death, to the human world of family and the land.

Part II

Possessing and Dispossessed

4

Dispossessed Possessor
The Displaced Patriarch

America was founded upon a moment of physical, psychological and symbolic parricide, becoming a country by displacing the patriarch and the patriarchy: the fatherland England, and the English father, the monarch. It is, therefore, not surprising to find that the early centuries of the country and its literature, are marked by the absence of the patriarch. Ironically the paradigm of the lost father is abetted by a number of American systems set up to dispossess others: the slavery of African Americans; the extirpation of the Native American; and the consequent clearing of the American landscape. Each of these American systems displaces a marginalized Other, but the process of displacement also results in a destabilized identity for all Americans. The would-be American patriarch thus finds himself displaced by the very systems he creates to displace others. Added to the dilemma of the potential American patriarch, the eventual liberation of slaves and women further destabilized patriarchal authority. A number of texts exhibit this pattern, as well as invoking the Gothic to express the anxiety provoked by such moments of dispossession.

Displacement of the English Father and Appropriation of English Land

The American Revolution was clearly influenced by the Enlightenment promotion of individual resistance to communal traditions and truths, as well as by the Romantic valorization of the rebellious youth, displacing the autocratic father. In *Prodigals and Pilgrims*, Jay Fliegelman asserts, "The relationship of the American colonies to England had long been accepted by both the British government and its subjects in America as analogous to that of a child's relationship to its parent" (Fliegelman 93). From the perspective of the aristocratic English authorities, the Revolution signified the illegal rebellion of the ungrateful, parricidal child, "unnatural ingratitude" (96) to the powerful father. Fliegelman explains, "Despite Blackstone's own formulation that 'the empire of the father' must give place to 'the empire of reason,' English law insisted that 'the tie of nature is not dissolved by any misbehavior of the parent'" (95). Yet, the Americans insisted on the replacement of "the empire of the father" with "the empire of reason"; the "call for filial autonomy and the unimpeded emergence from nonage echoes throughout the rhetoric of the American Revolution" (Fliegelman 3). Complicating the issue and compounding the guilty anxiety of the American revolutionary was the alignment of the figure of the patriarch with the figure of God in the eighteenth century; so the rejection of the king was theocide as well as parricide. As Fliegelman indicates, the rejection of the king was also aligned with the rejection of the notion of a wrathful God within American Protestantism: "The most powerful Revolutionary polemic ... implicitly identified England with an unreasonable Jehovah" (157).

Adding to American anxiety was the sense that the revolutionaries had stolen the land from the English. Young Americans, anxious about dispossessing the land of the Native Americans, also had to face misgivings about appropriating the same land from the English monarch. In "The American Road to Capitalism," Charles Post explains that "Britain ruled its North American possessions indirectly" (465), through systems meant to enforce long-distance ownership. Yet the English systems were successfully countered by the colonists who actually lived in North America: "Independent farmers and artisans ... resisted the commodification of landed property" (465), that is, they resisted the English notion that land could be owned though title only. "Most settlers ... could not obtain legal title to the land, and [instead] illegally occupied ('squatted' on) lands owned by private owners" (471). The small farmers of the colonies thus appropriated English land even before the Revolution by establishing their possession through living and working land to which they had no title. The British militia was "ineffective in ... preventing European setter populations from illegally occupying lands on the frontier" (465). The militias "were rarely deployed against legally free populations" and were "unwilling and unable to enforce legal claims to land against other small farmers" (466). After the Revolutionary War, resistance to the local army continued the trend and so the land was still effectively owned by squatters. (Ironically the relationship of the settlers to the land was similar to that of the Native Americans who also rejected formal ownership and considered themselves proprietors of any land they used.) Not until the Whiskey Rebellion of 1794 in Western Pennsylvania was the U.S. government in Washington able to impose the power of the central government, "closing off access to free or inexpensive land on the frontier" (Post 479).[1]

The new systems of property acquisition worked against the reinstatement of a patriarchal society or economy based on inheritance as the main means of property transfer: "The existence of unoccupied land within easy reach of most settlers, combined with the inability of landowners to craft state institutions that could impose legal titles, made the creation of a social monopoly of land impossible in the seventeenth and eighteenth centuries" (Post 471). As Post indicates, land acquisition based on labor and physical possession (rather than on inheritance and arranged marriage) prevented the consolidation of land into great estates. Additionally, as Post indicates, the removals of the Native Americans resulted in the almost unlimited availability of land, which meant that social and economic power could not be consolidated in the hands of a small group. Thus in the early years of American agrarian life, the figure of the English patriarch could not be readily revived. The powerful, possessive, and evil father, the figure who haunts the English Gothic from the eighteenth century on, disappeared from the social and economic landscape of America, and from the American Gothic.

Headless

The disappearance of the patriarch plays a significant role in Washington Irving's "The Legend of Sleepy Hollow" (1820). Ichabod Crane, a hapless young man, is ostensibly the central character, his story the legend to which the title refers. However, there is another legendary figure in the story, the presumably supernatural headless horseman. Writing decades after the American Revolution, Irving deploys the horseman to depict the new Americans, lacking the king, their former head. The missing head of the horseman also evokes the figure of the headless French king, decapitated in 1793 during the French Revolution. Irving directly associates his horseman with the American Revolution. In describing Sleepy Hollow, he tells his readers that "the British and American line had run through it during the war" (289). The headless horseman is said "to be the ghost of a Hessian trooper, whose head had been carried away by a cannon ball in some nameless battle during the revolutionary war" (273). Legend has it that his specter, known as "The Headless Horseman of Sleepy Hollow," "rides forth to the scene of battle in nightly quest of his head" (273). Thus the absent head of the specter, more than his actual ghostliness, is his distinguishing and most frightening quality.

In "Rip Van Winkle" (1819–20), Irving also uses a supernatural narrative to advance the theme of headlessness in new America, highlighting the instability of patriarchal authority and identity in a young country founded on parricide. Rip lives as an English colonial in a little village before the war, "while the country was yet a province of Great Britain" (29). He fails to successfully perform the role of the patriarch; he is lazy and passive, dominated by his wife. Like Ichabod Crane, he is curiously boyish, more inclined to the telling of tales that manly labor. Yet, Rip clings to the old failing model: as a young man he finds refuge in "the strong hold" (32) where the patriarchs of the village gather; later in his old age he is "reverenced as one of the patriarchs of the village" (40). Though a patriarch manqué, Rip is nevertheless a father, husband and land-owner. However, this failed English patriarch is completely undone—dispossessed of his self and his identity—one mysterious night when he drinks with the Dutch spirits who inhabit the Catskill mountains. Rip falls into a twenty years' sleep, awaking to discover that he has lost his gun and his dog. Rip soon learns that he has also lost his political and personal identities. Like Brown's Edgar Huntly, Irving's Rip is dispossessed of his spatial, social and psychological identity through the dispossession of sleep.[2] As in Brown's *Wieland* (1798), Rip's experience connects the destabilization of the patriarch with the disorientating madness of the patriarch. After Rip's return, "Some always pretended to doubt the reality of it, and insisted that Rip had been out of his head" (41); the head of the family has, once again, lost his own head.

Rip discovers his political dispossession when he returns to his village. Although upon waking, Rip announces himself "a loyal subject of the King," his assertion to the villagers leads to accusations of treason: "A tory! A spy! Away with him!" (38). Finally Rip understands that he has been transformed. Neither subject to the king, nor spy, he unwittingly receives a new identity: American citizen. He is told that "there had been a revolutionary war—that the country had thrown off the yoke of Old England and that instead of being a subject of his majesty George the Third, he was now a free citizen of the United States" (38). Rip witnesses an outward manifestation of this odd political transformation with his own eyes, in the painted sign hanging outside the old Dutch inn that Rip used to haunt with his friends in his youth. When Rip returns to the old inn, he experiences an uncanny moment: "He recognized on the sign, however, the ruby face of King George under which he had smoked so many a peaceful pipe, but even this was singularly metamorphosed. The red coat was changed for one of blue and buff; a sword was held in the hand instead of a scepter, the head was decorated with a cocked hat, and underneath was printed in large characters GENERAL WASHINGTON" (37). In the image of the sign as palimpsest—in which the accouterments of the former leader, the English George, are painted over and replaced with the accouterments of the his uncanny double, the American George—Rip encounters an unsettling American reality: the English past—culturally, linguistically, politically familiar—repressed and reappearing in an new unfamiliar and thus uncanny form. The sign emphasizes that even a king can be dispossessed, repressed, and replaced in America; thus any patriarch is vulnerable in this new uncanny land. Yet, although his patriarchal identity is lost, Rip benefits by the transformations of time. He experiences a personal liberation that echoes the political liberation of his country: "there was one species of despotism under which he had long groaned and that was petticoat government. Happily that was at an end—he had got his neck out of the yoke of matrimony, and could go in and out whenever he pleased without dreading the tyranny of Dame Van Winkle" (40–41). Irving suggests that a lost patriarchal identity is a small price to pay for the promise of new American freedoms.

Rip also learns that he has been dispossessed of his personal identity; he has been forgotten and replaced by a man who appears to be his uncanny double. When Rip asks if anyone remembers Rip Van Winkle, a few townspeople answer: "'Oh to be sure—that's Rip Van Winkle—yonder.'" When Rip sees "the precise counterpart of himself.... The poor fellow was now completely confounded. He doubted his own identity and whether he was himself or another man" (38). His replacement, his own son and namesake, has appropriated Rip's name and position in the village, symptomatic of the new American tendency to replace the aged with the young. The former patriarch, seeing his own double reappearing from the past, actually becomes his own ghost, feebly returned from the dead. Rip also represents the ghost of the dead and repressed English past haunting the colonies. Irving highlights this theme in the name he gives his character, a name whose letters furnish the initials for the phrase that Irving uses when mentioning Peter Stuyvesant, "(may he rest in peace!)" (29). Rip's doubleness, his return as the old repressed form, touches on Freud's paradigm of the relationship between past and present in "The Uncanny." Freud emphasizes that the uncanny often re-appears through "doubling ... the self" (9) and that the "double" is a "creation dating back to a very early mental stage, long since left behind" (10). The return of the double is the "return of something repressed which *recurs* ... this uncanny is in reality nothing new or foreign, but something familiar and old" (12). Rip is then the old, familiar, though long-gone, figure of the English patriarch. His return to the village proves Freud's point that the old forms cannot be repressed indefinitely; they return as a slightly revised double, the uncanny form. Irving thus suggests that America is doomed to be forever haunted by the repressed English past.

The Uncanny Land

The disputed American land too is doubled and uncanny—and haunted by many ghosts—in Irving's story. The duality of the land surfaces in Irving's competing descriptions of the Catskill Mountains in colonial upstate New York. From the start Irving describes the Catskills as unrealistic and uncanny: Rip's "little village of great antiquity" lies at the foot of "fairy mountains" (28), invoking the supernatural of the old country. Rip first views the landscape through a natural frame of trees, which limits and contains the picturesque sight: "From an opening between the trees he could overlook all the lower country for many a mile of rich woodland. He saw at a distance the lordly Hudson, far, far below him, moving on its silent but majestic course, with the reflection of a purple cloud, or the sail of a lagging bark here and there sleeping on its glassy bosom, and at last losing itself in the blue highlands" (33). Shifting his gaze, Rip views the sublime landscape, the wild, uncontained double of the picturesque: "On the other side he looked down into a deep mountain glen, wild, lonely and shagged, the bottom filled with fragments from the impending cliffs and scarcely lighted by the reflected rays of the setting sun" (29). The dual description gestures to the opposition that Edmund Burke sets up in *A Philosophical Enquiry into the Origin of Our Ideas of the Sublime and the Beautiful* (1757). Irving, like Burke, opposes the unknowable, wild, sublime, and frightening landscape to the merely pretty, the picturesque, thus setting up the American landscape as uncannily doubled. The uncontrollable sublime landscape that Irving describes also exists outside the limits of human time, enduring longer than any human beings and human enterprises. When Rip returns after his long sleep he discovers many changes in the village: "everything was strange" (36). All of his old "haunts" are gone (36). Indeed now that he is a ghost, the entire region is his haunt. The landscape, however, remains unchanged: "there was every hill and dale precisely as it had always been" (36). The doubled landscape seems to reflect the doubled experience of young American. On one side they see the remembered past, the picturesque English countryside; on the other, the rugged sublimity of the present American land.

Irving also reminds his readers that the uncanny ghostliness of the landscape is a consequence of the many repressed ghosts who haunt the land: the Native Americans; the Dutch; and finally the recently dispossessed English. The story of the ghosts of the Native Americans, the first to inhabit the land, is the most fully repressed, deferred to a "Postscript," after the end of the actual narrative.

> The Kaatsberg or Catskill mountains have always been a region full of fable. The Indians considered them the abode of spirits who influenced the weather.... They were ruled by an old squaw spirit, said to be their mother ... there was a kind of Manitou or Spirit, who kept about the wildest recesses of the Catskill mountains, and took a mischievous pleasure in wreaking all kinds of evils and vexations upon the red men.... The favorite abode of this Manitou is ... a great rock or cliff in the loneliest part of the mountains [42].

Of course, by Rip's time, the Native Americans themselves have joined their spirits in the ghostly afterworld, as reflected by the belated placement of their story in the postscript. This structure suggests that Irving operates as an archeologist, or a psychoanalyst, first digging up what was last buried, getting to the deepest, most repressed, original layer last. The Dutch too are relegated fully to the realm of ghosts from the ancient past. When Rip returns to his village, an "ancient inhabitant" recalls that "the Kaatskill mountains had always been haunted by strange beings ... [including] the great Henrik Hudson ... with his crew of the Half Moon" (40). The Dutch spirits appear to Rip dressed in "the antique Dutch fashion" (34). In fact, "the whole group reminded Rip of the figures in an old Flemish painting" (34). Their haunt is set in "a cleft between lofty rocks" (33), leading into "a hollow like a small amphitheater, surrounded by perpendicular precipices" (34)—perhaps including the cliff of Manitou. In that fantastic space, the Dutch ghosts indulge in their old pastimes, drinking out of "a stout keg ... full of liquor" (33), "playing at ninepins" (34), and presumably still trying to destabilize the English, here in the person of Rip. In addition to their clothes and pastimes, even their "visages" seem "peculiar" to Rip, who is more accustomed to English colonial appearances. The last ghost to join the array is Rip himself, seemingly the first ghost to emerge from the dispossessed English tradition and people, the latest stratum in this heap of ghosts. In becoming a ghost, Rip enters the tradition of ghosts that haunt the Catskill Mountains. Irving thus presents a line of dispossession and repression, and the consequent spectralization of the repressed. Irving excavates this ghostly wave of succession to indicate that even ghosts are susceptible to dispossession as a result of historical and cultural change in America.

Irving thus reveals that in American culture, unlike that of England with its traditions and lineages, loss of identity and self is the norm, a liberating though unsettling state, especially to those who have held power in the old world order. Arthur Kopec identifies the appearance of yet another kind of destabilization in Irving's story: the newly American author's troubling loss of authority. Kopec suggests that Rip's situation reflects that of Washington Irving's and that "Rip" is "an allegory of authorial labor in early America"

(728). Rip, the character, is dedicated to story-telling and imagination, having "an insuperable aversion to all kinds of profitable labour" (Irving 30). In fact, Rip avoids only labor that would be of direct financial benefit to himself; he is always happy to assist others. Kopec asserts that he thus represents the American writer, detached "from the worlds of enterprise that increasingly mediated male identity" (728). Rip's re-awakening suggests the experience of the American writer, displaced in a new, tradition-less culture. In his essay, "English Writers on America," Irving highlights the obstacles that American writers face: "We are a young people, necessarily an imitative one, and must take our examples and models, in a great degree, from the existing nations of Europe ... especially England" (49). Irving asserts that, given their own cultural vacuum, American writers must accept the English influence as the foundation of American writing, using it as the basis for a new American literature, a solution that seems anxiously at odds with the notion of a fresh, rootless American identity.

The Reversed Dispossessions of Slavery

As the unnatural revolution against the English patriarchy resulted in the continuing destabilization of the American patriarch, so did the unnatural power reversals of slavery paradoxically disturb the stability of white male hegemony. In *Intricate Relations: Sexual and Economic Desire in American Fiction: 1789–1814*, Karen Weyler suggests slavery as the cause of masculine instability in Brown's *Arthur Mervyn* (1799). (Indeed Brown's entire opus is a litany of lost men.) In *Mervyn*, the destabilized eponymous protagonist wanders through a feverish and hallucinatory labyrinth, Philadelphia during the 1793 yellow fever epidemic. Weyler argues that Brown's representation of the plague adds a layer of "physical corruption" to "the moral rot already pervading the city" (161). The first outbreak of the yellow fever occurred at the city wharf; although some physicians believed the origin of the outbreak could be traced to the terrible hygiene in the city, others believed that the illness had been brought from the West Indies, through the slave trade. In *Gothic America*, Teresa Goddu too suggests that Brown links yellow fever to the slave trade. In the novel, the fever infallibly destabilizes the white men who experience it, and Brown might have been operating under a common misperception that African Americans were less susceptible to the disease. Thus Brown deploys the yellow fever epidemic as a powerful symbol of the destabilizing powers of the institution slavery, a theme that recurs in the literature of America and in the American Gothic.

The Dispossession of the Master in Uncle Tom's Cabin

Harriet Beecher Stowe's *Uncle Tom's Cabin* (1852) emphasizes the legal status of the slave as property. Chapters of her book are entitled "The Property is Carried Off" and "In Which Property Gets into an Improper State of Mind." The chapter entitled "The Unprotected" focusses on the dangers faced by the slave whose master has died. Yet Stowe ultimately emphasizes that the possession of slavery occurs on the economic plane alone, and that on the transcendent theological and moral planes, the slave never loses self-possession. Indeed, it is the master who is dispossessed of his essential humanity and property within this system. In her Introduction, Ann Douglas emphasizes the power of the moral and religious realities in Stowe's novel. Douglas reminds the reader of the solid Christian credentials of the author's family—the Beechers and the Stowes—and notes: "Like most of the Beechers, she saw life in terms of moral commitments" (7). Douglas adds, "in antebellum America, almost no one ... wrote about slavery in secular terms.... Slavery was a sin" (23), rather than an economic crime. Douglas further notes that Stowe claimed to have formed the idea of the book "as she was taking communion.... She had a vision of a saintly black man being mercilessly flogged and praying for his torturers as he died" (8). Stowe's vision serves as the culmination of the novel, and of the series of struggles that link Uncle Tom to Jesus. Indeed accusations that Uncle Tom is an example of the submissive and subservient African American ignore that, despite the parameters of nineteenth-century realism, Tom is not a typical, realistic slave; he is the slave *cum* the supernatural Jesus.[3] Stowe insistently places her narrative within a Christian context. Her protagonist also recalls Christian, the eponymous pilgrim in Bunyan's *Pilgrim's Progress* (1678), which Stowe mentions, along with "Milton's *Paradise Lost* and Scott's Family Bible" (244). Like Christian, and like Jesus, Tom journeys through various stations of trial and suffering, finally getting to the Celestial City. The escaped slave, Eliza, parallels the figure of Christiana, whose story follows that of her husband Christian in *Pilgrims Progress*; unlike Tom, whose pilgrimage ends in death, Eliza finds an earthly paradise in Canada, the sanctuary of the oppressed American slave.

Like Jesus, Tom begins his trials when he is sold for a sum of money; his economic value is necessary to save the family plantation, including his fellow slaves. He rapidly forgives those who have sold him, quoting to his children: "'Pray for them that 'spitefully use you,' the good book says'" (111). In arriving at his final station, Simon Legree's plantation, Stowe's Jesus descends to hell. Simon Legree is clearly the Devil, the nemesis in many an English Gothic novel.[4] He is "sun-burned" (477) and "demoniacal" (506);

George later calls him: "'The old Satan'" (590). Legree's possession of his slaves is described in language that evokes Satanic possession; as he purchases a slave, the narrator says, "he has got the girl, body and soul, unless God help her!" (479). One of his slaves calls herself "'a lost soul'" (522). Legree, ruler of his hellish space, is a tempter, in Satan's image (584), enticing Tom to cast off his Bible and "'Come ... join my church'" (553). He is the tempter whom Tom resists. When a fellow slave says, "'You are in the devil's hands ... and you must give up.... Everything is pushing us into hell. Why shouldn't we go?'" (511–512), Tom insists on emulating the model of Jesus: "'If we suffer with him, we shall also reign'" (514). As Tom is whipped to death, the narrator says, "the tempter (Legree/Satan) stood by him too,—blinded by furious despotic will" (584).

As the savior, opposed to the satanic Legree, Tom paves the way for the salvation of his people. He exerts "a strange power over them ... many would gather together to hear from him of Jesus" (559). George, the son of Tom's original master, comes to Legree's plantation in search of Tom and finds him as he is dying; in the view of a fellow slave, Tom is a "'sacrifice'" (589). The dying Tom is filled "with compassion and sympathy for the poor wretches by whom he was surrounded" (558). In his last words, Tom announces to George, "'*Heaven has come!*'" and sends a Christ-like message to his family: "'Tell 'em all to follow me—follow me!'" (590). Tom dies "a martyr" (577). His last words for Legree: "'I forgive ye, with all my soul'" (584). Finally, Tom ends with declaration of "love for all" (590). And his death does serve to redeem the other slaves on Legree's plantation. Additionally, George's witnessing of Tom's death promises a brighter future for many other slaves. In heightened biblical rhetoric, George swears at Tom's grave: "'I will do *what one man can* to drive out this curse of slavery from my land'" (593). The narrative voice reinforces this message: "of old, there was One whose suffering changed an instrument of torture [the cross] ... into a symbol of glory, honor and immortal life" (583), and reminds us "like his Master, he knew that, if he saved others, himself he could not save" (584). Even the two slaves who are the instruments of Tom's death—evoking the two thieves crucified alongside Jesus—are saved by his death. One of the slaves says, "'Hope Mas'r'll have to 'count for it, and not we.'" The other says, in confession, "'O, Tom we's been awful wicked to ye!'" They "washed his wounds" (584), and Tom also forgives them. Tom tells them of Jesus, and "They wept,—both the two savage men" (585). In fact, Tom is not only Jesus; he is the living Bible. When Eva's father buys him from Haley, he sums up Haley's voluble praise of his merchandise: "All the moral and Christian virtues bound in black morocco compete!" (234).

In the chapter entitled "Concluding Remarks," directly addressed to her readers, Stowe amplifies the discrepancy between biblical Christian values and "the legislative act of 1850," the Fugitive Slave Act, which required Northerners to return escaped slaves to their Southern masters. Stowe's novel thus sets in opposition two competing world views, represented by two opposing documents, the law and the Bible. The law allows the commodification of human beings; the Bible presents God as the sole master of all humans. A "poor heathenish Kentuckian" illustrates this opposition. When the poor man helps Eliza escape, the narrator ironically tells us: "he had not been instructed in his constitutional relations and consequently was betrayed into acting in a sort of Christianized manner" (119), unlike those "better situated and more enlightened" (119). Mrs. Bird, a Senator's wife, also makes this distinction. Berating her husband for supporting the law that criminalizes assisting runaway slaves, she tells her husband: "'I can read my Bible; and there I see that I must ... comfort the desolate; and that Bible I mean to follow'" (144). And when pages later the Senator, despite himself, is drawn to help Eliza when he sees her human plight, the narrator ironically calls him "a political sinner" (156), highlighting the inverted relationship between political law and Christianity in regards to slavery. Ultimately, Stowe promotes the greater power of Christianity's claims for possession of the soul over the attempts of the law to commodify bodies.

In fact, *Uncle Tom* demonstrates that (at least on the moral plane) the institution of slavery results in the dispossession of the white slave owner even more than it dispossesses the slave. Stowe asserts this perspective in the climax of the novel, during the struggle between Simon Legree and Tom. As Legree is "Riding by his slave quarters late at night," he hears Uncle Tom singing, "'When I can read my title clear / To mansions in the skies'" (557). Tom's song invokes the language of real estate possession, "title," to establish his spiritual ownership of his future space. As Walter Benn Michaels notes, Uncle Tom's "sense of heaven as 'home' is barely metaphoric" ("Romance and Real Estate" 102). Indeed on the Christian plane, Tom's statement is not metaphoric at all: the good Christian Tom knows that he will take possession of an eternal home, quite soon in fact, as he is dying. Thus "his home was in sight" (582). The dying Tom assures George that he is going to a far better place: "'The Lord's ... going to take me home.... Heaven is better than Kintuck'" (590). It is the evil Legree who will be dispossessed of heaven for eternity. For emphasis, Stowe highlights Tom's possession of his earthly home, built on love and faith, the space that provides the title of the novel. When we first meet Stowe's hero, it is in "the cabin of Uncle Tom" (66); he is a full human being, defined not by his master, but by his own place in his home and in his family, unstable as that place may be. His home is described in high domestic nineteenth-century style, surrounded by a garden that is "the delight and pride" (66) of his wife's heart, filled with happy children, and with good food. Even when couched in realistically material terms, Stowe shows that "home" is defined by Christian, rather than worldly, values. When the escaping slave George finds shelter with a Quaker family, we see their domicile from the perspective of George, who has never before "sat down on equal terms at any white man's table" (223): "This indeed was a home,—*home*," informed by "the light of a living Gospel" (224).[5] Stowe also reminds her reader that within the Christian world view, no one but God can possess a human being. Early in the novel, Tom's wife Chloe reminds her family that even the slave trader has "'*his master*'" (110), who will call him to account. When Legree announces to Tom: "'*I'm* your church now'" (482), this statement is opposed by a heavenly voice heard by Tom alone: "Fear not! Thou art MINE!" (482), thereby dispossessing Legree of his claim to ownership of Tom. When Legree commands Tom to beat another slave, Tom claims his right to refuse: "'my soul an't yours, Mas'r'" (508). When Legree, sounding as Satanic as ever asks rhetorically about Tom, his legal slave, "'Isn't he MINE?'" (578), we know the implicit answer. God's mastery of Tom deprives Legree of his property.

The strategy of Harriet Beecher Stowe's novel thus depends upon the convergence of the supernatural Gothic and the spiritual Bible, despite the hyper-realism of her text. An example of this conflation occurs late in the book when Tom, facing the spiritual and existential crisis that is slave life at Simon Legree's plantation, has a vision of the saintly child Eva, "reading to him from the Bible; and he heard her read" (498). As the vision passes, the narrator tells us: "Tom woke. Was it a dream? Let it pass for one" (498); the narrator's disinclination to insist upon the vision as a dream, suggests the spiritual nature of the vision, its supernatural aspect. Throughout the novel Stowe brings together the Gothic tradition and the tradition of the Christian Bible. Both texts present the struggle between Good and Evil in frankly supernatural terms; both concern themselves with issues, moral and material, of property possession, while condemning human power and wealth; and both often present fantasies of the liberation of the oppressed. Thus, ultimately, Stowe locates her work in the Gothic literary tradition by imagining an actualization of the Christian vision, as spiritual and supernatural powers overcome economic and legal mastery.

White Anxieties of Displacement: Benito Cereno and Pudd'nhead Wilson

White anxieties of being destabilized by the existence of slavery are evident in Herman Melville's *Benito Cereno* (1856), written in 1855 and taking place in 1799, not quite the distant past depicted in the English Gothic, but nevertheless an unusual American attempt at imagining a past moment. In the novel, "Captain Amasa Delano, of Duxbury in Massachusetts" commands "a large sealer and general trader" (37). Melville immediately sets up his point-of-view character as a powerful and established citizen of young America. Delano, although not young, is innocently oblivious of the presence of evil, which early Americans tended to associate with dark Europe; he is "a person of a singularly undistrustful good nature," lacking a tendency to dwell on the "malign evil in man" (37). Throughout the narrative, Melville emphasizes Delano's "simplicity" (53) and "guilessness" (57) which, in denying evil, allows it to rule. Melville explicitly indicts this world view, suggesting the danger of such attitudes; when challenged by the purpose of a tied rope, Melville depicts his hero with "knot in hand, and knot in head" (66), and condemns him for being "oblivious of any but benevolent thought" (70).

The innocent American, Delano, is too good for his world, an evil world in which human beings are bought and sold. Melville shows how a man who is himself innocent can be implicated in the inversions and artifices of the institution of slavery, and by his own blithe and unexamined assumptions about the capacities of "Negroes" and Spaniards. His attitude of unskeptical innocence leads Delano to unwittingly cause grave harm as he completely misinterprets the situation he observes on a strange ship that he encounters in the harbor of "a small, desert, uninhabited island" (37) off the coast of South America.[6] Where Delano sees mystery and confusion—the ship first appears to him, obscured by "the vapours partly mantling the hull" (38)— his unskeptical nature blinds him from the reality in front of him: he is actually witnessing a deadly slave mutiny.[7] An innocent, "his surprise ... lost in pity" leads him to believe that the ship he encounters is "evidently reduced from scarcity of water and provisions [thus] impairing the Spaniard's authority over them [the slaves]" (42).

A consequence of Delano's innocent lack of skepticism, Melville demonstrates, is his inability to weigh the evidence in front of him and to challenge the truisms of his world. Thus, when Delano encounters the captain of the strange ship, the eponymous Benito Cereno, he notes "the debility, constitutional or induced by hardships bodily and mental, of the Spanish captain," who seems dejected and mentally "unstrung" (42). Delano's unoriginal mind leaps immediately to the stereotypes of Spanish Catholics that he has inherited from his culture, including the stereotypes of the English Protestant Gothic, coalescing in his time. He assumes that the mental instability of the captain is a consequence of being "shut up in these oaken walls, chained to one dull round of command" like "some hypochondriac abbot" (42); he also sees

Cereno as "half-lunatic" (43), a common Gothic figure. The distaste for the Catholic aristocrat (also inherited from the Gothic tradition and from the ideologies of post–Revolutionary America) also leads Delano to dismiss the seriousness of the captain's plight. In fact, because Cereno is a scion of a powerful Spanish family, Delano actively distrusts him, furthering his inability to discern the actual situation. Speaking from Delano's perspective, the narrator deploys Gothic imagery to diminish the Spanish Catholic (the untrustworthy villain of many an English Gothic novel): "there seemed something so incongruous in the Spaniard's apparel as almost to suggest the image of an invalid courtier tottering about London streets in the time of the plague" (48). Delano dismisses Cereno's expressions of grief and fear as "sad superstition which associates goblins with the deserted body of man, as ghosts with an abandoned house" (51). Delano decides that "the dark Spaniard" (using the English Gothic tactic of conflating the dark Spanish or Italian Catholic with the menacing African) is more disturbing than the black slaves; Cereno is "the central hobgoblin of all" (59). Unable to recognize the new world horror of slavery, in which he is immersed, Delano remains stuck in the old Gothic motifs. He worries about being "murdered here at the ends of the earth on board a haunted pirate ship by a horrible Spaniard" (67), and dismisses his fears about the "strange craft" by returning to the comforting old stereotypes: "as a nation all these Spaniards are an odd set" (68).

Additionally, Delano's prejudices about Africans (determined by the dehumanizing stereotypes necessary for the implementation of slavery) lead him to underestimate the mutinying slaves. He never considers that the Africans might possess the motive, intelligence and organization necessary to carry out a revolt. Convinced of African inferiority, he is certain that "the whites ... by nature were the shrewder race" (65). Because Delano underestimates the capacities of the blacks, and dismisses Cereno as an unreliable Spaniard, he completely misses the meaning of the terrible scene that plays out in from of him. At one point, he blindly mistakes a moment of danger and threat for an intimate moment between master and slave, as the slave takes a razor to his master's throat to shave him. As he watches the dangerous Babo searching for the "sharpest razor," and observes that Cereno "nervously shudders" (74), Delano only notes the subservient servant and the unnerved master. As far as he is concerned, it all makes sense: "there is something in the Negro which, in a peculiar way, fits him for avocations about one's person" (74). For a moment Delano comes close to comprehending the reality, recognizing in the image before him "a headsman" with his victim "at the block." This notion he shakes away as an "antic conceit" because it unsettles his modern certainties. Only when the obtuse American leaves the strange ship to return to his own, does "a flash of revelation" sweep over "the long-benighted mind of Captain Delano" (88), disabling the stereotypes that have blinded him. By the end of the narrative, it becomes clear that every powerful white in the novella, as well as the reader, has been fully destabilized by the masquerade of the enslaved Africans, and by the fictions that establish the foundation of slavery: the misconception that Africans lack the humanity to desire freedom; the misguided notion that Africans are intellectually inferior to whites. Cereno loses his comrades, loses control of his ship, and is dispossessed of (and by) much of its rich cargo, the slaves. Even during the mortal battle between the American and Spanish sailors, and the Africans, we are reminded: "to kill or maim the Negroes was not the object. To take them, with the ship, was the object" (90). Like the ship, the "Negroes" are a valuable commodity, to be protected and preserved for future economic use. The status of the Africans as property is reinforced by a catalog of the blacks on the boat, listing "names, descriptions, and ages" (93).

Melville suggests that by losing his mastery over the Africans, Cereno has been dispossessed of his masculinity. In a brief summation of some outstanding details at the end of the narrative, we learn that Cereno's "silver-mounted sword, apparent symbol of despotic command [and phallic power], was not, indeed a sword, but the ghost of one. The scabbard, artificially stiffened, was empty" (103). Ultimately Cereno emerges, at only twenty-nine, a broken man "reduced" (91) and haunted for the brief remainder of his life by his encounter with slavery. Delano, blind to the end, declaims to Cereno "'you are saved: what has cast such a shadow upon you?'" Cereno's answer: "'The Negro'" (103). The institution of slavery thus destabilizes the American ship master, depriving him of the ability to reason and to discern reality for the entire narrative. Because of his naïveté, his acceptance of the legal fictions of his society, Delano almost loses his ship (the blithely named "Bachelor's Delight" 50) and his life to the Africans. Melville quite explicitly indicts the sunny American innocence that prevents Delano from interrogating the fictions of slavery, the false certainties and stereotypes of race that sustain the institution. Blindly, he accepts as real the "the fictitious story dictated to the deponent [Cereno] by Babo" (97)—the narrative of the subservient slave and the unstable Spaniard. Delano reveals his almost willful ignorance, his overreliance upon the clearly fallible law, in the need for a legal "investigation" (91) to determine "the truth" (92) of the events he has witnessed, and to establish the criminality of the Africans' actions. Melville's indictment of this one moral white American can easily be extended to his countrymen, who from the time of Delano to the time of Melville were blithely, willfully, ignoring the horror in their midst.

Clearly, the true master in this unstable web is Babo the slave, the "ringleader" (93), the murderer of his own "master," Aranda. Babo's ambition is to be "captain of two ships," dispossessing Delano as well as Cereno. He is "the plotter from first to last" (99). The dual meanings of Babo's "plot" are at play here. Babo plans "the act of revolt" by the Negroes [who] made themselves *masters* [italics mine] of the hatchway" (93). But he also weaves the "plot," the fiction, that dupes Captain Delano, scripting a masquerade that the foolish Delano accepts as real. Babo thus exhibits the doubled epistemological power of the subaltern, who sees his own reality as well as the false reality of the master. At the moment of Babo's fall, his capture, the narrator tells us that he had a "slight frame" and that it was "his brain, not body, [that] had schemed and led the revolt with the plot" (103). Melville thus also provides us with details that re-humanize Babo, working against the truisms of slavery. His revolt is an act of final desperation, the only chance his people have to fulfill their dream of "returning to Senegal" in "liberty" (94). That is, the Africans are brave enough, intelligent enough, to fight against their masters to attain freedom. Not only does Melville reverse the situation of slave and master; he creates a disconcerting confusion in the mind of the American reader who is grounded in the ideology of the noble rebellion against cruel mastery. Any distinction between the rebellion of the Africans and that of the Americans, only decades before the action of the novella, seems like yet another American fiction.

The national implication of Melville's story becomes clear at the end; when the scales are "dropped from his eyes," and "the mask torn away," Delano sees the emblem of the mutiny—previously covered by a "canvas shroud." From Delano's confused perspective, we see "death for the figurehead, in a human skeleton, chalky comment on the chalked words below, FOLLOW YOUR LEADER" (88). The skeleton is that of Cereno's friend, the slave owner Don Alexandro Aranda. Aranda was killed earlier in the mutiny and his decaying body "had been substituted for the ship's proper figurehead" (95), the image of Christopher Columbus: the first European patriarch to dominate the non–Europeans of the Western hemisphere. The meaning of the motto represents a threat by the Africans—a reminder that any Spaniard who plans to fight back will end up following Aranda in death. The master is subverted by the slave as Babo threatens, "'keep faith with the blacks from here to Senegal, or you shall in spirit, as now in body, follow your leader,' pointing to the prow" (95). But at the end of the story, the motto takes on another meaning. We are told that some months after the trial of the mutineers, Babo, the leader of the African rebellion is hanged and his "body was burned to ashes" (103). The narrator also informs us that "three months after being dismissed by the court, Benito Cereno, borne on the bier, did, indeed, follow his leader" (104). Melville ends his narrative with these words, and with this ambiguity: who exactly is the "leader" that Cereno follows?: Aranda the dispossessed and murdered master, or Babo who led his people in a desperate attempt for freedom, and who during the rebellion was the true master of the ship and of its captain. Just as we readers are left in the dark throughout the narrative, benighted as we are by the blindness of Delano, the point of view character, we are left with this uncertainty at the end of the narrative. Like the two captains we readers are also destabilized by the ambiguities and fictions of slavery.

* * *

Mark Twain's *Puddn'head Wilson* (1894), written well after Emancipation but set during the 1830s (another unusual instance of American historical Gothic) also reveals that the system of slavery can destabilize even the most powerful certainties, including the certainty of stable white male identity. Like Melville's *Cereno*, Twain's *Wilson* avoids the supernatural. But, like *Cereno*, *Wilson* is haunted by the dark shadow of slavery, and exhibits a core Gothic anxiety: the fear of the instability and alienability of identity. This fear is amplified by the structures of slavery, a system that routinely dispossesses human beings of their identity. Twain's Preface, "A Whisper to the Reader," written in Italy, raises a question that recurs in nineteenth-century America: who is an American writer, and who is an American? Twain's convoluted narrative amplifies the complications of this question during the time of slavery as it traces the journey of young Tom, a "passing" black, who is an unlikely and uncanny double of Twain's quintessential white American boy, Tom Sawyer.

Although the supernatural is absent from *Wilson*, Mark Twain illustrates the American affinity for other Gothic conventions in his text, which involves mystery, murder and mayhem. A central location in the narrative is "'de ha'ntd house'" (50), avoided by most members of the community. In opening his story, Mark Twain deploys a strategy of horror that still operates to great effect in twenty-first-century literature and film. The reader is first presented with a sunny setting of domestic happiness: a neighborhood of "pretty homes," surrounded by carefully described flowers gardens. Each of these homes is "complete," marked by "contentment and peace" (5). After thus lulling his audience into a state of vulnerability, with this comforting description of domestic joy, Twain shocks the reader with a sudden shift to the horror of slavery: "Dawson's Landing was a slaveholding town." The narrator's description thus amplifies the horror of slavery by contrasting it with the happy life of the free white Americans, and by partaking almost completely in the erasures of slavery. The narrator focusses on the lush products of slave labor, while repressing the human slaves who are the producers. The setting is "a rich slave-worked grain and pork country" (6), a place where a humane man is kind to "his slaves and other animals" (14), and "only" sells his slaves locally, instead of "DOWN THE RIVER" (16). It does not take long for Roxanne, a young slave mother, to realize the true "terror" and "horror" (17) of her situation: at any moment a sale could separate her from her infant son forever. Her response echoes the melodrama of her life: "'yo' po' mammy will kill you fust'" (17). Reflecting the sad reality of her time, Roxanne declaims: "'we gwine jump in de river'" (18).

However, the horror at the center of the novel is not so much the horror of slavery, as the anxiety evoked by the instability of identity for everyone—white and black—within the structures of slavery. On the surface, the only alienable identity within the system of slavery is that of the slave who is dispossessed of name, personhood, property, mobility, family—indeed of everything. Yet, as Mark Twain illustrates, the presence of a system that destabilizes the identity of a significant part of the population endangers the identity of all. Twain sets up a pattern of confused identity in the novel, through the related Gothic themes of the double, and of the disguise. The most overt example of the double appears in the persons of the Italian twin brothers. Ironically, they are not completely identical: "One was *a little fairer* than the other" (34 italics mine). Based on this flimsy distinction, the twins, sporting their white privilege, take on distinct identities, as "the blond" and "the brunette." Thus arises a fiction of difference that echoes the racial fictions of slavery, which distinguished free "whites" from enslaved "blacks," without any reference to actual skin tone. Because of systemic rape within slavery, a slave could be physically fair and closely related to the family of the master; thus slavery too was based upon a fiction of unbridgeable difference. In addition to the fiction of difference the Italian twins enact other variants of slavery. Their life story includes moments of servitude akin to "slavery." Commodified and exploited as children when they were seized for the debts of their parents, and "placed among the attractions of a cheap museum" (35), they become the objects of the dehumanizing gaze of the crowd. Escaping from bondage at the age of twelve, the twins emerge transformed into "men" (35), achieving adult masculine identity (denied to slaves) by virtue of their freedom. The twins are again reduced to being objects of the popular gaze upon arriving in America. As boarders at the home of the widow Cooper, they are visited by a crowd of Americans. The first visitor in the "procession," stunned by their exoticism, greets them with "a devouring stare" (36). Twain thus creates yet another voracious American in the line of Mary Rowlandson, Edgar Huntly and Ned Higgins. Not surprisingly, Mark Twain's visual devourer is named "Higgins," to commemorate Hawthorne's young consumer, The celebrity of the twins ensures their commodification; after the gazers depart, the homeowner's daughter, Rowena, gloats about their connection to the twins: "they are ours—all ours" (37). In addition to raising doubts about the stability of identity through the duality of the twins, Twain shows us the fluidity of identity as the twins' "Western adventure" (143) unfolds. Because of their celebrity, and the resulting adulation of the town, the twins give "the regulation thirty days' notice, the required preparation for citizenship" (94), with the plan to run for town mayor. Mark Twain thus reminds us how unstable and permeable was the American identity in young America (as opposed to the rigid barriers imposed in our time to alleviate the anxieties of patriarchy). Twain also contrasts the situation of black Americans during slavery. Even though the Italians are exotic "foreigners" (105), as Europeans they can easily achieve the status of American identity, virtually inaccessible to enslaved Africans—another unveiling of the irrationalities that buttress the system of slavery. Finally, the situation of the twins reveals how hard it is to sustain identity, when the former celebrities are demonized as murderers. In fact the actual perpetuator is young Tom, the confounding black passing as white.

Mark Twain also deploys the trope of disguise to suggest the fluid instability of identity. Tom, the black slave, who is unknowingly passing as the young white scion of a slave owning family, is particularly adept at masking his supposed identity. He dresses as a white girl to avoid suspicion as he robs his neighbors, donning a dress "as a disguise for his raid" (58). Since the clothes belong to the black woman who is secretly his biological mother, his disguise indicates the fluidity of racial identity as well as the fluidity of gender identity. (Roxy, the slave mother, also expresses the fragility of gender identity when she disguises herself as a black man to escape detection as a runaway slave.) Tom adds to the gender and racial confusion (or interchangeability) by dressing as a black woman to avoid detection when he kills Judge Driscoll; he puts on "his suit of girl's clothes" and blackens "his face with burnt cork" (119). Mark Twain thus ironically leads us into the depths of masquerade and illusion, as a young man born black and raised white must darken his skin to appear black. After the murder, to escape detection, Tom, raised in wealth, engages in a masquerade of social class; he burns "his male and female attire ... and put[s] on a disguise proper for a tramp" (121). Wilson, the title character, the hero by default of the book, also experiences the instability of appropriated identity. Pudd'nhead Wilson's legal name is David Wilson; he is a double outsider in Southern America, "of Scotch parentage" (8), born and raised "in the interior of the State of New York" (8). Since he is too clever for the townspeople to understand him, they quite illogically decide that he is "'a fool'" (8) and "'a pudd'nhead'.... Within a week he had lost his first name: Pudd'nhead took its place" (9).

The recurring moments of destabilized identity underline Twain's contention. A nation dominated by an economic and social system which denies the concept of an unalienable core identity to a large segment of its population sets up a system in which no one is secure from the appropriation of identity. Mark Twain's narrative begins when the slave mother Roxy steals the white child from his family, usurping his identity as family scion, and bestowing that identity upon her slave child. To fully cover her tracks, Roxy passes off the white child as her slave son, thereby robbing the white infant of his freedom as well as of his identity. Roxy is able to do this because the two babies are identical, more alike, in fact, than are the Italian twins. Dressed in the white child's clothes, Roxy's child is indistinguishable from the white baby. Twain explains this seemingly surprising doubling of slave and master: the slave child is actually "thirty-one parts white [yet] he, too, was a slave and, *by a fiction of law and custom,* a negro" (13 italics mine). Twain thus stresses the fictions of identity upon which rested the code of racially defined chattel slavery. Like her son, Roxanne appears to be white woman: "Her complexion was very fair." And clearly she is one of the most intelligent characters in the book. Yet, as the child of a slave mother, Roxy is legally considered black and irrationally designated a slave. In a heightened irony, we later find out that the slave child himself is in fact, if not in legal fiction, an heir of the Southern aristocracy. His mother tells him that he was the son of a white gentleman, and that he descends from "'de Highest blood that Ole Virginny ever turned out'" (89). In a moment of merited family pride, Roxy refers to her family as "'De Smith Pocahontases'" (90), a hilarious parody of the pride of her presumed betters, and an example of the heartbreakingly dark humor that regularly punctuates the narrative voice.

For most of her son's life, Roxy keeps the secret of the usurped identity from everyone, including Tom, the new appropriated name of her unknowingly passing son. Roxy hopes to sustain his natural attachment to his mother, so that she may wield the alliance as a powerful weapon to fight the battles she constantly faces. But Tom, raised white, disappoints her, and so she informs him that she possesses dangerous knowledge about him. In a sudden reversal of power, the supposedly white Tom is reduced to "begging" her to reveal the secret. Roxy's reward is the unimagined pleasure of seeing a "'fine nice young white gen'l'man kneeling down to a nigger wench'" (49)—the irony being that he was actually born a slave. When Roxy reveals to Tom that he is, in fact, her son, a black slave, she hovers "above him like a Fate" (51), controlling his destiny. She thus reveals a shocking reality to the reader as well as to Tom: his identity as a white man is as unstable, as alienable as that of any slave; in fact he is a slave. "'You's a *nigger!—bawn* a nigger en a *slave!* En you ain't *got* no fambly name, beca'se niggers don't *have* em!'" Tom comes to the annihilating awareness that "'I am a nigger!'" (55). In addition to ripping away Tom's white identity, Roxy re-imposes his actual identity as slave, and his relationship to her: "'You'll call me ma or mammy'" (53). Roxy also restores Tom's paternity to him, although that lineage is virtually unchanged. In a moment of irony that is far from amusing, Roxy informs Tom that his biological father, like his presumed father, was a member of the Southern white aristocracy. "'Dey ain't another nigger in dis town dat's as high-bawn as you is'" (55), a bitter irony indeed. With this, Tom becomes a new being with a new awareness of race, and a new self-awareness; he has been unknowingly "passing" his entire life. This is all, of course, completely irrational, but it reflects the irrational legal reality of the South. Tom is still the same; his father is virtually still the same, but with the revelation that his mother is a black slave somehow, magically, as in a fairy tale, his identity is transformed. Roxy, wielding the power of the subaltern, has thus undermined the certainties of Southern aristocratic lineage, and revealed them as illusory fictions.

Roxy's superior intellectual and moral intelligence is apparent in that she alone (unlike Melville's Delano) recognizes the fictions of slavery. Reflecting uncomfortably on having consigned the master's child to a life of slavery, she justifies herself by invoking the precedent set by white America: "'Tain't no sin—*white folks* has done it'" (19). The American insistence on the alienability of identity sets the precedent for the usurpation of the white master's identity, overriding morality and reality. But Roxy is too smart to believe in these fictions. At the end of the tale, the narrator conflates Roxy's heartbreak with an aside about the original white Tom, upon whom she "had inflicted twenty-three years of slavery" (143). We sense that this statement describes her subjective reality. For her, consigning a person to slavery is a moral problem, though ironically not so for the slaveholders. Roxy's power thus lies in her ability (an ability lacked by Melville's Delano) to recognize that the boundary between "the slave" and "the human" is false. Later in the novel, when Roxy offers to let her son sell her to pay off debts, she asserts that the love of a black mother is identical to that of a white mother: "'In de inside, mothers is all de same'" (102). The analogous interchangeability of the two children at birth, and throughout their lives, amplifies the point that the distinction between white and black, master and slave is a fiction with no rational support.

Mark Twain stresses that it is the legal system of slavery itself, rather than inherent nature, that creates the distinction between master and slave. Tom, the slave child (the narrator calls him "the usurping little slave" 22) who usurps his master's status, is raised to become the white master. He is spoiled from infanthood, "indulged in all his caprices" (23). Because he is allowed to torment Chambers (the actual white child transformed into a slave) and to denigrate Roxy, his secret biological mother, young Tom rapidly learns to be a bully. Into young manhood, Tom is "petted and indulged and spoiled," growing into adulthood as an "indolent" (30) gambler. He ends his tenure as a white man by killing the man who has raised him, his presumed uncle. He also twice shows his willingness to sell Roxy "down the river" (103), even after he knows that she is truly his mother. On the other hand, Chambers, the white boy raised as a slave, learns early on—through "convincing canings" (25)—the imperative of slavish subservience. His body, the source of his value as a slave, is well-cared for; he becomes "strong because he was coarsely fed and hard worked about the house" (25). But his spirit and his mind are crushed. When he finally is identified as a free white male, he is as debilitated by his upbringing as Tom by his. He speaks in the dialect of slaves; "his gait, his attitudes, his gestures, his bearing, his laugh—all were vulgar and uncouth; his manners were the manners of a slave" (144). Being subjected to the upbringing of a slave has made Chambers (the original white infant) into a creature of paradox: a "pure-white slave" (46). Here too we see Twain's bitter humor. As we know from the ancestry of Roxy and her son, a slave might be racially black only by the smallest percentage of maternal ancestry; most of the genetic heritage could be inherited from white progenitors. Slaves whose blackness was thus racially diluted remained slaves as long as they inherited the one iota of blackness from their mother that prevented them from being "pure-white."

While the central Gothic anxiety of *Pudd'nhead Wilson* is the fear of lost identity, Mark Twain introduces a number of other themes that serve to link his novel to the Gothic tradition. The text's anxiety about the loss of property, related to the loss of identity, mimics the English Gothic of Walpole's *Otranto*. Walpole's text reveals an English faith in unalienable noble identity; once his true high birth is revealed, Theodore, the aristocrat raised as a peasant, immediately shows himself to be a deserving heir to the property, overcoming the usurping owner who is himself of servant ancestry. In Mark Twain's narrative the false heir, Tom the undeserving slave, also usurps the property of the legal aristocratic (white) heir. However, Twain reveals a healthy American skepticism about the power of aristocratic breeding, and the unalienability of noble character: Chambers (the original white child) fails to rise to his proper status once he is revealed as the legitimate, white heir. The wily Roxanne experiences the instability of property. After being freed, she works for years, only to lose her life savings when "her bank had gone to smash" and she becomes "a pauper and homeless" (42). Her dream of getting support from her son is shattered when she learns of his constantly impoverished state. The imagery Mark Twain uses to describe Roxy's disappointment evokes the conventional Gothic castle, as well as the image of the castles in the air found in the Preface of Hawthorne's *Seven Gables*: "Roxy's pet castle ... was tumbling to ruin before her eyes" (44). Additionally, the unstable and dysfunctional family, also a Gothic trope dating back to Walpole also appears, with the twist of slavery, in Twain's narrative. Tom murders his presumed uncle, and is willing to sell his biological mother. Within a few lines of text, we are reminded that Tom has two sets of relatives: we hear of Tom's white, legal "aunt and uncle," acquired through his usurpation of their real nephew's identity, as well as "his mother," Roxy, his biological black mother (100). Ultimately both the black family and the white family are blasted by the curse of slavery.

The consolidation of Gothic effects in the text, underscores the change of tone at the conclusion. Like Edgar Allan Poe, who moves from the mysteries of the Gothic to the solutions of rational authority, Mark Twain's novel leaves the world of the Gothic to conclude in the world of science and reason—although this world is hardly enlightened, morally or emotionally. Mark Twain's marginalized title character proves his intelligence by deploying the rationality of science to supplant the fictions of slavery. Through his scientific study of fingerprints, Puddn'head (by now the irony of his name is well-established) re-stabilizes the identities of the two young men who were switched at birth. Like the authorities of the town, the perpetuators of the *status quo*, Wilson is a lawyer, but he is a lawyer devoted not to upholding the inscrutable fictions of slavery, but to the truth. One of his "fads" is an interest in "fingermarks" (11), which he discovers can be used to definitively establish identity. Thus, he scientifically and logically deduces the switch. He observes the only discernible difference between the two men: "'the baby's [original prints] don't tally with the others!'" (132). From the discrepancy between the prints on record for the baby Tom, the original white baby, and the prints he has for the adult Tom, the original black baby, Wilson deduces the solution to the "mystery" (132). The narrative thus moves from the irrational Gothic world (in which slavery is legal) to the enlightened world of reason and order, the world in which the law promotes truth and justice. At the murder trial of the twins, Wilson attempts to prove that Tom is the actual murderer of his Uncle the judge, and that he is also an imposter. Wilson logically and clearly explains the fingerprints; each set is unique to one individual. There can be "'no duplicate of it among the swarming populations of the globe'" (137). Even in the case of twins "'one twin's patterns are never the same as his fellow-twin's patterns'" (137). Thus: no more confusing doubles; no more slippage of identity. At last identity can be definitively determined, through science. The trial is attended by a white mob in the making; the newspaper that reports on the murder of the judge adds "The assassin will probably be lynched" (121). But Wilson transforms the attitude of the crowd from irrationality to reason. He painstakingly traces the process of fingerprinting to all those attending the trial to prove that the twins are innocent and that the usurping Tom is the criminal. Mark Twain thus enters the world of modern science to solve the problem of identity that had long roiled the Gothic, and the patriarchy. Having fingerprinted the two children, both before and after the switch, Wilson possesses the means to scientifically re-establish their original identities. At the same time, Wilson discovers a method that definitively alleviates the anxiety that drives much of the Gothic plot: the fear of illegitimate infiltration of the patriarchal dynasty through usurpation of identity. At the end of the trial, wherein the identities of slave and master are restored, the narrator tells us, "the clock struck twelve" (143); presumably we are witnessing the happy, definitive resolution of the Cinderella fantasy of disguise.

Mark Twain seemingly concludes his book with a solution that is satisfying to the patriarchal *status quo*. Magically, in a conservative fantasy of restoration, the characters are satisfyingly returned to their original identities and situations; the identity of the white man is finally restored, and so his lost property is also restored. Wilson's language heightens the magical nature of this transformation. Speaking of the original white Tom (turned into a black slave) he says: "'Within a quarter of an hour he will stand before you white and free!'" (142). The subversion of the black slaves who tried to undermine the system is also suddenly revealed, and order is restored. Roxy's usurping son, long disguised as Tom, quite magically "'became a negro and a slave'" (142). Yet, the joy of restoration that accrues to the white patriarchy, is tragically countered by the pain experienced by Roxy and both of her sons—the true and the false. Roxy's life and spirit are destroyed; her "heart was broken" (143). Having lost both sons, she retires to a secluded life, the only "solace" for her is "her church and its affairs" (144). Although identity and property are returned to the true Tom, his slave upbringing has rendered him unable to fill his new role, and he too lives an isolated life, exiled from his former community of black slaves, and from his present white social circle. And, even though the false Tom (now again the slave Chambers) is a scoundrel,

Mark Twain emphasizes that he was a beloved baby, ruined by his upbringing, and that, despite his many flaws, he is a fully-developed human being, about to endure the inhuman suffering of slavery. Yet, Twain seems to follow the biases of the slave system in denying any inner life and real humanity to Chambers, the false slave. The last words of the novel tell us, somewhat blithely, that Chambers (the usurping Tom now restored to his original slave identity) was "sold down the river" (145), disappearing from the record, and from the rolls of humanity.

The ambivalent conclusion of *Wilson* taps into the Gothic narrative pattern, beginning with Horace Walpole's *Otranto*, which almost immediately moves from order to disorder, indulging in a ludic central narrative that features fleeting fantastic moments of joyful and chaotic subversion, only to end with a stifling restoration of order, to the dismay of readers and characters alike. Variations of this narrative pattern are visible in Lewis' *The Monk*, and in the American Gothic tradition in Hawthorne's *House of the Seven Gables*, Brown's *Edgar Huntly*, Poe's "Masque of the Red Death," Irving's "Rip Van Winkle," and "Legend of Sleepy Hollow," as well as Melville's *Cereno*, and other texts previously discussed. Similarly, the conservative restoration that concludes *Wilson* is disappointing and even tragic: social and economic order is restored in a comfortingly definitive manner, but the immediate consequence is personal tragedy for characters the reader has come to know intimately. The horror of the reader of *Wilson* is heightened by the comic and sly tone of the narrator, who clearly relishes this tale of subversion. The comic narrative voice, visible in a number of passages quoted above, is abetted by the overt comedy of the excerpts from the imaginary "Puddn'head Wilson's Calendar" which furnish the epigrams for the chapters of the narrative. These epigrams usually condense the point of a chapter in a humorous way. The epigram for the chapter on the boys' disparate upbringings: "Training is everything. The peach was once a bitter almond; cauliflower is nothing but cabbage with a college education" (28). The chapter that comprises the story of the twins' triumph in the community, and Tom's female disguise begins: "One of the most striking differences between a cat and a lie is that a cat only has nine lives" (38). The chapter that features the judge's condemnation of Tom's reluctance to fight a duel, because a court trial is undignified, begins: "When I reflect on the number of disagreeable people who I know have gone to a better world, I am moved to live a different life" (77). The chapter in which Tom murders the judge begins: "Few things are harder to put up with than the annoyance of a good example" (116). Thus the narrative is permeated with humorous versions of quite weighty matters. Sustaining the seemingly benign tone with which the text begins, Twain continues to lull the reader into a false sense of comfort, only to startle the reader with a tragic and horrifying reality. *Wilson* thus manages to achieve the Gothic horror of the slave narrative, without a single description of physical torture or gore.

* * *

The image of the unstable or absent patriarchy endures throughout nineteenth-century America, instigated by the American Revolution and abetted by the system of slavery. However, by the end of the century, by the time Twain wrote *Wilson,* it was clear that the restored Southern aristocracy would be joined by a new set of American patriarchs, the robber barons who made productive use of the economic changes that occurred in the wake of the Civil War to accumulate previously unheard of wealth in the United States.

5

Masterless
The Anxieties of Freedom

While the English Gothic flirts with the dangers of the supernatural, often the ultimate figure of fear in the English Gothic is the human male tyrant—the dangerous and decadent aristocrat or his authoritarian counterparts: the patriarch and the priest. While the aristocratic patriarch still posed real dangers to the poor and powerless in eighteenth-century England, and continued to appear as the villain and nemesis of the young in the English Gothic, the dispossession of King George III and of the monarchy and the aristocracy in America removed that threat from American life, and from the young protagonist of the American Gothic text. In fact, in the American Gothic, a major source of fear is the absence of authority, the *horror vacui* that follows revolution and parricide. The fear of dispossession, that is, the fear of *not* being possessed, left to flounder without a guide, thus informs much of the nineteenth-century American Gothic.

Jay Fliegelman, whose analogy of the American Revolutionary as parricide is mentioned earlier, calls American post–Revolutionary society "postpatriarchal" (*Prodigals and Pilgrims* 262), arguing that the remaining American fathers were cut from a mold different from that of the autocratic and tyrannical patriarchs and monarchs of England. Fliegelman points to the model of Washington as benevolent Father of his country and asserts, "it is a parent's grief, not anger, authority or indifference, that is feared in the postpatriarchal family" (262). The absence of the strong and harsh patriarch from American life and literature ironically creates anxieties for the newly-free young American. Liberation from the displaced ruler results in the anxiety of young men who have lost their guardians. In the essay "The Spirit of Place" (*Studies in Classic American Literature* 1923), D.H. Lawrence also invokes the family model: "Somewhere deep in every American heart lies a rebellion against the old parenthood of Europe" (10) to explain why the American "isn't a European still, like his father before him" (9). Lawrence identifies the anxiety provoked by deposing the patriarch—the monarch, and the old English father—and appropriating his land at the core of American identity. Lawrence further notes the paradox of this anxiety. Liberation from the patriarch, to "be masterless" (9), was the expressed goal of those who left England, the expression of "a frenzy for getting away from any control of any sorts" (10), to be free of "the old authority of Europe" (10). Yet, Lawrence continues in "Fenimore Cooper's White Novels": "When America set out to destroy Kings and Lords and Masters, and the whole paraphernalia of European superiority, it pushed a pin right through its own body" (49). This is because being "masterless" is not the same as being free, which Lawrence defines as the state of "obeying some deep, inward voice ... obeying from within.... Not ... escaping to some wild west" (12). And so, in Lawrence's formulation, young Americans, having cast off the external masters of Europe without yet discovering the mature state of self-determination, are stuck in an anxious limbo of "masterlessness." In "Romancing the Shadow," Toni Morrison also notes the discomforts of freedom; she remarks on the "dour ... troubled ... frightened and haunted ... early founding literature" troubled by "Power—control of one's own destiny" (35). Like Lawrence, Morrison concludes that it is "the terror of human freedom" (37) that results in Gothic meditations on "problems of human freedom." Americans are haunted by the vacuum that is freedom, by the fear of what it means to be "masterless."

The new American Gothic reflects this anxious dilemma, the struggle of young people who find themselves in a chartless country and society, lacking the comforting, though limiting, structures of the old world. Compounding this anxiety are the reasons for the absence of the patriarch, whose authority has been displaced in the young country through military, political and cultural revolution. As Susan Manning notes in her introduction to Washington Irving's *Sketches*, "Having rejected the father—as America symbolically did in the colony's rebellion against King George III, and as Irving himself had in fleeing from a steady career in Law to the unsettled prospects of literature" (viii)—the son is left with the anxiety of being alone through his own choices. Indeed, the young American man, freed in life and in literature from the looming presence of the dark patriarch, is far from carefree. In the absence of the dangerous patriarch who is the conventional villain and major obstacle of the English Gothic, the young man is threatened not only by the unmapped wilderness and the spectral Native American, but also by his own unlimited, lawless self, that threatens to create chaos without the guiding and repressive hand of the father. Added to the challenges faced by the rudderless young man is the need to independently acquire fortune and identity, without the assistance of the old patriarchal systems of patronage and inheritance. The economic master-plot of the eighteenth-century English Gothic is the restoration of appropriated property to its rightful owner, often a young man whose identity as heir is belatedly discovered, or who marries the young heiress, or both. These avenues to success do not exist in the American world or in the American Gothic text. In the absence of any legacy, property or family business, in the absence of a bequeathing father, or a marriageable heiress, the displaced young man must seek, or create, his fortune in the new world. The conventional Gothic journey toward the unknown is reframed in the American novel as the search to discover or create an identity or vocation.

The Anxieties of Young Benjamin Franklin

Although he evolved to become an American patriarch, the quintessential self-made American man, young Franklin, as reflected in his (most certainly non–Gothic) *Autobiography* (1771–1789), illustrates the anxieties of his time and generation. Fliegelman discusses the concerns that Franklin displays in leaving his father's home and control, noting "the crucial relevance of the parable of the prodigal son to the concerns of later eighteenth-century Anglo-American culture" (113). The early pages of the *Autobiography* detail young Ben's search for vocation and thereby identity and a livelihood, a search during which he was often at odds with his father, and determined to make his own way. The father cannot afford "to support the expense of a college education," but he does actually have two trades to bequeath to the son, "tallow chandler and soap boiler" (63); Ben refuses both. Significantly, Ben's father "was not bred" to that vocation but himself became a self-made man in America in response to commercial demand. In an attempt to dissuade Ben from his dream of being a sailor, like his older brother, the father takes his son on a search for a vocation: "he sometimes took me to walk with him and see joiners, bricklayers, turners, braziers, etc., at their work that he might observe my inclination and endeavor to fix it on some trade that would keep me on land" (66). Yet ultimately Ben chooses his own path: to be a printer. William Andrews locates a deeper meaning in Franklin's search for the right vocation, linking that search with the beliefs of his Puritan New England ancestors. Like them, "Franklin believed that God's will was for everyone to have a calling, a vocation, through which each person would seek not only to fulfill the self but also to benefit the community" (Andrews Introduction *Classic American Autobiographies* ix). Thus as Andrews continues, the notion of the self-made man, the man who creates his own identity, is an American innovation:

"the act of remaking oneself, the perpetual reinvention of one's role and image in the social order." This is clearly an act that is simultaneously liberating and frightening. Indeed, Franklin's *biography*, if not his *Autobiography*, reveals the dangers of an economically fluid society. As detailed in Jill Lapore's *Book of Days*, Ben Franklin's sister, Jane, and her family fared far worse in the American economy than he did.

Brown's Wandering Young Men

The dark misery of Jane Franklin's story is closer in tone to Brown's novels than to Franklin's cheerful *Autobiography*. Brown has a far less sanguine view of American society and the possibilities for American youth than that presented by Ben Franklin, even though Brown "grew up in the Philadelphia that Benjamin built," a center of education and culture and "a marvel of commerce, both legal and illegal," featuring a "freshwater port" and "two banks" (Norman Grabo Introduction *Edgar Huntly* vii). Grabo suggests that Brown's boyhood during the Revolutionary War predisposed him to a more gloomy view of the America of his day. His Quaker family attempted to be neutral in the war against the British, but this made them seem like outsiders to their revolutionary neighbors. In return, Brown associated the Revolution with "riot, excess, violence, fear, and death" (Grabo ix). Like Franklin, and like his character Edgar Huntly, Brown had to search for his own vocation, rather than inherit it. He was not temperamentally suited to the line of work of his family, merchants and government workers. Nor did he find fulfillment when he was apprenticed to a law firm as a young man. Finally in his twenties, he found a vocation that truly called to him, literature. But the question remained: could this be a vocation, providing him with a livelihood, or was it merely an avocation, to fill in any free hours between commerce and the law?

Thus, the Native Americans are not the only characters dispossessed in Brown's *Edgar Huntly*. The complicated and anxious odyssey of young, fatherless, Edgar, whose search for identity and livelihood offers a counter-example to the straightforward success of Franklin's *Autobiography*, illustrates how the search for vocation in a trackless society can go awry. The central movement of the title character of the novel, when he is not waylaid by the dangers of the wilderness and the "savage" Native Americans, is his search for a place in his world. Huntly is in a precarious economic and social position. His parents have been killed and his home farm destroyed during an attack by Indians. In order to marry his equally impoverished fiancée Mary, who ekes out a living doing sewing, Edgar must identify a source of income. When the novel begins, he is dependent on his uncle, living on the uncle's farms with his two surviving sisters. This does not represent a stable long-term plan as the uncle's son will inherit the farm upon the death of the uncle, which does occur at the end of the novel: "My uncle's death will transfer this property to his son, who ... is an enemy of us" (149). When the novel opens, Huntly's best prospect is the mysterious $7500 that has appeared in the bank account of Waldegrave, his friend, the brother of Huntly's fiancée. Since Waldegrave has died without leaving a will, his heir, his sister Mary, takes "possession" of his "property" (135) and stands to inherit the money which would allow her and Edgar to marry; as her husband, Edgar would come into possession of the money, thus finding his fortune, and economic and social stability. Yet the ownership of this property (the money) is disputed, in typical Gothic style. Another friend of Waldegrave claims that the money in the bank account is his, thus depriving Edgar of the English route of acquiring property and status through inheritance and marriage. There is yet one more traditional avenue to wealth available to Edgar; acquiring a wealthy patron. An old "preceptor" (89) of Edgar's, Sarsefield, conveniently turns up. Edgar invokes the old hierarchal language, calling him "My master! My friend!" (89), reminding him: "It is Edgar Huntly, your pupil, your child" (233). Until the end of the novel, Sarsefield is encouraging and Edgar is hopeful about his prospects under his protection. Yet, a late blunder on the part of Edgar results in the premature termination of the pregnancy of Sarsefield's wife, resulting in the death of the child who would have implicitly been a competitor of Edgar for Sarsefield's favors. The loss of the unborn baby of Mrs. Lorimer and Sarsefield impels Sarsefield to cut Edgar off. Thus at the end of the novel, Edgar has failed at his attempts to earn his place the old English ways: through marriage and inheritance, or patronage.

Elizabeth Jane Wall Hinds notes the accuracy with which Brown reflects the transitory economic situation of his times, the change from the old forms of English wealth to the new American forms of wealth. She notes the transition in America from an economy of landownership to an economy of paper currency and speculation run by a decidedly entrepreneurial class:

> [During the] "federalist" decade of the 1790's ... this previous land-based economy arguably paralleled the most long-lived aristocracies of the Old World, depending as it did on the patrimony of inherited property and social connections to support the insular economy of colonial America.... Throughout the 1790's, this power base began to erode as the U.S. economy turned to fuller practice of market capitalism [resulting in] a new social order ["Charles Brockden Brown's Revenge Tragedy" 52].

Brown thus taps into the social anxieties typical of the Gothic mode to capture the fears engendered by change in the wake of the Revolutionary War. The transformation of the old forms is also visible in the failure of Huntly's plans to acquire economic stability in the old European ways: through inheritance, sponsorship and marriage. Ultimately *Huntly* is about a masterless young man's unsuccessful search for a benefactor so that he can live without discovering the vocation that Ben Franklin so forcefully pursued in becoming the self-made American. As Hinds notes, throughout the novel Huntly "becomes increasingly disinherited" (54) due to his reliance on the old ways. Edgar's error is that he is counting on the old order of the economy as others evolve to embrace the new. Indeed, Brown clearly indicts his protagonist for failing to adapt to these transformations, despite Grabo's contention that "Edgar's hopes are blasted through no fault of his own" (xxi).

Throughout the novel, Brown carefully provides commendable illustrations of American men, contrasted to Edgar, who pursue economic stability through the new channels afforded in America—labor, capitalism, commerce, and the practice of the emerging professions. As Gillian Brown observes, Brown promotes the acquisition of wealth based upon individual accomplishment, which "signified a break from past structures of society and economy, and an advance for individual opportunities in a capitalistic order" (109). The successful American landowners, Edgar's uncle and his neighbor Inglefield, are not aristocratic absentee-landlords; they are farmers, working the land. The most successful agent within the economic framework is Weymouth, the authentic possessor of the mysterious money; he is the quintessential capitalist. In accordance with the new models of acquiring wealth, Weymouth earns capital through labor and commerce: "'I earned my bread by daily labour.... I saved ... a few hundred dollars ... turned it into a bulky commodity and loaded a small vessel, and went with it to Barcelona.... I was not unsuccessful in my projects,'" achieving wealth "'sufficient to the supply of all my wants.'" The old ways are reserved for the old country; Weymouth continues: "I then resolved to return to my native country, and, lay ... out my money in land" (136–137). Admittedly, his luck turns, as he loses his ship and cargo at sea; Brown thus reminds us of the Gothic distrust in the stability of material possessions. Yet, all is not lost, as Weymouth still possesses his capital, the mysterious $7500. Other men in the novel are less economically successful, but nevertheless persevere in pursuing a vocation. In speaking of Waldegrave, Weymouth tells Edgar, "'His religious duty compelled him to seek his livelihood by teaching a school of blacks'" (135–136), thus illustrating Ben Franklin's conflation of religious and professional calling. Even Clithero, the murderous madman, upon fleeing Ireland feels unworthy of being the beneficiary of Mrs. Lorimer, and earns his own way by becoming a "'servant'" (14) in America. At the peak of his madness, as the narrative ends, he manages to acquire "'food and clothing ... by labouring on a neighboring farm'" (276). Sarsefield, an ambiguous model of success in the novel, perhaps most closely illustrates Brown's economic ideal. Far from being a self-made man, Sarsefield is in a position to be benefactor to Edgar because he is the beneficiary of Mrs. Lorimer. When he was young, he was denied permission to marry Mrs. Lorimer by her family because "his birth was mean and he was without fortune" (56). But the two lovers are reunited after Sarsefield spends twenty years in the east, during which time Mrs. Lorimer, through age, inheritance and widowhood (also old world methods), has become "disengaged and independent" (58). The two then establish "a confidential intercourse" (58), leading to a marriage based on love, that also yields the old world reward to Sarsefield: "The bounty of Mrs. Lorimer soon divested her friend of all fear of poverty" (58). Yet for twenty years, Sarsefield forged his own way in the world, intermittently practicing his profession "that of a surgeon" (56); he takes a job in "the East-India company" (56) thus partaking of the colonial enterprise. During his adventures in the east, his profession affords him only "a precarious subsistence" (57) although during one adventure he saves his own life through "a seasonable display of his chirurgical skill" (58). Thus Sarsefield differs from Edgar in a number of key ways, even though Sarsefield achieves the goal to which Edgar can only aspire: coming into a windfall. Unlike Edgar, Sarsefield has a vocation; he is a surgeon. Also unlike Edgar, Sarsefield attempts to make his own way by joining the East-India company—admittedly with Mrs. Lorimer's assistance. Thus Sarsefield reveals activity, a willingness to pursue his vocation and his economic success, whereas Edgar only acts in pursuit of a passive sinecure. We can see that in rewarding Sarsefield with the economic happy ending of which he deprives Edgar, Brown suggests that active pursuit is what it takes to become a successful American. The languid ways of the lazy aristocrat are proper only in Europe.

Indeed, Brown stresses the inactivity of the life that Edgar desires. In meditating on American commerce, Edgar writes, "Our countrymen are prone to enterprize, and are scattered over every sea and every land in pursuit of that wealth which ... when gained, by no means compensates them for the hardships and vicissitudes endured in the pursuit" (147). His dismissal of the pursuits of his fellow Americans rationalizes his own failure to endure "hardships and vicissitudes." His attitude implies an aristocratic laziness that he can ill afford. When Edgar writes to Mary, his impoverished fiancée, he tells her: "Thy love of independence and ease, and impatience with drudgery are woven into your constitution" (149). The reader wonders if, perhaps, this description might not apply all too readily to Edgar himself. In fact, never once does Edgar consider the possibility of acquiring money the American way, by working for it, by pursuing a vocation. The only other men in the novel who do not earn a living or pursue a vocation within the dominant economic system are the marginalized, spectral Native Americans. Edgar's economic situation is yet another instance in which he is doubled by the Native Americans. In the scene where he quite savagely eats the panther he has just killed, he echoes the Native American way of life, eating off the land instead of farming or engaging in commerce. In fact, Edgar is, like the Native Americans, exiled from his land and from the narrative of history. Like them, he is homeless and without a livelihood, since the murder of his parents and the pillaging of the house and grounds. Like the Native Americans, Edgar becomes an outsider, not fitting into the economic and social norms of his own community: "Our scheme was, for the most part a patriarchal one. Each farmer was surrounded by his sons and kinsmen" (14), reflecting the "family-based agriculture" (454) observed by Charles Post. In the system which is currently coming to an end, all the other farmers, including his uncle, have sons and heirs to take over the farms; all the other young men have fathers to bequeath their land. Only Edgar, the American of the future, is left masterless, without father or farm as a legacy. In this Edgar emblematizes the new young American, cut off from support, and on his own. Edgar's failure to find a vocation illustrates the daunting challenges faced by these masterless young men.

* * *

In addition to focusing on the difficulties of pursuing material possession in America, Brown picks up another English Gothic theme: the slipperiness of intellectual property, also subject to appropriation. Clithero, the mysterious and mad Irish servant, possesses an intricate sealed box, which contains what Clithero calls "'a treasure.... Inclosed in a box at Inglefield's, were the memoirs of Euphemia Lorimer'" (262), who was his protector in Ireland. Edgar Huntly also possesses a box of dangerous writing, the letters from Waldegrave that express his religious skepticism—"pollution and depravity" (127)—from which Edgar wishes to protect Mary. Waldegrave himself wished to acquire his own letters: "to gain possession, to destroy, or secret them was the strongest of his wishes" (131). Both sets of papers go missing in mysterious ways and end up in the possession of others. At the end of the novel, we learn that each owner, Clithero and Edgar, hid his own manuscript while sleepwalking. Experiencing personal dispossession through sleep, each dispossesses himself of the writing that had been his. The theme of narrative dispossession is further achieved on the meta-narrative level by Brown's adoption of the standard strategy of Gothic narrative: the use of multiple narrators. This strategy disputes intellectual possession, in that it dispossesses the authority of the reader (and sometimes the writer and characters) to fully apprehend the narrative. *Edgar Huntly* unfolds through a series of narratives. The first, the central narrative, comprises a letter that Edgar writes to Mary. Embedded within Edgars letter are the narratives of others that Edgar retells to Mary: the stories of Clithero, Sarsefield, Weymouth and Inglesfield—thus exhibiting Edgar's narrative control, for the moment. The conflicting narratives of Sarsefield and Clithero illustrate the Gothic interrogation of the Enlightenment reliance on certainty and knowledge, on the ability of the (usually rational) male mind to possess reality. Both Sarsefield and Clithero acknowledge Clithero's madness; yet their interpretations of this fact differ. Clithero, who receives empathy and forgiveness from Edgar, presents a plausible account of his actions. His explanation for making an attempt on the life of Mrs. Lorimer is that he wanted to spare her the miserable death he was certain she would experience on hearing of the death of her beloved brother. He addresses the sleeping Mrs. Lorimer: "'Yes. It is my power to screen thee from the coming storm: to accelerate thy journey to rest'" (78). Using the language of demonic possession to describe his madness, Clithero dissociates himself from his action: "'It was the daemon that possessed me'" (79). Brown thus invokes the common Gothic trope of madness, highlighting that, despite Enlightenment ideals, the human subject is not fully in control of mind or actions. In fact, in a rebuke to Enlightenment valorization of the power of thinking, Clithero presents a modern, non-supernatural analog to demonic possession—the obsessiveness that is a consequence of overthinking: "'Now my liberty, in this respect, was at an end. I was fettered, confounded, smitten with excess of thought'" (70). The end point of all this seemingly reasonable thinking is the irrational plan to kill Mrs. Lorimer. Sarsefield's narrative reveals a divergence of opinion; he holds Clithero morally culpable for his actions. Unlike Edgar, Saresfield feels no sympathy; he is furious with Clithero, calling him a "madman" and liar (253), "an agent from Hell" (266). Sarsefield questions the logic of Clithero's actions: "'Kill the brother whose existence was interwoven with that of his benefactress and his friend? Then hasten to her chamber and attempt her life?'" (266). In fact, the failure of Edgar to achieve his final goal that is within sight toward the end of the novel—to be the protégé of Sarsefield—is the result of his inability to determine that Sarsefield's perspective is accurate and that Clithero is, indeed, an immoral homicidal maniac, a threat to Mrs. Lorimer and her pregnancy. Edgar is undone by the presence of multiple narratives in his story and in his life. Nor does Edgar, as protagonist, manage to sustain the narrative integrity of the novel. His letter to Mary, which composes the bulk of the narrative, ends before the novel does. It is succeeded by a series of numbered letters. Letter one is from Edgar to Sarsefield, warning that Clithero is on his way to New York to see Mrs. Lorimer. Letter two is a follow up letter in which Edgar recounts to Sarsefield his final encounter with Clithero that has convinced Edgar that Sarsefield is correct in judging Clithero to be "a maniac"; Clithero tells Edgar that he must kill Mrs. Lorimer to fulfill "my evil destiny" (280). The book ends with letter number three, in which Edgar cedes narrative control to Sarsefield. Previously all the other narratives have been embedded within Edgar's letters; Edgar has exerted narrative control in revealing the narratives to us, the reader. Sarsefield takes possession of the narrative in composing letter number three, addressed to Edgar. Sarsefield berates Edgar for his "rashness" (284) in sending the previous two letters. After receiving letter one, Sarsefield left his home to try to waylay Clithero. In his absence his wife (Mrs. Lorimer) opened letter two from Edgar. The information in it about the imminent advent of the mad Clithero caused her to deliver her baby in "an untimely birth," and the death of the child "has blasted my fondest hope" (284). Saresfield concludes by telling Edgar that Clithero is dead, a suicide by drowning, and ends with the hope that "this be the last arrow in the quiver of adversity" (285). Sarsefield then ends with one word to and for his erstwhile protégé, "Farewell" (285). The abruptness of that word spells Edgar's doom—it holds no hope for future reconciliation, ending his last hope for a sinecure. Nor does Edgar attempt to encompass Sarsefield's words within his own. Edgar's silence strongly suggests that he is completely undone; dispossessed of narrative power and of hope for his own future, he is reduced to silent nothingness. Ironically, the young man loses his last hope of attaining a master by acting against the older man's advice; for once in his life, he rebels against authority, and makes his own decision, with dire consequences. Or, Brown suggests, he has lost all by depending on the advisor in the first place, instead of forging his own way.

* * *

Ironically Edgar does succeed in the conventional Gothic quest—the journey of the (young) innocent to encounter and to know evil. He discovers that the murderer of Waldegrave was one of the Native Americans with whom he, Edgar, had been contending. He writes to Mary: "It was the fate of thy unhappy brother to encounter this ruffian" (271). Moreover, Edgar manages to defeat this emblem of evil, having killed a number of Native Americans during the course of the novel he speculates that "the assassin has himself been killed and probably by my own hand" (271). Edgar also finally encounters and recognizes the evil in Clithero as he writes to Sarsefield in letter two:

"Clithero is a maniac. The truth cannot be concealed" (280). Yet he fails in his economic quest to consolidate an income for himself and his future wife. Indeed, the darkest, most Gothic aspect of the novel is Edgar's complete failure and effacement at the end of the narrative, and the message that is enforced by the conclusion: the possession of property, in America as well as in England, is unstable and unreliable. The new American story, the story of a young masterless American man searching for possessions, and for the vocation that will lead him to become a possessor, is set against the backdrop of the dispossession of the land by the Native Americans and the English. The new land is inhabited by the ghosts of the dispossessed, including the young who fail to find a vocation in a land in which the paths are not yet clearly defined.

The Anxiety of Masterlessness in Wieland

Brown also considers the dangers and anxieties of masterlessness in *Wieland* (1798), another novel of madness and murder. As Norman Grabo notes in his introduction to *Huntly*, "popular fiction in the eighteenth century, dwelling obsessively as it does on the mutual obligations between parents and children" was as much about the developing political independence of "the infant colonies" (xvi), as it was about actual family relationships. In *Wieland* (1798) Brown addresses American anxieties of revolution, framed as anxieties about patriarchal authority and its absence. The novel is set outside Philadelphia, and Brown takes care to inform us that "these events took place between the conclusion of the French [French and Indian War, ending 1763], and the beginning of the [American] revolutionary war" (Preface 4). As Charles Post reminds us, this was a time and place when property ownership was disrupted: "The landowners' inability to enforce legal title to land was evident in the countryside surrounding Philadelphia" (Post 471). Because squatting was widespread, "in 1765, the Penn family and their allies ceased all attempts to enforce their legal title to lands in the hinterlands of Philadelphia" (Post 474). Daniel E. Williams notes that Brown is also careful to remind his readers of the social context of his novel. In fact, there were a number of actual cases of fathers murdering families in the years before *Wieland* was written.[1] Williams notes that these crimes challenged "the optimistic republican faith in the individual's capacity for self-government" ("Writing under the Influence" 646), leaving the "citizens of the new nation ... to sort out the meaning—and limits—of liberty" (666), including the problem of the absent ruler. Williams amplifies the significance of the voice of Carwin, a trickster ventriloquist, in influencing the actions of Wieland, the title character, a patriarch manqué who has lost his own father. In a republic where authority was awarded to "those who can persuade the most voters, the power of the human voice to manipulate perception becomes the primary means of securing authority. The force of words, rather than the privilege of high birth, frames the power-structure of the new nation" (666). Hence the dangers of democracy—in which the principle of equality undermines the power of authority—and the vulnerability of a country where leaders are chosen by an electorate, instead of by appointment or divine right.

Wieland begins during a time of turmoil, the end of the French and Indian War, which is only experienced at a distance by the main characters. In fact, the distance creates the kind of safe thrill that Burke describes in his work on the Sublime: "The sound of war had been heard, but it was at ... a distance.... The Indians were repulsed on the one side and Canada was conquered on the other. Revolutions and battles, however calamitous to those who occupied the scene, contributed in some sort to our happiness, by agitating our minds with curiosity, and furnishing causes of patriotic exultation" (24). The odd separate peace of the four young friends reflects their personal status. All their parents are dead, leaving the young generation to rule themselves at will. The young brother and sister, Wieland and his sister Clara, live happily—parentless, masterless—without any adult leadership or authority. Their friends, the Pleyels, are also orphans. Despite the pleasures of freedom from parental control, Brown suggests that the absence of parental guidance makes the four young people vulnerable to the disembodied voices that they begin to hear. Ultimately, the absence of the absolute law of the father results in a freedom that is fatal to the children.

The violent displacement of the family patriarch, years before the action of the novel, had indeed been catastrophic. The elder Wieland had died in a mysterious way; all the reader and the witnesses know of his death is that it was precipitated by some force involving "a blazing light," "a cloud impregnated with light," and "a very bright spark" (16–17). The cause and the motive for the father's death are never clarified in this consistently ambiguous novel. W.M. Verhoeven speculates that the elder "Wieland is convinced he is going to meet with a 'strange and terrible' fate 'in consequence of deviation from his duty,'—to convert the natives on the shores of the Ohio" ("Gothic Logic: Charles Brockden Brown and the Science of Sensationalism" 97). Indeed, Brown does place a clue leading toward this interpretation. As a young man, the father "had imbibed an opinion that it was his duty to disseminate the truths of the gospel among the unbelieving nations.... The North American Indians naturally presented themselves as the first objects for this species of benevolence" (*Wieland* 9). On coming to America "a nearer survey of savage manners ... shook his resolution" (10), and he is side-tracked by establishing a family and farm. Eventually, "his ancient belief relative to the conversion of the savage tribes, was revived with uncommon energy" (10) but to no avail: "The license of savage passion and the artifices of his depraved countrymen, all opposed themselves to his progress" (10). When there "appeared no reasonable ground to hope for success" (10), the elder Wieland gives up the pursuit, turning instead to developing his own personal religion and building a "temple of his Deity" (11).

But a compelling case can be made for an alternate interpretation of the father's crisis, by recalling additional information about the events leading to the father's death. The father, who has created his own form of religious expression, spends much time in his temple until he reaches a crisis. Clara, the Wieland daughter who narrates the tale, describes this episode in an elliptic way that is typical of her narration: "A command had been laid upon him, which he had delayed to perform.... The duty assigned to him was transferred in consequence of his disobedience, to another, and all that remained was to endure the penalty.... He was likewise haunted by the belief that the kind of death that awaited him was strange and terrible" (12). This is all we learn from Clara's opaque narrative. But there is a key to this riddle that may be found in Clara's recounting of her family history. She tells of "an ancestor [who] may be considered as the founder of the German Theater. The modern poet of the same name is sprung from the same family" (6). The "modern poet" to whom Clara alludes is "Christoph Martin Wieland ... an important German poet.... Wieland's *The Trial of Abraham*, a treatment of the story of Abraham and Isaac, was published widely in America in the 1760's and 1770's" (*Wieland* 190 Note 6). Clara's indirect allusion to this poem opens up an explanation for the death of her father and the subsequent central event of the novel: the younger Wieland's murder of his own wife and children. The allusion to the poem invites the reader to infer that "the duty assigned to him [the father]" was the same that was committed to the patriarch Abraham in the biblical story: the commandment to kill his own son to prove fealty to his God. Unlike Abraham, who intends to obey God's command, the elder Wieland rebels against the order: "he had delayed to perform it" (12). As Clara tells us, "in consequence of his disobedience, [the duty is assigned] to another." And this statement prefigures the course of events that transpires in *Wieland*. The younger Wieland, son of the rebellious father, does obey the original command that has been transferred to him. He obeys the voice of supernatural authority (or madness—the text equivocates) and slaughters his entire family.

The popularity of Wieland's poem of near-filial sacrifice in pre–Revolutionary America reveals contradictions within the psyche of a country that was contemplating overthrowing its patriarch, the monarch. The figure of the biblical Abraham is complex and subject to a number of interpretations. From one perspective, the patriarch, who is willing to sacrifice his son to his own ideology, may be read as an emblem for the conventional frightening dark and dangerous patriarch, his presence a justification for the parricide of revolution. But Abraham may also be read as the emblem of the Enlightenment revolutionary; the Bible first depicts him as an iconoclast, a young man who abandons his father's homeland and gods, to create his own system in his own new land. The biblical Abraham follows a disembodied voice that he alone hears, which he assumes is the voice of an external God. The consequences of his obedience to his own ideals, conveyed to him through the disembodied voice, are dire. Abraham almost kills his son, and certainly marks him for life; the Isaac of the bible never appears to move beyond the trauma of his youthful experience, never becomes the hero his father was. Either reading of the biblical story results in anxiety and despair. The voice of Abraham's new God betrays him and tempts him to death and destruction, as does the voice of the elder Wieland's new God. The story of Abraham and the story of Wieland, then, express the question of the Enlightenment revolutionary: if the individual listens to the voices he hears in his own head, will the result be rational orderly transformation, or anarchic and violent destruction? Without the stabilizing authority of the patriarch, can the individual be trusted to correctly interpret the voices he hears? In *Apparition in the Glass*, Bill Christopherson argues that these questions were amplified by the violent and horrifying events of the French Revolution that occurred between the time of the action of the novel, and the time of the writing of *Wieland*. The events in France recast revolution in an unfavorable light and generated concerns that the rational trust in the goodness and lucidity of the human mind, used as justification for revolution, was unfounded. The main action of *Wieland*, then, is set within a pattern of multiple revolutions—multiple displacements of authority—resulting in the chaotic consequences of unguided masterlessness.

Brown suggests that without the absolute steadying authority of the father, the king, the children will be led astray by disembodied voices that may be untrustworthy. There are numerous disembodied and dispossessed voices in the novel, including the voices of various narratives; these destabilized voices require interpretation, and without the single law of the father, there is a danger that they will be misinterpreted. Carwin—the dark biloquist with quasi-supernatural powers, the foreigner from Europe whom Emory

Elliott, drawing on Toni Morrison's writing, identifies with "the racial Other" (*Wieland* Introduction xxvii)—is the original source of vocal possession and dispossession. He ventriloquistically appropriates the voice of Catherine, the wife of Wieland and the sister of Henry Pleyel, confusing and troubling her brother and husband. Carwin tricks Clara Wieland, the narrator, into believing that she hears the voices of two thieves in her closet. Carwin then appropriates Clara's voice so that Henry thinks she is flirting inappropriately. Carwin's biloquism—his ability to speak with two distinct voices—aligns with the Gothic trope of the double. In stealing the voices of Catherine and Clara, Carwin becomes their vocal double; he steals their identity and their agency.

But Carwin's biloquistic power does not explain all the disembodied voices in the novel. Carwin convincingly disclaims responsibility for the voice that commands Wieland to kill his family; indeed, we witness, through Clara's narrative, a debate that Wieland holds with a silent interlocutor that only he hears—clearly Carwin is not part of this dialogue. As Clara describes, "After a silence and a conflict which I could not interpret, he lifted his eyes to heaven, and in broken accents exclaimed, 'This is too much! Any victim but this, and thy will be done'" (141). In his confession to his crime, Wieland insists that he heard the voice of God, "'my deed was enjoined by heaven; that obedience was the test of perfect virtue'" (161). These words connect Wieland's monstrous act to the earlier crisis of his father. Seemingly both Wielands, father and son, hear the voice of their God, or their madness (linking them to the American revolutionaries who followed the internal voices of their consciences). The older Wieland defies the divine command, and thus sacrifices himself. The younger Wieland, masterless, obeys the voice he hears and massacres his family.

The cacophony of voices in Brown's novel also results in the loss of Clara's sense of self-possession. If her brother could be swayed by the voice of madness, why not she: "What was my security against influences equally terrific and equally irresistible?" (165). Brown suggests that in fact Clara can have no assurance, that without the anchor of absolute, paternally sanctioned truth, the masterless individual is capable of confusing madness for inspiration—a frightening thought to a nation that has recently enacted violence and parricide in order to follow its vision.

Charles Brockden Brown and Washington Irving: A Search for Vocation

Brown's tragically Gothic *Edgar Huntly* and *Wieland* are countered by a number of comic—though nonetheless Gothic—"sketches" that appear in

Washington Irving's *The Sketch-Book of Geoffrey Crayon, Gent.* (1819–20) including "The Legend of Sleepy Hollow." Irving's story also features a fatherless, patronless young man, who, like Huntly is in search of an old-world sinecure. Irving, like Brown, found personal relevance in this topic. Irving also had to persevere to discover that he could make a living at the vocation that truly called him, the life of letters. In 1815, on a visit to a brother in England, Irving discovered that his family's business was in trouble. Out of a sense of loyalty, he remained with the failing business and ultimately found himself "adrift in England … lacking either literary or business prospects, and implicated in the shame of commercial failure" (Manning Introduction ix). Ultimately though, Irving, like Ben Franklin, did manage to save himself by following the American method of self-determination: "Resisting his family's attempts to secure him employment by patronage, and determined to support himself he [Irving] set off on a tour around Great Britain and began making notes for a new literary work" (Hedges Introduction ix), *The Sketch Book*, which became a success. Thus, we can see that Irving, like Brown and Franklin disdained the traditional path for a young man, going into the family business and depending upon established social and economic connections. Instead, each of these young American men carved out his own economic and intellectual path as a writer.

In fact, Irving was one of the first professional writers in America; he was "able to earn a decent living by literary labor alone" (Hedges viii). Manning emphasizes that in pursuing his vocation, Irving took a "risk" (ix), since at that time British writers and readers scorned American writers. Hedges amplifies: "British contempt for American literature had reached a climax in January, 1820, only two months before the first volume of *The Sketch Book* appeared in England, when the celebrated clergyman, reformer, and wit, Sydney Smith asked.… 'In the four quarters of the globe, who reads an American book?'" (viii). Irving bravely responds to this dismissal in his sketch, "English Writers on America." Irving also had to ward off American resistance and skepticism in the form of Puritan prejudices "against the seeming frivolity of certain kinds of writing, fiction and drama especially" (Hedges ix). Added to the obstacles placed before the American writer was the notion that writers did not typify the brawny, active male who, to some, epitomized American identity. There was a tendency to conflate writing with the passive idleness that Irving (like Brown in *Huntly*) disdained himself. Irving thus works to represent writing as a legitimate and challenging vocation. In "English Writers" he writes of the young American writers "labouring" at their task (Irving *Legend of Sleepy Hollow* Penguin 46). Irving's work did pay off; while Brown is considered the inventor of the American novel and the American Gothic,

"Irving is generally credited with inventing the short story as a distinct genre" (Hedge viii). In "Irving, Ruin, and Risk," Andrew Kopec points out that the risk Irving took was financial as well as artistic, noting that Irving "spoke of his project as if it were a financial speculation" (717), and traces the sense of economic anxiety that underlies the *Sketches* to Irving's uncertain financial situation. This anxiety was exacerbated by the transitional state of the American economy during Irving's time (as in Brown's); in the late 1810s Kopec identifies "the erosion of a mercantilist economy and the subsequent rise of a paper money one" (710). In this "brave new economic order," Kopec adds, "identity was not static, but fluid, not given but achieved" (710), resulting in the pressure on Irving and his characters, like Brown and his characters to achieve an economic identity in uncertain times, what Kopec calls "the identity imperative governing subject formation for enfranchised men in early America" (716).

Two Hungry Writers, Two Voracious Young Men

Brown and Irving, who both lived during transitional economic moments, both re-enact in their work their own struggles, as young men in search of vocation. The hunger that drove the authors to succeed is re-imagined as a voraciousness that focuses on consumption without the accompanying production displayed by the authors. Both Edgar Huntly and Ichabod Crane display an inhuman, unnatural, and frightening appetite, echoing the blood-thirst of Mary Rowlandson, and anticipating the hunger of Ned in *Seven Gables*, and other Americans to follow. Edgar's "ferocious" (156) hunger develops when he finds himself trapped in the cave and is driven to kill the panther and consume the "yet warm blood and reeking fibres of [the] brute" (160). Edgar displays the engulfing hunger that drives him to attempt to parasitically consume anyone who might serve to his benefit. He also resists the kind of planning and labor required for farming and industry, European methods of sating hunger. Thus Huntly again shows himself to be the double of the "savage" Native American who lived off the land. Similarly, Ichabod Crane displays an appetite that is disturbingly inhuman. Irving tells the reader that "one might have mistaken him for the genius of famine" (274) because of his "lanky" and "spindly" build. He was "a huge feeder, and though lank had the dilating powers of an Anaconda" (275), that is, a serpent that can consume prey far larger than itself. Additionally Ichabod displays a cold-blooded tendency to translate most of what he experiences into a form of food for his consumption. We learn about his great "appetite for the marvelous, and his powers of digesting it.... No tale was too gross or monstrous for his capacious swallow" (277). On an autumn ride in the country, his eye is "ever open to every symptom of culinary abundance" (285). The apples on the trees, and the pumpkins in the fields remind him of the "ample prospects of the most luxurious of pies" (286), as the Indian corn and buckwheat fields make him think of "slap jacks, well buttered" (286). The narrator tells us that Ichabod is "feeding his mind with many sweet thoughts and 'sugared suppositions'" (286) about his future. When he visits the homestead of Katrina Van Tassel, the lovely heiress who represents his chance of attaining the aristocratic life of ease, through marriage, he reduces everything he sees to food. As he scrutinizes the animals trooping around the farm: "The pedagogue's mouth watered, as he looked upon this sumptuous promise of luxurious winter fare. In his devouring mind's eye ... the pigeons were snugly put to bed in a comfortable pie ... the geese were swimming in their own gravy ... in the porkers he saw carved out the future sleek side of bacon ... and even bright chanticleer himself lay sprawling on his back, in a side dish, with lifted claws, as if craving that quarter, which his chivalrous spirit disdained to ask while living" (279). This passage exemplifies Irving's masterfully comic version of the Gothic—quite amusing, but upon closer inspection, quite horrifying. Ichabod Crane wields a gaze that is death-dealing. Under his eye, every living creature becomes a corpse upon a plate. Indeed, from Ichabod's perspective, Katrina herself is just another "tempting morsel" (278)—leading seasoned readers of the Gothic to fear for her happiness (and even safety) as his wife. In the eyes of her would-be suitor, Katrina is "plump as a partridge; ripe and melting and rosy-cheeked as one of her father's peaches" (278). Ichabod is thus, like Edgar, pure appetite. He desires to possess and to consume, to reduce all around him to objects of consumption. Irving's iteration of his comic figure makes it clear just how close he comes to the conventional Gothic villain, the aristocratic patriarch, who also exists to possess and consume, destroying the lives of those around him, without actually producing anything. This iteration of the young American male, set within this context is troubling indeed. New America has disposed of the patriarch, the king, the aristocrat, and well-meaning guiding parents, left behind in England when the young migrated. Yet America has not gotten rid of the human hunger to possess that drives the Gothic in America, as it did in England.

* * *

It is not entirely necessary to know that Irving created his hungry hero in homage to Brown's; certainly the type is not uncommon in American literature, or sadly, in American history. Yet a telling detail does seem to link the two texts: the great old elm tree in *Huntly*, and in "Sleepy Hollow." (This image also recurs in later texts including *House of the Seven Gables*.) The vivid image of the tree seems to exist for the sole purpose of linking the two texts. In *Edgar Huntly* the elm plays a central role. Huntly carefully describes the unique properties of the "fatal Elm" where Waldegrave was mysteriously murdered: "The remarkable bulk and shape of its trunk, its position in the midst of the way, its branches spreading into an ample circumference, made it conspicuous from afar" (9). The sleepwalking Clithero returns to the elm to bury and dig up his mysterious boxes. Sydney J. Krausse provides an intriguing explanation for the elm in *Huntly*. He argues that for Brown's contemporary readers, the elm would have evoked "the long honored symbolism of the legendary 'Treaty Elm' under which, tradition has it, William Penn ... negotiated a treaty of friendship ... with the Lenni Lenape" in 1682. Krausse adds: "these were the same Delawares whose dispossessed descendants" haunt *Edgar Huntly* (464). The treaty was beginning to come apart by 1701 when Penn left America, and was further weakened by the underhanded dealings of William Penn's sons with the Native Americans. Krausse suggests that the occurrences of burying, digging up, violence, and loss of consciousness at the base of the tree in *Huntly* signify the psychological repression and guilt associated with the treatment of the Native Americans. "The Legend of Sleepy Hollow" also features a powerful elm, found in the "strong hold" (279) of Old Baltus Van Tassel, the father of the desirable Katrina. Irving's narrator describes the tree: "A great elm tree spread its broad branches over it [the strong hold], at the foot of which bubbled up a spring of the softest and sweetest water" (279). There is a second giant tree in "Legend," that also invokes the tree in *Edgar*, "Major André's tree": a tulip tree which, like the elm in *Huntly*, stands oddly "in the centre of the road." It is a ghostly tree, "which towered like a giant above all the other trees ... and formed a kind of land mark. Its limbs were gnarled, and fantastic, large enough to form trunks for ordinary trees" (291). The tulip tree, like Huntly's elm, is linked to a death, that of "its ill-starred namesake" (291).

* * *

The protagonist of Irving's story, Ichabod Crane, is certainly of Edgar Huntly's camp when it comes to his desire for an easy situation. When we meet him, Ichabod is a school teacher, but far from devoted to that vocation. In describing him as "a conscientious man" (275), the narrator addresses Ichabod's assiduous application "of the birch" in chastisement, rather than the care he employs to educate his charges. His role of "singing master" attracts more of Ichabod's attention, but although he may feel a calling, he lacks the ability that is an essential part of a true vocation. In fact, the narrator suggests, his voice is so bad that "quavers ... from the nose of Ichabod Crane ... may even be heard half a mile off ... of a still Sunday morning" (276). In his economic life Ichabod also displays a lack of focus; like Rip Van Winkle he prefers to play a supporting role, helping others at their work, while failing to attend to any vocation of his own: "He assisted the farmers occasionally in the lighter labours of their farms" (276). He even puts aside his manly pride in order to assist with the small children in their farm homes: "He would sit with a child on one knee, and rock a cradle with his foot, for whole hours together" (276). The narrator, perhaps ironically, considers all Ichabod's activities as "vocations" (276). Yet, while they keep him busy, and help him to curry favor with the more established members of the community, they reveal a lack of initiative; he is content to contribute to the economic growth of others, without forging his own path, or his own identity.

Ichabod's only notion of contributing to his own growth is reminiscent of Edgar Huntly's. Like Edgar, Ichabod plans to avoid the risk and labor attendant on a true vocation. Instead, also like Edgar, Ichabod hopes to revert to the aristocratic model of the old country: to acquire wealth through marriage to an heiress. He means to marry Katrina Van Tassel, and to partake of her bounty: "his heart yearned after the damsel, who was to inherit these domains" (280). Fittingly, the narrator's description of the Van Tassel farm is closely aligned with the description of the old world landscape in Irving's "Rural Life in England," as opposed to Irving's other descriptions of the wild American landscape. On the Van Tassel farm, all is regulated and ordered. In England: "The manner in which property has been distributed into small estates and farms has established a regular gradation from the nobleman through the classes of gentry ... down to the laboring peasantry" ("Rural Life" 52–53), as opposed to the American farms of Brown's *Huntly*, where each landowner struggles for a tenuous foothold in the disordered and wild land, susceptible at any moment to dispossession through Native American raids.

Unfortunately for Ichabod, the intellectual, cultured, quasi-European male, with European aspirations of marrying property, he must face a manly and active all-American rival in the form of Brom Bones. Ichabod's ultimately unrequited pursuit of Katrina rouses the ire of the competing suitor: "A deadly feud gradually arose between him and the preceptor of Sleepy Hollow" (283). Under cover of the supernatural "Headless Horseman," Brom unseats Ichabod from his "steed" and his quest. Having rid Sleepy Hollow of its un–American intellectual and superstitious male, the brawny Brom gets the girl and the property.

Ichabod as New American Dynast

Yet Washington Irving comically modifies the figure of the lost and hapless young American man, defeated by his failure to adapt to the meritocracy of the new country. Even early details of Ichabod's character reveal traits that, for better or worse, mark him as more suited than Edgar Huntly to carve his own way. In his classroom and in his courtship, Ichabod's characterization suggests that he, unlike Edgar, has the potential to grow into the role of adult male as tyrannical patriarch. In his classroom Ichabod is very much the tyrannical figure who haunts the European Gothic text. He sits, "enthroned on the lofty stool.... In his hand he swayed a ferule, that scepter of despotic power." On his desk sit "sundry contraband articles ... such as half munched apples, popguns..." (284), the cherished possessions tyrannically appropriated from his subjects. Irving prepares the reader for Ichabod's aristocratic bent earlier in the story, when we are told of the "dominant dignity and absolute sway, with which he lorded it in his little empire, the school" (276). Indeed, within this context, Ichabod's tendency to see everything as food to sate his voracious appetite, also aligns him with the Gothic villain of the English text, the aristocratic who seeks to possess all that he sees. Whereas Edgar consumes the wild panther, unowned by anyone else, Ichabod seeks to consume the domestic animals on Van Tassel's farm, as well as Van Tassel's daughter. Ichabod's plan for the Van Tassel farm also betrays his incipient capacity as dynast and tyrant. He desires the farm and its accouterments not for its material pleasures, but to advance his territorial, and quintessentially American dream: "His imagination expanded with the idea, how they might be readily turned into cash, and the money invested in immense tracts of wild land and shingle palaces in the wilderness" (280). Ichabod imagines himself an American patriarch with Katrina and a pack of children "mounted on the top of a wagon ... setting out for Kentucky, Tennessee, or Lord knows where" (280). Ichabod's dream reveals that, unlike the boyish, ambitionless Edgar, he has a plan that does involve labor and risk, and his plan takes him very close to becoming the possessing patriarch of the English Gothic, or the successful American male—two characters that, as the next chapter suggests, are not entirely dissimilar.

Brom Bones, Ichabod's rival, is also a potential American tyrant. Significantly, his name is a "Dutch abbreviation" of Abraham, the name of the first biblical patriarch (whom Brown also recalls in *Wieland*). He is a bully, "broad-shouldered," with a "Herculean frame and great powers of limb" and great "skill in horsemanship" (281). Yet Brom, who ends up possessing the woman and the property is, like Ichabod, a comic American transformation of the old type. The narrator tells us that "he has more mischief than ill will in his composition; and with all his overbearing roughness, there was a strong dash of waggish good humor at bottom" (281). He is the source of "many a madcap prank or rustic brawl" (282). When his courtship with Katrina is stymied by Ichabod, Brom responds with "boorish practical jokes" (283), rather than the dangerous and fatal strategies of the tyrant of the English Gothic text. Even when Brom appears in the guise of the frightening Headless Horseman, his weapon of choice is a pumpkin which only damages Ichabod's pride. Yet, W.M. Verhoeven connects Carwin, the source of murder and tragedy in *Wieland*, with 'the con artist" (98) and "the trickster" (99)—Brom's type. Verhoeven thus suggests that a trickster like Brom is capable of real harm. In "'Not in the Least American': Nineteenth-century Literary Regionalism," Judith Fetterly suggests the cultural significance of the triumph of Brom Bones. Fetterly writes: "Irving poses the question of who will be given possession of Sleepy Hollow, that imaginative space which inspires our stories, and who will be driven out. Irving identifies the masculine Brom Bones as the decisive victor, the effeminate Ichabod Crane as the figure to be driven out and the tall tale ... [as] the quintessential American story" (893–894). Irving thus banishes European stories of goblins and ghosts that Ichabod and the village women favor from the American canon, although the American Gothic continues to pervade American literature.

But Ichabod's success, or the rumors of it, provide a conclusion for the story. He disappears from Sleepy Hollow with whatever "money [he] possessed" (295). An old farmer returns from New York with a report that Ichabod "had kept school and studied law ... had been admitted to the bar, turned politician, electioneered, written for the newspapers, and finally had been made a Justice of the Ten Pound Court" (296). Irving leaves us with the plausible, though not certain, possibility that his protagonist has transcended the old European model of possession through marriage, and has become the new American version of the successful male: the self-made man, living by his wits, pursuing a true vocation. As Hedges suggests, Ichabod transforms from being an idle storyteller to a [laboring] writer (xviii), illustrating Irving's contention that despite Puritan distrust, the creation of fiction is an honorable profession. Ichabod's fate thus provides an "artful comment on authorship or storytelling in a rapidly expanding democratic and commercial society" (Hedges xix). Nevertheless, the catalyst for Ichabod's transformation is the supernatural, or at least his fear of it. Again, the Gothic hovers around the margins of this comical and realistic American story.

The Comic Gothic Return from the Dead

Perhaps the divergence of Edgar and Ichabod, and the literary modes of their authors, is most visible in the way in which each young man undergoes a conventional Gothic experience: the return from the dead. In Brown's novel, Edgar is presumed dead in the wilderness by the friends who have gone to rescue him. Having seen Edgar in a faint, Sarsefield believes that he was killed by the Indians. When Edgar does return from his wanderings, he is an object of fear. Sarsefield shrinks from him "as if I were an apparition" (232). Upon hearing Edgar's version of events, Sarsefield tells him: "You had risen from the dead" (246), and once more at the end of his recounting, Sarsefield tells Edgar, "You were dead ... you had risen" (251). Despite the Christological connection Sarsefield makes, Edgar's return is presented as an unwelcome revival. And the premature death denoted by his time in the wilderness seems a foreshadowing of his social and economic death at the end of the novel. Conversely, Ichabod's return from the dead reads like comedy. In the climax of the story Ichabod finds himself chased through the woods; confronting his pursuer Ichabod is "horror stuck on perceiving that he was headless! But his horror was still more increased on perceiving" (293) that the horseman is carrying his own head. As Ichabod is about to achieve the bridge that represents safety, the "goblin rider" hurls his head. The narrator provides this obscure concluding sentence: "It encounters his cranium with a tremendous crash—he is tumbled headlong into the dust ... the black steed, and the goblin rider, passed by like a whirlwind—" (294). The rest is silence. Until the next paragraph and "the next morning," when Ichabod's old horse returns to its "master's gate" (294). But there is no sign of Ichabod and the consensus is that "Ichabod had been carried off by the galloping Hessian" (295). Indeed, despite the report that Ichabod has become a lawyer, "the old country wives ... the best judges of these matters, maintain to this day, that Ichabod was spirited away by supernatural means; and it is a favorite story.... The schoolhouse ... was reported to be haunted by the ghost of the unfortunate pedagogue" (296). Thus we have a double comic ending. The practical, realistic version has Ichabod discovering his vocation and achieving success by the new American terms; in the supernatural version, Ichabod finds his place within one of his own beloved supernatural stories.

Irving's version of the comic Gothic appears in another of the sketches, "The Spectre Bridegroom," set in a European equivalent of Sleepy Hollow, "The Odenwald, a wild and romantic tract of upper Germany" (121). In this narrative, the promoter of supernatural tales is a benevolent patriarch, "who loved to tell long stories about the stark old warriors" (123), including a "history of the goblin horseman that carried away the fair Leonora; a dreadful but true story"

(128). This story seems to prefigure the courtship of his own daughter, the pretty heiress who is "a pattern of docility and correctness" (122). The reader and the characters are led to believe that the "tall gallant cavalier" (126) who comes to woo and win the heart of the daughter is her dead betrothed. The suitor chillingly announces to the Baron: "'the worms! The worms expect me! I am a dead man—I have been slain by robbers'" (129). Indeed, it seems that the girl is carried off by the specter bridegroom. She disappears from her room, the clatter of horse's hoofs is heard, and the narrator reminds us that "events of the kind are extremely common in Germany" (131). Yet as in "Sleepy Hollow," Irving substitutes the practical joke for the tragic supernatural conclusion. And here too, the readers, as much as the characters, are the objects of the joke. For the next morning, the horseman and his bride return, explaining away the supernatural: "though her husband was of a hostile house, yet thank heaven, he was not a goblin" (132). The disfavored lover had actually been inspired to spirit his bride away from hearing the Baron's story. Thus the Baron himself ironically becomes the source of the anti-patriarchal, anti-dynastic ending in which his daughter marries for love rather than dynasty. What promises to be a sad, dark, Gothic ending, ends as a revolutionary practical joke.

Irving, like Brown, does not completely disallow the old forms of coming into wealth. Irving's Brom Bones, and the "spectre bridegroom," like Brown's Sarsefield, all follow the old pattern: acquisition of wealth through marriage to an heiress. But the two writers deny this path to their two American protagonists. Instead, they force Edgar and Ichabod to confront the problem faced by their creators: how to forge a path in a country in which inheritance is not a ready path toward success. Both writers turn to the Gothic, with its tradition of examining anxiety-provoking material matters. Irving imagines a solution for his protagonist, thus creating a comic American Gothic of sorts, while Brown cannot. In doing this, Irving also seems to succeed in the ongoing project of the nineteenth century, to create a distinctly American literature. But Irving's comic Gothic does not engender a thriving American literary tradition. The gloomy Gothic favored by Ichabod himself, and by Brown, as well as his English precursors, takes root in America, setting the tone for much of American literature that follows.

"The Fall of the House of Usher": No Patriarch, No Future

The Gothic of Edgar AllRan Poe most certainly follows Brown's darker strain, as does his exploration of the masterless, fatherless young man. An exemplar of this situation is Roderick Usher, the orphaned last of the line in "The Fall of the House of Usher" (1839). Poe's story reveals yet another problem with displacing the dynasty and the patriarch. Without a patriarch and progeny, without the continuation of the line, there can be no future. We meet the family of Usher just as it is about to be extinguished.[2] The setting of the story follows the tradition of the English Gothic. The dark looming house is doubled by its mirror image in a "black and lurid tarn" (88)—into which the house finally collapses; the house itself is filled with "dark and intricate passages" (90); Roderick Usher's mind radiates darkness (92). The characters who are ultimately entombed in their patriarchal dwelling, Roderick and his sister Madeleine, the last of the Ushers, are part of some vague, depleted aristocracy, the victims of a hereditary disease, forshadowing Hawthorne's later American aristocrats, the Pyncheons.

Despite seeming to be a quasi-European dynasty, this "very ancient family" (89)—the consequence of the "undeviating transmission from sire to son, of the patrimony" (89)—lacks a patriarch, and is drained of the masculine, patriarchal, albeit malevolent, energy that drives so many dynasties, and so many Gothic tales of dynasty. The "last of the ancient race of the Ushers" (92) are a brother and sister still in "the maturity of youth" (95). Although Roderick is the "master" (92) by default, he is far from being a patriarch. Both siblings, twins, are sickly and enervated, clearly incapable of forging a future for the dynasty. Nor is there any other hope for the perpetuation of the Ushers. The family never produced an "enduring branch" (89), a strong and healthy offshoot of the main family line (like Hawthorne's Phoebe Pyncheon); in fact, the entire family "lay in the direct line of descent" (89). The only other character in the story, a childhood friend of Roderick Usher, and thus also young, does not mention any family or forbears. When we first encounter him, he is "alone" (88) on horseback. When we last see him, he is alone, the only survivor of the collapse of the house. These three young people exist in a vacuum with no family members to represent the past, and with no sense of a future.

The course of the story follows the family in its last gasps before it ceases to exist. As in the case of *Wieland*, the family collapses upon itself, imploding, like a black hole, without having any impact upon the world outside. Roderick inadvertently entombs his dying sister Madeleine when she is not quite completely dead. When she manages to return, dying, she falls "heavily inward upon the person of her brother" (98), who instantaneously dies. The house collapses into its reflection, also leaving no trace behind: "the deep and dank tarn at my feet closed dully and silently over the fragments of 'The House of Usher'" (98). As in the case of *Wieland*, the author invokes the old Gothic trope of the destroyed house, reflecting the depleted House (the dynastic family) to further emphasize the total destruction of the family and the collapse of the family line. Thus Poe, like Brown and Irving, interrogates the displacement of the patriarch and the patriarchy as a source of liberation and hope for the future, suggesting instead that in disposing of the old malign patriarch, the young risk destroying their own future. *Edgar Huntly* ends with the erasure of Edgar; there is no reason to suppose that he will recreate himself as an economic entity and manage to marry his fiancée, let alone have descendants. While *Sleepy Hollow* concludes with the economic success of Ichabod, we do not hear of any marriage and heirs in his life. Only Katrina and Brom Bones, who follow the patriarchal European path, marry and produce heirs who will inherit their property. Wieland, lacking the guidance of a father, mistakenly believes the voice of Carwin (or his own madness) to be divine, and obeys the command to kill his wife and children, and finally himself, thereby putting an end to the Wieland family line.[3] In typical Gothic fashion, the end of the family line is echoed by the destruction of the family home. Wieland's house burns down, as Huntly's has before the action of the novel. The Usher house collapses and entombs its inhabitants. These scenes pose the unsettling, and seemingly unsolvable, conundrum of American revolutionary politics. In a new country which has displaced its patriarchs and the patriarchy, how can masterless young men create lives and futures for themselves and their country? The narratives of the young men liberated from the old patriarchs reveal little hope for an enduring American model of the non-patriarchal family.

Fears of the Masterless Woman: Alcott's "Perilous Play"

By now, most readers know that Louisa May Alcott, the seemingly demure author of *Little Women*—the nineteenth-century novel that served as a guidebook for the proper young American girl—had her own dark anti-domestic side. Partially to make money, but perhaps also to explore her creative possibilities, Alcott wrote many Gothic potboilers that were published in ephemeral magazines, lost until their discovery by Madeleine Stern, who then published them in her collections. These stories, including "Perilous Play" (1869), explore the dark underside of American womanhood, imagining the dangers that await young women (and young men) who are newly independent of the supervision of their elders (and no longer challenged by the dangers of a raw new country or by the rigors of the Civil War).

The narrative focuses on a "young party" (686) of men and women, who seem to live in a world devoid of adult authority. Bored and aimless, they decide to eat "bonbons" containing "hashish" (687), given to them by a physician, Dr. Meredith, who, far from being an elderly man of science and authority, is notably "a young man" (686). Alcott easily slips into the Gothic fascination with altered states, and the distrust of the scientist who gains power through having knowledge of the hidden levels of human experience. Dr. Meredith medicalizes the hash by calling it "'your dose'" (688), and plays the role of the dark tempter: "'Six can do no harm, I give you my word. I take twenty before I can enjoy myself, and some people even more. I've tried many experiments, both on the sick and the well, and nothing ever happened amiss, though the demonstrations were immensely interesting,' said Meredith, eating his sugar-plums with a tranquil air, which was very convincing to others" (687). In addition to the conventional Gothic trope of the unleashed and dangerous scientist, Alcott brings in just a bit of racial anxiety to further unsettle her American readers. The physical description of the young woman who finds romance in the story hints at the possibilities of forbidden miscegenation. Rose, a beauty from the South, is racially ambiguous: her "clear olive cheeks contrasted well with darkest hair; lips like a pomegranate flower, and delicate, straight brows, as mobile as the lips," her hair in "loose black braids" (687). Rose's dark complexion is explained by the mention of her Spanish mother, but her parentage also suggests an intermingling: she is the child of a "Spanish mother" and an "English father." She wears an ornament of exotic design: "a golden bracelet of Arabian coins on the slender wrist" (687). Rose is also the inspiration of Dr. Meredith's dangerous plan, which comes to him when he observes that she is "reading the legend of 'The Lotus Eaters'" (686).

The young party thus finds itself in a psychic situation reflecting that of the masterless youth of nineteenth-century America. They encounter new and exotic (psychic) space, and explore unfamiliar and dangerous territory: "'Oh, yes; it's that Indian stuff which brings one fantastic visions, isn't it? I've always wanted to see and taste it, and now I will,' cried Belle, nibbling at one of the bean-shaped comfits with its green heart" (687). In addition to the wild territory of the mind, the misguided young people also explore the wilderness of the sea. The narrator observes that "a boat put off mysteriously from a point nearby, and sailed away like a phantom through the twilight" (689). Far more unnerving than the ghostly mystery of this scene, is the knowledge that the little boat is commanded by a solitary woman, Belle. Ironically, despite the certainty of Rose and Mark that "she was not fit to take care of herself!" (689)—affirming the nineteenth-century stance on all women, sober or not—Belle manages to return safely on her own. The party with a male member is the one that goes astray. Having gone out to rescue Belle, Rose and Mark find themselves quite literally lost at sea in a small boat. They are thus unmastered in a number of ways: free from authority they are unable to master the sea or themselves. Explaining his inability to maneuver the boat, Mark says: "'I am [a skilled boatman] when I am myself; now I am rapidly losing the control of my will'" (691). As self-possession and even identity are eroded by the power of the hashish, reason and propriety are overcome by sensuality and romance.

> How lovely it was! All the indescribable allurements of a perfect summer night surrounded them: balmy airs, enchanting moonlight, distant music, and, close at hand, the delicious atmosphere of love, which made itself felt in the eloquent silences that fell between them. Rose seemed to yield to the subtle charm, and leaned back on the cushioned seat with her beautiful head uncovered, her face full of dreamy softness, and her hands lying loosely clasped before her. She seldom spoke, showed no further anxiety for Belle, and soon seemed to forget the object of her search, so absorbed was she in some delicious thought which wrapped her in its peace.
>
> Mark sat opposite, flushed now, restless, and excited, for his eyes glittered; the hand on the rudder shook, and his voice sounded intense and passionate, even in the utterance of the simplest words. He talked continually and with unusual brilliancy [689–690].

At this point, the reader does not yet know that they have both taken hashish and we are led to believe that their sensations are the symptoms of romantic passion. Yet Dr. Meredith has already described similar symptoms caused by hashish use: "'Your pulse will rise, heart beat quickly, eyes darken and dilate, and an uplifted sensation will pervade you generally'" (688). Indeed, in a double confession, Mark declares: "'Then I shall follow you, for I am mad, Rose, with love—hashish!'" (691). Rose's confession reveals that she too is doubly mastered: "As if swayed by a power more potent than her will, Rose bent to meet his lips. But the ardent pressure seemed to startle her from a momentary oblivion of everything but love. She covered up her face and sank down, as if overwhelmed with shame, sobbing through passionate tears, 'Oh, what am I doing? I am mad, for I, too, have taken hashish!'" (692).

Mark and Rose are thus quite literally swept away by their passion and by the hashish. Adrift in their small boat, the two young people find themselves helplessly journeying on the Gothic quest to the unknown—the unknown human heart, and the unknown wild American space, the sea. In true Gothic form, the sea becomes increasingly dark and stormy; the lovers are trapped between "threatening heavens [and] treacherous sea" (691), and Mark acknowledges that they are in "'great danger'" (691). Their conversation is silenced as "a rattling peal of thunder drowned his voice, and then the storm broke loose. Rain fell in torrents, the wind blew fiercely, sky and sea were black as ink, and the boat tossed from wave to wave almost at their mercy" (692). Alcott's description of the storm and the stormy passion closely reflects the Gothic trope John Ruskin dismisses in *Modern Painters* (1843–60) as the "pathetic fallacy": the artistic presumption that external nature reflects internal human emotion. Ultimately, the two lost lovers are rescued from the chaotic and irrational darkness by a guide, a lighthouse keeper, and taken to the sanctuary of light and reason, the lighthouse.

Throughout much of the story Alcott is ambivalent, and even condemnatory, of the free behavior of her young characters, demonstrating her ongoing commitment to nineteenth-century female propriety. She inserts a number of voices of disapprobation into the narrative: "'I advise you not to try it. People do all sorts of queer things when they take it. I wouldn't for the world,' said a prudent young lady warningly, as all examined the box and its contents" (687). Within moments of eating the bonbons, "Evelyn, a shy girl, [is] already rather alarmed at what she had done" (688). Indeed, the twenty-first-century reader may also be alarmed by the promised effects of the hashish; Dr. Meredith counsels his friends, "'here are two ladies who have imbibed, and in three hours will be in such a seraphic state of mind that 'No' will be an impossibility to them'" (688). The narrator highlights the unpleasant after-effects of the "perilous play" of her young characters; their actions, when freed from the constraints of authority, cause them some pain. Alcott details Mark's penance for his moment of rebellion, and the resulting hangover: "All night he lay motionless, with staring eyes, feverish lips, and a mind on the rack, for the delicate machinery which had been tampered with revenged the wrong by torturing the foolish experimenter." Rose too suffers the consequences of free play: "All night Rose wept and sang, talked and cried for help in a piteous state of nervous excitement, for with her the trance came first, and the after-agitation was increased by the events of the evening" (693).

Yet Alcott seems to cede grudgingly that the joys of freedom outweigh the dangers of masterlessness. The young lovers can reveal their mutual love and begin their romance only in the altered, irrational state induced by the hashish, free from the social rules imposed by their absent elders. Stranded on the uncharted sea, in a small boat, on a dark, stormy night, they are free to act outside the bounds of social constraints. Alcott shows how difficult it is for these proper and reasonable young people to resist their social training. The narrator tells us: "Something in his tone terrified her; she snatched her hand away and drew beyond his reach, trying to speak calmly, and to meet coldly the ardent glances of the eyes which were strangely darkened and dilated with uncontrollable emotion" (690). Mark, too, initially clings to the old rules, explaining, "'I meant nothing; it's the moonlight; sit down, I'll control myself—upon my soul I will!'" and Rose properly responds: "'Are you mad, sir?' cried Rose, trembling with indignation." Yet ultimately the drug compels the two to repress the rational conventions of their elders' society, and to succumb to the delights of freedom and romance. Mark returns to the forbidden topic, "'Say you love me'" (692), to which Rose responds: "'I do; but I should not own it now'" (692). All of this ends in a free, passionate, and forbidden kiss. Both lovers confess that, for each, the goal of the hashish experiment was freedom from the social dictates governing the behavior of youth of both genders. Rose says, "'I hoped it would make me soft and lovable, like other women. I'm tired of being a lonely statue,'" to which Mark responds, "'And I took it to gain courage to tell my love. Rose, we have been near death together; let us share life together, and neither of us be any more lonely or afraid'" (694). In fact, any quiet condemnation that Alcott has tried to articulate is negated by Mark's words, the last words of the story: "'Heaven bless hashish, if its dreams end like this!'" (694). Alcott concludes her text in the world of the Romantic Gothic, by bravely dispelling anxieties about the happiness and future of youth left without rational adult guides. In her story, Alcott overtly refuses the *horror vacui* consequent to the absent patriarch articulated by other American writers. Alcott's story concludes with a strong sense of hope for a progeny-rich future for her newly liberated young Americans.

The Dangers of the Masterless Servant: James and Wharton

The vacuum left by the absence of the patriarch, the master, leads to another anxiety: the fear that his absence will allow members of yet another suppressed group, the servants, to rebel and to appropriate the property of the absent master.[4] An ongoing question of American canon-formation is whether Henry James, who spent most of his writing life in England and who died an English citizen, fits into the American canon. In "The Art of Fiction" (1884), James attempts to refuse this question by erasing the distinction between American and British literature. Yet clearly there are themes and concerns unique to the American Gothic tradition, including the anxieties evoked by unmastered Americans, an anxiety that replaces the fear of the ever-present tyrannical patriarch in the English Gothic tradition. Moreover, as Poe's "Usher" and "Masque" and Wharton's "Mr. Jones"—discussed later in this chapter—demonstrate, European setting alone does not make for a non–American text. Thus James' *The Turn of the Screw* (1899), though inhabited by English characters and set in England, locates itself within the American Gothic tradition by displaying American anxieties of the absent master.

In James' text, the governess, the point of view character of the central narrative, is clearly possessed—by her obsession to obey her master fully, and by her obsessive need to exorcise the ghosts of the servants that she believes are haunting and corrupting the children in her care. She tells Mrs. Grose, the housekeeper, "I was carried away in London" (282), where she met the master who convinced her to take sole responsibility for two orphaned children in an isolated setting. The terms of the master are that he remain absent, that the governess not consult him. She is thus forced to take the place of the absent master; but his very absence unravels and obsesses her. When the governess begins to observe the ghosts of the previous servants, she writes, "A portentous clearness now possessed me" (293); the governess herself describes her fixation as "my obsession" (312). This is a telling word; "obsession" originally meant the possession of an innocent person by an evil spirit. In the evolution of this word from the external supernatural to the internal psychological, we see the evolution of the site of horror in James' fiction, an evolution that will continue in the twentieth century.

The Gothic resonances illustrate that James' text itself is possessed, haunted by the ghosts of the English Gothic tradition, despite James' dismissal of long and complicated novels as "loose baggy monsters" (Preface to *The Tragic Muse* 84). Though James attempts to escape those monsters by tightening up his narrative—in the Preface to *Turn*, he states that its strength is its tight "perfect homogeneity" (xlvii)—the story, its setting, and its characters remain haunted by the English past, as does much American Gothic literature. Bly, the country manor setting, is the typical Gothic haunted castle complete with "an old machicolated square tower" (282), and dark secrets from the past. Indeed the text of Charlotte Brontë's *Jane Eyre* (1847) is the unnamed, almost invisible ghost that hovers over James' narrative, emerging spectrally at a number of moments. For example, the name "Miles" echoes the name of the school "master" (*Jane Eyre* 7) of John Read, Jane's cousin, who like James' Miles is sent home from boarding school under a cloud of suspicion. The haunting of the governess by her own history of reading is the source of many of the echoes from *Jane Eyre*. Upon arriving at the rambling house, she recalls the specters of Radcliffe and of Brontë: "Was there a 'secret' at Bly—a mystery of Udolpho or an insane, an unmentionable relative kept in unsuspected confinement?" (288). The governess evokes Brontë's novel when she walks the grounds of the estate, remembering her absent "master," who is described by Douglas—the friend in "possession" (278) of the governess' manuscript—as "such a figure as had never risen, save in a dream or in an old novel" (278–

279) before the governess. As she walks, the governess considers that "it would be as charming as a charming story suddenly to meet someone. Someone would appear there at the turn of a path and would stand before me and smile and approve" (286). This scene pointedly recalls the scene in which Jane first encounters Mr. Rochester. Walking in the "evening calm," Jane sees a vision that seems to be a "North-of-England spirit, called a 'Gytrash'"; the apparition, mounted on his phallic horse, coalesces into a more prosaic sight—an unknown "traveler taking ... [a] short cut" (Brontë *Jane Eyre* 143–144). In the following scene this unknown traveler solidifies into the person of the patriarchal Mr. Rochester, who lends meaning and purpose to Jane's journey. James' governess seems even closer to fulfilling her fictionally induced fantasy when she, like Jane, discerns a seemingly supernatural figure—perched upon a phallic tower. The governess' desire to echo Jane's ultimate ascension, as possessor of Thornfield Hall, emerges as she walks the grounds of Bly, "almost with a sense of property." However, the narratives of the two governesses diverge; the vision of James' governess fails to materialize as her master, the object of her desire, despite her initial hope that her "imagination had, in a flash, turned real" (286).

The haunting of the governess by the ghost of Jane Eyre—the anonymity of the governess leaves a vacuum filled by Jane's unspoken name—is one way to account for the action that follows. For it is the governess' fixation upon her absent master and her desire to please him, informed by her reading of *Jane Eyre*—in which the master, Mr. Rochester, is ever-present—that leads her to mishandle her responsibilities. In crediting the reading of Gothic novels for the unfolding of disaster, James follows in the shadow of another ghost, Jane Austen, whose *Northanger Abbey* (1817) indicts foolish female readers who are unduly influenced by novels of Gothic romance. In exorcising the ghost of Brontë, and discrediting her influence, James invokes the ghost of Austen and her morality tale of the dangers of the Gothic text.

Shoshana Felman astutely identifies a pattern of narrative dispossession in the recurring trope of "purloined letters" ("Turning the Screw of Interpretation" 138) that fail to convey their meaning in James' text. Felman observes that the various levels of embedded narration in the novel support a pattern of narrative dispossession. James disconnects the text from the authority of any single narrator by establishing three distinct narrators: the "I" of the frame; Douglas; and the governess. Each of these narrators addresses a distinct audience, and a distinct motive in narrating. James thus creates a masterless narrative, dispossessing each narrator of "the authority of its author" (Felman 127). Indeed, as Felman notes, James relinquishes his own narrative authority, and thereby mirrors the master of Bly who—like the English monarch, absent from the colonies—abandons his own property. Felman cites passages in which James addresses the levels of authorial displacement:

> Dispossessing himself of his own story, James, more subtly still, at the same time dispossesses his own story of its master. But isn't this precisely what the Master does in *The Turn of the Screw*, when, dispossessing the governess of her Master (himself), he gives her nothing less than 'supreme authority'? It is with 'supreme authority' indeed that James, in deconstructing his own mastery, vests his reader. But isn't this gift of supreme authority bestowed upon the reader as upon the governess the very thing that will precisely *drive them mad* [206].

Thus James returns to the great American theme of the nineteenth century: American masterlessness (legal or literary) presents an array of opportunities—including anxiety and even death.

James' confusion of narratives also leads to confusion on the part of literary critics who, as Felman indicates, struggle with each other in competing attempts to apprehend the single—master—meaning of the text. James' recognition that the role of the critic and the careful reader involves grasping for interpretation and textual apprehension appears in the Preface to *What Maisie Knew* (1897): "To criticise is to appreciate, to appropriate, to take intellectual possession, to establish, in fine, a relation with the criticized thing and make it one's own" (*Art of the Novel* 155).[5] Felman locates the beginning of the contest for hermeneutic possession of *Turn* in the "Freudian reading" developed by Edmund Wilson in 1934. Wilson was the first to argue that the specters are manifestations of the governess' psyche, her hysterical madness; his reading contests the interpretation of the "anti–Freudian" critics who read the visions as old-fashioned "real" ghosts. The extent to which this debate was framed as an either-or proposition was demonstrated in 1960, through the exclusion of *Turn* "from [an] ... edition of the collected James ghost stories" (Kathryn Cramer "Possession and 'The Jolly Corner'" 19) by the noted James scholar and editor, Leon Edel. This editorial decision indicates that the "anti–Freudians" had lost the battle for hermeneutic possession—the ghosts of the story are exiled from the realm of the old fashioned ghost story and definitively fixed within the Freudian space of the hysterical psyche. It is not just the critic whose reading is maddened by *The Turn of the Screw*; any reader of this text treads on unstable ground. As Felman writes, James' narrative "is *the story of the subversion of the reader* ... a *trap* designed to close upon the reader" (184–185). Like its looser and baggier predecessors, James' Gothic text entices and imprisons the reader who enters in pursuit of meaning. In fact, James adopts the unsettling framing structure deployed to great effect by Ann Radcliffe, the mother of the English Gothic. As in Radcliffe's *The Italian*, *The Turn of the Screw* presents an opening frame and then omits a

5. *Masterless*   137

stabilizing end frame that would close the framing narrative. James' story begins with the conventional framing structure of the embedded narrative: in the outer frame the unnamed "'I'" tells of a group "gathered round the fire" in an "old house" listening to ghost stories (277); within this frame we hear the indirect report of Douglas' introduction to the manuscript; at the center of these narratives is the manuscript of the governess, read by Douglas to his listeners. Yet James' story ends within this embedded level—with the report by the governess of the death of Miles. We hear nothing more of "'I,'" or Douglas, or his auditors. We are deprived of their stabilizing response to the story, a complementary frame to their opening conjectures. The absence of a closing end frame leaves the reader alone and confused; we miss the comfort of other voices telling us what to make of the ambiguous ending to this ambiguous story. Like the governess, the reader is left without a master to anchor the meaning of the narrative.

Felman follows the path of possession and dispossession in *The Turn of the Screw* to a conclusion that is aligned with the project of the volume of *Yale French Studies* in which her work appears: "to familiarize the American public with the new theoretical orientation of modern French psychoanalysis" ("Foreword" *Yale French Studies* 4). In her distillation of the various moments of possession and dispossession of property, self, and narrative in James' story, Felman discovers a conclusion that is inevitable from her perspective:

> the governess' narrative tells of the *loss of the proprietor of the house*, of the 'Master' (by virtue of which loss the house becomes precisely *haunted*, haunted by the usurping ghosts of its *subordinates*), so does the framing prologue convey, through the reader's (vocal) rendering of an authorship to which he has no title, the *loss of the proprietor of the narrative*. And this strange condition of the narrative, this strange double insistence, in the frame as in the story, of the absence of the story's master, of the owner of the property, cannot but evoke, once more, the constitutive condition of the unconscious, itself a sort of obscure knowledge, which is, precisely, authorless and ownerless, to the extent that it is a knowledge which no consciousness can *master* or *be in possession of* [127–128].

And here we see Felman fall into the very trap that she sees laid for other critics in *Turn*: the temptation to discover a single, essential meaning, the meaning of the master, the author.[6] In insisting that possession and dispossession in *Turn* point to the unpossessable unconscious, Felman attempts to limit and contain the text within the confines of one particular critical approach. As her essay indicates, the psychoanalytic approach reveals many secret places within the story, but in ignoring the political and social repressions in James' Gothic story, and in suggesting that all roads in the story lead to the psychoanalytic reading, Felman denies the value of other critical approaches. And indeed, an investigation of the expression of the American political and cultural unconscious in James' story reveals secrets unavailable to Felman's reading.

A focus on the political context of this story reveals the significant detail that links James' text to the tradition of the American Gothic: the malevolent spirits are the ghosts of servants. The unreliable narrator of the central text is a servant (as a governess, an uncomfortably liminal one) and the benevolent but useless housekeeper is a servant. The master of them all, the "proprietor of the house" as Felman figures him, is absent before the governess' embedded narrative begins. *Turn*, then, is a post–Revolutionary story that reveals a *horror vacui*, detailing the chaos that ensues in the absence of the patriarch. In this story, as in post–Revolutionary America, the former head in his absence "*becomes a ghost*" (Felman 206); the former subjects are in charge, leading to dire results. In his prologue Douglas tells his listeners that since the master relinquishes his control: "the governess would be in supreme authority" (279); she would "take the whole thing over and let him alone" (280). This abdication of power is not the first on the part of the master. The reader and the governess learn from Mrs. Grose that earlier "the master went, and Quint was alone.... Alone with us.... In charge" (293); Quint, in the words of Mrs. Grose, "was much too free" (294)—a critique applicable to the post–Revolutionary American. Although the most relevant meaning of "free," the meaning that Mrs. Grose suggests, portends class impropriety, with a touch of sexual impropriety, the word gestures to the larger political freedom that Quint's rebellion suggests. James' text expresses the anxiety that we see in the American Gothic canon: the fearful conjecture about what evil and chaos may follow revolution, what occurs after a nation, a people, lose the master who guides them.

When placing the political reading within the context of Felman's psychoanalytic reading (a move that illustrates the uses of reading James' fiction through "many windows" (Preface to *The Portrait of a Lady* ix), we can see that the convergence of the two approaches sheds further light. Felman, taking the Freudian perspective, suggests that the absent master represents the absent phallus and thus the absent referent of essential meaning (172); in the absence of the Law of the Father, meaning unravels. The necessity of the present master to provide fixed meaning is presumed by a number of characters in the story; at various moments the governess, the children, and Mrs. Grose attempt to contact the master, inviting him to join them, to help them stabilize the meaning of their situation. Although the governess tries to fill this vacuum of meaning, as Felman notes: "Meaning's *possession* is itself ironically transformed into the radical *dispossession* of its possessor" (174). Since "the governess is herself essentially a *reader*, engaged in an interpretative enterprise"

(183), she is distanced from the center of hermeneutic authority. She fails to understand the meaning of the evidence she sees, and her unguided interpretive enterprise ends in death and despair. Here too, we can see an American political subtext and a political anxiety, a fear that without a central authority to dictate order and meaning the liberated American citizenry will lose its way.

Once again, we see an inability to imagine a future for a non-patriarchal system. Like *Wieland* and "Usher," *The Turn of the Screw* emblematizes the lack of a future in the loss of the children; under the influence of the ghosts (or the governess), they are "lost" (299). The last words of the governess to Flora are "'I've lost you. Good-bye'" (327). This valedictory is reversed in her last words to the dying Miles: "'I have you ... but he has lost you forever!'" (338). Yet the governess too loses the dying Miles: "his little heart, dispossessed, had stopped" (338). Miles himself becomes masterless, freed from the competing influences of the ghosts and of the governess, but at what cost? Once again an American Gothic text suggests a secure future as the price of freedom.

* * *

Edith Wharton's ghost story, "Mr. Jones" (1937), echoes James' story in its evocation of American anxieties regarding the dangers of the ruling servant, who represents the rule of the masses[7] within democracy. Wharton's story sets up a struggle for possession of property between an exemplar of the English aristocracy, Lady Jane Lynke, and her unruly opponent, the servant Mr. Jones, whose title, position and common name mark him as a man of the people. Wharton's story, which also features English characters and an English setting, is visibly haunted by the ghost of James: in the Preface to *Ghosts*, the collection of short stories in which "Mr. Jones" appears,[8] Wharton writes, "For imaginative handling of the supernatural no one, to my mind, has touched Henry James in 'The Turn of the Screw'" (4). Wharton, it appears, is not of the Freudian camp; the struggle in her story emphasizes the actuality of the specter, and highlights the economic and social roots of haunting, rather than psychological causes. "Mr. Jones," like *The Turn of the Screw*, is also haunted by other ghosts of the English Gothic, displaying many of the familiar motifs: the struggle for possession of narrative and text; the setting of an old English structure; the imprisoned wife kept in "close seclusion" (192); the aristocratic demon-husband with the "Byronic throat and tossed-back curls" (171); the supernatural; dark secrets from the past. Wharton consolidates her debt to the English Gothic tradition by setting the embedded narrative of the imprisoned wife in the past, during the early years of the nineteenth century, the time of the high Gothic. The framing narrative is appropriately belated, occurring a century later during Wharton's own time.

Wharton's story begins, as any good English Gothic text, with matters of inheritance. Lady Jane, already wealthy, belongs to an aristocratic family that manages to effortlessly accumulate wealth; they are a family to whom "considerable possessions had accrued." Lady Jane discovers that she has become even more wealthy and powerful, as she inherits Bells, "the beautiful old place" with a "moat" (170) set in the English countryside, which had been in her family for hundreds of years. Lady Jane thus takes "possession of Bells" in the old aristocratic manner, although ironically she dismisses her female predecessors who accumulated wealth, "mostly by clever marriages[,] with a faint contempt" (171). That is, Lady Jane *thinks* that she has taken possession of Bells. She finds herself locked in battle for possession with an ancient servant, Mr. Jones. From the start, he resists Jane's authority as owner; when she first attempts to enter, she is informed by a young frightened servant that "Mr. Jones says that no one is allowed to visit the house" (173). Jane assumes that he is merely a long-term proprietary "caretaker" (174) as she learns that "he was in possession" (174) of the house at least thirty years before her attempted entrance. Even when Lady Jane establishes herself at Bells, she has to struggle for control with Mr. Jones, as rooms she wishes to explore remain inexplicably locked to her. The contest is unconsciously defined by Lady Jane when she is forced to leave a "freezing" attic room: she says, "the muniment room was really untenable" (189). Although she means simply that the room is too cold to stay, her language captures the essence of her situation: she has just lost a battle in the war with Mr. Jones. Her home has become a fortress and her ability to hold it is strongly contested. In fact, the struggle for the estate—in particular for the blue room, "the warmest room of the house" (181), and the muniment room in which the family documents are stored—is a struggle between two opposing forms of property possession: legal possession and ghostly possession. Lady Jane bases her claim upon the legal rights of inheritance and property as she comes into "possession of Bells" (195) upon inheriting it from a distant relative. In this Wharton touches on the aristocratic mode of property acquisition that is a preoccupation of the Gothic and the question of female inheritance of property that is central to Ann Radcliffe's Female Gothic and its successors. Mr. Jones founds his claim to Bells upon equally compelling terms. His "possession" (174) is based upon the terms of ghostly possession; he is actually the ghost of the former steward of the property.[9] Wharton's story asks whether Lady Jane's legal possession will prove more powerful than the ghostly possession of Mr. Jones. The reality of Mr. Jones ghostliness is well established in the story; he is no figment of a hysterical female imagination, even though he inhabits a twentieth-century text. Even before Lady Jane and the reader realize that Mr. Jones is indeed a ghost, Lady Jane recognizes that there is something intangible about his tenure; never seeing him directly, Jane only catches brief glimpses of a very old man—she calls him "my invisible guardian or rather the guardian of Bells" (179). Mrs. Clemm, the housekeeper who knows of Mr. Jones' spectral identity, ambiguously informs Lady Jane that he is "more dead than living ... between life and death, as it were" (177–178). Finally a servant reveals that Mr. Jones is actually dead "in his grave in the churchyard—these years and years he is" (196).

In addition to struggling for the possession of Bells, Mr. Jones and Lady Jane also struggle for possession of the household documents, and thereby for the embedded narrative of Juliana, the sad-faced, "inconsolable" (185) woman whose portrait was placed in the blue room after being painted in 1818, and whose place in the tomb with her husband is indicated only by the anonymous "Also His Wife" (171). The familiar English Gothic motifs of the missing or effaced document, and the silent, effaced wife appear in Wharton's story in the form of family records that detail the story of Juliana and her husband Peregrine. These records are appropriated by Mr. Jones who hides them in the blue room and then are re-appropriated by Lady Jane; in the words of the narrator, the letters are "purloined by Lady Jane" (195). In uncovering the letters written by Juliana, another Gothic instance of suppressed women's writing, Lady Jane wins one battle for possession, and liberates Juliana (or at least her story) decades after she had been imprisoned by Mr. Jones. In his pre-ghost steward days, he was her human "keeper" (194), the emissary of her husband Peregrine, the young aristocrat who owned the house at the turn of the eighteenth century. Jane gives Juliana an identity and a voice that she never had in life; her letters to Peregrine reveal that she was deaf and mute and that her love for him was unrequited because he married her for her money. We also learn that Peregrine confined Juliana, possibly because he was ashamed of her disability, although she begged to be allowed to meet other people. Mr. Jones perpetuated this imprisonment, obeying Peregrine's "express orders" (193). Thus in the core of a story that bears all the traits of an English Gothic tale, we can detect an American fear, expressed by an American writer: the fear that the free populace will, in the absence of the patriarch, enact a system more malign than the cruel order that inspired revolution.

Paradoxically, or perhaps obviously, it is Mr. Jones ghostly status that allows him to win the war, although he loses some skirmishes. As Jane ultimately learns, Mr. Jones "still rules" (179). He is, in fact, a powerful murderous ghost, who will kill to maintain his hold over the property. As the story ends Mr. Jones appears to be the victor; he has just murdered Mrs. Clemm, the living servant who has failed to serve him correctly, and Mrs. Clemm's niece explicates the source of his malevolent and enduring power: "'That's the terror of it … that's why she always had to do what he told her to … because you couldn't even answer him back'" (196).

*   *   *

Wharton's story, like James' and like much American Gothic literature, thus expresses post–Revolutionary anxieties of possession and power. As in James' ghost story, the structures of ownership in "Mr. Jones" echo those of a post–Revolutionary system, where the former underlings are in charge. The masters of Wharton's Bells all abdicate their authority: the property is owned by a series of absentee landlords, including Peregrine who dies in Aleppo, leaving Juliana and Bells under the care of Mr. Jones; a more recent master "had forsaken [Bells] sixty years before [Jane's arrival] to seek his fortune in Canada" (170)—admittedly, he too might have been vanquished by Mr. Jones. Before she learns the secret of Bells, Jane refers to the stewardship of Mr. Jones with unconscious irony: "'They were lucky, all these absentees to have someone to watch over their interests so faithfully'" (178). Mr. Jones is no loyal servant; he is the fearful figure of the revolutionary, the usurping subject who fills the void left by the absent master, the dangerous rebel who abuses his newly acquired power. Wharton thus expresses the American fear that the rule of the revolutionary, the liberated servant, will prove to be as vicious and chaotic as that of the displaced aristocratic master.

6

The Return of the Master
The New Patriarch

The Robber Baron: Re-Emergence of the Aristocrat

In the late nineteenth century, changing business and technological conditions led to an unprecedented consolidation of wealth and power in America. Howard Zinn observes that in the late 1800s most of the wealth in the country was held by dynasts such as J.P Morgan (256). Attendant to this rise of wealth was the rise of "consumerism," with a focus on the consumption of material goods, as exemplified by the "'cottages' in Newport and the extravagant philanthropies developed to support and dignify the local *nouveaux riches*" (Patrice Higonnet 173). Cal Jillson records the anxiety which greeted this change: in 1873, a speaker warned the "University of Wisconsin class of 1873 that property rights were again threatening to overwhelm human rights," reducing Americans to "'the feudal serfs of corporate capital'" (Jillson 120). The disparaging name given to the new American dynasts, the robber barons, made clear the imaginative connection to the archaic hierarchies of Europe. The original medieval robber barons were, as Richard John notes, "warlords who had defied the Holy Roman Emperor by illegally collecting exorbitant tolls on river-borne traffic.... Like their medieval forebears, the modern robber barons blocked commerce and flaunted [sic] the law" (5). The image of the medieval robber barons was thus appropriated as part of a critique of the big business that dominated the American economic scene from the 1880s. Richard John, who traces the origins of the term in the United States, argues that it originated in 1869 in a letter from Charles Francis Adams, Jr. Adams himself was as John notes, a member of the American social aristocracy, descended from John Adams. His coinage expresses his alarm at the new lawless model of dynastic wealth that was emerging. The term was picked up by his equally blue-blooded cousin, Josiah Quincy, Jr., who "four years later ... invoked the epithet in a popular address" (3), connecting a financial technique "known as stock watering" to "'the robber barons of the middle ages,'" whose treachery, Quincy suggested, was surpassed by the financiers of his day. As heirs of the American revolution, Adams and Quincy were horrified at the return to European modes of generating and consolidating wealth. Indeed, "anti-monopolists could be found all across the political spectrum" (6). John notes that the term "gilded age," a term that was not "popularized until after the First World War ... is explicitly pejorative" (32), and that its use tends to mask the "public revulsion" (32) during the period in which the barons ruled.

As the Wisconsin speaker suggested, the direct result of the accumulation of American wealth was "a new hierarchy ... that excluded blacks and most immigrants, as well as women. At the top were gigantic industrial firms dominated by WASPs (White Anglo-Saxon Protestants)" (Higonnet 166). At the bottom was everyone else. Howard Zinn adds that during this time "industrial and political elites" (253) wrested economic, social, and political power from the rest of the American people.[1] Zinn also points to the economic exploitation of "the new immigrants" (266) and "women immigrants" (267). The exploitation of immigrants was particularly cynical, since as Jillson notes, during "the gilded age.... America continued to be a beacon of freedom and opportunity," as emblematized by the Statue of Liberty, "erected on Ellis Island in New York harbor in 1886" (125). Jillson gestures to the terms of social Darwinism, an anti-egalitarian misconception of the day: "the concentration of power and wealth reward[ed] society's fittest for their successful competitive efforts [and] kept power and wealth out of the hands of the unfit" (132). This tautological logic worked to sustain the *status quo* and to ensure the continued economic exploitation of women, blacks and immigrants. Clearly the post–Revolutionary picture of a republican democracy was fading, being replaced by the old European model headed by the powerful white male: the patriarchy. Thus, as Poe had feared almost a century before, America was enacting a return to patriarchal aristocracy. Those at the top of the new hierarchies were represented by villainous figures like Jay Gould. Richard John resorts to Gothic language to describe this new American villain as "an agent of destruction" (John 19), who orchestrated "the takeover of Western Union" (John 12) in 1881. Continuing to evoke the excessive rhetoric of the Gothic, John recalls "the magnitude of Gould's perfidy" (16), and the aristocratic arrogance of William H. Vanderbilt, infamously memorialized by his anti-democratic statement: "'the public be damned'" (John 26).

The unmatched power of the men running this system was complemented by the powerlessness of women, evidenced by the twin myths of the proper woman, and "The Angel in the House," popularized by the 1854–62 poem of that name by the English poet Coventry Patmore. The poem was immensely popular in America and perpetuated the imperative of the pure nineteenth-century woman. The lot of the angelic woman was confinement in the domestic sphere of her own home; she was thus rendered ghostly as well as angelic. The prescribed confinement also ensured that women did not sully themselves by being exposed to worldly affairs, perpetuating their continued disempowerment in public life. Jillson notes that "the federal courts were consistent in upholding state and federal laws that barred women from the practice of law," quoting a judge's statement: "'nature herself,' along with 'the divine ordinance,' indicated 'the domestic sphere as that which properly belongs to the domain and functions of womanhood'" (153). As a corollary, "women's suffrage ... was associated by its enemies with promiscuity, divorce, and national decline" (Higonnet 174), and thus suffrage did not occur until 1920.

As John notes, "the origins of the robber baron epithet were literary" (7); certainly the robber baron evokes the dark dangerous patriarch who is the source of danger and fear in most eighteenth- and nineteenth-century English Gothic novels. With the absence of this villain from the American scene in the early history of the country, the fear of the villain is replaced by the anxiety evoked by his absence, the fear of being lost without a guide. However, the return of the powerful and dangerous patriarch to the scene of American public and economic life alters the terms of danger in the evolving American Gothic. Americans no longer need to fear being without a strong leader; with the return of the strong and malignant leader, American literature returns to the old patterns of the threatening patriarchy. In the light of John's reading, the return of the patriarch was not immediately acknowledged; historians "relegated the robber baron to the dustbin of history [where] he has mostly remained, at least for business historians" (John 2). Of course, whatever is repressed by the official narrative bursts forth into the chaos of the Gothic text. Hence the return of the patriarch to American Gothic literature in the wake of the robber baron. The Gothic figure of the dangerous patriarch emerges in American literature at the turn of the twentieth century to challenge and to correct the romanticizing of the robber barons during the graceful gilded age.

Fitzgerald's "The Diamond as Big as the Ritz": The Rise and Fall of the Dynastic Monopoly

Although he is not exactly a mainstay of the Gothic tradition, and the title suggests a jazz-age confection, F. Scott Fitzgerald's short story, "The Diamond as Big as the Ritz" (1922), unfolds a horrifying tale of the re-emergence of the American patriarch in the early twentieth century. The title image of the narrative is quite literal; the wealthy American family in the story possesses a mountain that comprises a single mammoth diamond. Fitzgerald deploys the image of the immeasureably valuable diamond as a concisely accurate metaphor for the monopoly, the economic strategy used by the dynasts to consolidate their economic and hence social power in the late nineteenth and early twentieth centuries. The luxuries that exclusive ownership of the diamond entails reflect the unbridled excess of the lives of the robber barons.

Fitzgerald creates two hellish Gothic spaces to represent the gilded lives of the rich, and imagines an appropriate Gothic ending for at least one of them. The first Gothic hell is "Hades—a small town on the Mississippi River" (1), evoking images of slavery and of those American innocents, Tom Sawyer and Huckleberry Finn. This Hades, the hometown of the point-of-view character John Unger,[2] like Dante's hell, is furnished with gates, emblazoned with an unspecified "old-fashioned Victorian motto" (2). Despite his "look of passionate frankness," John bears the "dark face" common to many Gothic villains. When he goes off to school, John's father gives him an "asbestos pocketbook stuffed with money" and tells him "'we'll keep the home-fires burning'" (1). Fitzgerald's narrator distinguishes (or tries to distinguish) the new American Hades from the original "that was abolished long ago" (35). The new Hades seemingly revises the moral stance of the old hell. In this American Hades, Capitalism, rather than Evil, reigns—though Fitzgerald's story works to blur the distinction. John's wealthy family sends him away to "St Midas' School near Boston"—an appropriately named training-ground for scions of the gilded age. St. Midas' is the "most expensive and the most exclusive boys' preparatory school in the world" (2). On meeting his rich friend, Percy Washington, John, a frank boy from the American heartland, announces that he is very fond of jewels, and that "'I like very rich people'" (3). In Percy, John has discovered his ideal; Percy explains, "'my father is by far the richest man in the world'" (2), possessing "'a diamond bigger than the Ritz-Carlton Hotel'" (3). The monolithic diamond composes an entire mountain that is "'one cubic mile without a flaw'" (9).

Percy's family—whose estate is the second hell of Fitzgerald's story—thus has a monopoly on the world's diamonds; the economic value of their possession dwarfs the value of all the diamonds outside their domain. The treasure had been discovered during the Civil War by an ancestor of Percy's family, the Washingtons. The ancestor estimated that "the diamond in the mountain was approximately equal in quantity to all the rest of the diamonds known to exist in the world" (12). This early Washington realized that he must be discreet in selling small "samples" (11) of the diamond, to protect his secret, and also to avoid flooding the market and causing "the bottom to fall out of the market" (12). Like the robber barons, he fears that "the Government" (12) might somehow intervene to dispossess him of his near-monopoly. In fact, he fears that the government "might take over the claim immediately and institute a monopoly" (12) of its own, and so he keeps his huge possession a secret, thus sustaining the exclusivity and value of his diamond. Eventually, when the Washingtons accumulate enough wealth to live in "unparalleled luxury for generations" (13), the son of the first dynast "did a very simple thing—he sealed up the mine" (13), thereby preventing the discovery of his secret, and the devaluing of the commodity; that is, he ensures the value of his monopoly.

The limitless wealth of the Washingtons allows them to live in unequaled luxury. Fitzgerald enthralls his readers with lavish descriptions of unimagined comfort, implicating, perhaps, his readers and himself in the greedy appetite of the American dynast. We experience this excess through John's relatively unjaded eye. On his first night in the "exquisite chateau" (7), he encounters "many colors ... quick sensory impressions [and] music soft as a voice in love" (8). He explores rooms whose floors change colors "from lighting below, patterns of barbaric clashing colors, or pastel delicacy ... or of subtle and intricate mosaic" (8). Some floors are composed of aquarium windows, some of fur. At dinner, John finds that "each plate was of two almost imperceptible layers of solid diamond between which was curiously worked a filigree of emerald design" (8). As he drifts off to sleep, John is engulfed by the sensation of "jewels, fabrics, wines, and metals" (8). The next morning John encounters more material extravagance, and the luxury of "a large negro" attendant "in a white uniform" (9) curiously named "Gygsum" (10), who gently shifts his body into a decadently lavish bath; the walls of the bath room are the glass walls of aquariums. Sunlight filters through glass in the ceiling. The energy Fitzgerald applies to these descriptions suggests that he is more than half in love with this excessive luxury, despite the taint of its source.

For, as John quickly learns, the Washington family is—in the tradition of the English Gothic—an evil patriarchal dynasty. Its aristocratic credentials are quite impeccable. The father of Braddock, the present Mr. Washington, was "a direct descendant of George Washington" (11). Any reader with a modicum of knowledge of American history will immediately spot the error; Washington had no children. Perhaps the family is perpetuating a lie. Or perhaps Fitzgerald is reminding us that we are outside the realistic world of history, and in the fantastic world of the Gothic. Whatever the case, Braddock looks very like his "ancestor," George: "white haired" (8) with "intelligent eyes set in his good-looking vacuous face" (16). As in the conventional Gothic patriarchal dynasty, the Washington mother is practically absent. She first appears as a silent, almost invisible cipher, a beautiful object: "Amber light flooded out upon the darkness, silhouetting the figure of an exquisite lady" who "silently held out her arms" (7). The sisters of the family, of no dynastic use, are also objects, possessions: one is named "Jasmine," the other "Kismine." The last syllable in each name makes clear their status as family property.

The setting, the palatial Washington property is also located within the confines of the English Gothic; the chateau is a Gothic labyrinth in which John and Percy wander "through a maze of ... rooms" (8). In accordance with the conventions of Gothic setting, the estate is located outside the known world. Percy first vaguely describes his family's estate as being somewhere "in the West" (2); when they arrive, Percy further explains that the Washington property begins "where the United States ends" (6). In fact, the manipulations of the family ensure that they own "'the only five square miles of land in the country that's never been surveyed'" (6). Fitzgerald also carefully delineates the conventional immorality of the dynasty. The father of Braddock brings his younger brother into his scheme, putting him in charge of his "colored following," the African American servants. However, after the older brother marries and has a son, he is "compelled ... to murder his brother" (13) to ensure the safety of the dynastic monopoly. This dynasty, founded on fratricide, proceeds to enact additional atrocities, as Braddock Washington continues to safeguard his family's gilded possessions by dispossessing others. Braddock Washington thus creates a Gothic space which is heaven for his own family, but hell for everyone else. To protect the fortune, Braddock Washington imprisons any pilot who happens to fly over the hidden estate in a modern version of the dungeon: "a large cavity in the earth ... covered by a strong iron grating" (17). Passing the grating John hears the voices of the prisoners calling, "'Come on down to Hell'" (17). Fitzgerald emphasizes the class exploitation of his time by explaining that "John could tell from the coarse optimism and rugged vitality of the remarks and voices that they proceeded from middle-class Americans" (18). In fact, the Washingtons have no qualms about sacrificing anyone less wealthy than they, meaning everyone. John discovers that all the guests who are invited by members of the family are killed at the end of their luxurious stay, but not before the family can selfishly "'get all the pleasure out of them that we can'" (24), all to preserve the secret lode of wealth. John, himself, is at the point of being executed by "three naked negroes" (27) when the crisis of the story explodes.

Despite the echoes of the English Gothic text, Fitzgerald's narrative ultimately distinguishes itself as an American story of hierarchy and inequality, including the race exploitation practiced by the American aristocracy. The Washington estate echoes the hierarchal structure of the antebellum plantation. Braddock's father came west from Virginia with "two dozen of the most faithful blacks, who, of course, worshipped him" (11), "darkies who never realized that slavery was abolished" because "he read them a proclamation that he had composed which announced" (12) that the South had defeated the North in the Civil War. Thus the black attendants who serve Percy and their hosts think they are slaves, and are treated as such. Their dehumanization in the eyes of the Washingtons is expressed by Kismine when pilots suddenly arrive and bomb the estate, including the "slave quarters" (16): "'There go fifty-thousand dollars' worth of slaves ... at prewar prices. So few Americans have any respect for property'" (28). Fitzgerald thus also locates slavery as the foundation of American wealth: the slaves do the manual labor of digging into the mountain for fragments of the diamond; the slaves translate the diamonds into the daily comforts enjoyed by the Washington family. In turn, the slaves are completely dependent on the Washingtons; isolated from the rest of the world, they speak to each other in an "extreme form of the Southern negro's dialect" (5), not unlike plantation slaves during slavery.

Fitgerald's dynastic American monopolist is so arrogant that he considers his only equal to be God himself. When the estate comes under attack from airborne bomber pilots, John observes an odd interchange. "The white man [Washington] addresses the heavens: 'You out there' ... there was something in the man's whole attitude antithetical to prayer" (31), for prayer suggests the subservience of an inferior. Braddock considers himself God's equal and so he offers "a bribe to God!" (31). "God was made in man's image.... He must have His price" (32). To John, Washington looks "like a prophet of old—magnificently mad" (32). Fitzgerald thus captures the megalomania of a class that would justify the sacrifice of other Americans to ensure their own happiness. In true Gothic tradition, the grand estate, representing the consolidated wealth and power of the tyrant, is destroyed at the conclusion of the text. The Washington estate comes under fire from "aeroplanes" manned by middle class aviators who have been alerted by an escaped prisoner. Fitzgerald ironically uses modern technology, the tool of the robber barons themselves, to undo their cohorts. Moreover, the dynasty of the Washingtons is also undone by the selfishness of the family. In one last greedy act, Washington blows up the mountain so that its spoils cannot be possessed by the pilots: "the chateau threw itself into the air, bursting into flaming fragments" (34)—a preview, perhaps, of the destruction of wealth during the impending Depression. The dark dynasty that was housed by the estate is also destroyed: "the dark glittering reign of the Washingtons would be over" (29). Only the two daughters, irrelevant to the patriarchy, survive as newly reduced members of the "middle class" (34). The rest of the dynastic patriarchy—father, son, and nearly-invisible mother—along with their human property, is destroyed. John witnesses the end of the dynasty as slaves and master are entombed within the ruins of wealth and power:

> a broken, white-haired man ... followed by two gigantic and emotionless Negroes who carried a burden between them which still flashed and glittered in the sun ... two other figures joined them.... Mrs. Washington and her son ... the negroes stooped and pulled up what appeared to be a trap-door in the side of the mountain [that is itself the eponymous diamond].... Into this they all disappeared.... Before their eyes the whole surface of the mountain had changed suddenly to a dazzling burning yellow ... the intolerable glow ... disappeared, revealing a black waste from which blue smoke arose slowly, carrying off with it what remained of vegetation and of human flesh [33].

In Fitzgerald's version of the destruction of the dynasty, the interment of slave and master within the actual wealth itself, we hear echoes of patriarchal destruction beginning with the spectacular conclusion of Horace Walpole's *Castle of Otranto* (1764), although the Washington mountain is destroyed because it is "wired" and not because of supernatural intervention. At the same time, we are reminded of the American revisions of this trope, in response to the realities of slavery: the actual immurement of the body. Fitzgerald thus gestures to the continuation of slavery in his time through the Jim Crow laws, and the sharecropper system. He aligns the predations of the robber barons with those of the slaveholders, and traces the never-ending expansion of the great American hunger.

At a time when America was returning to the old hierarchal social and economic forms of Europe, when the evil patriarch was re-emerging as an American force, Fitzgerald returns to the English Gothic novel, which is driven by the fear of the tyrant, and the fantasy of his destruction. Fitzgerald restores the patriarch to American literature, as he resurfaces into American public life. Like his precursors, Fitzgerald turns to the Gothic text to peel away the rich patina of the patriarchy, revealing the horror at the root of a seemingly polite and beautiful society.

William Faulkner's Absalom, Absalom! *The Rise and Fall of the Dynastic Patriarchy*

William Faulkner's *Absalom, Absalom!* (1936), written a decade later than Fitzgerald's "Diamond," at the height of the Depression, also draws upon the tropes of the English Gothic to explore the returning American patriarchal dynasties. As Ian Watt observes, "In Faulkner's *Absalom, Absalom!* ... the central pattern is very clear" (169). Faulkner's text, haunted by the ghosts of its cultural past, continues the Gothic focus upon dynastic possession and transmission of property. As with Fitzgerald's American Gothic text, Faulkner's return to English forms amplifies distinctly American anxieties. *Absalom* is thus doubly haunted by its literary precursors: the ghosts of the American literary past, as well as the ghosts of the suppressed English tradition. Haunting texts such at Walpole's *Otranto* and Nathaniel Hawthorne's *House of the Seven Gables*[3] loom beneath the surface of Faulkner's text that is inscribed as a palimpsest over its precursors. The presence of these haunting texts illustrates the challenge of modernism: to bear the burden of cultural history while also following Ezra Pound's dictum to "make it new."

Anxieties of textual authority and narrative possession inform Faulkner's novel as the text interrogates problems of inheritance of myth, as well as inheritance of land. The story of Thomas Sutpen is told through a densely ambiguous web of narratives: Rosa Coldfield's spoken and written narrative to Quentin; the letters of Quentin's father; Quentin's narrative to Shreve; Shreve's reconstruction of the narrative that he tells back to Quentin. The result is a labyrinthine narrative structure, much like that of the conventional Gothic novel: circular and repetitious, leading not to meaning but to confusion. Faulkner sets up a variety of narrators and auditors who narrate and comment upon the numerous events in the novel. Each narrator and auditor must recreate and re-imagine the narrative; together they (and the reader) work to reconstruct the fragmented history of the Sutpen dynasty. In typical Gothic form, this modernist narrative is ultimately revealed to be beyond the possession and apprehension of any single narrator, and resistant to hermeneutic containment on the part of the reader. The dispossession of the narrative is highlighted by the conclusion of the novel: the story, like the property, is left in the hands of a non–American outsider, Shreve McCannon, the Canadian roommate of Quentin Compson. This tale of the American South is thus completely dispossessed: dislodged from its Southern origins; narrated in the frigid and alien North; its last proprietor, a Canadian, a cultural and political ally of the English, whose possession of the American story is so strenuously opposed by the American text.

Faulkner's fragmented and confusing modernist locution also links his text to his Gothic precursors. The famously circuitous style and structure of the novel, usually associated with modernist poetics, certainly owes a debt to the labyrinthine and fragmented conventions of Gothic writing, as does the modernist interest of Faulkner's narrative in the question of inheritance of story and of myth.[4] Indeed, Faulkner's use of tropes inherited from the

English Gothic in his modernist American text reveals a number of surprising affinities between Gothic literature and the modernist tradition: both seek to repress the past and to create a new tradition free of haunting precursors; both reveal a sense of belatedness and nostalgia for an idealized past, a common yearning for deep essential meanings, a solipsistic search for these meanings, and a skepticism that such meanings can be achieved and conveyed through textual narration. Richard C. Moreland gestures to the connection between modernism and the American Gothic mode in his essay on "Faulkner and Modernism," arguing that Faulkner's modernist phase, which includes *Absalom, Absalom!*, draws on two dimensions of modernism: the urge of the writer to escape the contaminating practices of the world that he has inherited, and the awareness that the refused historical world always returns, however repressed. This troubling awareness, as we have seen, also haunts the Gothic text. Thus the structure of Faulkner's indeterminate narrative is informed by the indeterminacy of the Gothic tradition as well as it is by modernist principles.[5]

Thomas Sutpen, the villain of Faulkner's novel, uncannily reflects the dark, dynastic, and demonic patriarch who wreaks havoc in the Gothic novel, beginning with Walpole's monomaniacal Manfred, and continuing with Hawthorne's Judge Pyncheon,[6] and Fitzgerald's Braddock Washington. Rosa, Sutpen's sister-in-law, with whom he desperately seeks to perpetuate his line in an act of quasi-incest reminiscent of Manfred's, calls him a "'demon'" (4), a "'devil'" (107), "'an ogre, some beast out of a tale'" (128). Shreve McCannon (the Canadian outsider who hears the story of Sutpen from Quentin Compson, a fellow student from Sutpen's part of Mississippi) also considers Sutpen a "'Faustus, this demon, this Beelzebub'" (145). Sutpen is certainly the typically demonic husband and father of the English Gothic; to promote his dynastic "design," his plan for "money, a house, a plantation, slaves, a family—incidentally of course, a wife," he abandons his first wife and child because in words that recall Manfred's purpose in trying to abandon his first wife and daughter, "'it [was] impossible that this woman and child be incorporated in my design'" (*Absalom* 212). Sutpen echoes Manfred's strategy: he means to use the body of his second wife to perpetuate his dynasty; in Shreve's words "'breed him two children'" (145) whose lives he destroys.

The core of Sutpen's villainy is that of the tyrannical Gothic patriarch: the obsessive struggle to preserve and transmit his suspiciously acquired property. As in the case of Manfred, the Pyncheons and the Washingtons, Sutpen's obsessive attempts to engender a dynastic line fail; his patriarchal line falters. Sutpen's son Henry becomes a fugitive after killing Charles Bon; Rosa spurns Sutpen's overtures to revive his line with her; the child he engenders with the descendant of a squatter on his property is killed by the squatter, who also kills Sutpen. In accordance with Gothic convention, the depletion of the Sutpen line is accompanied by the destruction of the Sutpen property. The fate of Sutpen's property and dynasty reflect the Gothic paradigm as modified by the contingencies of history: after succumbing to ruin and decay during the Civil War, Sutpen's house is finally burned down in 1909. Clytie, Sutpen's dispossessed daughter, also illustrates the Gothic influence: like Bertha Rochester (of *Jane Eyre*), she burns down the house of her oppressor. Quentin imagines her: "'the tragic gnome's face ... against a red background of fire, seen for a moment between two swirls of smoke'" (300). Yet the description of Sutpen's property focuses upon the American surface of Faulkner's palimpsest, and works to obscure the English and Anglicized-American texts that lurk beneath. Unlike the Pyncheon house, Sutpen's mansion does not reflect the typical structure of the English Gothic. The "dream of grim and castlelike magnificence at which Sutpen obviously aimed" (29) is denied by the French architect: "the little grim harried foreigner had singlehanded given battle to and vanquished Sutpen's fierce and overweening vanity..." (29). Sutpen's dream of an aristocratic castle is denied as Faulkner re-locates the American sublime to the American countryside. Like Hawthorne's Maine wilderness and Brown's Pennsylvania wilderness, the vast Sutpen's Hundred is the new American version of the darkly mysterious, dangerous and ultimately unpossessible Gothic property. In addition to revealing its literary antecedents, Faulkner's text, like its Gothic forebears, responds to the historical and economic contexts of its time and place. In noting the preoccupation of Sutpen and his text with the transmission of property, Norman Rudich argues that Faulkner's concept of "the sin of property" derives from his historical moment: "Faulkner discovers the artistic significance of this theme in the 1930's when the Great Depression at home and the spread of socialist ideas both here and abroad reveal that the institution of private property is facing a critical historical challenge" ("Faulkner and the Sin of Private Property" 56).

The closure of *Absalom* moves Faulkner's text further from the haunting influence of the English Gothic text toward the haunted American canon. In the conventional Gothic dénouement, the destruction of the contested property, and the failure of the dynastic line are ameliorated by the inexorable movement of the narrative toward a conciliatory marriage. The Gothic closure turns to the time-honored mechanism of the aristocracy—the union through marriage of the two competing families. Through this conservative alternative to revolution, the usurped property is returned to its rightful aristocratic heir without violence. Thus in *Otranto*, Theodore, the heir to the dispossessed

Alfonso, marries Isabella, who had been the apparent (competing) heiress. At the conclusion of Hawthorne's *Seven Gables*, Holgrave, the descendant of the poor landowner, consolidates his inheritance by marrying Phoebe, the heiress of the usurping Pyncheons. In these narratives the marriage of the authentic heir to the heiress of a competing line works to consolidate the restoration of the property, promising a stability that will endure beyond the closing frame of the text. Faulkner, however, denies the possibility of regeneration and unification through marriage; his narrative disrupts the conventional pattern in presenting an unending series of interrupted weddings and marriages, beginning with the first (that is, by the chronology of the events) interrupted union, the marriage that is disrupted when Sutpen casts off his first wife and son, Charles Bon, in response to the discovery that "'she was not and could never be, through no fault of her own, adjunctive or incremental to the design which I have in mind'" (194)—the design Sutpen means is for a racially white American dynasty. Charles Bon, acting as his father does, abandons his marriage to a woman "with a face like a tragic magnolia" (91) and deserts her child. The proposed marriage between Rosa and Sutpen is canceled when Sutpen suggests that they determine whether they can produce a son together before actually marrying, eliminating any doubts about his motives. In fact, the central event of the novel, the murder of Charles Bon as he returns to marry Judith, Sutpen's daughter by his second wife, is Faulkner's reworking of the motif of the interrupted wedding. This wedding presents the possibility of the conventional Gothic resolution within Faulkner's text. The potential marriage would perpetuate the line of Sutpen's dynasty, resolving the conflict between the two competing Sutpen lines generated by his two wives. The marriage would work to legitimate and consolidate the position of the secret heir, the first-born Charles Bon, as marriage does for Theodore and Holgrave, the secret heirs in *Otranto* and *House*. This possibility is promoted further by the repudiation of "'home and birthright'" (84) by Henry, Sutpen's acknowledged son. Yet this wedding too is interrupted, by Sutpen's prohibition and finally by the murder of Charles Bon by Henry, Judith's brother.

As Faulkner's narrative moves toward its climax, a number of possible reasons for the objection of father and son to the match are raised; each of these objections is typical of the barriers to marriage that arise in the Gothic narrative, and each is discounted as an obstacle to the match. The apparent problem of bigamy, Charles Bon's previous marriage to "the octoroon" (246), is clearly not problematic for Sutpen; Charles Bon's bigamous second marriage would simply be a re-enactment of his own. Nor is this evidently a problem for Henry; in the final retelling of Quentin and Shreve, Henry's visit to Bon's first wife makes little impression on him. The incestuous nature of a marriage between Bon and his half-sister, Judith, is also dismissed as an obstacle to the marriage.[7] Henry explicitly accepts the incestuous nature of his sister's future marriage to Charles Bon; citing the aristocratic precedent of "'kings and dukes'" (273) and invoking the aristocratic model for his American dynastic family, Henry is prepared to embrace his brother as his sister's husband.

There is, in fact, only one insurmountable obstacle to the marriage of Judith and Bon, a particularly American obstacle that distinguishes the unsettled end of *Absalom* by disallowing the conventional consolidating marriage. The obstacle to marriage that neither Sutpen nor Henry, his son, can accept is the fact, revealed by Sutpen to Henry, that "'it was not until after he [Charles Bon] was born that I found out that his mother was part Negro'" (283). As Charles Bon says to Henry, "'it's the miscegenation, not the incest, which you cant bear'" (285). And it is the fear of miscegenation that leads Henry to shoot the brother he loves, thereby interrupting the wedding of his sister, as it has caused Sutpen to abandon his first wife and son. In fact, the final failure of Sutpen's dynasty is based on his failure to reconsider the essential whiteness of his "design," the racial imperative by which Sutpen tries to define his legacy. Clytie, cast off because her mother is a black slave although she bears the "Sutpen face" (22), definitively ends the white line of the Sutpen dynasty. In burning down Sutpen's house, she kills Henry, who is hiding in the house. It is, then, the Sutpen refusal to accept black lineage into the family, a refusal transmitted by Thomas Sutpen to his son, Henry, which prevents the enactment of the marriage that would serve the conventional role of providing stability to the family and conservative closure to the narrative. Because the American tyrant Sutpen cannot modify the racism of his "design," the destruction of his property and depletion of his dynasty cannot be reversed.

The failure of Sutpen's patriarchal dynasty, the empire that is "built on the backs of his slaves" (145) after he appropriates the land for his vast estate from "a poor ignorant Indian" (145), marks the departure of *Absalom* from the English Gothic tradition. In his American Gothic text, Faulkner modifies the representation of the conventional Gothic villain, redefining his evil greed as racist exclusivity. Faulkner thus transforms and Americanizes the Gothic portrayal of the degenerate dynast, who traditionally emblematizes the decay and failure of aristocratic ideology. The problem with Sutpen's line is not aristocratic overbreeding, but the infusion of African blood or, to be more precise, the rigid inability to absorb this infusion. Sutpen's failure to redefine his dynastic imperative and his attempt to repress the presence of the racial blackness that is part of the American reality ultimately leads to the downfall of his dynasty. Ironically, the only line of Sutpen's dynasty that does endure, albeit in a degenerate and dying form, is that which he attempts to deny. At the conclusion of the novel, the last remaining Sutpen heir is Jim Bond—the defective and black (son of a black mother) descendant of Charles Bon—whom Quentin describes ironically as "'the scion, the heir, the apparent'" (296). Shreve, the Canadian outsider who is able to respond to Quentin's story without the constraints and biases of American expectations, foresees the end of all racist hierarchies and dynasties: "'in time the Jim Bonds are going to conquer the western hemisphere ... and so in a few thousand years, I who regard you will also have sprung from the loins of African kings'" (302). Although Shreve cannot bring himself to imagine the end of all hierarchy, dynasty, or patriarchy, he allows the narrative to end with the vision that Sutpen attempts to repress: the vision of racial synthesis, of the erasure of the racial distinctions that are the dark legacy of American slavery.

Sutpen is thus an American villain because he is a racist. The narrative of Faulkner's Gothic constructs racism as the supreme evil that incapacitates the conventional closure of the Gothic, and subverts the Gothic capacity to fantasize an end to boundaries and barriers. In revealing racism as the core of evil, Faulkner gestures toward the racial anxieties that lurk beneath the surface of many Gothic texts, English and American. The physically dark villains of the English Gothic, the Italians and the Spanish, allow these anxieties to appear, as they do in the American texts discussed previously. But in those earlier texts, racial anxieties are repressed, veiled in evocative metaphor.[8] In creating a villain who attempts to construct his evil dynasty in explicitly racial or racist terms, Faulkner revises the conventional representation of evil to encompass racism, an American reality that is far more frightening and dangerous than the imagined horrors of the supernatural.

Shirley Jackson's Hill House: *The Haunting Power of Patriarchal Property*

As argued and evidenced by Ruth Franklin's biography, *Shirley Jackson: A Rather Haunted Life* (2016), the long-repressed literary reputation of Shirley Jackson is being deservedly resurrected. Seen through the lens of twenty-first-century feminism, Jackson's Gothic narratives of post–World War II femininity play a meaningful role in American literature of the second half of the twentieth century, as they trace a new stage in the re-emergence of the American patriarch and patriarchy. In America, the decade after World War II saw major reactionary change in the balance of power between men and women. Because of demand for labor during the war, women had been liberated from the imperatives of domesticity, becoming, like the iconic "Rosie the Riveter," mainstays of the home front. Upon the return of the men from war, women, no longer necessary to the economy, found themselves again delegated to the domestic sphere, performing monotonous, often meaningless, unpaid labor. Isolated from the centers of economic and intellectual life in the newly proliferating suburban tracts, possessed of higher levels of education and more leisure time (due to new domestic technologies) than their mothers, American women of the fifties found themselves experiencing the angst Betty Friedan identified in *The Feminine Mystique* (1963). While home ownership was the goal of the middle class woman, for many the home became a prison. While the young husbands returning from a brutal war were not necessarily the evil patriarchs of the past, their return presaged the re-imposition of the archaic values that constrained female behavior. Shirley Jackson presents this dilemma in Gothicized form in a number of her works, including the terrifying *The Haunting of Hill House* (1959).

In this novel, Jackson makes it clear that the quasi-patriarchs of the second half of the twentieth-century America were not exemplars of evil power, as were their earlier counterparts. The most extreme model of raw (though ridiculous) masculinity in *Hill House* is Arthur. A schoolmaster whose exaggerated masculinity is a source of humorous contempt rather than fear, he arrives to experience the haunted house carrying his "'golf clubs, just in case'" (181). He also brings a second phallic marker of the patriarch manqué: a "'revolver'" to "'patrol the house'" (195). Arthur ambiguously talks about serving as a model of masculinity for "'the fellows at the school [who] look up to one a bit, you know'" (184), and also explains his imposition of heteronormative masculinity upon the occasional "'bad hat [with] no taste in sports ... [Arthur] knock[s] *that* out of them fast enough'" (185). Further expanding upon his pedagogical strengths as a model of masculinity, he tells his fellow diners: "'No fancy sauces for *me* ... tell my fellows it's the mark of a cad.... Fancy sauces, women waiting on you. *My* fellows wait on themselves. Mark of a man'" (217). When asked how many "fellows" are in his school, he provides the tally "'not counting milksops'" (217). Arthur may be an ogre, but he is also a clown. Another failed contender for the status of patriarch is Luke Sanderson, the heir to the Sanderson family, descendants of the servant who possibly usurped the property from the family of the original owner. Luke is introduced to the reader as a "liar" and a "thief" (9). But he is only a young scoundrel, neither villain nor patriarch. The head of the diverse household, John Montague, a "doctor of philosophy" (4), who has brought together the various characters to study their reactions to the hauntings of Hill House, leads his group in a nonthreatening, nonpatriarchal manner. A clear-headed "man of science" (5), he takes a rational approach to the supernatural; he is interested in "the analysis of supernatural manifestations" (4) and is both "knowledgeable and stubborn" (60). A number of aspects of the professor disqualify him from full-blown patriarchy: he is a kind and benign "little man" (60), with a domineering and ridiculous wife, who herself is less curious scientist than avid fan of Gothic literature. Indeed, based on her vast experience of reading bad literature (yet another reader led astray by the Gothic), Mrs. Montague is convinced that she has received ghostly messages from a nun walled up alive, unlikely in an American mansion, yet making much sense to her since "'the figure of a nun is fairly common ... do you suppose that a nun would deliberately *pretend* to have been walled up alive when she was not?'" (188–189). Dr. Montague is also perhaps influenced by his reading; during the course of the novel, he reads *Pamela* and plans to move on to *Clarissa*. Both novels by the eighteenth-century novelist Samuel Richardson are appropriately about young woman endangered, not by ghosts, but by the patriarchy.

Thus Jackson's novel lacks any truly dangerous patriarchal figure to threaten its female characters. Nor are most of the women in the novel likely to succumb to danger. In addition to the liberated Mrs. Montague, Theodora also rejects all attempts at social control. Theodora is the eager and voracious young American who recurs in the American novel, this time in the guise of a strong, non-feminine young woman. On the first morning at Hill House she pounds on Eleanor's door, announcing, "'I'll starve to death'" (95). Theodora's upbringing has trained her to resist social and patriarchal control. She grew up on her own, at boarding schools, to which she was consigned even "during vacations" (45). Theodora is sexually ambiguous, signing her name as "'Theo'" (8), apparently emerging from a lover's argument with her female roommate, to whom she returns at the conclusion of the experiment at Hill House. When asked if she is married, "there was a little silence, and then Theodora laughed quickly and said, 'No'" (88). Theo rejects any gendered compartmentalization; she flirts with Eleanor, calling her "'my Nell'" (137), but she also sustains a flirtation with Luke. Theo, a rebellious woman, rejects the vestigial haunting of the patriarchy. She fights for her right to an identity, a profession, ownership of her space and body: she has her own "apartment" and "shop" (8). The narrator informs us that "duty and conscience were, for Theodora, attributes which belonged properly to Girl Scouts" (8). Duty and conscience ultimately destroy Eleanor Vance, the point of view character, who insistently follows the female imperative. She had a benevolent father who died when she was a child, bringing sudden grief to Eleanor, who "could not remember a winter before her father's death on a cold wet day" (15). Yet Eleanor is destabilized, not by any individual male, but by a social system that still bears the vestiges of gender inequity and patriarchy. After the death of her mother, she loses the space that was both sanctuary and prison; at the beginning of the novel, she is literally homeless and infantilized. As she confesses to the others at the novel's end, "'I haven't any apartment.... I sleep on a cot at my sister's, in the baby's room.... I haven't any home'" (239). At thirty-two, Eleanor is still a child, destroyed by a lifetime of fulfilling the feminine ideal: devoting herself to the care of her demanding invalid mother. The influence of a more rigid patriarchal past—not very far removed from Jackson's 1950s—is evident in Eleanor's relationship with her family. Before her sister and brother-in-law give her the shockingly necessary permission to accept Dr. Montague's invitation to Hill House, they need "to make sure that this doctor fellow was not aiming to introduce Eleanor to savage rites not unconnected with matters Eleanor's sister deemed it improper for an unmarried young woman to know" (8). This unmarried "young" woman is thus still subject to the Victorian patriarchal imperative of propriety for women. To her, it is "daring" to include "two pairs of slacks" (41) when she packs for the visit. Even without the presence of a Victorian patriarch, Eleanor is haunted by the still-current, though archaic messages, from those times.

As a consequence, Eleanor arrives at Hill House lacking a stable adult identity. When the little group comes together for the first time, they play an identity game to get to know each other. As Eleanor announces "'I *am* Eleanor,'" Theo "soberly" explains: "'Therefore *you* are wearing the red sweater'" (61). The circular and flimsy logic at play destabilizes Eleanor's certainty about her identity, as indicated by her own identity shifts during the game. At one point, in spite of herself, Eleanor blurts out: "'I love my love with a B'" (61), resulting in more playful comments about shifting identity. Eleanor herself partakes of this slippage, declaring her fantasy identity: "'my affairs are the talk of the cafés'" (62). Later in the novel, as the cohesiveness of the group, and of Eleanor's mind, begins to unravel, they return to this game, which has now become more spiteful and destabilizing. Theodora announces: "'I am Eleanor ... because I have a beard.... I am Eleanor ... because I am wearing blue'" (222–3). Eleanor herself expresses her lack of a stable identity: "'I *hate* seeing myself dissolve and slip and separate'" (160). Mrs. Montague also seems to sense Eleanor's personal fragmentation; when she has one of her "'little session[s] with planchette'" (186), "a device similar to a Ouija Board ... a form of automatic writing" (187), planchette refers to "'Eleanor Nellie Nell'" (192). Planchette thus articulates Eleanor's fragmented identity, her hopeless feelings—"'Lost. Lost. Lost'"—and her deepest desire:

"'Want to be home'" (192). Eleanor's mental fragility, the destabilization of her identity by patriarchal imperatives, makes her vulnerable to the dangers of the old ways, whose values continue to haunt Hill House; she is, thus, representative of the haunted docile woman of the 1950s.

Hill House clearly emblematizes the old patriarchal order. When Theodora, free from the conventional social restrictions, first sees the house, she says, "'It's altogether Victorian'" (50). Perhaps influenced by her own reading, or by her intuition, Theodora also knows what should be done with a house like this: "'what fun it would be to stand out there and watch it burn down'" (45). She senses that the house represents all that she works to resist. Jackson emphasizes the patriarchal past of the house in the brief history Dr. Montague provides. The house was "'Built eighty-odd years ago'" (75), which locates its construction at around 1870, the time of the robber barons. It was built by a wealthy patriarch, Hugh Crain, as a country home, "'where he hoped to see his children and grandchildren live in comfortable luxury'" (75). A little vignette later in the novel gives us a sense of Crain's parenting style; Luke finds a grotesque book in the library, made by Crain for the edification of his daughters. Crain created the book by deploying a standard patriarchal strategy. He appropriates the work of others: "'He has clearly cut up a number of fine old books to make the scrapbook'" (168). The book contains a number of horrifying images, guaranteed to frighten Crain's two little girls into the submission of Victorian childhood and womanhood. The professor notes, "'a Goya etching; a horrible thing for a little girl to meditate upon'" (168). The book is signed in "'Hugh Crain's blood'" (170). Crain ensures that his daughters will be haunted by his little book, and its oppressive message for the rest of their lives.

In Dr. Montague's telling, Crain's wives fare no better in the beautiful patriarchal house. Crain's "'high hopes for a dynasty'" (77)—the dream of every dark patriarch—are thwarted when his first "'young wife died minutes before she set eyes on the house,'" in a carriage accident "'in the driveway,'" leaving Crain with two daughters, of little dynastic use, as we know. Dr. Montague adds that although Crain married a total of three times, "'He seems to have been—unlucky in his wives. The second Mrs. Crain died of a fall, although I have been unable to ascertain how or why.... The third Mrs. Crain died of what they used to call consumption, somewhere in Europe'" (76). The pattern and the hesitation in the doctor's speech allow us to wonder if Crain was unlucky or malign. The death of each wife could easily been plotted by Crain, who could have caused the carriage accident, pushed his second wife, and spirited this third wife away to dispense with her. In any event, Crain died soon after his third wife, leaving only the two daughters. This unpromising dynasty rapidly declined. The older unmarried sister, "'who resembled her father strongly ... she genuinely loved Hill House,'" came to live in the house and "'she eventually took a girl from the village to live with her, as a kind of companion'" (77). In typical Gothic fashion, there is a struggle over property; the two sisters fight over their father's possessions. After the older sister dies, the companion insists "'that the house was left to her'" (79)—following in the tradition of the usurping Gothic servant. Montague continues: "'The companion won her case at last'" (79), and the younger sister and her husband were dispossessed; "'The villagers believed ... that the younger sister was defrauded of her inheritance by the scheming young woman'" (80), the servant. This house is not kind to women: the companion ultimately commits suicide, prefiguring the later suicide of Eleanor. The companion is "'maddened by the conviction that locks and bolts could not keep out the enemy who stole into her house at night'" (81). The companion's relatives, the "'Sandersons spent a few days in the house ... and then abruptly cleared out'" (82), and the house remained abandoned for almost one hundred years. Hence the old abandoned house of the English Gothic, relocated to American literature.

Dr. Montague's embedded narrative of Hugh Crain and his legacy solidifies the dynastic, patriarchal, and Gothic identity of the house. The three dead wives, possibly murdered by their patriarchal husband, the autocratic and unloving father, the absence of a male heir, the declining dynasty, disputed property, the decay of the property, the suicide and madness—all align with the conventions established in the English Gothic, to critique the depredations of the English aristocrat. Jackson establishes that Hill House is haunted by the traditions of the archaic dynastic, aristocratic, and malign, patriarch. Our first sight of the house establishes its character: "No human eye can isolate the unhappy coincidence of line and place which suggests evil in the face of a house" (34). The malign gaze of the house reminds us of the exterior of Poe's House of Usher; Jackson describes the "watchfulness from the blank windows" (34). As she first approaches it, Eleanor sees a house "without kindness, never meant to be lived in, not a fit place for people or for love or for hope" (35); she tries unsuccessfully to identify the "badness" (35) of the house. In fact, this haunted house perpetuates the dangers of the patriarchy even in the absence of the patriarch. As Dr. Montague notes, Hill House explicitly reflects the mind of its builder: "every angle is slightly wrong. Hugh Crain must have detested other people and their sensible squared-away houses, because he made his house to suit his mind'" (105).[9] It is the malign house itself that is the source of danger—only fleeting, unthreatening, supernatural phenomena appear: a little ghostly creature that leads the two men of the party out of the house, leaving the women alone; an uncanny ghost "picnic party" that appears to Eleanor and Theodora. They vividly hear "the laughter of the children" and "the affectionate amused voices of the mother and father" (176). But this ghostly domestic group does nothing to harm the two young women. In fact, rather than seeming to be of the house, this happy family appears to be the spirit of domestic happiness that has been exiled from the house. The house itself induces the more spectacular threats: manifestations such as disembodied banging and crashing on the doors; a "sickening, degrading" cold that invades the body with "icy little curls of fingers" (130). At one terrifying moment, "the house shivered and shook ... and the floor shook under their feet" (203); the room seems to fall away and then "right itself" (203). As Eleanor is cast out of the house it watches "arrogant and patient" (243).

As Theodora correctly points out, "'It [the house] never hurt *us*'" (200)—just frightened the inhabitants out of their wits—a metaphor literalized by Eleanor's fate. The house never hurts Dr. Montague, or Luke, or Theodora, but it does gradually destroy Eleanor, the least stable and most normatively passive female of the group, the most susceptible to patriarchal influence. She experiences events that might be her own hallucinations: she hears her mother calling her name, and spends one terrifying night holding Theodora's hand for comfort, only to awake to Theodora's denial of the experience. Eleanor, aghast, questions: "'whose hand was I holding?'" (163). This could have been a dream, and it is also possible that Eleanor, losing her sanity, creates the manifestations she experiences: the red blood that is poured over all of Theo's clothes; the "red letters" on the wall over Theo's bed reading, "Help Eleanor Come Home Eleanor" (155). Jackson is ambiguous about whether Hill House or Eleanor causes these frightening phenomena. Eleanor has motivations for hostility toward Theo: Theo's relationship with Luke; Theo's refusal to take Eleanor into her home when the summer ends. Theo has already expressed suspicion regarding Eleanor after an earlier writing episode: "She looked at Eleanor with a bright smile. 'Maybe you wrote it yourself'" (145). Indeed, Eleanor might be the source as she is reduced to a ghostly state by the patriarchal powers that linger in the house. On her last night, reduced to the ghostliness of the suppressed woman, she haunts the house, wandering through the empty darkness. On this night, the house is welcoming; it is "drowsily, luxuriously warm" (228), because on this night Eleanor has become the proper woman of the patriarchal order, infantilized and ghostly. She wanders downstairs but remembers that she is not "allowed" (228) in the library, having childishly internalized the patriarchal rules of the house. She wanders upstairs to the nursery in search of her mother. In fact, Mrs. Montague believes that Eleanor is a ghost, and comically calls to Eleanor through her closed door: "'I am your friend; I intend you no harm. Come in and tell me what is troubling you'" (229). When the entire household wakes, Eleanor's ghostly figure evades them, darting "into the drawing room; 'Hugh Crain,' she said, 'will you come and dance with me?'" (231). Eleanor's descent into madness is thus accompanied by her complete submission to the patriarchy. She dances in front of the "huge leaning statue" (231) of Crain. The night culminates with Eleanor climbing the phallic tower, where the "companion" had long ago hanged herself; "time is ended now" (232). She is rescued by Luke, the heir of the house, who is driven by the madness of the moment to become quite patriarchal himself: "'Perhaps I will just push you over the ledge…. Let you smash down there on the floor'" (235). Within her madness, suicide poses salvation for Eleanor; death will allow her to stay forever in what she has come to believe is her only home: "the only house I ever knew where you don't have to worry about making noise at night" (227), a great asset in the home of a ghost. As she climbs the stairs of the tower she thinks, "I have broken the spell of Hill House and somehow come inside. I am home" (232). But Hill House, the misogynous home of the patriarch, offers false sanctuary. Even though she insists that "'the house wants me to stay'" (240), the doctor and the others insist that she must leave, find her way "'home'" (240). They mean to preserve her sanity and safety, despite her insistence that she has no home. In her car as her exile begins, Eleanor continues to resist her return to the world of the fifties, where patriarchy is beginning to be challenged: "Hill House belongs to *me*" (245), and clearly she is possessed by Hill House. Ultimately, Eleanor is more willing to "relinquish my possession of this self of mine" (204) than to relinquish her (soon to be ghostly) possession of the house. She turns the wheel "to send the car directly at the great tree at the curve of the driveway" (245), thus becoming part of the fabric of Hill House: at least the second woman to die by her own hand, and the second woman to die in a driving accident. Docile Eleanor belongs in and to Hill House.

Ultimately Dr. Montague, the scholarly man of science, gets it right. He says: "'Essentially the evil is the house itself…. It has enchained and destroyed its people and their lives. It is a place of contained ill will'" (82). Jackson leaves the reader with one final statement about the nature of the house. After Eleanor dies and the others leave, we read in the final paragraph: "Hill House, itself, not sane stood against its hills, holding darkness within; it had stood so for eighty years and might stand for eighty more. Within, its walls continued upright, bricks met neatly, floors were firm, and doors were sensibly shut; silence lay steadily against the wood and stone of Hill House, and whatever walked there, walked alone" (246). These words echo almost exactly the words in the opening paragraph of the novel. (The exception: in the first paragraph "its walls" reads simply "walls"; this might have significance, but might also be an editing oversight.) By the second iteration, we know that what walks alone in Hill House, what engenders its malignancy, is the spirit of the solitary malign patriarch, still-established, and capable of exuding dangerous influence well into the twentieth century.[10]

Morrison's A Mercy: *Revisiting History, Revising the Patriarchy*

Toni Morrison's novel *A Mercy* (2009) also presents a late re-examination of the archaic figure of the patriarch and his malign influence. Looking back at the seventeenth century from the twenty-first, Morrison argues that the system of patriarchy—ebbing and flowing according to the times—lies at the root of American evil as much as does the "original sin" of slavery. The novel begins with a mysterious voice addressing an unspecified audience: "'Don't be afraid. My telling can't hurt you in spite of what I have done and I promise to lie quietly in the dark—weeping perhaps or occasionally seeing the blood once more'" (3). The reader does not yet know the identity of the "I" or of the "you"; the situation of the telling will not become clear until the conclusion of the narrative. However, by the first lines of the novel the reader can be certain that Morrison's narrative is set in the paradoxically familiar and mysterious world of the Gothic: the world in which mystery is as expected as darkness, blood, chaos, and confused identity.[11]

As the mists of the text clear, we discover that "I," who tells the central narrative is Florens, a young African American slave living in late seventeenth-century America. The letter is addressed to one of the powerful and cruel patriarchs of the novel, the blacksmith, a free black man whom Florens has loved, and whom she possibly has murdered; thus her first comforting words to him. Florens had been sent by her mistress to find the unnamed blacksmith so that he could cure the mistress of smallpox. Florens willingly takes this assignment, even though it means encountering the dangers of the early American woods, because she is eager to join the free African blacksmith whom she passionately loves. The central action of the novel thus suggests an exciting twenty-first-century revision of the epic journey of discovery, adventure and romance, or a *bildungsroman,* tracing Florens' development from abandoned girl to self-possessed women—undergoing the blossoming suggested by her name. However, *A Mercy* ultimately collapses back into the dark, antique Gothic, as Florens' journey leads back to her own dark and despairing past, and to the dual inherited curses: slavery for blacks; patriarchy for women; and for black women, both.

Each stage of Florens' journey, the various stations of her failed pilgrim's progress, is an imprisoning Gothic space. Her childhood home, Jublio plantation, is a Gothic home in the tradition of Simon Legree's slave plantation in Harriet Beecher Stowe's *Uncle Tom's Cabin*. Jublio is located in Catholic Maryland, a dangerous place from the perspective of Jacob Vaark ("Master"), a trader from the North: "The palatinate was Romish to the core. Priests strode openly in its towns; their temples menaced its squares; their sinister missions cropped up at the edge of native villages" (13). Morrison thus aligns the sensibility of her American Gothic text with the anti–Catholic discourse of the English Gothic. Horace Walpole, Ann Radcliffe and others expressed their irrational English Protestant fear of Catholics by creating Catholic villains lurking in monasteries and convents. Fittingly, the master of Jublio is Catholic, and Jacob is appalled by "the graven images" that fill his house. Yet, far more shocking, is D'Ortega's ownership of slaves, and his dehumanization of his "property"; D'Ortega complains to Jacob about the capital he loses as a consequence of 'cargo' dead of ship fever" (17). Jacob sees that his house slaves eye him with fear. We later learn from Florens' mother, whom Florens calls *a minha mãe* (Portugese for my mother), that in this space, enslaved women experience rape far more often than romantic love. Although Florens never learns this, her mother sends her forth from this house of horrors to protect her. As Florens' mother kneels before Jacob, begging for salvation, Jacob sees "the terror in her eyes" (26). The mother chooses well: Jacob is himself opposed to chattel slavery, and takes the child from her mother out of kindness, as a mercy.

Like Morrison's earlier masterpiece, *Beloved* (1988), *A Mercy* is an outraged indictment of the evil inclination to possess human beings through slavery. The two novels show startling similarities, most notably the event coiled at the center of each narrative: the dreadful decision by a mother to give up a daughter to save her from a life of slavery. In *Beloved*, Sethe attempts to kill all four of her children in order to protect them from slave-owners. She succeeds only in killing her third child, her older daughter; yet this action results in the liberation of the rest of the family, as the white men determine that Sethe is too damaged to be taken back into slavery.[12] In *A Mercy*, the mother of Florens, faced with the possibility of being traded to Jacob away from her daughter and young son, begs Jacob to instead take her daughter from the harsh plantation and from a future of sexual slavery. The consequences of these desperate choices are brutal: Sethe is haunted by guilt and ostracized by her community; the forfeited Florens spends her life believing that her mother has rejected her in favor of her baby brother.[13]

The inability of the enslaved to communicate with each other is also a source of heartbreak to Florens' mother, the second speaker in the novel. Although the reader hears her narrative, the mother has no hope of conveying her meanings to the daughter she longs to reach. When Florens describes the fateful moment of her mother's mercy, she shares an incoherent memory of *a minha mãe*, "'Saying something important to me, but holding the little boy's hand'" (8). Throughout her time at Vaark farm, Florens envisions her mother silently speaking, "'As always she is trying to tell me something'" (137). Even when Florens has given up on all happiness, and possibly on life itself, she returns to this loss: "'I will keep one sadness. That all this time I cannot know what my mother is telling me. Nor can she know what I am wanting to tell her.'" And then, in the last lines of her narrative, Florens turns away from the unloving blacksmith, speaking directly to the mother who loves her, sharing a little family joke: "'Mãe, you can have pleasure now because the soles of my feet are hard as cypress'" (161). Unlike Florens, the reader has only to turn the page to read the words that the mother longs for Florens to hear, the words that explain that what Florens saw as a rejection was "a mercy," the mother's only way of saving Florens from a place in which "there was no protection" (162), that the stolen lessons in reading and writing were the mother's attempt to help Florens find her own way in the world, that in giving Florens to Jacob, she was counting on his humanity to recognize the humanity in Florens, counting on his ability to also offer "a mercy" (167) to a small unprotected child. The final tragic and futile words of the book: "'Oh Florens. My love. Hear *a tua mãe*'" (167). In particularizing the tragic suffering of mothers and children, as in *Beloved*, Morrison invites us to consider how many slave children, like Florens, lived their lives believing that somehow lack of maternal love accounted for their expulsion from the paradise of their mothers' arms.

The reader experiences a brief moment of horror in the Jublio plantation episode; but most of *A Mercy* takes place in "the freezing hell" (8) of Jacob's New York State farm. When Florens arrives up north to the farm, located near a town significantly named Milton,[14] she discovers one of Toni Morrison's doomed female communal paradises—like the brief paradise at 124 in *Beloved* before the slave-owners track down Sethe and her children, or the community of *Paradise*, also destroyed by men who cannot tolerate female independence. The re-enactments of paradise lost and found in *A Mercy* begin with Florens' exile from what she imagines was the sanctuary of her childhood home, and her mother's embrace. However, Morrison reveals paradise and hell to be relative and variable. For the hell of exile and expulsion (a word that recurs throughout the text) soon turns into a regained paradise of family and community, as the various exiles and outcasts of Jacob's farm, each coming from a different lost paradise, come together to build a communal home. Lina, a Native American woman, had been taken in by "the Presbyterians" after her village was wiped out by smallpox. But when the sexually free activity allowed by Lina's culture offend her benefactors, they "abandoned her without so much as a murmur of fare well" (48), and "Sir [Jacob] bought her" (51). Lina, the first and only slave whom Jacob buys outright, is thus rescued as much as bought. Sorrow, the "daft girl" who is "accepted not bought by Sir" (51), had been found as a castaway, and given away by the first family to take her in. In fact, the master and mistress, Jacob and Rebekka are exiled outcasts themselves. Before inheriting his land and the aristocratic title of poltroon from a distant and unknown Dutch uncle, Jacob was a London orphan—his English mother dead; his Dutch father gone—searching for a better life in the New World. Vaark's farm is thus a diverse community of men and women, black, Native American, white, all working together. Although the people are not officially equal, none of the traditional hierarchical categories—race, gender, sexual affinity, sexual activity—is invoked to impose harm.[15] In addition to this diverse community, Morrison also presents one of her female paradises, the community of outcast women who support Rebekka on her voyage of exile to America.[16] The Vaark community is a paradise because it is free of the original sin of America: the greed for property and power, exemplified by slavery. Sadly, this paradise, like Morrison's other sanctuaries, proves to be false and is thus lost. The community falls apart, its members dispersed. *A Mercy* ends in the cold hell of Jacob's abandoned house, with the isolated, incommunicable despair of Florens and of her mother, with the greater hell of institutionalized slavery still ahead.

A number of critics articulate disappointment with Morrison's bleak and despairing closure. Cheryl Miller faults Morrison: "America is thus envisioned as a nation of orphans, separate, lonely, alone" (64)—a seemingly unfair critique given the narrative of American history. Wyatt Mason asserts that the Gothic end anticipated by Florens, the fiery destruction of the house by Lina, proves that "the novel embodies the belief that the only way for the children of slaves to transcend their patrimony is to burn down the white man's hollow house to its insufficient foundation, that we might start again" (37). These readings mistakenly take the conclusion of *A Mercy* as Morrison's final statement on the history of African Americans. But, or course, the history of African Americans did not end in 1690, nor does Morrison's statement. The imperatives of history dictate that Morrison could not conclude a novel about slavery in 1690 with a hopeful statement about the future of those about to enter the inferno. Recognizing the intertextual relationship between *A Mercy* and *Beloved* allows the reader to conclude that Morrison's *Beloved* yields the final statement about the descendants of those African Americans who passed through the false paradise of the seventeenth century into the hell of the eighteenth and nineteenth centuries, finally to be reborn[17] into the (relative) paradise of freedom in the late nineteenth century. By the end of *Beloved*, the ghost of slavery still must be exorcized but, significantly, the American house no longer needs to be burned down because its inhabitants provide an "alternative vision to ... patriarchal control" (Askeland 802), a community of equals, a rebuilt African American family, whose freeborn daughter is poised to embark upon a full, human life.[18]

Morrison's commitment to historical reality, no matter how dismal, is also illustrated by the relative benevolence of Jacob's farm, indicating that *A Mercy*, a Gothic text that takes on the power of myth or fable, derives its narrative force from the reader's understanding that the events it describes did broadly happen, although the details might be imagined. Ira Berlin's essay, "Time, Space, and the Evolution of Afro-American Society on British Mainland North America," underscores the historical accuracy of Morrison's novel. Berlin's observation that slavery developed differently in different times and different parts of the country aligns with Morrison's. The distinction Berlin makes between the relatively benign "Northern non-plantation system" and the horrifying "plantation system ... around the Chesapeake" (Berlin 46) is illustrated by the contrast between Jublio plantation and the Vaark farm. As Morrison indicates, during the time of *A Mercy*, Northern slavery was a relatively fluid and humane system of servitude; the status of "slave" was not yet linked to racial identity. Jennings remarks that "economic expediency led the shift to non-white slavery.... Race slavery was not an inherent ideology" (647).[19] As we see in *A Mercy*, until the late seventeenth century, there were free blacks and Native Americans; Europeans were likely to serve side-by-side in bondage with Africans. The unit of servitude in the North functioned more as a household as opposed to the factories of the large Southern plantations. Only starting in the 1680s (the time in which Morrison sets her story) did a loose set of laws develop that over time would concretize into the harsh, brutal and racialized system of slavery of the eighteenth and nineteenth centuries. Morrison's refusal to provide *A Mercy* with a happy restorative ending reflects her commitment to historical accuracy. For Africans of the late seventeenth century, there were no happy endings. As the historian Jon Butler notes, "by 1700 the free Africans had disappeared—fled or been re-enslaved, no one knows" (37).

These humble words of the historian, "no one knows," offer an invitation to the writer of literature to imaginatively access the narrative that remains unavailable to research,[20] to turn to myth in order to answer the questions raised by history. Jean Wilson explains that this strategy aligns Morrison with Northrop Frye, the influential theoretician of literary criticism of the mid-twentieth century. Wilson argues that *Beloved*, a "history book" (238), is also "what Frye would describe as 'a vision of reality that is something other than history or logic'" ("Toni Morrison: Re-Visionary Words with Power" 238). *A Mercy*, too, offers "a vision" of reality that is "something other than history." Morrison works to fill the lacunae of history by drawing on the Gothic trope of the fragmented narrative—the trope that disputes the possibility of a single correct version of any event—to imagine voices not recorded in the documents of history.[21] The voices we hear in *A Mercy* belong to the voiceless: the poor, the female, the dark, the enslaved.[22] None of these voices speaks directly to the reader; they are haunting ghost voices—whispering to themselves, whispering to others, and we must strain to understand the confusing utterances. Most of the characters—Jacob, Rebekka, Lina, Sorrow, Willard and Scully—do not actually voice their stories. Their perspective is presented by a third-person narrative that positions them one by one, as the point-of-view-character. Only two of the characters, Florens and her mother, speak in the hope that they will be heard.

Morrison's representation of slavery during its relatively "humane" early moments acts to highlight the cruelty of the patriarchy—the institution that bears the full brunt of her indictment in *A Mercy*—which Morrison portrays as a root of American evil, and a gateway to slavery. Morrison plants early clues to suggest that Jacob is not the benevolent father figure that he seems. He has acquired his own wife through a sale; sold to Jacob, a stranger who could afford to feed her, she is rescued from the brutal London of her childhood. We learn that "Rebekka's mother objected to the 'sale'" (74), a transaction based on the patriarchal commodification of women. The sale is also based on the imperatives of the aristocracy. Although he truly loves his wife and is a good husband to her, Jacob's prime motivation for marrying is dynastic: "taking over the patroonship required a wife" (20). Another clue to Jacob's patriarchal tendencies is his name: Jacob is one of the biblical patriarchs; "Vaark" is the Dutch word for pig. His assessment of his own character is that he "continues to feel a disturbing pulse of pity for orphans and strays" (33). That Jacob finds the impulse "disturbing" indicates his future. In fact, Jacob is yet another patriarch on the path to corruption. As Lina observes, Jacob is a "poor farmer" (49) because he is not patient; he is actually drawn to the quick profits of the capitalist trader, an affinity that Morrison aligns with the usual evils of capitalism. It is Jacob's affinity for capitalism that leads to the decline of his community, as he allows himself to be corrupted by his brief visit to Jublio. Although at Jublio, "Jacob sneered at wealth dependent on a captured workforce" (28), a brief conversation at an inn nearby, with a man meaningfully named Downes, convinces Jacob that "there was a profound difference between the intimacy of slave bodies at Jublio and a remote labor force in Barbados" (35). Conversely, as Morrison suggests, there was very little difference between a benign small-scale slave owner, and a murderous possessor of many commodified human beings. The tendency toward patriarchy is only the beginning of Jacob's decline. We witness Jacob's moral turning point, as he ceases being a part-time farmer and "a small-scale trader for the Company with a side line in fur and lumber" (33), and embarks on a lucrative career as a capitalist in the rum trade, which was supported by the suffering of those unknown slaves in the West Indies, whose expendable bodies were "like firewood, what burns to ash is refueled" (30).

Jacob's capitalistic greed drags him and his community from the world of the pastoral to the world of the Gothic, the world of the dark patriarch who destroys everything in his path, so that he can acquire a grand property, and a dynastic line to inherit it. Like his Gothic precursors, Jacob builds his patriarchal house for power and for pride, because, he thinks, "What a man leaves behind is what a man is" (89). As Lina recalls, the building of his second, penultimate house was reasonable: "The first house ... dirt floor, green wood—was weaker than the bark-covered one she herself was born in." The second house, a simple farm house, did not involve a wasteful use of natural resources: "He tore down the first to lay wooden floors in the second." However, "There was no need for a third. Yet ... he meant to build another, bigger, double-storied, fenced and gated like the ones he saw on his travels ... a profane monument to himself" (44), a monument to his patriarchal power that unnecessarily "required the death of fifty trees" (43). Rebekka recognizes the aristocratic pride and greed that the house represents: from her point of view, the house is "Something befitting not a farmer, not even a trader, but a squire" (88). Like all Gothic structures built on pride and on the backs of others, Jacob's last house is doomed to haunting and decay. It remains uninhabited; by the time it is completed, all of Jacob's children are dead and so he has no dynastic line to occupy it. Jacob himself dies in the house. The women drag him there in the rain to fulfill his last wishes; he orders them to "lift him from the bed and lower him onto a blanket. All the while he croaked, 'hurry, hurry'" (89). Morrison connects the end of the dynastic line, the earlier death of Jacob's beloved last-surviving child, a daughter aptly named Patrician, to the construction of the monument. Rebekka thinks of the death of her child: "Men, barrows, a blacksmith, lumber, twine, pots of pitch, hammers and pull horses, one of which once kicked her daughter in the head." Rebekka also

6. The Return of the Master

connects the building of the house to Jacob's death: "The fever of building was so intense she missed the real fever, the one that put him in the grave" (89). Some of the characters believe that Jacob's ghost will maintain possession of the building. Lina thinks, "Now having died in it he will haunt its rooms forever" (44). Willard and Scully, the two bondsmen who work on the farm, believe that "Jacob Vaark climbed out of his grave to visit his beautiful house" (143). They see a shadow and convince themselves it is Jacob: "His glow began near midnight floated for a while ... moved ever so slowly from window to window" (145).

Indeed, the house is haunted, but not by Jacob. The living ghost of the house is Florens, returned to the farm after enduring a heartbreaking rejection by another brutal patriarch, the blacksmith whom she loves, and who seems to promise her a happy free life. The glow that Willard and Scully see is the glow of Florens' lamp, as she writes the narrative, directed to the blacksmith, that only we readers ever see. Writing with a nail, she uses the primitive literacy she secretly acquired in her childhood from the "Reverend Father" (159). She writes first on the floor and then moves to the walls: "'There is no more room in this room. These words cover the floor. From now you will stand to hear me.... I am holding light in one hand and carving letters with the other.... I am near the door and I am closing now. What will I do with my nights when the telling stops?'" (160). Florens is thus writing her life to keep herself, like Scheherazade, alive. She knows that she is to be sold out of the farm community, likely into a more brutal form of slavery. The servant Sorrow wants her to run away with her but Florens writes, "'She wants me to go with her but I have a thing to finish here'" (159). Since Florens has already told us that she is finished with the writing, is the thing she needs to finish here her life? Has she accepted that in her future life in slavery she is to be only a "thing" and has she decided to end an existence that has been marked by rejected and exile? The historian Jon Butler provides evidence to support this speculation: "Unlike inanimate property, Africans could and did destoy themselves, a prospect owners feared and resented" (*Becoming America: The Revolution before 1776* 41). Certainly Florens knows that her narrative will not last.[23]

In the image of the slave writing her story on the walls of the grand house, Morrison pointedly conflates the house of the patriarch with the silenced narrative of the oppressed. Florens' narrative of her journey—from Jublio plantation to the Vaark farm, to the blacksmith's home and back to the farm—is addressed to the blacksmith, who might have been killed when Florens attacked him with a hammer. This is the narrative that is inscribed on the walls of the grand house, that Florens knows is doomed to burn. Anticipating the conventional ending of the patriarchal Gothic space Florens writes: "'Lina will help. She finds horror in this house and as much as she needs to be Mistress' need I know she loves fire more'" (161). Thus the grand house of the poltroon, Jacob Vaark, is destined to suffer the conventional fate of the Gothic property; it will be burned to the ground, in anticipation of the destruction of the structures of oppression that it represents.[24] And it will take Florens' narrative with it.

In addition to d'Ortega's Jublio plantation, and Jacob's unnamed grand house, there is one additional hellish patriarchal Gothic space in *A Mercy*: the home of the unnamed blacksmith, a free black man in possession of himself and of his space. It is the home to which Florens journeys in search of sanctuary, although "'my journey to you is hard and long'" (137). When she arrives at the homestead of the blacksmith and sees "'the yard, the forge, the little cabin,'" Florens believes that finally she has discovered a true home: "'Here I am not the one to throw out'" (136–137). But as we know, patriarchal spaces are never sanctuaries for women. The blacksmith's behavior validates the suspicions of the reader who wonders about the reliability of an ardent lover who goes off without a word, and stays away from almost a year, and the skepticism of Lina who realizes in retrospect that "she should have seen the danger [of the blacksmith] immediately because his arrogance was clear" (45). It is the arrogance of the patriarch, not of the free black. The perceptive Lina defines his legal status: "He had rights, then, and privileges, like Sir. He could marry, own things, travel, sell his own labor" (45). In other words, despite his race, he can become a patriarch. The blacksmith ultimately literalizes Florens' romantic metaphor: "'Before you know I am in the world I am already kill by you'" (38); he is the traditional murderous Gothic patriarch, interested in property and dynasty rather than in romance. Immediately after seeing the blacksmith, Florens sees his little foster son. The sight of this little boy sends Florens back to the central moment of her first rejection: the moment when her mother kept her brother and sent her away: "'This happens ... before. The first time it is me around my mother's dress hoping for her hand that is only for her little boy.... I am expel.'" Throughout her life, Florens has held the mistaken belief that her mother's decision was based on her preference for her male child, a preference that would have reflected the values of the patriarchy. However, this time Florens is quite correct in guessing that she is to be discarded in favor of a little boy. As the blacksmith explains that the boy is "'a foundling.... My mouth goes dry as I wonder if you want him to be yours'" (136). As Florens senses, the blacksmith's cabin, despite its humble appearance, is the home of the Gothic dynast whose need for a woman lasts only until his need for an heir is fulfilled. In this too, Walpole's Manfred sets the tone, eager to divorce his loyal wife and to rape the fiancée of his dead son in order to engender an heir. We see this model alive and well, revised as an African American man, in the character of Luther Nedeed in Gloria Naylor's twentieth-century novel, *Linden Hills*. We know that the blacksmith, a "free man from New Amsterdam," is such a dynast with his own long lineage. He has inherited his trade from a long line of forebears: "'The glory of shaping metal. Your father doing it and his father before him back and back for a thousand years'" (69). This ancient history suggests a link between the blacksmith and the Roman god of the forge, Vulcan, also famed for his progenitive powers. Florens immediately understands that within the patriarchal code, once this man has a son (perhaps his own biological child), he no longer requires a woman for breeding; the supposed foundling has replaced her in his life. She notes how "'you offer and he owns your forefinger. As if he is your future. Not me'" (136). Florens accurately senses that she is no longer to have access to the blacksmith's phallus or to his future. Once ensured of his heir, the blacksmith no longer requires Florens' sexuality. All fears are fulfilled when the blacksmith returns just as the young and inexperienced Florens accidentally injures the child, who is the midst of a tantrum. The blacksmith is convinced that she is of no use, even as a foster mother. The blacksmith makes his choice clear: "'I am lost because your shout is not my name.... No question. You choose the boy. I am lost'" (141). Cheryl Miller argues that the blacksmith helps Florens in rejecting her: "Florens' insane jealousy costs her the love of the blacksmith" ("Mine, Mine, Mine" 64). The blacksmith does seem to tell her some truths. She cannot stay with him, he says, "'Because you are a slave.... Own yourself woman'"; he calls her "'a slave by choice'" and blames her for making herself a slave to her masters and to himself. Ultimately he blames the victim of slavery and patriarchy; dehumanizing Florens, he tells her, "'Your head is empty and your body is wild'" (141). Perhaps the cruelty of the blacksmith's rejection can be best understood when compared to the compassionate acceptance of Sethe by Paul D in Morrison's *Beloved*. Sethe has done far worse than Florens, killing her own child to evade slavery. Yet Paul D, who understands that a woman's value does not lie in her ability to create a biological line, tells Sethe that she, rather than her child, is her own "'best thing'" (*Beloved* 273).

    The blacksmith's treatment of Florens is evil because he abuses the power that Florens' love allows him; in casting her away into the living death of slavery, or suicide, the blacksmith sends her back into the worst horrors of the patriarchy. Morrison returns to the biblical imagery of paradise lost to highlight the demonic aspect of the blacksmith's patriarchy, ultimately aligning him with the iconic figure of transcendental supernatural Evil, and frequent Gothic character, Satan.[25] She deploys a variety of strategies to identify the blacksmith with the iconic font of evil.[26] The Roman god Vulcan to whom the blacksmith is linked by trade, is a mythological precursor of the devil. Like Satan, Vulcan is flung from Heaven by a deity (in Vulcan's case, his mother Juno); both demons land in the depths of the earth (Vulcan underneath Mount Etna in Sicily), inhabiting realms of fire. Florens says to the blacksmith: "'The first time I see it [his naked back] you are shaping fire with bellows'" (137). Although less familiar than some of the other symbols of Satanic iconography, the bellows is one of Satan's fiery tools.[27] When Florens arrives at the blacksmith's home one of the first things she sees is the "forge" (135), the fiery oven in which metal is melted at hellish temperatures. The blacksmith's handiwork also suggests devilish associations. He enters the narrative when he is brought to the farm by Jacob to create a "sinister gate" for the doomed mansion. The gate is decorated by "two copper snakes [that] met at the top," reminding us of Satan's appearance in Paradise. There is no question about the association of these gates with the gates of hell; when Lina goes through them to bring Jacob into the house to die, "she felt as though she were entering the world of the damned" (51).

Morrison's representation of the villainous patriarch of her story as a free black man adds a link to the long chain of dark Gothic patriarchs.[28] From Walpole's Manfred on, the typical villainous Gothic patriarch is a swarthy Catholic Italian or Spaniard, the Other to the English Protestant reader and writer. In addition to Manfred, Ann Radcliffe's dangerous men are dark Southern Europeans. Charlotte Brontë's English hero/villain/patriarch, the swarthy Mr. Rochester fits this mold, as does Emily Brontë's Heathcliff.[29] In her twentieth-century American Gothic, *Linden Hills* (1985), Gloria Naylor suggests an interrogation of this pattern in creating a Gothic system in which all the characters, evil patriarch, imprisoned wife, and suffering populace— are black. In amplifying the racial darkness of the Gothic patriarch, Morrison, like Naylor, revisits the question of race in the Gothic. The villains of their novels are not powerful white men; they are African American patriarchal dynasts. Delores Keller notes that this is similar to Morrison's strategy in *Paradise* where her "sermonic purpose" is "to convey the atrocities that can occur when black patriarchs imitate the racist, oppressive, and exclusionary ideologies of white society" ("Toni Morrison's Sermon on Manhood" 46).

Morrison's examination of the conventional link between race and moral identity revisits and interrogates a long-standing Gothic trope: black equals evil; white equals good. She also thus contests the ideological underpinnings of slavery: the essentialist notion that racial identity should be the sole indicator of freedom or slavery. Morrison suggests that freedom, like moral character, like patriarchy, should not and cannot be determined by race.[30] In fact, Morrison's stated project for the novel is to "'separate race from slavery to see what it was like ... where your status was being enslaved but there was no application of racial inferiority.'" The book thus "challenges us to historicize the racialized political momentum that ushered in perpetual servitude based on non-whiteness and to meditate on the analogous forms of early colonial servitude, formal and informal, that might have united rather than divided persons" ("Toni Morrison Discusses *A Mercy*" with Lynn Neary. National Public Radio Book Tour. Oct. 27, 2008. Quoted in La Vinia Delois, 645). In *A Mercy*, then, good and evil are determined not merely by racial identity, but by deployments of power. Evil derives from the malign abuse of power that begins with the patriarchy imported from Europe, and then blossoms in American chattel slavery. Morrison states the moral of her book in the unheard voice of Florens' mother: "'to be given dominion over another is a hard thing; to wrest dominion over another is a wrong thing; to give dominion of yourself to another is a wicked thing'" (167). These words, that Jennings calls "the benediction of the novel" ("*A Mercy*" 649) apply to all systems of power, including slavery and patriarchy. The words might as well be the curse of the novel. For the patriarchs who abuse power in *A Mercy* destroy their entire world as well as themselves. Lina, foster mother to Florens, also contributes a condemnation of the greed and power of the dynast run amok. She tells Florens a mythic story of a traveler who discovers a beautiful countryside. "The traveler laughs at the beauty saying, 'This is perfect. This is mine.'" The word "mine" booms and "swells" over the countryside. The traveler then "strikes a mother eagle, displacing her from her nest and orphaning her babies" (62). Of course, this myth is the story of Lina's Native American people, and of the oppressed and dispossessed people who will follow. As Wyatt Mason notes, this story is "a creation myth. The eagle, our emblematic bird, symbol of liberty and freedom, sits far above ... a world ... jammed with beauty.... Alas, the traveler is ... a consumer, a childish one ... his 'evil thoughts' betray a drive to possess" (35). And, alas, this traveler is just one in the long line of greedy, devouring Americans, young and old, black and white, who view America and other Americans only as food to sate their hunger.

Part III

*Gothic Conversations:
Transgressing the Boundaries
of American Cultures;
Crossing the Atlantic*

7

Textual (Dis)Possessions
Hannah Crafts a Textual Labyrinth

The American Gothic text is often acutely aware of the influence of its precursors, both English and American. Because of the common ground created by common tropes, strategies, and preoccupations with various modes of possession and power, the Gothic canon becomes a shared space where disparate writers can gather to discuss and debate, exchange and appropriate, uphold and revise the conventions of the genre. *The Bondswoman's Narrative*, written between 1853 and 1860 by the pseudonymous Hannah Crafts, presents a rich and multi-textured example of such literary discourse. In *Narrative*, the writer deploys intertextuality not just to tell of the horrors of slavery, but to establish her narrative power; to define herself as an authentic American writer, a legitimate contributor to the canon.

When the novel was published in 2002, having been recently rescued from obscurity by Henry Louis Gates, Jr., it did not seem a strong candidate for a place in the canon of American literature. Even less certain was the placement of its author within the panoply of American authors of the nineteenth century. The name "Hannah Crafts" that appeared on the title page of the manuscript is likely a fictionalized clue as to the actual identity of the author.[1] In 2013 Gregg Hecimovich, a Southern scholar of Victorian literature, identified the novelist as "Hannah Bond," a slave whose existence was documented. The consolidation of the author's identity alleviated the "skepticism" manifesting, even in the twenty-first century, regarding whether a book like this could actually have been written by "a black woman" who was also a slave (*New York Times* Thursday 9/19/2013 A3). Hecimovich himself expresses this doubt in an interview with Hannah Winston in *The Chronicle of Higher Education*: "I didn't know it was possible that a slave could have this kind of literacy" (*The Chronicle of Higher Education* Sep 20 2013 A22). In fairness, this skepticism was based on historical reality; literacy was illegal for slaves and so a slave writer was rare indeed. In the nineteenth-century sensibility, the slave was a commodity and object, not the subjective source of ideas and feelings to be captured in writing.[2] Bond's gender was an additional obstacle; the female writer—white or black—remained a figure of suspicion in America of the nineteenth century. In addition to being dispossessed of the authority of the author by virtue of race, social status and gender, Harriet Crafts (to use her pseudonym), was also displaced from an easy sinecure in the Western tradition by virtue of her nationality. As an American in the nineteenth century, Crafts was part of another group of writers who had not yet been wholly accepted as creating a distinct and valuable national literature; Americans were still *arrivistes* to the Western tradition.

Crafts evidences a self-conscious awareness of her unstable position, and goes about establishing her credentials in a logical and painstaking way. She first establishes herself as a reader, a primary role for any serious writer. Additionally Crafts works to counter her authorial dispossession: highlighting her writerly identity as a woman, a black slave, and an American. Ultimately, Crafts also proves herself to be a scholar, adept at discerning patterns and meanings in the writing of others. By the end of her novel, she has succeeded in seizing the power of American authorship for herself.

The Incipient Reader and Writer

From the first sentence of *The Bondswoman's Narrative*—before defining her gender, race or social status—Hannah Crafts establishes her identity as a writer, albeit an insecure one. Belying her humble possibilities and skills, Crafts opens the book with a rhetorical flourish, disingenuously disclaiming her talents in order to forestall the criticisms of her reader, while simultaneously revealing her sophisticated self-awareness and her possession of the qualities necessary for a writer to succeed. Crafts anticipates and disarms readers' criticisms in the first words of her book: "It may be that I assume to[o] much responsibility in attempting to write these pages. The world will probably say so, and I am aware of my deficiencies. I am neither clever, nor learned, nor talented" (5). These criticisms aired and diminished, Crafts quickly moves to tell us, in an inverted, subtle, manner that she indeed has the very qualities to make her a authoritative writer. Again, she begins with seeming humility: "I had none of that quickness and animation which are so admired in children" (5). Rather, and here is the payoff, she possessed "a silent unobtrusive way of observing things and events, and wishing to understand them better than I could" (5). In other words, she was a budding writer, possessing the essential qualities of perceptiveness and curiosity. As Lawrence

Buell sees it, even her pseudonym, Hannah Crafts, reads as "a declarative sentence" ("Bondwoman Unbound" 16), a statement of what she does.

The observant child, Hannah, is also a determined reader. Echoing Frederick Douglass' account of needing to steal literacy, Crafts tells us that "I was determined to learn if not in a regular, approved, and scientific way" (6), even if that led to punishment by "my master [who] never permitted his slaves to be taught" (6). Indeed, the first episode of the book recounts a scene of (attempted) reading. Young Hannah is discovered at her favorite activity: "I would quietly steal away ... to ponder over the pages of some old book or newspaper" (7), even though she had not yet learned to read. "One day while sitting on a little bank, beneath the shade of some large trees" (7), she is discovered with her book by a kind woman who agrees to teach her to read. This first scene echoes not just Douglass' *Narrative*, but also Charlotte Brontë, a writer who had her own anxieties about writerly dispossession, The first page of *Jane Eyre* reveals the eponymous young girl also engaged in a hidden scene of reading.[3] Separated from her group, Jane also retreats and "I soon possessed myself of a volume" (Brontë *Jane Eyre* 5). Withdrawing "into the window-seat," Jane reads until she too is interrupted, in her case by her horrid and unsympathetic cousin. An important divergence in these two scenes reflects the observation of Charles Brockden Brown regarding the transformations of American literature: the American slave girl reads in a natural bower, "beneath the shade of some large trees," while the English orphan reads in a window seat protected by a "red moreen curtain" (5). In fact, Crafts provides another scene of reading that is even closer to Brontë's. Having achieved literacy, Hannah comes under the rule of a kind mistress who "indulged me in reading whenever I desire" (37). Hannah takes advantage of this liberalism to take a position even more reminiscent of Jane's, overtly proclaiming her equal position in the canon: "I descended to the parlor, and seated myself with a book behind the heavy damask curtains that shaded the window" (37). Here, in her indoor reading nook, like Jane, Hannah is interrupted by an unpleasant scene, involving an unpleasant representative of the patriarchy, in Hannah's case, the slave-hunter, Mr. Trappe. Hannah provides yet another scene of interrupted reading earlier when the slave overseer barges into the house of her tutor's family as Hannah is "sitting with them, and reading from the book of God" (12). The similarities of the scenes of reading traced by the two authors seem to move beyond mere coincidence. Harriet Crafts clearly invites us to note the comparisons between herself and this other young, isolated reader, Jane, who becomes the author of *her* novel *cum* memoir. Like the slave Hannah, forced by her society to steal her literacy, Jane is perceived as a thief by her cousin, John Reed, who tells her: "You have no business to take our books ... for they *are* mine" (8). John, of course, though only fourteen years old is yet another possessive tyrant in the making. Like Brontë, Crafts turns to good Christian texts to authorize what is, in the society of each, a subversive appropriation of literature and literacy. Both allude to John Bunyan's *The Pilgrim's Progress* (1678), the allegory in which the protagonist, Christian, journeys through allegorically named settings, engaging with allegorically named people and challenges, until he finally reaches "The Celestial City," a journey followed by his wife Christiana in the second part of the text. Brontë follows this model, as her protagonist journeys through allegorically-named places like Lowood and Thornfield, meeting people with names like Miss Temple, finally achieving happiness in Ferndean. Jane, or Brontë, further establishes her Christian credentials by allowing her righteous cousin St. John Rivers the last words: "Amen; even so come, Lord Jesus" (398).[4] Hannah Crafts establishes her literate familiarity with her predecessors, and her credentials as a good Christian, by tracing a similar narrative arc for her protagonist. Hannah (whose name is the Hebrew word for Grace) journeys from misery to ultimate happiness, meeting on the way the allegorically named, evil Mr. Trappe and the good Mrs. Wright. Additionally, Crafts reveals her familiarity with the Bible to validate her morality and cultural literacy. Many of her chapter epigraphs derive from relevant biblical texts.[5]

Crafts thus establishes herself as a serious reader and a good Christian, and so authorizes her necessary, and even moral, appropriation of literacy and literature. Her frequent borrowings from the literature of others visibly settle questions about her legitimacy as reader and writer, thus establishing her authority as an author.

The Haunting of Bleak House

If Crafts' goal is to validate her authority by highlighting her familiarity with other literary texts, she surely succeeds. In their Introduction to the collection *In Search of Hannah Crafts* (2004), the editors Henry Louis Gates, Jr., and Hollis Robbins note that "Crafts alluded to a remarkably impressive range of British and American works" found in the library of John Hill Wheeler (x). In Gates' collection, a number of scholars point to literary echoes from "Walter Scott's *Rob Roy* (1817), Charlotte Brontë's *Jane Eyre* (1847), Harriet Beecher Stowe's *Uncle Tom's Cabin* (1852), and William Wells Brown's *The Escape, or A Leap for Freedom* (1858)" (xi). As attested to by the Gates collection and by subsequent critical writing, the set of borrowings that seems most noticeable and that draws the bulk of critical attention comprises the many allusions in Crafts' novel to Charles Dickens' *Bleak House* (1852–53). A number of essays in the Gates collection point to the influence of the Dickens novel. Hollis Robbins' essay aptly traces the textual relationship in "Blackening *Bleak House*: Hannah Crafts' *The Bondswoman's Narrative*." Scholarship published after Gates' collection also tends to emphasize the relationship of *The Bondswoman's Narrative* and *Bleak House*. R. J. Ellis begins his paper "'so amiable and good': Hannah Crafts and *The Bondswoman's Narrative*, its Lineages" with a promising discussion that ultimately succumbs to the temptations of "the inescapable debts" (145) to Dickens' text. Despite all this, Rachel Teukolsky finds new material to mine: "The major literary work I examine is Charles Dickens' *Bleak House*" ("Pictures in *Bleak House*" 492). In the *New York Times* article, Hecimovish contextualizes the influence of *Bleak House* in asserting that Hannah Bonds served on a plantation that kept boarders from a nearby school: "The curriculum there required the girls to recite passages of *Bleak House,* allowing Bonds access to this novel." Certainly, a consideration of *Bleak House* as an influence on *Bondswoman's Narrative* has much to offer.

A significant example of Crafts' use of *Bleak House* to reinforce her themes occurs in a shared trope: the rediscovery of the missing mother—an important element in both texts. The trope of the missing or absent mother (sometimes rediscovered), which originates in the work of Horace Walpole and Ann Radcliffe, recurs frequently in Gothic fiction, most often signifying the legal and social powerlessness, and invisibility, of the mother in society and law. The absence of the nurturing and proper mother is also helpful in allowing freedom and its interesting consequences to the female protagonist. The trope takes on additional meaning within the system of slavery, in which mothers were often separated from their children, and many writers of slavery, including Toni Morrison, invoke this trope to highlight the horror of slavery. Additionally, Harriet Jacobs highlights the image in her slave narrative, *Incidents in the Life of a Slave Girl* (1861). Hannah Crafts reminds us that she too has experienced this void in her childhood. Like Harriet Beecher Stowe's Topsy, Hannah too "was not brought up by any body in particular" (5). "I had no mother, no friend" (8). Yet Crafts' novel (like Jacob's narrative) culminates with the joyous and unanticipated discovery of the mother. When Hannah asks her reader: "Can you guess who lives with me?" (244), the ongoing absence and silence of her mother leaves the reader with little basis for a correct guess. But the answer actually is: "my own dear mother, aged and venerable, yet so smart and lively and active" (244). We have not had any reason to think of this mother since the first pages of the novel when we learn that "[o]f my relatives I knew nothing. No one ever spoke of my father or mother" (5–6). Yet, as Hannah explains, her mother remembered her, and recognized her by "certain marks on my body" (244). This is all the explanation Crafts affords her readers. Seemingly even she lacks the narrative energy to spin the yarn that would account for this miraculous reunion, telling us only that "[w]e met accidentally, where or how it matters not" (245). The reunion is thus solidly placed within the realm of fiction, of fantasy, specifically the unbelievable Gothic tropes of randomly recovered identity, and the often-metaphorical return from the dead, another set of tropes developed by Horace Walpole in *The Castle of Otranto* (1764).

Although Crafts does not pave a realistic path toward this reunion, she does create a literary, thematic foreshadowing for the happy closure of the novel, which follows the pattern of Ann Radcliffe's Female Gothic. When Hannah is cast into the depths of prison, she enjoys "a blessed dream of ... my angel mother" (82), only to wake to the reality of another missing mother, Mrs. Wright, "the mother [torn] from her children for no crime but yeilding [sic] to the dictates of humanity" (85). The fantastic reunion of Hannah and her actual mother echoes an earlier miraculous mother-daughter reunion that Hannah experiences. When Hannah is a child, the maternal void is filled by the "aged woman" (7), Aunt Hetty, who teaches her to read and welcomes her into her home, as well as cultivating her "moral nature" (10). Hetty disappears, spirited away in punishment for nurturing a slave. Hannah imagines a Gothic fate for Aunt Hetty and her husband: "[m]y fancy painted them as immured in a dungeon for the crime of teaching a slave to read" (13). Yet this lost mother is also ultimately rediscovered. After many trials and tribulations, in flight yet again, Hannah is discovered half-drowned by a woman. Hannah unknowingly calls to her: "[m]other, good mother" (233) and discovers that it is Aunt Hetty, her old mother figure who helps her escape. Thus in the stories of Aunt Hetty and in Hannah's biological mother, we have a doubled instance of the Gothic trope of the return of the missing mother. Nor is Hannah the only daughter to discover her lost mother. The mistress of Lindendale also unexpectedly discovers her absent mother. Raised as the daughter of a white couple she had been taught to "consider her mother as dead." Her discovery of her biological mother, and thereby of her own true identity, though is doubly tragic; she learns that "her mother was a slave then toiling in the cotton feilds [sic] of Georgia" (45), and that she is therefore a slave. Thus Hannah Crafts creates a happy ending for her protagonist that is clearly unrealistic, but in its fantasy, it is also self-consciously literary, aware of literary conventions, thus reinforcing the authority of its narrator to craft any ending she chooses.

Similarly, Crafts turns to *Bleak House* to reinforce the literary thematics of her conclusion, and to validate her own credentials as a writer. Dickens' novel also tells the story of the recovery of the missing mother. During the course of the novel, the reader discovers that Lady Dedlock—whose own name, as John C. Ward notes, is belatedly revealed in Chapter 54 as "Honoria" ("The Virtues of Mothers" 42 Note 10)—is the mother of Esther Summerson. As in Crafts' story of the mistress of Lindendale, Dickens realistically tempers the joy of this discovery; the flight and death of Lady Dedlock preclude a permanent reunion with her daughter. And so, not only does Crafts prove her literary knowledge, she proves that she is a strong writer in the Bloomian sense, able to appropriate and revise the text of her precursor.

The House of the Seven Gables *and* The Bondwoman's Narrative

An oddity of the scholarship on Crafts is that while many scholars focus on the influence of *Bleak House*, few dwell on the significance of the text that lurks behind *Bleak House*, the text that haunts Dickens' novel as well as *The Bondswoman's Narrative*: Hawthorne's *The House of the Seven Gables* (1851). Certainly, the connection between Crafts' novel and Hawthorne's has not completely escaped critical attention. A number of scholars note the similarities without developing a fuller comparison of Crafts' and Hawthorne's texts. "Missing Intertexts: Hannah Crafts' *TBN* and African American Literary History" provides a typical example of the scholarship. Gill Ballinger, Tim Lustig, and Dale Townshend, present a compelling reading of the Gothic context of Crafts' novel, and pay glancing tribute to "one of the key texts here being Nathaniel Hawthorne's *The House of the Seven Gables*" (220). But the final energy of the paper is devoted to the observation that "Crafts' more notable intertext is, without question *Bleak House*" (220). As Gates and Robbins note in their Introduction to *In Search* there are "many points of similarity" between the novels of Crafts and Hawthorne, including "the storied old house, the glowering portrait, the curse and the old tree, the name Clifford, the preoccupation with documents and inheritance, the sudden gurgling death" (x-xi). They further note that the Wheeler family, with whom Crafts lived as a slave, "like the Pyncheon's in Hawthorne's tale, [owned land] first granted to a family named Maule" (xi). Other writers in the collection also note links between *Bondwoman's Narrative* and *Seven Gables*, especially the shared preoccupation with family portraits. In "The Problem of Freedom in *The Bondwoman's Narrative*," John Stauffer compares portraits in Crafts to "those in Hawthorne's fiction" ("The Problem of Freedom" 57), noting that in her consideration of the haunting effect of the portraits of the dead, Crafts echoes "Hawthorne's language in *The House of the Seven Gables*" (57), and recognizes the powerfully prophetic nature of the portraits. In "Trappe(d): Race and Genealogical Haunting in *The Bondswoman's Narrative*," Robert Levine, observes that Crafts "shares many of the gothic tropes and unmasking strategies of ... Hawthorne's *House*" (278), including the trope of the family portrait as a representation of two competing and yet entwined family lines. Levine also notes the significance of blood in the curses invoked upon Hawthorne's Pyncheon family and Crafts' Vincent family by the victims of the family patriarchs (284). Yet Levine does not include the House of the Seven Gables on his list of important "'white' houses" in nineteenth-century American literature.

A major consequence of the scholarly focus is the critical sense that Hannah Crafts is connecting mainly, or largely, to the English tradition, as articulated by Lawrence Buell: "With the possible exception of Poe and Stowe, the now-canonical white writers who seem to have caught Hannah Crafts' eye were all British: Horace Walpole, Ann Radcliffe, Walter Scott, Charles Dickens, among others" ("Bondwoman Unbound: Hannah Crafts' Art and Nineteenth-Century U.S. Literary Practice" 28). In fact, Bernier and Newman, pursuing their argument that Crafts is an immigrant, perhaps Irish, ask: "Is it possible that Crafts was writing for a translatlantic audience?" ("*The Bondswoman's Narrative*" 154). The result of these Hawthorne-free readings is thus to detach Crafts from the American tradition, unfortunate indeed as she clearly works, in her many allusions to Hawthorne to establish herself as an American writer, writing for an American audience about American issues, in response to the American tradition.

* * *

The oddity of this omission is heightened by the presence of the many connections that link *The Bondwoman's Narrative* and *The House of the Seven Gables*. The missing document of Emancipation in Crafts' novel echoes the missing deed for the Pyncheon land in Maine. In both cases, "no positive proof could be adduced that such an article had ever been in existence" (Crafts 240). The proud mistress, stalked by Trappe, "the old gentleman in black" (31–32) recalls Hawthorne's proud Alice, harried by Matthew Maule with his "black" look (188).[6] The profession of Crafts' evil Trappe, the law, aligns him with Hawthorne's villainous Judge Pyncheon. Both books open with an image of an imposing tree that makes the comparison almost inevitable. Hawthorne begins his book with a description of the eponymous house with "an elm-tree of wide circumference rooted before the door ... the great elm-tree" (5).

In fact, we find ourselves within a virtual literary forest, as this tree surely evokes those in *Edgar Huntly* and "The Legend of Sleepy Hollow"—all trees associated with past crimes. Crafts provides an elaborate story for her tree, a linden growing on the Lindendale plantation. This linden "was chosen as the scene where the tortures and punishments [of the slaves] were inflicted" (20–21). Indeed, both texts are linked by their representations of the system of slavery, although in this we can see that Crafts foregrounds a topic repressed by Hawthorne's novel. Whereas Crafts large topic is the curse of slavery, this subject surfaces in Hawthorne's novel only in the marginal figure of "Black Scipio" (192), and in the image of the Jim Crow cookie devoured by Ned, the little American boy. Indeed, the gustatory journey of the voracious boy, a creature of appetite who begins as "the little cannibal of Jim Crow" and ends as an omnivore, devouring and destroying every creature he encounters, anticipates Crafts' representation of slavery as cannibalism. In describing the search for a runaway slave, Hannah says: "The dogs were long, gaunt, and lean, inexpressibly fierce with a cannibal look that made me tremble" (149). That the cannibalism of the dogs is shared by their masters, devouring their own kind, is made clear by an aside that follows, in which a slave master tells of his wife who "actually killed two or three of the best gals I ever had. Just worked them to death" (150).

* * *

The closure of *The Bondswoman's Narrative* also reveals the influence of Hawthorne's text. Just as the dark passages of *Bondswoman's Narrative* echo those of *Seven Gables* (as well as those of *Bleak House*), so does the sudden and unexpected sunny conclusion link Crafts to both of her predecessors. Milton R. Stern's qualification regarding Hawthorne—"the endings of his fictions [exemplified by *Seven Gables*] often seem curiously, even outrageously, inorganic impositions upon and contradictions of the stories which led up to them" (Introduction xxvi)—anticipates William Andrews' critique of the improbably happy closure of *Bondswoman's Narrative*: "No slave narrative in the history of African American literature comes to such a marvelously happy, yet curiously hazy, ending" ("Hannah Crafts' Sense of an Ending" 36). Indeed, that is because the text is positioned as a novel, an artifice, and the closure is modeled upon the novels of Dickens and Hawthorne, rather than on the conventions of the slave narrative.

In the penultimate chapter, we see Hannah on a steamboat heading North, alone in the world: "there is no desolation so deep as that you feel when surrounded by a crowd" (238). Yet in this chapter, Crafts plants the seeds of her random happy ending, for on the steamboat, Hannah overhears a conversation between two strangers conveying the news of the death of Mr. Trappe. And then suddenly, in the last chapter, we find Hannah living "a life of freedom" (244), happily installed in "a neat little Cottage," a destiny shared by her fellow former slave, Charlotte, who ends her journeys in "a tiny-white cottage" (246). Hannah is no longer alone, as she has a "companion … a fond and affectionate husband" (245). Even more unexpected is Hannah's discovery of her long-lost mother. The discordance of this unexpected happiness at the close of a dark and tragic narrative echoes that of Hawthorne's closure, which also rapidly moves from darkness to light, finding his characters established in a comfortable home in the bright countryside. Towards the end of his novel, Hawthorne's character Clifford declaims that a home reduces its inhabitant to "a prisoner for life in brick" (260). This describes the situation of the family while they live in the gloomy House of the Seven Gables, as well as literalizing the system of slavery in which the slave is actually a prisoner in the home.

* * *

Crafts actually initiates an intertextual conversation with Hawthorne even before her narrative begins. In her very brief Preface, she considers many of the concerns that emerge in Hawthorne's more expansive Preface to *Seven Gables*, utilizing language that clearly echoes that of her precursor. In the Preface, Hawthorne adopts a frankly defensive posture, deflecting possible charges of making an unauthorized entrance into the canon of the novel, long-claimed by his English predecessors. Hawthorne insists that his work, a lowly "Romance" rather than "a Novel" (Hawthorne Preface 1), does not aspire to the heights of the novel. He imagines himself "laying out a street that infringes upon nobody's private rights and appropriating a lot of land which had no visible owner, and building a house of material long in use for constructing castles in the air" (3). Hawthorne thus claims for his American narrative the disclaimed and disavowed site of the Gothic Romance.[7] In the Romance, in the Gothic, Hawthorne asserts his freedom to write as he likes, unconstrained by the conventions of the novel, and of the English tradition.

Like Hawthorne, Crafts uses her Preface to address her writerly anxiety, and to consider and justify her status as a writer. Like Hawthorne, Crafts creates a dividing line between the fantasy of Romance, and the truth of history and of the realistic novel. But Crafts diverges from Hawthorne in finding safety and security as a writer on the other side of the divide. Taking a stance that connects her to the realism of other female American writers of her century, Crafts humbly opposes her work to the poetics of Romance, linking it instead to simple history and memoir: "Being the truth it makes no pretensions to romance" (Crafts 3). In aligning her text with history, rather than with Romance, Crafts takes what she sees as the less offensive path. She confesses her "diffidence and self-distrust" to her reader: "How will a literary venture, coming from a sphere so humble be received?" Her solution to this quandary is to insist that her production is a "record of plain unvarnished facts" relating "events as they occurred." Thus by defining her text as history and memoir, Crafts shields herself from *ad femina* attacks on her authority as a writer; she cannot be held responsible for the contents because history, or fate, was the author of the events described.[8]

Despite the disavowal of his Preface, Hawthorne works in his first chapter to establish the veracity and credibility of his tale: his narrator cites "my occasional visits to the town" (5), and suggests that the events he describes are the culmination of a long chain of history, "extending over the better part of two centuries" (5). Hawthorne's transgression of the generic boundaries that he sets is echoed by Crafts. For although she asserts the veracity of her tale, the strategies she deploys—hints of the supernatural, clashes between transcendent good and transcendent evil, critiques of a decadent aristocracy, unrealistic coincidences, doubling of character and event—recall the artificial Gothic Romance which she disclaims, far more than suggesting an unelaborated record of history.[9]

Crafts even more explicitly aligns her Preface with Hawthorne's in invoking her chosen genre to disclaim a moral for her text, while ultimately acknowledging the moral. Hawthorne invokes the Romance to deny any overt lesson in his narrative: "When romances do really teach anything ... it is usually through a ... subtle process"; he claims that he does not wish "to impale the story with its moral" like a butterfly (2). Yet, Hawthorne does obliquely acknowledge a moral for his story: "the Author has provided himself with a moral;—the truth namely, that the wrong-doing of one generation lives into the successive ones" (2). Crafts similarly initially rejects the moral possibilities of her chosen genre: "relating events as they occurred it has no especial reference to a moral." Yet, she too ends in conceding that her text does, in fact, have a moral, and the moral is actually a reworking of Hawthorne's: "those of pious and discerning minds can scarcely fail to recognise the hand of Providence in giving to the righteous the rewards of their works, and to the wicked the fruits of their doing" (3). Crafts' revision of Hawthorne's moral indicates that although she presents herself as a diffident author, she will not shy from responding to her predecessor. Her presentation of the moral returns Hawthorne's secularization of the biblical invocation to its religious source, emphasizing the language of theological sin and curse that both writers invoke.[10]

Crafts also diverges from Hawthorne in her figuring of the inherited curse. In her Preface, Crafts turns to Hawthorne's overarching trope of the curse, referring to slavery as "that institution whose curse" (3) blights its victims. She amplifies the inherited nature of this curse later in her text: "The greatest curse of slavery is its hereditary character. The father leaves to his son an inheritance of toil and misery, and his place on the fetid straw in the miserable corner, with no hope or possibility of anything better. And the son in his turn transmits the same to his offspring and thus forever" (205). Crafts thus revises Hawthorne's notion of the inherited curse. In Hawthorne's novel, the inherited curse is biological, a disease passing through the Pyncheon line that results in a blood-choked death; the Pyncheon family curse is punishment for the sin of misappropriating land, passed down to the descendants of the original usurper. Thus, the curse is ultimately the ownership of property passed from father to son.[11] Crafts reverses Hawthorne's model by demonstrating that, under the system of slavery, the situation of *being* property is the curse transmitted through the generations. In making this connection, Crafts ironizes a cultural trope which Hawthorne repeatedly references: the depiction of the United States as happy and sunny—free from the stains of history, bathed in the light of the Enlightenment. In his Preface Hawthorne limns his present time (1851) as a moment of "our own broad daylight" (2).[12] Crafts appropriates Hawthorne's own language to reverse his assertion, emphasizing that the "curse" of slavery "rests over the fairest land the sun shines upon ... [blighting] the happiness of the white as well as the black race" (3).

Both writers develop the motif of contrasting light and darkness to describe their respective texts in the prefaces. Hawthorne asserts his right as the author of romance "to bring out or mellow the lights and deepen and enrich the shadows of the picture" (1). He states the attainment of "a picturesque effect" as his goal (2) and contrasts the "fancy-pictures" of his romance with "the realities of the moment" (3). Although Crafts is more subtle, she also draws upon the language of pictorial representation when she wonders whether she has succeeded in accurately "portraying" (3) the institution of slavery. Both Hawthorne and Crafts thus turn in the prefaces to the image of light to align the written text with the pictorial representation. Each creates an emblem for the metaphorical contrast between political and personal light and darkness: the central image of a family portrait, introduced early in each text. Hawthorne's narrator observes that the "stern immitigable features" of Colonel Pyncheon "darkly mingle the shadow of their presence with the sunshine" (21).[13] Hawthorne's representation of the interplay between light and darkness thus acknowledges that the taint of past wrongs does continue to cast a shadow over contemporary life. Crafts also points to the interplay of light and dark in her description of the ancestral portrait, yet her representation seems less harsh about the haunting effect of the past upon the future. As Hannah gazes at the portraits of the dead Vincent family, "a golden light of sunset penetrate[s] through the open windows [and …] set[s] each rigid feature in a glow" (16), seeming to animate the dead faces.[14]

Each writer employs the preface to painstakingly develop the larger themes of the book to come. Each also considers the placement of the novel within the literary tradition: Hawthorne thinks of the English novel, and Crafts thinks of Hawthorne. Ultimately though, Hannah Crafts is less deferential in her preface. While Hawthorne timidly promises not to appropriate any previously owned cultural territory, Hannah Crafts bravely meets Hawthorne on her terms, initiating a meaningful dialogue with her great precursor, thus proving herself to be capable of entering the literary conversation in America.

* * *

The power of the imagination to animate the dead also connects Crafts to Hawthorne in a meaningful way. His invocation and containment of the ghosts of the Gothic novel moves *Seven Gables* away from haunted England to the sunny rational America that he works to represent. At the end of the novel, Hawthorne suggests an exorcism: "Wise old Uncle Venner … fancie[s] that sweet Alice Pyncheon … had given one farewell touch of a spirit's joy upon her harpsichord, as she floated heavenward from the House of the Seven Gables" (319). In ridding the House of its ghost, who is, in fact, never witnessed and only "fancied," Hawthorne works to rid his American text of the actual supernatural ghosts that haunt his English predecessors. Even before the exit of Alice's ghost, an exorcism that is deferred until the last page of the novel, Hawthorne transforms and Americanizes the Gothic convention of the supernatural destabilization of legal property possession. When repressed ghosts do surface, Hawthorne works to contain them, never allowing his reader to forget that his narrative takes place in the sunlit place of reason. As we see in the passage in which Alice's departure is imagined by Uncle Venner, Hawthorne presents ghosts as subjective phenomena, safely situated within the mind of the narrator or the character, and thereby ultimately subject to the control of rational mental processes[15]: the House "*would* afford the ghost of [Mathew Maule] a kind of privilege to haunt its new apartments" (9), but this ghost remains conditional, never actually appearing, except as his flesh and blood incarnation, Holgrave. Later in the novel Hawthorne presents an extended episode in which the power of the narrator's imagination

7. Textual (Dis)Possessions

and reason opposes the power of the supernatural, with somewhat ambiguous results. As Judge Pyncheon lies dead in the parlor of Seven Gables, the narrator, arrogantly confident of his own rational power to keep the supernatural at bay, decides to play a little mental game with himself and with the reader: "We are tempted to make a little sport with the idea. Ghost-stories are hardly to be treated seriously any longer" (279). He thus allows himself to imagine the ghosts of the Pyncheon family assembling in the parlor. Although the narrator works to sustain his contention that the ghosts fall within his rational narrative power, these ghosts dispute his claims to possession and comprehension, as ghosts are wont to do. Although the narrator claims to control the ghosts, once conjured they resist and refute his control. He is mystified by their approach to the picture frame hanging on the wall: "What do these ghostly people seek?" (280), he asks. And further mystified when he sees the ghost of Judge Pyncheon's son, whom the narrator thinks is still alive. He is forced to concede his loss of rational control: "Indulging our fancy in this freak, we have partly lost the power of restraint and guidance" (280). Finally by the end of the passage, the narrator, weakly declaring that "the fantastic scene, just hinted at, must by no means be considered as forming an actual portion of our story," is forced to admit defeat: "We were betrayed into this brief extravagance by the quiver of the moonbeams; they dance hand-in-hand with shadows, and are reflected in the looking-glass, which, you are aware, is always a kind of window or door-way into the spiritual world" (281). By night, the narrator is unable to resist ghostly possession, the appropriation by the ghosts of his narrative and of his reason; only with the arrival of day is he able to re-appropriate the narrative and steer it back to the day-lit world of rationality. The attempts of Hawthorne and his narrator to exclude the supernatural from his gloomy, castle-like House thus emblematize the American aspirations toward reason. Hannah Crafts also sets up the opposition between reason and the imagination, but she, unlike Hawthorne, cannot allow herself even a momentary indulgence in superstition. Without noting the connections to Hawthorne's strategies, Patricia Wald observes that "Crafts foregrounds the play of her own imagination," rather than presenting actual "spectral haunting" ("Hannah Crafts" 218). In discussing the analogous ghostly portrait scene in *Bondswoman's Narrative*, Wald notes that Crafts refuses "to be haunted by the portraits," refusing to "surrender her agency" (220). The visages of the Vincent ancestors that she observes are not ghosts, they are realistic and material representations of the dead. It is the mind of the observing Hannah that lends an air of the supernatural to the material; but it is also her mind that allows her to fully contain the supernatural. Like Hawthorne's narrator, Hannah asserts the primacy of the rational, with even greater success. Looking at the portraits, she tells us, "I could think and speculate. In their presence my mind seemed to run riotous and exult in its freedom" (17). As Hawthorne uses his imagined and contained supernatural to declare his independence from European superstition, so does Hannah take the opportunity to declare that, even as a woman and a slave, she is a rational and intellectually free being, countering the voice of the housekeeper who interrupts her: "'as if such an ignorant thing as you would know anything about them [the pictures]'" (18).

* * *

Crafts also alludes to the death of Judge Pyncheon (and the earlier death of Colonel Pyncheon) in a number of ways. The image of the isolated dead body of the evil patriarch is echoed twice in her novel. Mr. Trappe is discovered alone in his "country seat" (242): "The door was shut; [his employee] knocked loudly, there was no response.... Mr. Trappe was lying with his face downward to the floor ... a bullet had penetrated his brain" (242). Earlier, Hannah's master also remains "silent and solitary in his apartment" (75) until the door is forced open and his dead body is discovered. Not only does Crafts recall Hawthorne's image, the narrative voice she deploys in retailing the death of the patriarch echoes Hawthorne's. As the master is lying dead, awaiting discovery, Crafts' narrator seems surprisingly indifferent and somewhat confused: "Is there no significance in the hours as they pass away, and still he comes not forth?" (75). Craft's tone clearly echoes that of Hawthorne's when he tells of the death of Judge Pyncheon. Hawthorne's previously omniscient narrator coyly adopts an air of confusion, finding himself unwilling or unable to grasp the latest turn of his own plot: "the Judge cannot be asleep. His eyes are open! It is odd that [he] ... should linger thus in an old, lonely mansion" (269). The narrator wonders, "has he forgotten all the other items of his memoranda" (271). Like Hawthorne's narrator, Hannah details the many obligations—the dinner, the waiting carriage—that the newly-dead man misses. Like Hawthorne's narrator, Hannah displays a fittingly cavalier attitude in response to the death of the evil patriarch.

Dickens and Hawthorne

Despite the variety of direct connections between *Seven Gables* and *Bondswoman's Narrative*, this link tends to be obscured by the looming presence of Charles Dickens' *Bleak House*, published 1852–1853, that is, after the publication of *Seven Gables* in 1851. Because *Bleak House* and *Seven Gables* are so closely related, a number of motifs that seem to connect *Bleak House* with *Bondswoman's Narrative*, actually originate with *Seven Gables*. The story of the unusual and unexpected relationship between Dickens' and Hawthorne's texts opens up new perspectives on the American struggle for narrative possession and power, as played out in the Gothic canon. Much has been written on the fraught relationship of English and American literature in the nineteenth century and of the permutations of the American attempt to escape the haunting influence of the parent culture. As Robert Weisbuch notes in *Atlantic Double-Cross*, the nineteenth-century American writer usually "begins from a defensive position" in regards to "the achievements of British literature and British national life" (xii). Raoul Granqvist develops this insight in *Imitation as Resistance*, arguing that the imitation of the English by the Americans "involved acts of creative resistance and inversion" (10), reflecting the "relationship of the dominant culture and the Other" (18), meaning English and American culture. Yet, the relationship between *Bleak House* and *Seven Gables* reverses this situation, with the American novel serving as the source and inspiration for the English one. Of course, as Weisbuch notes, Dickens' novel certainly does not pale in comparison. In fact, "at times, in relation to *Bleak House*, Hawthorne's *House* seems afflicted by the fate that Harold Bloom categorizes as the rare case in which a subsequent text so subsumes its influential predecessor that the latter text comes to appear the source of the former" (*Anxiety of Influence* 39). And so, at times, *Bleak House* overshadows *Seven Gables* as a major influence of *The Bondwoman's Narrative*. Yet a number of motifs in Crafts' novel that seem to originate with Dickens, actually can be traced back to Hawthorne.

Weisbuch bases his argument for the influence of the Hawthorne novel upon Dickens on the many correspondences he observes between the two texts, including the title, and the echo of Hawthorne's Preface in Dickens prefatory statement: "I have purposely dwelt upon the romantic side of familiar things" (Dickens 43). Weisbuch observes that the case of Jarndyce v. Jarndyce illustrates "Holgrave's complaint" (36) about the dangers of inherited property, and notes other similarities between characters and situations: Esther recalls Phoebe in their impossibly virtuous domesticity; Esther's suitor Woodcourt recalls Phoebe's suitor, Holgrave; and both couples finally depart to "pastoral Edens" (37), thereby ameliorating the "the simulacrum of original sin" (37) that shadows both texts. For Weisbuch, the most compelling case for influence is the language of the ancestral curse placed by the ancient Lady Dedlock upon the Dedlock line: "When calamity, or when disgrace is coming ... let the Dedlocks listen for my step" (141). In "Double Exposures," Ronald R. Thomas adds to the list of correspondences between Dickens' and

Hawthorne's texts although he does not directly link the two; instead, he considers preoccupations that both novels share. Thomas focusses upon the representations in each text of portraiture in various forms, and with the nineteenth-century technologies of pictorial representations that were developing to supplement, or supplant, the old form of the painted portrait. Both novels, Thomas asserts, reveal a "politics of representation that informs the replacement of a painted portrait with a photographically-reproduced print reflect[ing] ... cultural conditions and concerns" (92). Thomas further indicates the political aspect of this cultural evolution in that both texts associate the middle class with the new technologies of representation, and the aristocracy with the old forms.

In addition to the correspondences noted by Weisbuch and Thomas, a number of additional striking similarities illustrate the extent of the debt of *Bleak House* to *Seven Gables*. Both novels feature a major character with a secret identity: Dickens' Lady Dedlock recalls Hawthorne's Holgrave. The flight of Lady Dedlock echoes the flight of Hepzibah and Clifford Pyncheon. Although Weisbuch asserts that Hawthorne's novel lacks a counterpart for Dickens' elderly and sinister lawyer, Tulkinghorn, "who combines the roles of pertinacious investigator of secret guilt and self-ordained agent of retribution" (Weisbuch 37), Hawthorne's sinister lawyer, Judge Pyncheon, does his share of spying and entrapping. The mysterious and sudden death of Judge Pyncheon in the parlor, is echoed in the calamitous stroke that befalls the Dedlock patriarch who is discovered in the library of his house, "lying on the ground like a felled tree" (Dickens 817), echoing Hawthorne's emblematizing of the aristocratic Pyncheon line in the image of the great elm tree. As in *Seven Gables*, the text and characters in *Bleak House* fixate on important missing documents and contested property: the deed to the Maine land in the former; the missing Jarndyce will in the latter. In each text, by the time the document is discovered its potency to establish property ownership is dissipated. Both texts feature dark ancestral houses haunted by ghosts wronged in the past by the aristocracy—Hawthorne's Matthew Maule and Dickens' ancient Lady Dedlock—and Dickens, like Hawthorne, relocates his central young couple to a sunny country home (set up an opposition to the gloomy ancestral manse), thereby appending an improbably sunny ending to his tale.

Dickens, Hawthorne and Crafts

As the careful reader will note, Crafts also deploys many of the characters, plot points, and images shared by Dickens and Hawthorne. Thus, the lawyer Trappe, a dark descendant of Tulkinghorn, is also the heir of Judge Pyncheon, a stalking lawyer in his own right. Hepzibah recognizes his malicious drive, when addressing the judge; referring to Clifford she says: "You hate him! You cherish, at this moment, some black purpose against him, in your heart!" (228). The theme of sudden, violent, and justice-dispensing death links Crafts to Dickens, as indicated by Robbins, who notes that the deaths of both Crafts' Trappe and Dickens' Tulkinghorn represent just "revenge" ("Blackening *Bleak House*" 78). So, too, of course does the death of Hawthorne's Pyncheon patriarchs. Indeed, in many cases, it would be difficult to determine whether the source of a particular moment in Crafts is Hawthorne or Dickens. And ultimately, it may not fully matter. What matters is to note that Crafts establishes her situation as a reader, a writer, and even a scholar, by displaying familiarity with both of these major texts, and that she draws upon the American as well as the English tradition.

Indeed, a close look at one of the major tropes in the novels reveals the interplay between the texts, which Crafts observes, and joins. Hawthorne, the first of the three writers, develops the image of the blood curse in the character of Matthew Maule, who having been dispossessed of his property by Colonel Pyncheon declaims: "'God will give him blood to drink!'" (8). Milton Stern notes that Hawthorne himself did not originate the story: an ancestor of Hawthorne's was "one of the sternest of the hanging judges" (viii) during the time of the Salem witch trials. Stern adds that Hawthorne read an account of a woman convicted by another judge, who pointed at his ancestor and announced: "'God will give him blood to drink'" (xviii). In the novel, the fictional curse is fulfilled as Colonel Pyncheon dies mysteriously, and is discovered "with blood on his ruff ... his hoary beard was saturated with it" (15). Over the centuries, other Pyncheon patriarchs undergo this bloody death, culminating in Judge Pyncheon, discovered with "a bloody shirt-bosom" (295). In keeping with his affinity for the rational, Hawthorne provides a scientific explanation for all this. Holgrave, the descendent of the Maule's and possessor of the secrets of his family tells Phoebe: "Old Maule's prophecy was probably founded on knowledge of this physical predisposition in the Pyncheon race" (304). Later this theory is reinforced by the narrator who tells the story of the death of a previous Pyncheon: "the old bachelor had an hereditary liability; he seemed to choke with blood" (311). The influence of Hawthorne's image may be discerned in Dickens' novel. We hear the story of a curse placed on the Dedlock family by the wife of an earlier ancestor, "who had none of the family blood in her veins" (140): "When calamity, or when disgrace is coming to it, let the Dedlocks listen for my step!" (141); the sound "a curious echo ... very like a halting step" (140) becomes a presage of tragedy for the family. Additionally, the fatal illness of Richard Carstone echoes the deaths of the Pyncheons. After having essentially sacrificed his life to greed (like the Pyncheons), he is at the point of speaking "in a fierce voice to the Judge" when "he was stopped by his mouth being full of blood" (Dickens 924).

Hannah Craft's deployment of this recurring image illustrates how she appropriates the two previous texts, weaving them into a work that is uniquely hers. As in Hawthorne's text, the source of the curse is a powerless person who is victimized by the patriarch and by the patriarchy, in this case, the slave Rose, who is tortured to death, gibbeted on the linden tree. Her last words recall the warning of Lady Dedlock: "'I die as a curse to this house, and I will come here after I am dead ... when death, or sickness, or misfortune is to befall the family ... ye will assuredly hear the creaking of its [the linden tree's] limbs'" (Crafts 25). The death of Hannah's master echoes Hawthorne's bloody image: "his garments and the carpet [are] saturated with the red stream that still oozed slowly from a ghastly wound in his throat" (76). Similarly, the death of Hannah's mistress (after discovering that she is a slave and subject to sale) results from a "ruptured ... blood vessel ... the sofa pillows were tinged with blood that bubbled from her lips" (103). Earlier in the book, Crafts takes the image further than either of her predecessors. The mistress, speaking of Trappe says, "he drinks my blood" (69). Crafts' reworking of Hawthorne's curse removes it from the realm of history, and firmly plants it into the space of Gothic horror, emphasizing the vampiric, ghoulish nature of the slave holder, and by extension, of the grasping patriarch.

A Web of Texts: Horace Walpole and the Gothic Tradition

The line of textual allusion set up by Hannah Crafts extends beyond Dickens and Hawthorne. The blood curse, as well as the ghostly portrait, and the collapse of the evil dynasty link Crafts' novel to the original English Gothic text, Horace Walpole's *The Castle of Otranto* (1764), and thereby to the larger Gothic canon. Crafts draws on the web of interconnected texts and tropes that compose the Gothic canon, with its long history of intertextual borrowing. She deploys a number of Gothic staples—madness, murder, death, and horror. Her text reveals a number of Gothic preoccupations, especially the anxious focus of the Gothic on ownership of various types of commodified property—real estate, the bodies of slaves and women, and intellectual property—and on the flimsy and disappearing documents needed to establish ownership in the world of law. Crafts' reenactment of the repression and return of the mother reworks Manfred's plan to imprison the mother of his children in *Castle*, and revises Ann Radcliffe's revival of the dead mother in *A Sicilian Romance* (1790). Crafts also finds inspiration in the Gothic tendency to deploy the supernatural as a code for the horrors caused by real legal systems, and as a sign of the ultimate impuissance of these horrifying legal structures as they inevitably collapse. A number of moments in the *Narrative* clearly deploy conventional Gothic tropes, including a scene in which Hannah finds herself imprisoned by a slave catcher. She is confined to a "large building" that looms "dark and gloomy," featuring windows "garnished with iron gratings" and a bolted "iron door." Inside, this dungeon features "bleak walls ... iron fetters and other uncouth implements designed for still more inhuman purposes" (78). The jailer enhances the hellish nature of this place: "His hair was red as fire" and he displays "a ghastly grin" (79) as he deploys the keys to the various cells. In the absolute darkness, Harriet starts up in "horror" to feel "a huge rat that was nibbling at my cheek" (81). Of course, this Gothic prison also contains a madwoman who, despite her irrational state, knows, unlike many characters in the book, that "nothing could be more wrong and unjust" than slavery (87).

* * *

In Walpole's novel, the Gothic curse that deposes Manfred, the sitting patriarch, takes the form of "an ancient prophecy, which was said to have pronounced, '*That the castle and lordship of Otranto should pass from the present family, whenever the real owner should be grown too large to inhabit it*'" (Walpole 15–16). This prophecy is augmented by an additional warning—drawing on the image of blood—discovered on an ancient sword: "'Alfonso's blood alone can ... quiet a long-restless prince's shade'" (79). Walpole's curse, like Hawthorne's reveals a preoccupation with blood that is particularly apt since each act of usurpation is dependent upon the misuse of the aristocratic blood line. In each text the corruption of the aristocratic blood line is figured in Darwinian terms: Conrad, Manfred's depleted son—"homely ... sickly" (15), dismissed by his own father as "a sickly puny child" (22)—is the end product of aristocratic intermarriage, as are the overly inbred chickens of Seven Gables. The narrator's judgment upon the chickens applies equally to the Pyncheon family, as exemplified by the depleted Hepzibah and Clifford: "It was evident that the race had degenerated, like many a noble race besides, in consequence of too strict a watchfulness to keep it pure" (Hawthorne 89).

Hannah Crafts would have likely had access to Walpole's novel, which was also found in John Hill Wheeler's library, a source of much of her reading

("Textual Annotations" *Bondswoman's Narrative* 247). Neither *Seven Gables* nor *Bleak House* is found in the catalog compiled by Bryan C. Sinche (*Bondwoman's Narrative* Appendix C), but as Gates notes regarding *Bleak House* (357–358), this missing book could have been acquired, and the internal evidence that Crafts was familiar with both books is compelling. A cursory glance at *Otranto* reveals that many of the tropes that descend from Hawthorne to Dickens and to Crafts are derived from Walpole. Whether they originate with him or if he too recycles old material (*Hamlet* for instance) is open to critical debate. The biblical evocation of "the sins of the fathers" emerges in each of the novels. The editors of *Bondwoman's Narrative* note this as an echo of *Bleak House* (*Bondswoman's Narrative* 261 Note 44). Each presents a dark contested and haunted property—Seven Gables, Bleak House, Chesney Wold, Lindendale (as well as the dark contested bodies of the slaves in *Bondswoman's Narrative*)—originating with Walpole's Castle of Otranto. The dark villains, representing all that is wrong with the lawfully empowered patriarch—Colonel and Judge Pyncheon, Tulkinghorn, Trappe—descend from Manfred, the tyrant who attempts to rape his dead son's fiancée and to make his wife disappear by placing her in convent, so that he may perpetuate his dark, ill-gotten dynasty. The unquiet portrait of the usurping patriarch also originates in *Otranto* and moves through the other novels.

Inheritance of Property

The question of the inheritance of property is central to the English Gothic, and to Walpole's novel, which articulates the fear of dispossession that hovers over all Gothic real estate and property. In the case of Walpole, the sign of anxiety is the blood curse which alludes to a secret regarding property ownership. Manfred is not the legal ruler of Otranto; his grandfather usurped the title and property from Alfonso, the legitimate owner. Alfonso's legal heir, the true owner of the Castle, Theodore, has been raised to believe himself to be a peasant. Thus Walpole sets up the masterplot of the English Gothic—the dispossession of property from the (seeming) aristocrat, and the movement of property to the (seeming) peasant, thereby highlighting the instability of legal possession of material property; this instability is also sometimes represented by ghostly appropriation of the property, also a motif in *Otranto*. Thus, the ghost of Horace Walpole hovers over *The House of the Seven Gables*, which presents an uncanny return to *The Castle of Otranto*. In "Time and Family in the Gothic Novel," Ian Watt recognizes the line of tradition that runs "from *The Castle of Otranto*, to 'The Fall of the House of

Usher' [another American Gothic text with a European cast], and *The House of the Seven Gables*, where the supreme power is the patriarchal authority of the long-dead lineal ancestor, who is still the real, though invisible, master of the house and its occupants" (157); each text, Watt suggests, deals with the problems and anxieties of property ownership and inheritance, a problem that is of course amplified by the repressed ghosts that haunt American culture.

Hawthorne's representation of the contested Pyncheon property is also in keeping with English forms: even though the property has originally been hewn from the American wilderness, by the opening of the narrative the estate is more closely aligned with the structures of Walpole's Europe than with Brown's raw American landscape. The eponymous House is described as a "gray, feudal castle" (10), haunted by past injustice and murder, and possibly haunted by ghosts as well. Conversely, Hawthorne's description of the other disputed Pyncheon property, the Maine land, works to repress the old English image of real estate, replacing it with the new American form. The disputed Maine wilderness with its "vast, and as yet unexplored and unmeasured tract of land" (18) thus operates as the uncanny American double for the disputed House of the Seven Gables. Hawthorne's evocation of the Maine wilderness, thus revises the American Sublime (as Brown and Fiedler suggest); the wilderness, like the English castle or abbey, is unpossessible epistemologically as well as legally. Hawthorne also revises the English terms of property acquisition and transmission in his description of the disposal of the Maine lands. Although generations of Pyncheons claim the Maine land, their possession is based on the English aristocratic terms of the absentee landlord, confirmed only by a (missing) legal document. The transmission and possession of the Maine property, in fact, takes on American forms: in an act that recalls Matthew Maule's original act of appropriation, the land is "partly cleared and occupied by actual settlers." Hawthorne continues: "These last [the settlers], if they ever heard of the Pyncheon title, would have laughed at the idea of any man's asserting a right—on the strength of mouldy parchments, signed with the faded autographs of governors and legislators, long dead and forgotten—to the lands which they or their fathers had wrested from the wild hand of Nature, by their own sturdy toil" (18-19). In this Hawthorne posits a new American model of property possession and transmission, based upon Locke's notion of labor, rather than on legal documentation or aristocratic appropriation. Thus in the image of Phoebe and Holgrave—retreating to their country estate to begin a new, healthy and sunny American line—in the image of the Maine lands—possessed and transmitted through labor—Hawthorne constructs a counter-narrative to the English

Gothic, a new myth of futurity, and of social and historical continuity that represses memories of past tyranny and revolution, disjunction and turmoil. In the chronological framework of Hawthorne's text, a narrative that ultimately looks forward to a new beginning, rather than hoping to reconstruct a lost past, another repression emerges, the repression of the memory of the pre-narrative idyllic moment that precedes usurpation. The nostalgic English Gothic typically remembers and yearns for this moment: we know that before Otranto was usurped by Manfred's grandfather, it was ruled by "Alfonso the Good"; the reinstatement of Theodore is a return to this moment. But in *House* the memory of the past only yields a doubled moment of usurpation: the Pyncheon usurpation of Maule property and the Maule appropriation of land "hewn out of the primeval forest" (7). The pre-narrative idyll, valorized and longed for by the English Gothic, is erased from Hawthorne's text because if the American historical and literary narrative were to follow the traditional Gothic course, the end of the story would detail the departure from the continent of the usurping Americans, heirs to the British usurpers; the American land would be restored to the original rightful owners, the Native Americans. The absolute erasure of this original ownership is emblematized by the missing "Indian deed" (316) to the Maine lands, "the connecting link [that] had slipt out of the evidence, and could not anywhere be found" (18). *The House of the Seven Gables* thus represses and transforms the English Gothic myth of restoration, representing an uncanny transformation of this myth in accordance with the imperatives of the new American ideologies of possession.

As an American writer, Hawthorne thus simultaneously evokes and represses the English forms that inform *The House of the Seven Gables*. Although Walter Benn Michaels indicates uniquely American anxieties of property possession at the root of the narrative,[16] *Seven Gables* is a text that evokes the forms of English property possession and the conventional, aristocratic roots of Gothic anxiety. Hawthorne's text begins in the conventional moment of stolen property in a context of troubled and troubling social hierarchy: the theft by the "prominent and powerful" Colonel Pyncheon of the land owned by the "obscure" Mathew Maule (7). In typical Gothic form Hawthorne begins his narrative belatedly, after an earlier moment of disruption: by the opening of the narrative, the property has already been appropriated from the Native Americans, colonized and "hewn out of the primeval forest" by Maule. The narrative represses this quintessentially American theft of property from the Indians, the theft that blurs the boundaries between owner and usurper as we saw in *Edgar Huntly*, and focuses instead on the more conventional (more English) misappropriation by the aristocratic Colonel Pyncheon, whose claim is visibly unsound and dishonest. Hawthorne also draws upon the Gothic conventions of family discord and family secrets: the transmission of the property is further thrown into disarray, and the family relationships further complicated, by the death of a subsequent Pyncheon, a wealthy old bachelor who is rumored to be contemplating the return of the property to the Maule family (22). He has apparently been killed by a nephew, his heir (Clifford), who is then replaced by a new and (as we later find out) inauthentic heir, Judge Pyncheon, ultimately revealed as the cause of the old bachelor's death. The narrative of *The House of the Seven Gables*, the story of the movement of the land and house through the hands of various improper owners, is then the old story of the instability of real estate, the alienability of property, going as far back as Walpole's novel.

Hawthorne's closure also illustrates the American attempt to come to terms with the English influence. In Walpole's novel, Theodore, a seeming peasant, is restored to his aristocratic identity, revealed as the descendent and heir of the displaced aristocratic family. In Hawthorne's more American, more radical approach, the lowly descendent of the dispossessed peasant re-appropriates the property, without losing his middle-class identity. Both Walpole and Hawthorne further consolidate this restoration by having the heir marry the heiress of the appropriating line. The confusion of the American text—in which the peasant remains peasant while also becoming property owner—is reflected in the unstable figure of Holgrave, the character who fervently expresses a hope for a new future in which old forms of property possession and transmission are abandoned: "'we shall live to see the day ... when no man shall build his house for posterity.... If each generation were allowed and expected to build its own houses, that single change, comparatively unimportant in itself, would imply almost every reform which society is now suffering for" (183–184). Yet, the populist, Holgrave, succumbs to the tradition of the English Gothic and comes close to transforming into the American aristocrat patriarch. As the novel ends, Holgrave is in double possession of the old property: through restoration of his identity, and through his dynastic marriage. The narrator remarks upon this irony; he tells us that all the characters of the novel become rich, including "that sworn foe of wealth and all manner of conservatism—the wild reformer—Holgrave!" (313). Thus in *House*, Holgrave re-enacts the role of Theodore in *Otranto* and shows the insufficiency of Hawthorne's repression of past models; like Theodore, Holgrave is the authentic and displaced heir, a previously marginalized character, who recovers his property in reclaiming his identity.

Yet in restoring the property to Holgrave, the previously unknown descendant of the Maules, Hawthorne does renegotiate the paradigm. In Walpole's narrative of restoration, the appropriated property is restored to an aristocrat who thinks he is a peasant. Walpole thus enacts a fulfillment of Freud's "family romance": here is a child who is indeed the unknown descendant of the lord of the manor. Hawthorne's post–Revolutionary revision of this old model is more complicated and less stable. For Holgrave is not the ignorant and simple peasant that Theodore is before being identified; although neither the Pyncheons nor the reader are apprised of his identity, Holgrave always knows exactly who he is. He is not an aristocrat in disguise, but the descendant of the man who has carved the estate out of the wilderness. Hawthorne's conclusion, then, is a re-enactment of American Revolution, as opposed to Walpole's re-enactment of restoration: the American land goes to the real owner who is not the aristocrat but the person who stakes his ownership to the land in the method endorsed by Locke, through his labor. Hawthorne further consolidates Holgrave as a revolutionary figure in his vocation as a daguerreotypist whose medium is the light that Hawthorne associates with the American Enlightenment, "our own broad daylight" (2).[17] And yet the figure of Holgrave as the sunny revolutionary inheritor is ultimately destabilized by Holgrave's reactionary darkness, by the dark secrets of his past and by his eventual transformation into an American man of property. Walpole's text ends with the fixing of stable identity—the booming declaration by the voice of divine authority that defines Theodore as heir. Hawthorne's text, however, establishes Holgrave's identity in a more oblique manner: through his possession of the secret of the Maules. When Phoebe Pyncheon asks him how he knows of the spring behind the portrait, Holgrave indirectly responds: "'how will it please you to assume the name of Maule?'" and informs her that the secret "'is my only inheritance'" (316). Ultimately, then, rather than defining a new American heir, the figure of Holgrave marks Hawthorne's unstable struggle to appropriate new narratives and to create new forms of property possession. Hawthorne's struggle is also visible in his description of the disposal of the property after it is returned to Holgrave. In the conventional Gothic closure, the property, like Walpole's Castle, is destroyed; this motif typically works to undermine the effect of the restoration of the property, and to further problematize the stability of real estate. Hawthorne, however, revises this trope, repressing the conventional closure with its dark echoes of revolutionary destruction. The House of the Seven Gables (like the castle in *Sicilian Romance* for one of numerous examples) is left abandoned and unpossessed at the close of the narrative, as the remnant of the Pyncheons and the Maules happily moves to Judge Pyncheon's country home that becomes (in another nod to the uncertainties of property possession and the instability of dynasty) the property of Clifford and Hepzibah, through the death of Judge Pyncheon's only child. Thus, having come to the end of their line, and the end of the Pyncheon line in the old, depleted and haunted ancestral place, the remaining characters move on to the country to reinstate the Maule line. This new territory where, we are told, Phoebe and Holgrave will establish a new, wholesome and sunny dynasty of their own,[18] represents the new model of American property available beyond the frontier: property that is imagined as having no past and no past possessor. Here too, the seemingly stable closure reveals instability: for the imagined ownerlessness of the American territories is based upon the repression of the figure of the Native American.

Property in The Bondswoman's Narrative

Like her predecessors, Harriet Crafts works to redefine the terms of property possession and dispossession. Like Hawthorne and Walpole, Crafts invokes the old conventional forms, most notably Lindendale, the Southern plantation house, a mansion that is "large and irregular ... built in a kind of rambling style that precluded the occupant of one part from knowing anything of the other" (178). This conventionally labyrinthine structure typically eludes the epistemological apprehension even of its owner. This house also slips away from the material possession of its possessors, passing from the cursed Vincent family to the Cosgrove family, equally deserving of curses. However, Crafts clearly diverges from her predecessors in focusing upon a different kind of property, human property, slaves, whose perspective dominates the novel. Crafts begins her novel with a story calculated to unsettle any white reader; a narrative of a privileged woman who considers herself white, until she discovers that she is actually the child of a slave woman, and therefore subject to sale in a system in which slavery is inherited through the blood of the mother. Trappe informs her, "'I may yet possess you on my own terms'" (41). Like Mark Twain in *Pudd'nhead Wilson*" (1894), Crafts tells the story of the exchange of two babies, reminding her readers of the instability of all identity in the face of a system in which the human self is alienable. Crafts' message is later confirmed in the story of the white Mrs. Wheeler whose skin turns black in response to some unadvisedly administered face powder. Even the husband of the privileged woman, now slave, with his "aristocratic name" (13), is powerless to rescue his wife from this system, since he is actually "impoverished" (13) and is unable to purchase her. Similarly we hear of the next family that takes over Lindendale, in which the husband keeps a number of slave mistresses and their children a secret from his wife. When she disturbs the situation, he reproaches her for meddling with "'my property'" (190). Crafts takes the opportunity to present a disingenuous critique of the economic system that allows this man to live in great comfort: "We [slaves] thought our master must be a very great man to have so much wealth at his command, but it never occurred to us to inquire whose sweat and blood and unpaid labor had contributed to produce it" (14). Indeed, it is only the older and wiser Hannah Crafts, the *author*, who thinks to raise this critique.

Hannah, the slave, is subject to the many indignities of possession. Yet Hannah, the person (and certainly Crafts, the author) refuses the status of property, refuses to be subject to possession by others. Even at a moment when she is about to be sold into prostitution, she asserts: "my soul was beyond their reach" (106). In fact, she is her own owner, and if others claim her, they are appropriating property that is not theirs. Crafts thus casts the Gothic trope of misappropriated property in a new light, thereby creating a highly literary critique of the system of slavery. For the defining feature of Gothic property is that it has been misappropriated from its authentic owner, hence the constant contestation of ownership, as evidenced in *Otranto*, *Seven Gables*, and *Bleak House*. More significantly for Crafts' uses, each text reveals the illegitimacy of the seemingly legitimate owner's claim. As the conclusion of *Bleak House* reveals, the imperious Lady Dedlock is an imposter, and indeed, by the end of Dickens' novel all legal claims to property are rendered inauthentic and preposterous. The closure of *Otranto* reveals that Manfred, the seeming lord of Otranto is an imposter, the descendent of a usurping servant. The aristocratic Pyncheons too are, of course, descendants of a thief. Crafts powerfully adapts this literary pattern for her critique of slavery. By locating her novel within the web of its precursors, Crafts announces that no Gothic owner is as inauthentic as the slave owner, who has no moral right, and should have no legal right of ownership. And no Gothic property has been as egregiously misappropriated as the slave, whose unalienable right of self-possession has been looted by a system that hides itself behind the veil of legal respectability.

* * *

Despite Hannah's identity as a slave, and her identification with many of her fellow slaves, she displays a discomforting class prejudice when confronted with the field workers, as revealed in her description of the degraded field slaves, and her repugnance at the thought of marrying the coarse slave Bill, with his "hidious [sic] grin" (214). This attitude might be race betrayal on the part of Hannah; but also might be read as a conventional trope rather than an authentic expression. Crafts' precursors, mostly socially comfortable men, often turn to the convention of the comic, dehumanized servant, a convention Walpole locates as borrowed from Shakespeare, his inspiration and indeed the inspiration for much Gothic literature. Walpole, Hawthorne and Dickens present the servant as a buffoonish clown. In his Preface, Walpole notes that his peasants are present to "excite smiles" and to heighten suspense when the action is "delayed by their coarse pleasantries" (10). Hawthorne, too, suggests a certain lack of sympathy for the oppressed, repressing from his tale the figure of the black slave, as well as the Native American. The one representative of the lower classes who plays a recurring role in *Seven Gables* is Ned, the comically voracious boy. In *Bleak House*, Dickens also reveals a lack of sympathy for the serving class; he unkindly turns to the subaltern for comic relief when he wryly describes the Snagby's servant, Guster, who is sometimes "found with her head in the pail, or the sink, or the copper, or the dinner, or anything else that happens to be near her at the time of her seizure" (180). But each of these writers tempers the portrait of the poor with sympathy. Dickens' portrait of Jo certainly merits the comment of Frederick Douglass cited by Robbins: "'Dickens has ever been the faithful friend of the poor'" (Robbins 73). Indeed, the trope of the revelation that the seeming peasant is really an aristocrat in disguise reveals a grudging sympathy, and even admiration for the poor. Walpole's Theodore, a supposed peasant, noble in spirit, emerges as the descendent of Alfonso the Good and the true heir of Otranto. Hawthorne's seemingly marginal Holgrave reveals himself as a Maule descendent and thereby the true heir of Seven Gables. Dickens revelation of Esther Summerson as the illegitimate daughter of Lady Dedlock, is certainly a variation of this trope. And certainly this sympathy for the oppressed on the part of the authors inspires Hannah as much as does their disdain.

The Sins of the Fathers: Inherited Property as Sin

Each writer within this web of texts turns to the Bible to establish the sinful nature of property possession and inheritance, an assertion that Crafts develops for her unique purposes. In the Preface to the first edition of *Otranto*, Walpole (speaking in the guise of an imaginary editor about an imaginary author) states somewhat obliquely: "I wish he had grounded his plan on a more useful moral than this; that '*the sins of fathers are visited on their children to the third and fourth generation*'" (5). These words gesture to the sin of Manfred's usurping ancestor; the punishment for this sin is, indeed, visited upon Manfred and his children. Hawthorne responds with a secularized American restatement in his Preface: "the Author has provided himself with a moral;—the truth, namely, that the wrong-doing of one generation lives into the successive ones" (2). In his reworking, Hawthorne attempts to repress the religious pre-Enlightenment foundation of his statement,[19] although he does not entirely succeed. His novel begins, like the Bible, with the original biblical sin of appetite and greed: Colonel Pyncheon (yet another voracious American) devours the property of Matthew Maule. Other biblical themes appear in Hawthorne's text: the seven gables of the House recall the seven deadly sins; the Pyncheon descendants are punished for the crime of their ancestor. Indeed the biblical context is appropriate for both Walpole and Hawthorne: the novels of each display the Gothic fascination with inheritance, family chaos, past wrongs, and generational reconciliation—motifs that dominate the earlier biblical narratives. As the editors of *The Bondswoman's Narrative* observe, without additional comment, Dickens also obliquely turns to the biblical notion of inherited sin. "This phrase also appears in chapter 17 of *Bleak House:* 'I think,' said my guardian, thoughtfully regarding her, 'I think it must be somewhere written that the virtues of the mothers shall, occasionally, be visited on the children, as well as the sins of the fathers'" (*Bleak House* Textual Annotations 261 Note 44). Dickens' statement, which feminizes as well as secularizes the biblical statement, certainly reflects his times and temperament, as well as anticipating the fate that befalls a number of descendants in his book.

Crafts, however, appropriates the secular versions of Hawthorne and Dickens by recontextualizing the phrase within its original biblical setting. For the epigraph of Chapter 4, Crafts returns to the original words of the Bible, "'The sins of the fathers shall be visited on the children,'" simply attributing these words from the ten commandments to "Moses" (44). No Enlightenment influences, or nineteenth-century biblical scholarship for her; she consistently establishes Hannah as a woman of faith in her novel. This chapter deals with the punishment dealt to the children of slavery. We learn that the white master, descendent of wicked slave-owners, has unknowingly married a slave—a discovery that will lead to the death of the master. In this chapter, we also see the moment of revelation as the mistress herself discovers that she is actually the child of a slave who switched her with a dead white baby—the wife thus discovers that she is the inheritor of the sin of her mother, as well as the inheritor of the curse of slavery, leading to her death as well.

Restless Ancestral Portraits

Each writer in this interconnected web also connects the notion of the sinfully acquired property with the haunted and haunting ancestral portrait, representing the legacy of the guilty ancestor who cannot rest quietly in death. This image, too, begins with Walpole. In fact Walpole creates two images of unquiet representation: the portrait of the usurping ancestor, and the statue of the last legitimate owner. The prophecy cited above, that "*the castle and lordship of Otranto should pass from the present family, whenever the real owner should be grown too large to inhabit it*" refers to the statue that portrays Alfonso the Good, the dispossessed owner of Otranto. The unraveling of Manfred's illegitimate dynasty begins when the prophecy is fulfilled. Giant pieces of the statue of the "'real owner'" start raining down on the castle: a giant helmet lands on Manfred's son; a giant arm appears in a hall. Thus the real owner, or his statue, is growing too large for the castle. The image of the portrait coming to life occurs in *Otranto* and recurs in *Seven Gables*. In both, the active portrait represents the active presence of the sinning past generation in the present of the descendants. In *Otranto*, the portrait of the original usurper, previously unnoticed and unmentioned, comes alive. As Manfred is assailing his dead son's fiancée, "the portrait of [his] grandfather ... uttered a deep sight and heaved its breast ... the picture ... began to move ... it quit its panel and descend[ed] on the floor with a grave and melancholy air" (23–24).[20] In *Seven Gables* the portrait of the Colonel, that has, for centuries, dominated the room in which he died, also comes alive, although in a way more commensurate with the realism for which Hawthorne's text strives. At the conclusion of the novel, Holgrave reveals the location of the missing deed to the Pyncheon family land in Maine: "he put his finger on the [secret spring]. In former days, the effect would probably have been, to cause the picture to start forward. But ... the machinery had been eaten through with rust; so that, at Holgrave's pressure, the portrait, frame and all, tumbled suddenly from its position" (315). In both cases the animation of the sinful ancestor accompanies the uncovering of repressed family secrets. Nor is the Colonel's portrait the only reviving image in *Seven Gables*. Hepzibah keeps a miniature of her brother, Clifford, as a young man in "a secret drawer" (31). This lifelike picture reveals his inner self, his "voluptuous emotion," his lack of "capacity of thought," as well as his effeminate "full tender lips and beautiful eyes" (32).[21] Similarly Holgrave's daguerreotype of Judge Pyncheon brings the demonic inner man to life. Dickens reworks the image of the living, haunting portrait; the aristocratic Dedlocks actually maintain an entire gallery of their family's revelatory portraits. Rachel Teukolsky notes that "the gallery functions as a part of *Bleak House*'s Gothic parody." The portraits are a "visual symbol of the genealogy of landed wealth passed down through generations" ("Pictures in Bleak Houses" 497). Except for the portrait of Lady Dedlock, that is. Here too Dickens feminizes a trope. Lady Dedlock is not fully one of the Dedlocks; she has married into the family with secrets of her own. Nor, as a married woman, does she possess any of the "landed wealth" of the family. In fact, Dickens hints at both her outsider status and her secret personal history in describing the sunlight shining on the portrait; "it throws a broad band-sinister of light" (204) across the portrait. As the Note in the Penguin edition indicates, the band sinister is "in heraldry one of the markings of bastardy" (957 Note 12.1). The portrait also performs a revelatory genealogical function, denoting her as an actual ancestor. When Mr. Guppy sees this "portrait of the present Lady Dedlock ... a perfect likeness" (138), it "acts upon him like a charm." Although he cannot identify the source of its uncanny familiarity to him, what he is responding to is the similarity of Lady Dedlock to her unacknowledged daughter, Esther.

The use that Crafts makes of the recurring trope of the haunting portrait reveals her genealogical relationship to her precursors, and to the entire Gothic tradition. The aristocratic portrait gallery links Crafts' text to Dickens. Three distinct sets of family pictures link Crafts' novel to Hawthorne's: the haunting portraits of the two patriarchs; the hidden pictures of Sir Clifford, and of the slave mother of the mistress; two representations of mothers that each author highlights. Crafts most certainly finds inspiration in the looming portrait of the patriarch in *Seven Gables*. The portrait of Crafts' Sir Clifford, like that of Hawthorne's Colonel Pyncheon, is an ominous, evil presence that looms over the household. Like Colonel Pyncheon, Sir Clifford dictates immortality for his image; he "ordered his portrait ... to be hung in the drawing room" (16). While in both texts the portrait eventually falls from the wall, Crafts presents a double and personalized revision of the image: a family catastrophe is heralded when "the portrait of Sir Clifford [falls] to the floor" (30); in keeping with her commitment to realism Crafts carefully explains this as the effect of the "corrupting canker [of time] over the polished surface of the metal that supported it [the portrait]" (30). Eventually the portraits of the Clifford's entire family are sold at auction, "publicly exposed in the market and knocked down to the highest bidder" (199), a poetic justice for the owners of slaves.[22] The hidden portrait revealed by the dark villain Trappe in Crafts' novel is also kept in "a secret drawer" (48), and also reveals a secret detail of identity: the mother's status as slave. The language Crafts uses links the maternal portrait to two other moments in Hawthorne's text: Trappe's secret drawer "opened with a spring" (48), echoing the moment in *Seven Gables*, when the dark hero, Holgrave, reminds Clifford of the existence of "a secret spring" (315), hidden behind the patriarchal portrait. In Hawthorne's text, opening the spring reveals a hidden document: the long-missing "ancient deed," now obsolete, which originally established the Pyncheon's ownership of "a vast extent of territory" (316). Similarly in Crafts' novel, the "paper ... old, and torn, and yellow with age" (48) that accompanies the hidden portrait establishes the legality of property. However, the property in Crafts' novel is the slave mother, and hence the mistress herself, whose relationship to her enslaved mother is established by her resemblance to the likeness depicted in the portrait (as in the case of Lady Dedlock and Esther). Thus in yoking her scene to Hawthorne's, Crafts indicates an important distinction between her novel and Hawthorne's. While both consider the evils of property possession, the property in question in *Seven Gables* is real estate; in *The Bondwoman's Narrative* the property is human.[23] Moreover Crafts' use of the portrait to consolidate family resemblance and identity connects her to Walpole's use of the statue of Alfonso, which is very like the visage of his descendent Theodore, and to Dickens' portrait of Lady Dedlock, that resembles her daughter. Crafts thus draws a straight line between two related and recurring Gothic tropes, the portrait, and the challenge of stabilizing identity.[24]

Hannah Crafts' Gothic Tendency

There is certainly no mystery as to why Hannah Crafts would turn to the tradition of the Gothic to find a space for herself as a writer. Crafts is not the only slave writer to note that the Gothic—with its tradition of horror, uncertainty, dehumanization, and the confrontation with absolute Evil—lends itself all too readily to descriptions of the slave situation. In their slave narratives, Frederick Douglass and Harriet Jacobs also tap into Gothic tropology as an accurate reflection of their lives, which include the torture and confinement that seem so unrealistic when appearing in Gothic fiction; a number of scholars, including Teresa Goddu in *Gothic America* (1997), have made important connections between American oppression and atrocity, and the American Gothic tradition.[25]

Yet the Gothic provides Hannah Crafts with more than a convenient pre-existing tropology. It offers her a canon and a tradition in which she—marginalized as a woman, a black, a slave and an American—can find a space as a writer. From its inception the Gothic has been the canon of the dispossessed, welcoming writers from the margins, attracting readers excluded from the centers of power and culture, especially women. In his eponymous biography of Horace Walpole, subtitled "The Great Outsider" (1998), Tim Mowl argues that, despite his seemingly secure social and economic position, Walpole, the originator of the Gothic, was actually an insecure outsider, as a consequence of his hidden homosexuality. Mowl asserts that Horace Walpole assembled the tropes of the Gothic in *The Castle of Otranto* (1764)—the return of past guilt; dark secrets coming out of the shadows; the lustful (heterosexual) man run amok, exposed, and stripped of family and property—to address anxieties associated with his homosexuality, in response to a piece of writing that essentially "outed" (185) him as a homosexual in his circle. Mowl writes of Walpole: "he might well have considered it expedient after being described as a hermaphrodite to bring out a rip roaring redblooded romance that included threats of rape in gloomy cellars and portrayed normally sexed young men falling in love normally, with beautiful high-born maidens in distress" (186). The status of the Gothic as an outsider tradition continued with the appropriation of the female writers who followed Walpole, most immediately Ann Radcliffe, whose novels of the 1790s served to consolidate the subgenre of the Female Gothic. One reason that marginalized and dispossessed writers were and are drawn to the Gothic tradition was that it was uncontested territory, dismissed as low culture, worthy only of low people. The writing of Gothic literature garnered little honor, and therefore it remained a canon open and available—there were no cultural gatekeepers blocking the path of the writer wishing to write in the Gothic mode.

* * *

The theme of narrative possession and dispossession emerges in the text of *Seven Gables* as well as in the Preface. The somewhat insecure narrator, who attempts to attain omniscience and clear-headedness, is destabilized in a number of ways, including by his own ghostly imaginings at the death of Judge Pyncheon. Occasionally competing narrative voices intrude to destabilize the narrator's voice, and to provide information that the narrator would repress. After the sudden death of Colonel Pyncheon, "there were many rumors," all unworthy of the narrator's "credence" (16). Similarly, after the death of Judge Pyncheon, "there was a hidden stream of private talk" (310–311) in which the submerged story of Judge Pyncheon's past crime surfaces. Indeed, Hawthorne intersperses his primary narrative with a chorus of communal voices commenting upon the actions of the main characters. An early customer of Hepzibah says of the novice shopkeeper, "'I was never so frightened in my life … if you could only see the mischief in her eye'" (54). Two such speakers, commenting on the good fortunes of the Pyncheons, provide the last lines of dialogue in the book. As they watch the Pyncheon entourage depart to the country, one says, "'If you choose to call it luck, it is all very well; but if we are to take it as the will of Providence, why, I can't exactly fathom it!'" (318). In addition to the competing speaking voices in the novel, Hawthorne introduces another writer and another text to interrupt the words of his narrator. At the end of Chapter 12, Holgrave invites Phoebe to listen to his story, inscribed on "a roll of manuscript" (186), and proceeds to read Chapter 13, "Alice Pyncheon" (187), telling Phoebe a story that is seemingly unknown to the omniscient narrator.

* * *

The tendency of the Gothic text to interrogate the capacity of the author, narrator, or reader to possess the narrative—illustrated by Hawthorne—poses a fruitful opportunity for Hannah Crafts. She can write without being suspected of cultural appropriation, of rising above her station, of taking on the kind of airs she is quick to dispel in her first humble lines. She can add herself to the line of dispossessed and marginalized writers who have contributed to the Gothic canon by borrowing from each other. The valorization of originality is alien to the Gothic, as each text transgresses the textual boundaries that separate if from the rest of the canon. Indeed, Crafts' pattern of borrowing is the technique that most links *The Bondswoman's Narrative* to the Gothic canon, that from its origins has been convention-ridden and intertextually repetitive. The tendency of Gothic literature to transgress boundaries—physical, categorical, national and generic—offers an opportunity to Crafts, who enters a transatlantic tradition that accepts her synthesis of the slave narrative and the Gothic novel. In "Gothic Liberties and Fugitive Novels: *The Bondswoman's Narrative* and the Fiction of Race," Karen Sánchez-Eppler, like other writers in the *In Search* collection considers the genre of the book and concludes it is a "hybrid" ("Gothic Liberties and Fugitive Novels" 257) that raises "questions about the nature of genre in the first place" (259). In fact, the same could be said of the entire Gothic tradition, which contests and transgresses all defining and confining categories and borders, including the category of genre.

Thus in the unpossessed, dismissed Gothic tradition, Hannah Crafts finds a place where she can take uncontested authorial possession, as a woman, a black, a slave, and an American. Because the Gothic is unpossessed and uncontested, Crafts can appropriate it, and revise it, making it into her own, while inserting herself into a literary tradition. As Augusta Rohrbach suggests, Crafts' borrowings indicate the place she wishes to stake in the literary canon: her "literary 'samplings' suggest the ... communities she wishes to connect with through her acts of intertextuality," in addition to "authenticating her literacy" ("'A Silent Unobtrusive Way'" 10).

Taking Authorial Possession—as a Woman

The texts that Crafts chooses as precursors indicate her security and vindicate her authority as a female writer. For while readers do accurately see echoes of Charlotte Brontë and Harriet Beecher Stowe[26]—and Crafts does emphasize the plight of the slave mother, as do Stowe and Harriet Jacobs—the most visible influences upon Crafts' novel are the great white male writers of the nineteenth century, Dickens and Hawthorne. Crafts extravagantly borrows language, images, characters and situations from Hawthorne's *Seven Gables* and from *Bleak House*, taking Gothic imitation to new heights. Yet (or consequently) the resulting text is radically original and creative, discovering new ground in the vast uncharted territory of the Gothic.[27]

Crafts bravely confronts and feminizes the texts of these two male literary pillars; showing herself to be a strong author, in the Bloomian sense; she makes these texts her own, taking on raw issues of rape and female vulnerability that do not find a place in the works of her male predecessors. The situation that finally precipitates Hannah into flight and into freedom is the prospect of being forced into marriage with a man she considers "vile, foul, filthy" (211). At the prospect, "my soul actually revolted with horror unspeakable" (211). The man with whom Crafts finally rewards her protagonist is very different from the near-patriarchal Holgrave who is Phoebe's prize; Hannah's husband is her "companion" who "sits by my side" in equality (245), a mild Methodist preacher, who seemingly accedes to her previous renunciation of maternity, and thus renounces the role of patriarch. Hannah's children are the students "of the school" (246). Hannah creates her female version of Eden, surrounded by "my mother, my husband, and by my friends" (246), liberated from the bonds of slavery, and from the responsibilities of maternity that weighed down so many nineteenth-century women, and so many heroines at the conclusion of the conventional Gothic novel.

In her more self-consciously literary moments, Crafts emphatically asserts the perspective of her gender, for example, when Hawthorne's painting of the patriarch, that defines genealogy and property, is countered by Crafts' portrait of the slave mother, that also establishes genealogy and property—the matrilineal line of slavery through which the child becomes property. Crafts' revision thus points to the unique form that property takes in her time and text. The representation of the patriarch in *Seven Gables* reminds us that the importance of the patriarchal family derives from its being the basis of inheritance and ownership of land. Crafts' representation of the slave mother, on the other hand, highlights the maternal basis of slave status. Crafts develops her feminization of Hawthorne's image of the portrait in her reference to another important scene. In the chapter "Governer Pyncheon" where Hawthorne's narrator imagines the appearance of the family ghosts, he invokes "the whole tribe" of Pyncheons, including "[a] mother [who] lifts her child, that his little hands may touch" (280) the Pyncheon portrait. Hawthorne's anonymous mother seems to be of little consequence, repressed in being figured as both a ghost, and a product of the narrator's imagination; moreover, she seems to exist only to serve the desire of her grasping male child. In Crafts' reworking of this scene, the ghostly mother enacts an uncanny return, taking on more substantial form as an actual portrait. Passing by "a long succession of family portraits" (15) in the Vincent portrait gallery, Hannah observes the picture of a young woman: "the long shining locks of a young mother waver and float over the child she holds" (17). Craft's reworking of the image of the mother refocuses the descriptive attention away from the male child, highlighting the mother with her "long shining locks" that threaten to obscure the child in her arms. Similarly the "granddames" (279) barely noticed in the fantasy of Hawthorne's narrator solidify into Crafts' single, humanized, "ancient dame" whose "frozen cheek ... seems beguiled into smiles and dimples" (17). Finally, to complement these two women—the mother and the old woman—to fill in the representation of the full cycle of female life (in the nineteenth century), Crafts adds a young female figure absent from Hawthorne's Pyncheon panoply: "Over the pale pure features of a bride descends a halo of glory" (17).[28] In fact, it is the male portrait model that Crafts elides. Whereas Hawthorne's array of Pyncheons contains a number of male types—"aged men," "clergyman," "shopkeeper," "gentleman" (279–280)—Crafts limits her descriptions of male portraits only to two masculine figures: the ruler and the soldier, Sir Clifford De Vincent, counterpart to Colonel Pyncheon, and a "veteran in the old-time war" (Crafts 17), counterpart to Hawthorne's "red-coated officer" (279).

Crafts thus reacts to the conventional Gothic repressions of the female, especially the mother, in Hawthorne's text; for while Hawthorne does present the conventional figure of the young woman, the heroine, in the form of Phoebe and the ghostly Alice (neither of whom is provided with a rich inner life) and to his credit, provides us with a rich and sympathetic depiction of an elderly woman, Hepzibah, no mother or wife, or woman in the full flush of life makes an appearance in his text. The patriarchs of the competing clans Colonel Pyncheon and Matthew Maule appear to have engendered their dynasties without the benefit of female intervention: there is no record of any Maule or Pyncheon ancestress in Hawthorne's introductory first chapter. Moreover, the long line of male Pyncheon descendents "gifted" with the "hard, keen sense, and practical energy" inherited from "the original founder" (19), along with the "ancestral house" that passes "from father to son" (20) perpetuates itself with no visible maternal input, with the single exception of a "great, great, great, great grandmother," whose sole contribution to the family is a "China tea set" (76–77). Alice Pyncheon, too, appears to emerge from the Pyncheon line with practically no trace of a mother. We do hear that "[s]he has brought a fair face from Italy" (188), and we might infer that this trait is inherited from her conventionally missing mother. But Alice's only visible parent is her father, Gervayse Pyncheon, who, like every Gothic patriarch who precedes him both within *Seven Gables* and in the Gothic canon, is willing to sacrifice his child to his dynastic imperatives. In a telling aside, we learn that the repression of the female line originates with the progenitor of the line, and that the Pycheon patriarchy fits quite comfortably into Gothic archetypes. The narrator's description of Colonel Pyncheon recounts that "an autocrat in his own household, [he] had worn out three wives, and merely by the remorseless weight and hardness of his character in the conjugal relation, had sent them one after another, broken hearted to their graves" (123). We can infer that Judge Pyncheon, "The Pyncheon of To-Day," also follows in this villainous tradition. Hepzibah tells Phoebe that Judge Pyncheon is "'the horror of my life!'" (131). When the judge is introduced, the narrator informs us that he had "wedded but a single wife, and lost her in the third or fourth year of their marriage," and somewhat skeptically and unsympathetically alludes to a "fable ... that the lady got her death-blow in the honeymoon, and never smiled again, because her husband compelled her to serve him with coffee, every morning, at his bedside, in token of fealty to her liegelord and master" (123). However, we have come to distrust the elisions and the skepticism of Hawthorne's narrator, leaving us to wonder what else Judge Pyncheon demanded of his wife during the truncated marriage. As the narrator reviews the responsibilities that the now-dead Judge Pyncheon is allowing to lapse, one duty he records is: "the renewal of Mrs. Pyncheon's tombstone" (271). The narrator returns to Judge Pyncheon's sanguine view of her life and death: "in spite of her nervousness, and the tears that she was so oozy with, and her foolish behavior about the coffee," she merits a repaired tombstone because she had the goodness to die "so seasonably," and it was better to need to replace the tombstone rather "than if she had never needed any!" (272). Certainly Hepzibah is correct in considering this man "a horror."

Phoebe seems to be the rare Pyncheon woman who will be spared the fate of her predecessors. Her Pyncheon father dying young after marrying a "a young woman of no family or property" (24), she is raised in the country with a non–Pyncheon step-father; we are reminded frequently that she has been spared Seven Gables and the Pyncheons. Phoebe announces, "'I have not been brought up a Pyncheon'" (74), an assessment confirmed by Hepzibah's unintended compliment: "'Phoebe is no Pyncheon. She takes everything from her mother'" (79). And yet, the closure of *Seven Gables* suggests that Phoebe, too, is fated to be subsumed by a dynastic patriarch. As she and Holgrave go off to the country to start afresh, we cannot entirely forget that Holgrave, secretive and manipulative, comes from the line of Maules with their "hereditary character of reserve" (26), and other inherited "mysterious attributes" (26), the line that engendered Matthew Maule, who used his terrible powers to crush and kill proud Alice Pyncheon. Holgrave himself suggests a return to the patriarchal model at the end of the novel: "'I have a presentiment, that, hereafter, it will be my lot to set out trees, to make fences … to conform myself to laws'" (307). In other words, Holgrave fully expects to return to the Gothic world where men rule over women whom they confine and control through physical and legal barriers. Holgrave's devolution into the conventionally dangerous Gothic patriarch does not bode well for Phoebe.

The absence of a full range of female models in *Seven Gables* accounts for Crafts' turn to the inspiration of *Bleak House* for a fuller array of female characters, including the mother who appears, albeit temporarily. Indeed, in "The Virtues of the Mothers," John C. Ward makes a case for the "'power'" (40 quoting Dickens) of Lady Dedlock and her daughter, thus suggesting the attraction of Dickens' novel for Crafts: *Bleak House* offers a model for the figure of the strong and fully-engaged woman. However, Crafts also turns to her own imagination (or some undiscovered sources) for the array of strong women who populate her book: the mentor who rescues Hannah from illiteracy and teaches her at great personal risk; Mrs. Wright who has lost all because she bravely assisted a slave girl to escape; Mrs. Henry, the benefactress whose home is an earthly paradise in which Hannah finds sanctuary. Crafts demonstrates her writing skill by refusing the nineteenth-century impulse to delineate a saintly one-dimensional portrait of the benevolent female character. Mrs. Henry is a very good woman, but she is also a rigid and legalistic woman. She refuses to break an oath she made to her father not to buy or sell a slave, even though, as Hannah notes, this is a cruel promise. "Since in a multitude of cases the greatest favor that a mild kind-hearted man or woman can bestow on members of the outcast service race is to buy them" (132). Mrs. Henry insists on following the letter of the oath, rather than the spirit of the oath, setting up her pride against her morality, and resulting in a richly multidimensional character. Mrs. Wright, who willing breaks the law to save slaves is an equally complicated character; the paradoxically illegal morality she deploys shows that she, too, is an exemplary literary character, reflecting complexities found in real, multivariate woman. And though the figure of Hannah's own mother is far less complex, she is an active agent, identifying and regaining Hannah as her child—as opposed to all the invisible and passive Gothic mothers who precede her. Crafts also creates a strong and complex woman in her protagonist, who renounces the conventional role of mother. She rejects marriage and sexuality, proposing "celibacy" for slaves, not only because a slave cannot fulfill the "responsibilities of marriage" (133), but also because slave marriage and sexuality tends "essentially to perpetuate that system" (212) by creating children to become future generations of slaves.. Thus although she happily finds her own mother, Hannah resists motherhood for herself, even at the moment of the novel's happy ending where no child is mentioned among her many blessings, because "it was my unalterable resolution never to entail slavery on any human being" (213).

Taking Authorial Possession—as an Enslaved African American

Crafts' revision of the Gothic trope of the recovered heir of the contested property identifies her as a radically original writer, carving out her own distinct place in the web of influence to which she links herself. Hawthorne reveals Holgrave as the secret heir of Seven Gables, following in the path of Walpole who reveals Theodore as the unknown heir of Otranto; both heirs take over the property appropriated from their forebears. But in Crafts' formulation, Hannah is both contested property and heiress, the belatedly revealed legitimate owner of herself. In this, Crafts radically redefines the notions of property and ownership, revealing that a slave who is figured as human property actually has a subjective reality and a voice, and that, therefore, ownership of human property is illegitimate.

There are a number of moments in the novel in which white characters betray a shocking disregard for the feelings of their fellow human beings. After Trappe and a slave trader haggle over her price in her presence as if she were an inanimate object, and order her to walk across a room to prove her value, Trappe, with evident sincerity asks her, as she is about to be shipped off to the unknown: "'What the devil are you crying for?'" (110). This callousness is repeated when the trader himself, who has already shown "kindness" by offering Hannah "some very nice cake, iced over with sugar, and highly delicious," asks, "'Don't you never smile?'" In response to Hannah's "'not lately,'" the trader tells her, "'I always like to hear my people sing, to have them laugh, and see them jovial and merry'" (117). Hannah is prevented from a reply, and indeed what reply can there be to such a statement. Earlier when Mr. Trappe reproaches her for weeping, she reports that she "had no voice to speak" (111).

Yet while the slave Hannah must suffer silently, the author Hannah Crafts gives her a voice and in doing so, takes possession of her text. As Gates and Robbins state in their Introduction, referring to Gayatri Spivack's silent subaltern, Crafts' character, Hannah, is "the subaltern who speaks" (xiii). In a powerful interlude at the end of the novel, when Hannah observes the field slaves and considers the "curse of slavery," Crafts lets loose a volley of reproach addressed to "Doctors of Divinity," demanding their empathy: "It must be a strange state to feel that in the judgement above you are scarcely human, and to fear that their opinion is more than half right, that you really are assimilated to the brutes" (207). The second-person address of this passage works in two complementary ways. On one hand, Crafts forces her readers to identify with the humanity of those figured by law as non-speaking working machines. On the other, Crafts refuses to join her characters in the position of the silent and objectified slave. She refuses to position herself as a mutely inanimate and mysteriously unknowable piece of property. She feels; she speaks; she refuses to be a silent and inanimate, commodified object. By looking at the situation of the slave from the perspective of the Doctors of Divinity, which she appropriates as their equal, Crafts achieves the empathetic connection whose failure, she suggests, lies at the heart of slavery.

Nor does Crafts allow her reader to forget that the body behind the voice is black, belonging to the racial Other. Reversing the social and cultural norms of speaking subject as white, and mute object as black, Hannah reminds us that the black body is human, and that it contains a human mind. As Gates and Robbins note in their Introduction, citing Porter, "the blackness of her characters [is] the default" (xxxviii); that is, Crafts creates a world where blackness is the norm, the human, and not the distanced Other. At some moments Hannah reveals that she has internalized the prejudices of the dominant society, perceiving the black to be inferior. A nemesis of Hannah is described as "a dark mulatto ... with black snaky eyes, and hair of the same color" (208). Bill, the field slave who wants to "marry" Hannah lives in a cabin that features "a large pool of black mud" and is "reeking with filth and impurity" (215). But more often, in a reversal akin to that described by Teresa Goddu in *Gothic America*, Crafts highlights the black disgust with the white body. When attending to the personal needs of the mistress, Mrs. Wheeler, she has to comb her hair which had not "been combed for more than a week," and discovers that it is "actually matted" (153)—an unsavory, and almost animal-like situation. When she finds herself working on a plantation, Hannah notes the overseer: "with a countenance grossly sensual and repulsive ... his person was extremely offensive and indelicate from want of cleanliness" (214). Thus, from Hannah's perspective, in Crafts' formulation, mystifyingly monstrous whites behave without humanity, and are correspondingly physically repulsive. Crafts' emphasis on the reversal of roles is most visible in the episode of Mrs. Wheeler, the mistress who mistakenly applies face powder that darkens her skin. Going to a political gathering, unknowingly so complected, Mrs. Wheeler is stunned by the disrespect with which she is treating. She is insulted by "'everybody,'" her marriage is disparaged and she is rebuffed in her attempt to advance her husband's career, told that "'it was not customary to bestow offices on colored people'" (173). It is no coincidence that this reversal occurs at a social gathering; Crafts taps into the trope of the masquerade, the literary moment when reversals and subversions occur, to emphasize the artificiality of cultural norms—in this case the racializing of power.

The story of Mrs. Wheeler suggests that Crafts is familiar with the literary convention of the masquerade, as she is certainly aware of the conventions of the Gothic canon. And clearly, Crafts as a writer is adept at appropriating and manipulating the conventions. In fact, ultimately Crafts' skill takes her beyond the roles of reader and writer; she writes as a scholar. She displays her wealth of knowledge of other texts, and of the patterns of relationship that exist between texts, allowing her reader to better understand the canon to which she alludes; additionally, Crafts offers literary and social commentary, based on her reading and on her keen observation of the world around her. Indeed, rather than being overpowered by the web of texts in which she locates her novel, Crafts masterfully manipulates the texts of her precursors, confidently revising them to reveal something rich and radically new. As Gates and Robbins note in their Introduction, "In her delicate and meaningful transformations, Crafts reveals ... her critical acumen" (xiii). Indeed, in her reworking of a web of texts from the Gothic tradition, Crafts reveals the true depth and breadth of her critical skills.

Hannah Crafts, American Writer

Hannah Crafts' self-consciousness as a writer, and her awareness of how she fits into the literary tradition, align her with her fellow American writers, who during her time were still grappling with their place in relation to the English literary tradition, responding to what Weisbuch calls "the burden of Britain" (ix). Weisbuch acknowledges that he is talking of canonical American writers—white males—and speculates that "women [and] Afro-Americans" would experience a "double bind. They would see themselves oppressed by the oppressed" (xx). If that is the case with Crafts, it is also the case that, like her American peers, she overcomes her sense of "intimidation" (ix) to create her work. Indeed, the new material and perspectives that enrich Crafts' art align with the American tradition that is constantly transforming the terms of the conventional English precursors. Just as Charles Brockden Brown transforms the old terms of the English Gothic to consider the journey of the young American subject, so does Hannah Crafts "transform" other texts "to craft her own tale of finding freedom" (Gates and Robbins Introduction xiii). Similarly, Crafts closely aligns herself with the Gothic tradition and its preoccupations with property possession and authorial authority as a way of dealing with her sense of displacement as a black, unfree, female American. Crafts thus locates herself firmly in the tradition of the American Gothic and presents an intriguing explanation for the strong overlap between the anxious Gothic mode, preoccupied with the instability of all possessions, and nineteenth-century American literature, still in search of a stable identity. Additionally the Gothic disdain for originality poses a solution for the American writer on a quest to create a new national literature, while haunted by the British past. The Gothic reliance on recurring tropes empowers a writer to legitimately imitate others. Indeed, Crafts' act of imitation represents a confident entrance into the constantly repeating Gothic canon and into the canon of nineteenth-century American literature which is so dominated by the Gothic. Crafts works to create an American text and to define herself as an American author, which is why it is so important to see the influence of Hawthorne hovering behind the many English novels that weave their way into Crafts' text. Hollis Robbins asks: is Crafts' novel "a British text or a Black one?" ("Blackening *Bleak House*" 82). Although Crafts does align herself to an interlinked web of texts, many of them English, *The Bondswoman's Narrative* is explicitly and self-consciously an American text in the American Gothic tradition. The recognition of the importance of the American influence in Crafts' novel, amplifies her significance as a literary writer, in that she synthesizes the Anglo and American influences in her novel, thereby highlighting the relationship between the two.

A seemingly random episode at the end of the Crafts' book sheds light on her self-aware *homage* to Hawthorne. Faced with a forced marriage that is akin to rape, Hannah finally decides to escape her bondage. Fleeing her role as slave, she also sheds her gender. She finds a "suit of male apparel exactly corresponding to my size and figure" (216), and transforms herself into the quintessential nineteenth-century American protagonist, the young white male "orphan" (218), parentless and masterless. Crafts thus emblematizes her appropriation of the role of American author, also defined as young, white and male in the nineteenth century, as, for example, by Melville in "Hawthorne and his Mosses." Nor is this reinvention Crafts' only commentary on her place in the American canon. For in the course of her escape, Hannah stumbles upon a loyal and fearful brother and sister who are also in "flight" (222). Suddenly, Crafts invades and raids Hawthorne's novel, appropriating, or indeed invading, the chapter, "The Flight of Two Owls." This chapter tells of the escape of Hepzibah and Clifford, another pair of hapless siblings. Crafts converges her novel and characters with those of Hawthorne, in order to grapple with his influence. In a move that may be read as Oedipal, after engaging Hannah with the two, Crafts kills off the pair of siblings in her novel; the escaping slave woman dies of disease, and her brother is shot. Only Hannah remains alive to continue her adventure and her solitary journey.[29] Having sacrificed the children of her precursor, Crafts proves herself his equal. Hannah steps into the quintessential American role: the solitary youth on the search for identity—though this youth is a woman, and unequivocally benefits from being masterless. Thus Hannah Crafts boldly defines herself as a legitimate American, and a legitimate American author. Rather than accepting her marginalized status, she links herself to the tradition of the American Gothic, staking a claim in that spacious canon and thus expanding the territory of this labyrinthine tradition.

8

Intertextual Voices in Gloria Naylor's *Mama Day*
Shakespeare, the Bible and the Dispossession of the Reader

In memory of Gloria Naylor, 1950–2016

Gloria Naylor's *Mama Day* (1988) is a more subtle appropriation of the Gothic form than is her novel *Linden Hills* (1985). Nevertheless, Naylor makes clear from the outset that her novel of 1988 (which ends in the twenty-first century) stakes a claim to Gothic space. Willow Springs, the barrier island off the shore of Georgia and South Carolina abides by the conventions of the Gothic setting, the space existing out of time and space. Although located off the coast of the United States, the island is not exactly part of the mainland country: Georgia and South Carolina have been trying unsuccessfully "since right after the Civil War to prove that Willow Springs belong to one or the other of them" (4–5). Nor do the residents of the island, descendants of slaves, consider themselves American citizens: "American ain't entered the question at all when it come to our land…. And we wasn't even American when we got it—was slaves" (5). Other Gothic conventions deployed by Naylor are the besieged young woman, the family curse descending through the generations, and despite the modernity of the setting, a strong dose of the supernatural, including the talking dead, and a matriarch (Miranda, Mama Day) who may, or may not, have divine powers. Naylor further consolidates her debt to the Gothic tradition in *Mama Day* by focusing her narrative on issues of possession: of land, of the body—in slavery and marriage, and of narrative and manuscript. In the American Gothic tradition, Willow Springs is suitably furnished with a haunted house, the Other Place, the abandoned house of the patriarchal slave owner, Bascombe Wade. The seeming project of the characters in *Mama Day* is the breaking of the vestigial Gothic cycle of family dysfunction that endure in the Day family. When George, the husband of Mama Day's grandniece, dies of a broken heart as do all the Day men before him, he ends the cycle, somehow.

Naylor radically revises the terms of the Gothic by modifying the structures of patriarchy and usurpation. *Mama Day* is a late Gothic text that begins more than a century after the destruction of the patriarchal dynasty of slavery. The slave-owner, Bascomb Wade, has been subverted by Sapphira, the slave woman who appropriated his property (including herself and her children) and founded the matriarchal dynasty whose descendants inhabit the island. The line of Day men who precede George disrupt the Gothic paradigm of demonic husbands—each is a good man whose heart is broken through love of his wife. In the world of *Mama Day*, the insular family, dominated by a powerful evil Gothic patriarch, is replaced by a large open community ruled by a powerful and benevolent African American matriarch, Mama Day, whose racial identity is solidified by her proud use of African American vernacular and by her reliance on magical traditions brought from Africa.

The Voices of the Island

Naylor effectively draws on the trope of multiple narrators in her novel, creating a number of narrators, including a communal voice that recalls the chorus of Hawthorne's *House of the Seven Gables*. Much of the action of the novel unfolds in a conversation between Cocoa and her dead husband, George. We learn that every year Cocoa returns to the island to visit George and to share with him, in an extended dialogue, the events that led to his death, and her salvation. As the two characters talk, with the reader eavesdropping, the story of what happened to them on Willow Springs unfolds. Yet because the two talk to each other, the meanings of the dialogue are not always clear. Sometimes the reader has to reread to determine whether a particular passage is spoken by George or by Cocoa. The narrative of Naylor's novel thus demonstrates the Gothic tendency to subvert narrative coherence and thereby to defeat attempts by characters and readers to fully apprehend the text.

The Privileged Reader

In a number of ways the reader of Naylor's novel is in a privileged position in regards to apprehending the mysteries of the text. The prefatory material of the book provides important information that is not accessible to any of the characters, including the almost omniscient matriarch, Mama Day. We encounter a genealogical table that begins with the name and birth-date of "Sapphira Wade (1799-)" (np). Naylor provides the names of the descendants in the five generations that succeed Sapphira, ending with the last living member of the last generation, "Ophelia b. 1953 (Cocoa)" (np), the female protagonist of the novel. The following page reinforces the notion that Sapphira was the slave of Bascombe Wade, who we later discover, was the father of her seven sons. Naylor provides the full text of a deed dated 1819, recording that Sapphira was "sold to Mister Bascombe Wade of Willow Springs" (np). The deed informs the seller, and the reader, that Sapphira, who is "inflicted with sullenness and entertains a bilious nature," has served as a "midwife and nurse, not without extreme mischief and suspicions of delving in witchcraft." Finally we read the "Conditions of Sale: one-half gold tender, one half goods in kind." Through these documents the reader knows more about the Day family than they do themselves, including the name of Sapphira. We next see this deed of ownership for the slave Sapphira late in the novel when Mama Day ventures to the Other Place, the deserted plantation, and discovers the old deed, hidden for centuries in the ledger in which Bascombe kept the records for the slave transactions. She cannot know how old the deed is; the year appears as "a 1 and half of what must be an 8, with the rest of the date faded away" (280). Since we know that the deed was dated "1819" and the action is occurring in 1985, we can deduce that the deed at the time of Mama Day's discovery is 166 years old. By the time Mama Day finds the document, it has deteriorated through age and neglect so that it is barely legible. Like Hawthorne, Naylor revises the conventional Gothic trope of the fragmented and illegible document; in their novels, the document is the illegible (and illegitimate) deed of property. As the missing and illegible property deed of *Seven Gables* destabilize the certainty of land possession in America, so does Naylor's fragmented deed destabilize the notion of ownership of human property. The fragmented remnant of the deed,[1] that was earlier available to the reader in its entirety, reveals only a few legible words. The full name of the slave is defaced, appearing only as "Sa" (280), leaving Mama Day to speculate in frustration: "She's staring at the name and trying to guess. Sara, Sabrina, Sally.... A loss that she can't describe seeps over her—a missing key to an unknown door somewhere in that house.... All Willow Springs knows that this woman was nobody's slave. But what was her name?" (280). The few remaining legible words of the deed also withhold the underlying truth. Miranda can only read: "Sold to Mister Bascombe Wade of Willow Springs, one negress answering to the name Sa.... Law ... knowledge ... witness ... inflicted ... nurse.... Conditions ... tender ... kind" (280). Mama Day is preternaturally wise and discerning yet even so these fragments resist her ample powers of interpretation; she is unable to accurately decipher or reconstruct the document. The fragmented and decontextualized words, "tender ... kind" belie their true, cruel, legal meanings, the meanings known only to the reader who remembers the entire document from the outer frame of the narrative.

Naylor's version of the reconstruction of the fragmented narrative transforms the trope to reveal problems of narrative reconstruction that are usually elided by the Gothic text. Typically, fragmentation indicates age, and the unreliability of narrative, but in fact, the meaning of the defaced manuscript somehow remains intact. In Clara Reeve's *The Old English Baron* (1777), for example, the occasional illegible pages in the discovered manuscript do not impede the recovery and ultimate rectification of the repressed history of murder and usurpation; similarly, although entire pages of narrative are purportedly missing from Charles Maturin's *Melmoth the Wanderer* (1820), the line of narration remains clear.[2] The traditional amelioration of the disruptive capacities of this trope may be read in the context of the conventional restoration of normalcy (and property) at the end of the Gothic narrative. This reading amplifies the conservative strain of the English Gothic, a strain that promotes the restoration of effaced meaning, as it promotes the restoration of usurped property. The proprietorship of the narrator and property owner appear to be disrupted, but the narrative unfolds to restore property and meaning. Naylor's refutation of the conventional restoration of narrative meaning suggests that the institution of slavery negates the possibility of restored meaning or identity, causing an irreparable schism between the present and the past. The lacunae in the history of many African American families can never be filled. The comfort offered with the restoration of property is not available when the property is human; stolen life cannot be restored.

* * *

The reader is also situated in a privileged position regarding the many narrative voices that circulate within the text. The voices of the dead, audible only to those who venture into the Willow Springs cemetery with a piece of moss in their shoes, are also audible to us. George speaks to Cocoa from beyond death, and Cocoa hears and replies; no other characters hear this exchange, but every word is available to the reader. Additional voices are a third person narrative voice, and a collective narrative voice that appears to emanate from the community; these two voices, too, are only audible to the reader. During at least one moment, the communal voice also allows the reader access to the (misguided) white perspective. When a young white deputy ventures across the Bridge into Willow Springs, he is challenged by Mama Day when he speaks disrespectfully to the people in the general store. The communal voice tells us: "Guess he only saw an old colored lady with a bag of groceries and a red straw hat cocked on her head" (80). By this point, the reader is shocked by this view of Mama Day, as we have come to know her as a socially, psychologically and perhaps magically powerful matriarch. Indeed, the mistake of the young white Sheriff's perception is confirmed when we learn that later that night, the sheriff finds himself "left alone wandering down in the cypress swamp," stranded with a non-working radio because of a quirk of weather inexplicable to the scientific mind: "Not a drop of rain or a bit of wind—just a sky lit up with them lightning bolts" (80). The white Sheriff may be oblivious, but the astute reader has enough evidence to guess that Mama Day is the source of this strange weather.

The Temptations of Allusion

The reader's position of privilege—of being in possession of knowledge and hearing voices unavailable to the characters of the novel—is heightened by the evocation of an additional set of voices, the intertextual voices that are evoked throughout the narrative. In these evocations, Naylor exemplifies Henry Louis Gates, Jr.'s observation regarding the doubleness of the tradition of the African American writer: "Anyone who analyzes black literature must do so as a comparativist, by definition, because our canonical texts have complex double formal antecedents, the Western and the black" (*The Signifying Monkey* xxiv). As a result, Gates argues, "The black tradition is double-voiced" (xxv). The textual voices that enter Naylor's novel, then, reflect the African American tradition, as well as the tradition of the Gothic text. The voices of the Bible and Shakespeare are particularly audible in *Mama Day*.[3] Importing these exemplars of the literary canon into her work provides Naylor with an external source of power and grace, while also amplifying the sense of privilege, particularly on the part of the educated reader who (in opposition to the inhabitants of Willow Springs) possesses the literacy necessary to recognize the many allusions.

Shakespearean Voices

Allusions to Shakespeare inform Naylor's text. In fact, the initials of the island name, Willow Springs, suggest the name of her precursor. The web of

Shakespearean allusions in Naylor's novel places her strongly within the Gothic tradition. In the preface to his seminal Gothic novel *The Castle of Otranto*, Horace Walpole delineates his literary debt to Shakespeare. Indeed, it is difficult to read *Hamlet* without identifying the many Gothic tropes that Shakespeare anticipates: the struggle of the innocent subject to identify evil; dysfunctional, incestuous family relations, cursed by the burden of secrets; the beleaguered young woman; familial and political jousting for power and possession; the haunted house and the supernatural; madness and death. Not surprisingly, Naylor, like Walpole, turns to *Hamlet* in her novel. The most direct invocation is the presence of a drowned, mad character named Ophelia, who is the mother of Mama Day and her sister Abigail. Naylor's Ophelia is another of the missing mothers of the Gothic tradition; she jumps into the Sound after her daughter, Peace, drowns in a well. Additionally, as in *Hamlet*, the ghosts of dead ancestors reveal important family secrets to the living in Naylor's novel. In typical Gothic tradition, Naylor imports a theme in order to provide a variation. Her great revision of *Hamlet* is to re-create the weak tragic figure of Ophelia as the strong protagonist, Cocoa, whose birth name is Ophelia. Unlike her great-grandmother and her Shakespearean namesake, Ophelia emerges from the text sane, alive, and assured of a future unmarked by the depredations of the patriarchy.

Naylor also references *King Lear*. Right before going on a date with Cocoa, George abandons his reading: "I had left King Lear naked and wandering on a stormy heath before coming to meet you" (59). George, who has a heart condition which eventually kills him, relates to Lear who essentially dies of a broken heart after the death of Cordelia. At the end of the play, Kent, in pity bids Lear: "Break heart; I prithee, break!" (V.iii.314). The language of Lear also connects him to the husband of the first Ophelia, John-Paul, the father of the dead daughter, Peace, who, like his slave-owning grandfather, Bascombe Wade, dies of a broken heart, grief-stricken at the loss of his wife. Here too, Naylor suggests a revision. While George also dies of a broken heart, in doing so he saves his beloved wife, Ophelia (Cocoa), and seems to break the cycle of broken-hearted men that is the curse of the Day family.

The allusions to these plays are important to *Mama Day*, but the play that seeps into the bones of the novel is *The Tempest*, despite Cocoa's dismissal of the relevance of the text and its author: "'Shakespeare didn't have a bit of soul—I don't care if he wrote about Othello, Cleopatra, and some slave on a Caribbean island'" (64). Naylor seems to explicitly counter Cocoa's skepticism, setting up a parallel that suggests how strongly Shakespeare anticipates issues central to the African American experience. *The Tempest* and *Mama Day* both present a central character named "Miranda"; both are set on remote islands with a history of slavery, islands that are haunted by disembodied voices. Both islands are ruled by a powerful magical figure, whose magic may be supernatural or possibly derived from psychological acuity. Like Shakespeare's aging Prospero, Naylor's aged, African American female protagonist, Mama Day, possesses power associated with a book and a staff, which she, like Prospero, ultimately relinquishes. At the end of the play, Prospero promises: "'I'll break my staff,/ Bury it certain fathoms in the earth,/ And deeper that did ever plummet sound/ I'll drown my book'" (V.i.63–66). When Mama Day turns to George for help in saving Cocoa, she "takes up the [slave] ledger and the walking cane" (295), which had been carved by her father. Additionally, both islands are visited by a "tempest" (*Mama Day* 256) which precipitates the complications and dénouements of both texts. In both texts, the power of the central figure is contested by a clownish character, Shakespeare's Caliban and Naylor's Dr. Buzzard. Indeed, Naylor creates a drunken scene that echoes the carousing of the drunken Caliban with the two sailors from the waylaid ship. When George agrees to play cards with Dr. Buzzard, he is treated to "clear liquid from an earthen jug" (209), moonshine that ensures his participation in the rhythmic clapping and singing, and his return to Cocoa unable to get into the house without "three pairs of ... soft ... arms ... guiding me up the steps" (215). Like Shakespeare, Naylor shows the depth of her sensitivity to her characters by providing her clown with a humanizing back story. We learn from Caliban's poignant speech to Prospero that he authentically loves the island that Prospero stole from him by playing on his good intentions: "'This island's mine by Sycorax my mother,/ Which thou tak'st from me. When thou cam'st first/ Thou strok'st me and made much of me.... And then I loved thee'" (I.ii.395–402). From Dr. Buzzard's conversation with George, the reader learns that Buzzard is not entirely the buffoonish usurper whom Mama Day and the narrator dismiss. Dr. Buzzard tells George: "'Yeah, I got a home. And it sits on the seventy-acres my uncle left me.... I got married too. But some folks can live here and some can't.... I stay away from there.... 'Cause if I was in it ... there wouldn't be nobody out here to miss it" (187–188).

Voices from the Bible

Important as Shakespeare's plays are to *Mama Day*, a number of key moments gesture to the Bible, and while the novel can be fully appreciated without knowledge of Shakespeare's plays, an accounting of the biblical allusions is essential in untangling some of its mysteries.[4] Even before the novel begins, Naylor presents a web of allusions to the Bible in the prefatory pages where we encounter the genealogical table of the descendants of Sapphira Wade. Knowledge of the Bible reveals that the first generation names are all derived from Hebrew Bible prophets, while the names of the second generation derive from the Christian Bible. Additionally, the surname of the family, taken by Sapphira herself—in resistance to Wade, the name of her owner/husband—is "Day," because "God rested on the seventh day and so would she" (np). In Sapphira's case, the seventh Day is her seventh son. This is but one of several links between Sapphira and the God of the Bible; there are more. Sapphira is godlike in that her name cannot be spoken because it is not known. Not knowing her actual name, people of present-day Willow Springs call her "the Mother who began the Days" (262). George says to Cocoa: "It was odd again the way you said it—she was the great, great, grand Mother—as if you were listing the attributes of a goddess" (218). Thus, as Naylor feminizes Shakespeare's Prospero, she feminizes the patriarchal God of the Bible. As the hurricane descends upon Willow Springs the narrator tells us that the massive tempest "could only be the workings of Woman. And She has no name" (251).

Naylor also feminizes Jesus, in the person of Mama Day, the descendant of the godlike Sapphira. Like Jesus, Miranda works through miracles of healing. When she is called to heal a baby dying of croup, she sits, "hour by hour, the baby cradled in her arms" (193), until she knows that with the help of God, "the child was gonna make it" (194). Even more miraculously, in some ambiguous way, Mama Day helps the infertile Bernice engender a child. In this major episode as in much of the book, Naylor straddles the line between psychological realism and supernatural magic, leaving the reader to wonder if Mama Day's power lies in her knowledge of folk medicine and human psychology, or in her possession of supernatural powers. To enable Bernice's pregnancy, Mama Day puts her on a complicated regimen involving pumpkin seeds, squash, saffron water, and dewberry juice. She tells Abigail, "'She got something to keep her busy, and now she got something to hope for.'" When Abigail responds skeptically, Mama Day says: "'The mind is a funny thing, Abigail—and a powerful thing at that. Bernice is gonna believe they are what I tell her they are—magic seeds. And the only magic is what she believes they are'" (96). So far we are in the scientific world of human psychology, the source of the power of the placebo.

However, the scene in which Bernice meets Mama Day at the Other place suggests that more than natural science is at play. In this strange and mysterious scene, Naylor mystically intones, "Space to space. Ancient fingers, keeping each in line. The uncountable, the unthinkable, is one opening. Pulsing and alive—wet—the egg moves from one space to the other. A rhythm older than woman draws it in and holds it tight" (140). And though the skeptical reader might dismiss the ritual at the Other place as part of Mama Day's attempt to manipulate Bernice psychologically so that she can relax and have a baby, we are left with the unaccountable fact that the resulting child looks like a little chicken. Despite his mother's irritation, people call him "Chick," because "That's what he looked like, toddling around: little pecan head sitting on a scrawny neck, two bright buttons for eyes, and a feathery mess of hair" (161). Mama Day, like Jesus, disavows her power—"I ain't in the business of miracles" (239).

The miraculous birth of Bernice's child is part of an extended allusion in the novel to a story in the Hebrew Bible that anticipates the story of Jesus: the tale of the prophet Elisha and the Shunamite woman. In the Bible, the prophet Elisha wishes to repay the kindness of the Shunamite woman who provides him with food and shelter on his wanderings. His servant Gehazi tells him "'she hath no child, and her husband is old'" (2 Kings 4.14). The prophet then tells the woman that in a year's time "'thou shalt embrace a son'" (2 Kings 4.16). The son is born and grows; one day he is out in the field and sickens. He is brought to his mother, laid on her knees, "and then died" (2 Kings 4.20). The mother puts him on the bed of the prophet, shuts the door and goes out, telling no one that the child has died. She "saddled an ass, and said to her servant, 'Drive and go forward; slack not thy riding for me'" (2 Kings 4.24). Finding the prophet, she confronts him and says, "'Did I desire a son of my lord? Did I not say, Do not deceive me?'" (2 Kings 4.28). The prophet responds to this reproach by sending his servant ahead to the boy with his staff (yet another powerful rod in this web of images), commanding the servant to "'lay my staff upon the face of the child'" (2 Kings 4.29). When Elisha arrives, he finds the boy dead, but he brings the boy back to life, and restores him to this mother. The story of Bernice revises, humanizes, and naturalizes this tale in a terrible way. Bernice's son, like the miraculously conceived son of the Shunamite woman, dies mysteriously, an ambiguous consequence of the hurricane, the tempest. Perhaps "a drowning in them gullies," or "live wires hanging from the electric poles" (256). Bernice takes the body of her son and puts him into her "white convertible" (256), evoking the ass of the Shunamite woman, while her husband, like the biblical father, stays at home. Slowly, Bernice drives to Mama Day, who waits for her, "old hands grasp[ing] the walking stick," recalling Elisha's staff. Mama Day greets her and the two woman stand face to face, Bernice holding aloft the body of her dead child. Time passes, from morning through evening and into the next morning, when Mama Day "stretches out her hand to touch the broken face of the other woman. 'Go home, Bernice. Go home and bury your child'" (259). Naylor thus amplifies the pathos of the death of the child, miraculously conceived but beyond the reach of resurrection or resuscitation. Not only does Naylor feminize the biblical story, substituting Mama Day for Elisha, she humanizes it. While the powers of Elisha transcend death, Mama Day is forced to encounter the limits of her power, supernatural, psychological, and medical. Later she considers the unsought for gift of healing—"Who made her God?"—and concludes that she is not supernaturally powerful: "most folks just don't know what can be done with a little will and their own hands. But she ain't never, Lord, she ain't never tried to get *over* nature" (262).

* * *

While the character of Mama Day mirrors the prophets and Jesus in her ability to heal, ultimately, it is George who fulfills the role of Jesus as savior in this novel. George resembles Jesus in a number of ways, starting with his heritage; he is the son of a young mother (a fifteen-year-old prostitute) with no visibly present father.[5] A series of dreams also connect George to Jesus. When he arrives at Willow Springs he has a prophetic dream that anticipates the climax of the novel. In the dream, George, who cannot swim, whose own mother died of drowning (one of the several drowning deaths in the book), hears Cocoa "calling me and calling me. And I was swimming across The Sound." As George feels his "strength giving out," he hears Mama Day. "Her voice came like thunder: 'No, Get Up And Walk'" (183). Angered at the absurd impossibility of this command, George lifts himself "out of the water to scream in her face, 'You're a crazy old woman!'" And, Jesus-like, "I found myself standing up in the middle of The Sound" (184).[6]

More significantly, only George seems to possesse the ability to save Cocoa when she has been cursed by the black magic of the witch-like Ruby, and to break the tragic cycle of her family, begun in the days of slavery: "one woman [Sapphira, left] by wind. Another [Ophelia, left] by water [causing] the blood from the broken hearts of the men who they cursed for not letting them go" (263). Mama Day explains that despite her great powers, she alone cannot save Cocoa, "'I got all that in this hand but it ain't gonna be complete unless I can reach out with the other hand and take yours'" (294). She needs George because he holds "in his very hands ... the missing piece she'd come looking for" (285). It is not entirely clear how George is to save Cocoa; Mama Day insists there are two ways, his and hers, "'Now I got a way for us to help Baby Girl. And I'm hoping it's the one you'll use'" (295). Mama Day gives him John Paul's carved "walking cane" and "Bascombe Wade's ledger" (293), and a mission. He must go to her henhouse and then, "'You gotta take this book and cane in there with you, search good in the back of her nest, and come back here with whatever you find'" (295). Carrying the cane, like the cross, George begins his Passion: "The last mile," covered in sweat, harried by mosquitoes and gnats, gripping the cane and ledger made slippery in the heat, falling and crawling, George makes his way to the chicken coop. And somewhere in the chicken coop, George's actions diverge from Mama Day's way. In the coop all he finds are his own hands. His modern rationalism cannot accept that as Mama Day's plan: "Could it be that she wanted nothing but my hands?" (300). As a chicken attacks George, ripping through his ankle with her beak, he feels the first of the various Christ-like stigmata he will receive: "a sharp pain through my ankle," followed by the sight of his "gouged and bleeding hands" (300). In anger and despair George resorts to (masculine) violence, wreaking havoc upon the offending chickens. We never learn the details of Mama Day's intended plan, but it most certainly did not involve the blood and violence that George unleashes. In following his own way, re-enacting the violence of the story of Jesus, George seals his own fate, dying of a broken heart, echoing the bleeding heart of Jesus. And George's way does work; as Mama Day thinks, "it wasn't wrong, just not hers" (295). After George's death Cocoa recovers, and there is a sense that the family curse has been broken; Cocoa achieves the peace not available to her ancestors. George's role as sacrificial savior is underlined after his death when, discovering that all of the photographs she had of him had been mislaid by Mama Day, Cocoa tells her son, his namesake, that "'he was named after a man who looked just like love'" (310).

The reader familiar with the Bible, including the stories of Creation, Elisha, and Jesus, are thus privy to meanings embedded in the novel. Identifying the parallels between George and Jesus especially adds to the reader's understanding and appreciation of the novel's conclusion. The biblical context provides the missing causal connection between the death of George and the healing of Cocoa, that is, the sacrifice of the one, and the salvation of the other; read without the biblical context, the novel's dénouement offers less meaning. Naylor's novel reveals additional dimensions to the Bible-literate reader, who can appreciate that when the hurricane is looming, Abigail reads Psalm 77: "'*I cried unto God with my voice*'" (77.1). The reader who can trace the intertextual web of Psalm 77 will recognize that the psalm evokes an earlier moment of storm and sea crossing, in the book of Exodus when the Hebrew slaves cross the Red Sea from slavery to freedom: "Thy way is in the sea, and thy path in the great waters, and thy footsteps are not known. Thou led thy people like a flock by the hand of Moses and Aaron" (Ps 77.19–20). This biblical story was of great resonance to African American slaves, offering hope that the divine would lead them, too, from slavery. The biblical allusions in Naylor's novel, in addition to providing meaning, are wondrous and inspiring, lending gravitas and grandeur to Naylor's humble characters and their story. Indeed, Naylor achieves the miraculous in presenting a modern story of twentieth-century America while preserving the mystery of ancient texts.

The Dispossessed Reader

Naylor's novel strongly suggests a female critique of the Bible, particularly an interrogation of the transcendent, unreachable, supernatural sublime in the story of Elisha, and the bloody violence in the story of Jesus. However, even with the biblical contexts, the actual meaning of Naylor's dénouement remains confounding. Ultimately, we are left with more questions than answers. What was Mama Day's presumably feminine non-violent way? How do George's misguided actions succeed in breaking the tragic cycle of Cocoa's family, especially since his personality, story and death seem to fall directly into the tragic pattern of the previous men in the family? What missing piece does George add? How does Cocoa actually achieve the "meaning of peace" at the end of the novel? Does any of this have anything to do with slavery, or is it just the story of one family's struggles? Is Naylor suggesting we focus on the message of Jesus' life, the healing, and not the message of his death? Naylor does not take the time to explain, and does not provide enough evidence for the reader to successfully connect all the dots; nor should she. Clear and rational explanations would take away from the spell of her work, as they would diminish the power of *The Tempest* and the Bible, two other texts whose thrall lies in their magic.

And so, ultimately, Naylor dispossesses her learned reader, the reader who seems to possess all the literary keys, but fails to discover the lock. Although it seems essential to possess the texts of the Bible and *The Tempest* in order to fully process *Mama Day*, by the end of the book, the reader knows no more than does Mama Day, and the unlettered people of Willow Springs. Indeed, we know far less. The folk wisdom and folk medicine that elevate the characters of Willow Springs is inaccessible to us. In fact, we are like Reema's "boy," the over-educated, "ruined," native son we meet in the prologue. Returned to Willow Springs "from one of those fancy colleges mainside" (7), he amuses the island's inhabitants by assuming that he alone understands a local island expression that has many uses: "He had come to the conclusion after 'extensive field work' (ain't never picked a boll of cotton or head of lettuce in his life…) that 18 & 23 wasn't 18 & 23 after all—was really 81 & 32, which just so happened to be the lines of longitude and latitude marking off where Willow Springs sits on the map. And we were just so damned dumb that we turned the whole thing around" (8). The collective narrator dismisses the motives and morals of "the people who ran the type of schools that could turn our children into raving lunatics" (8), and warns the reader of taking similar analytical approaches. Just talk to people, Naylor suggests, just listen, to discover the kinds of truths that are not to be found in even the greatest books.

Naylor concludes the ghostly dialogue between George and Cocoa with Cocoa's words: "What really happened to us, George? You see, that's what I mean—there are just too many sides to the whole story" (311). The novel ends then with the postmodern view, which is also the traditional Gothic view, that truth and experience are too fragmented and too sublime to be possessed by any single consciousness. Naylor makes sure to destabilize any character or reader who claims to possess a single truth: the rich developers, who think they understand more than the supposedly naïve islanders, fail to steal their property; the white sheriff, figure of authority, learns that he is not actually in control. In fact, as Naylor suggests at the end of her prologue, we readers, rather than possessing hermeneutic truths, are possessed—possessed by the characters, and the narrators, and the language of Naylor's novel: "Think about it: ain't nobody really talking to you." But you, the reader, have heard the whole story of Sapphira Wade and Willow Springs, seemingly related by the communal voice of Willow Springs. Yet, "Really listen this time; the only voice is your own" (10). Through the magic of her art, Naylor creates an entire world, a world that possesses us, as it continues to possess George, as Shakespeare's island still holds Prospero at the conclusion of the play.

9

Among Women
Convergences and Divergences in Gothic Space

The "double-bind" that Robert Weisbuch observes in *Atlantic Double-Cross*, applies not only to African American writers like Hannah Crafts, but also to other American writers who are members of "minorities." Weisbuch writes:

> I would hypothesize that, to the extent such writers identified themselves as members of an oppressed group, they encountered a double bind. They would see themselves oppressed by the oppressed so to say; they would join in the American attempt to defend New World possibilities against British taunts but they would also need to define those New World possibilities away from any homogenizing American ideal that would not recognize their particular social identity [xx].

How much more complicated is the situation of the American Jewish woman writer who is thrice marginalized: as an American, as a Jew, and as a woman writing within the patriarchal Jewish tradition.

The multiple tensions experienced by Jewish women writers—as members of an ethnic group belatedly arrived to the Western tradition, and representatives of a gender historically marginalized by their own tradition—are eloquently expressed by Allegra Goodman in her story, "Sarah" (1996). In an interior monologue, the eponymous character, a Jewish poet, thinks: "It has been difficult for her as a poet, to be influenced by Donne, Marvell, and Herbert, but to write about giving birth, a son's bar mitzvah, Yom Kippur" (221). To add to Sarah's complicated situation, Jewish women writers are also *arrivistes* in their own cultural tradition, which has historically dispossessed and silenced them. The traditional role of the Jewish woman, developed in the culture of Eastern Europe—a culture with continuing power and influence upon a people committed to its past—is marked by constraints, limitations and dispossessions. The traditional cultural paradigm is informed by a system of laws and customs, buttressed by the ritually impure state of the menstruating woman, and the primacy of female responsibilities to husband and children. Women are consequently denied access to the highest levels of Jewish observance available to men. Most telling for the Jewish woman writer is the dispossession of female language within the traditional paradigm. In Europe only the vernacular language Yiddish or the vernacular of the local populace were spoken by women (resulting in a canon of Yiddish texts read exclusively by women); the holy tongue, Hebrew, the language of scholarship and intellectual creativity, was used exclusively by men. The principle of *kol isha*, still observed in traditional communities, is also a direct limitation of the voice of the woman (the literal meaning of the Hebrew words). Within the guidelines of this principle, the voice of the adult woman is so seductive that it may not be heard publicly. Although much of modern Western culture has come to accept female power and the authority of women to be artists and scholars,[1] the place of women within Jewish culture is still controversial in some circles, as the continuing debate on this topic reveals ideological fault lines within the spectrum of Jewish observance. Contemporary Jewish women writing within their own tradition continue to grapple with the traditional powerlessness of women in Jewish culture and continue to search for ways to re-appropriate their own culture and their own voice.

Repossessing the Golem: Appropriating the Traditions of the Jewish Supernatural and the Western Gothic

The response of some Jewish women writers to the anxiety of authority[2] generated by their unstable cultural position is to engage in the kind of skewed response that Harold Bloom[3] characterizes in *The Western Canon* as a creative misreading of the powerful texts of their tradition, particularly the Eastern European folktales featuring the supernatural figures of the golem and the dybbuk. These folktales are comparable to the Gothic canon in a number of ways: they deploy the supernatural; they traditionally occupied a lowly position in the hierarchy of culture; they were dismissed by those (men) who pursued higher scholarship and writing. The folktales, thus, like the Gothic canon were available to the marginalized and dispossessed story-tellers who did not disdain to dwell in the lowlands of culture, including women who were not welcomed into higher levels of intellectual activity. Thus, the synthesis of the Jewish supernatural and the Western Gothic that finds its place in the writing of Jewish American women presents an intertextual conversation between two similar traditions. Like American writers before them,

Jewish American women writers transform the traditions, recreating them in ways that are simultaneously American, Jewish and female. And like American writers before them, they find within the subversive space of the Gothic a place where they can transgress confining categories of genre and national literatures—and gender.[4] In appropriating and recreating the narratives in their own image, Jewish women writers open up a narrative space for the figure of the creative, powerful, and vocal woman, and thereby write themselves into the tradition.

The figures of the dybbuk, a migrant soul that possesses the body of a living person, and the golem, a living creature made by men from clay, have long haunted Jewish folktales. Both figures represent unnatural appropriation. The dybbuk supernaturally appropriates the body of another, exerting the kind of ventriloquistic possession seen in *Wieland*. The golem represents the human appropriation of the powers of creation. In creating a golem—vivifying a creature of clay through the power of the holy word—a rabbi violates the second commandment prohibition against artistic creation, and subversively appropriates God's exclusive power to create life. Both the golem and the dybbuk are in fact monsters of language, appropriate to a culture that valorizes the power of the word. The dybbuk manifests itself as a torrent of uncontained language emanating from the possessed (usually female) body; the golem is created from clay, animated by the power of the word, mimicking the creation of the first human, Adam. Both figures and the tales that they inhabit manifest generalized cultural anxieties of dispossession, anxieties that were not limited to women in Eastern European Jewish culture where the situation of all Jews, men *and* women, was circumscribed. Jews were constrained by inner forces of God-imposed rules and constraints that limited and problematized the avenues of creative expression, and marginalized by outer forces of persecution and prejudice. Significantly both folk figures most powerfully captured the popular Jewish imagination during the sixteenth century, a time that heralded a renewed and reinvigorated persecution of European Jews.

* * *

In their revisions of the golem story,[5] Cynthia Ozick and Marge Piercy reconstruct the motif of the golem to re-appropriate the authority of creation (and sexuality, the basis of biological creation) for women. Rewriting the traditional texts to include female figures of authority and power, Ozick and Piercy reveal the possibilities of female creation and power that are suppressed by the traditional golem stories. They also gesture to the Western tradition of the Gothic, drawing on liberating models of transgression, generic and national. The golem stories originated in the (exclusively male) rabbinic literature, in which tales of the supernatural are prevalent, and became part of the Jewish folktale tradition, more accessible to both genders. Although there are many different versions of the tale, the most well-known is the legend of Rabbi Judah Loew, of sixteenth-century Prague; not surprisingly, this legend appears centuries after the rabbi's death. Many elements recur in each version of the legend: the golem is always a large powerful humanoid, created to save the Jewish people from some outward danger including the blood libel; the golem is always made from clay and vivified by a knowledgeable rabbi who uses the power of God's name inscribed on a piece of paper, inserted into the golem's mouth; the Hebrew letters *aleph mem taf, emet* (truth), are often inscribed on the golem's forehead. If the golem becomes dangerously powerful, he may be reduced to clay with the erasure of the letter *aleph*; the remaining letters spell *met* (death).

Although the primary function of the golem is to save the Jewish people from danger, some golems also assist with homely household duties like lighting the stoves of the Jews on the Sabbath and fetching water. These more mundane roles invite a reading of the figure of the golem as a veiled code for the woman in Jewish culture. In the Talmudic literature the word "golem" which literally means "unformed substance" is associated with women: "Thus an unmarried woman is called a golem, since her nature is not fully rounded until she is married" (Jacob Minkin "Golem" 43); for similar reasons, the word can also "refer to a woman who has not conceived" (Arnold Goldsmith *The Golem Remembered* 16). The golem is frequently speechless like women in traditional Jewish culture, and like women the golem is prohibited from participating fully in religious life; both women and golems, for example, are traditionally not counted in a *minyan*, the quorum of ten men required for public prayer. Many critics note the displacement of anxieties relating to women onto the figure of the monster.[6] The golem folktales paradoxically both express and allay male anxieties toward women: the encoded female character is monstrous, but is ultimately subject to the linguistic power of the male rabbi. The golem is always reduced to inanimate clay when, as often happens in the tales, the growing power of the monster threatens to endanger the Jewish community. Rachel Adler argues that the fear of the unleashed women, the fear of "rampant sexuality" functions as "a metaphor for the disequilibrating potential of female power ... [representing] to the rabbis all that is untamable, unpredictable and lawless in human beings" ("The Virgin in the Brothel" 103).[7] The folktale further works to limit the threat of female power by appropriating to the male rabbi the most powerful and thereby most anxiety-provoking act available to women in a traditional culture: the power derived from biology and sexuality to create life.

Mike Pinsky, writing of the "permutations" of the golem legends in a variety of texts, observes "although the golem itself always remains a fantastic creature, the purpose for which it is used reflects the culture of its time" ("The Mistaken Mistake" 215). This observation is exemplified in the uses that Cynthia Ozick and Marge Piercy make of the golem, as they transform the figure to rework a cultural icon that represents the dispossession of Jewish women. Ozick and Piercy conversely recreate the golem as a figure to celebrate the power of Jewish women as creators of myth and possessors of their own culture and voice, evoking Hélène Cixous' prophecy (echoing Lawrence): "When the 'repressed' of ... culture and ... society returns, it's an explosive, *utterly destructive*, staggering return, with a force never yet unleashed and equal to the most forbidding of suppressions" (Cixous "The Laugh of the Medusa" 886). Ozick and Piercy also deploy the transgressive figure of the golem to break through the boundaries of culture, negotiating a delicate balance between the two cultures—Jewish and American—that inform them. And both express a sense of cultural security and wit illustrating Cixous' exhortation: "You only have to look at the Medusa straight on to see her. And she's not deadly. She's beautiful and she's laughing" (885).

* * *

Anxieties of cultural dispossession and marginalization surface in Cynthia Ozick's fiction and in the essays in which she manifests the sense of displacement experienced by her characters. In her essay "On Living in a Gentile World," Ozick writes of the effort of negotiating between Jewish and Western cultures: "To remain Jewish is a process—something which is an ongoing and muscular thing, a progress or, sometimes, a regression, a constant self-reminding, a caravan of watchfulness always on the move; above all an unsparing *consciousness*" (168). Norman Finkelstein notes that Ozick's discomfort with Western culture is an expression of her fear of assimilation (*The Ritual of New Creation* 74), the minority fear of being engulfed by the majority. Ruth Puttermesser, the protagonist of the short stories that compose Ozick's *The Puttermesser Papers* (1997), enacts the struggle to enter the mainstream. As a Jew, she is marginalized at the "blueblood Wall Street firm" (6) where she is a lawyer. When she later moves to a job within the corrupt government of the evil, but cleverly named, mayor of New York, Malachy ("Matt") Mavett,[8] her adherence to Jewish ethics and Jewish texts further marginalizes her: "In New York, Puttermesser retained an immigrant's dream of merit: justice, justice shalt thou pursue" (30).[9] Puttermesser, who diligently reads Plato in bed at night, re-enacts her cultural dispossession in another story in the collection, "Puttermesser Paired," in which she unsuccessfully attempts to replicate

George Eliot's relationship with George Lewes. Ruth Puttermesser thus emblematizes Ozick's sense of dispossession, as a woman, from Jewish culture, and, as a Jew, from Western culture. This displacement is articulated in her essay "Notes toward Finding the Right Question": "In the world at large I call myself, and am called, a Jew. But when, on the Sabbath, I sit among women in my traditional shul and the rabbi speaks the word 'Jew,' I can be sure that he is not referring to me. For him, 'Jew' means 'male Jew'" (21). Cultural dispossession manifests itself in Puttermesser's deracination—"Her parents have no ancestry" (18)—and in her fruitless search for cultural roots. Significantly this search results in a fantasized attempt to learn Hebrew, the language of male scholars, from a long dead great-uncle.

Puttermesser's sense of cultural displacement is reflected and exaggerated in the golem she creates in the story "Xanthippe and Puttermesser" (*The Puttermesser Papers*). The golem, her monstrous daughter, rejects the Jewish name "Leah" over Puttermesser's objections and names herself "Xanthippe," in honor of Socrates' wife. As the struggle over the name indicates, Ozick appropriates the transgressive figure of the golem, deploying the golem's traditional resistance to categorization and possession, to negotiate tensions of cultural dispossession in her narrative. In becoming the first female golem creator, and creating the first female golem, Puttermesser takes possession of the ancient mystical power of the rabbis, traditionally the domain of male scholars. Puttermesser also takes possession of the secular world: with the help of her golem she is transformed from a marginalized city servant into the first female mayor of New York. Guided by the "immigrant ethics" of the Jewish tradition, Puttermesser emulates the God of the Jewish Bible; she creates a government that is an earthly Paradise. Gardens are planted; the subways are refurbished; "the youths who used to terrorize the subways put on fresh shirts and walk out into Central Park ... they dance. They have formed themselves into dancing clubs, and crown one another's heads with clover pulled up from the sweet ground" (76).

The feminization of both creature and creator indicates that the strategy of Ozick's narrative is to insert the female principle into the pre-existing narrative. Like Genesis, John Milton's *Paradise Lost*, and Mary Shelley's *Frankenstein*, the original golem folktales are birth narratives from which mothers are notably absent. Ozick's revision of the golem story reveals a poignant longing for the possibility of a female presence within the line of tradition, the line in which previous golem makers are all male.[10] Ozick's retelling reinstates the mother and the daughter into the narrative and into the culture. Puttermesser, distanced from her own uncomprehending mother (who writes from Florida of potential accountant suitors for her daughter), dislocated by an intellectual tradition that disinherits her, and marginalized by a political system that disempowers her, attempts to inaugurate a female tradition of power and creation. Puttermesser yearns for daughters—"She was not yet reconciled to childlessness. Sometimes the thought that she would never give birth tore her heart. She imagined daughters..." (36)—and Xanthippe appears, literalizing her creator's desires. Xanthippe is Puttermesser's intellectual clone, knowing all that Puttermesser knows, desiring all that she desires. But daughter-like, golem-like, Xanthippe resists Puttermesser's molding. Before Puttermesser breathes life into her golem, she is able to remold and refine her facial features. After Xanthippe comes to life her features are set; as when she chooses her own name, she resists her creator's control.

* * *

The inversion of genders is the only transgression enacted by Ozick's narrative; while feminizing the characters in the story, Ozick is respectfully conservative in preserving the details of the original folktales. The traditional narrative apparatus remains intact and the technologies of creation are an exact replica of the methodologies employed by the rabbis in the folklore. As in the original golem stories, Ozick's golem is created without the benefit of science through Jewish mysticism alone. Ozick's only revision is a comic updating: the soil from which Puttermesser forms her golem is taken from the flower pots in her apartment. As in the original stories, the golem's function is to assist its powerless creator to achieve justice; in Ozick's representation Mavett's corrupt New York is as dark and threatening as medieval Prague. Like her precursors, Ozick's golem grows in power, becoming a threat as she resists the power of her creator, who must then destroy her. Thus "Xanthippe" confirms Finkelstein's observation that Ozick's stories subordinate themselves in deference to normative religious beliefs (70).

Ozick's form of cultural appropriation, as enacted in "Xanthippe," thus admits the female presence while leaving the structures of power completely intact. Ozick's respectful subversion reflects her ambiguous feminist stance, her paradoxically conservative feminism.[11] Ozick resists the feminist impulse to celebrate the exclusively female power of creation, and focuses instead on the female appropriation of a traditionally male method of creating life. In Ozick's formulation, the feminist project is not to change social and cultural paradigms but simply to allow women entry. In "Literature and the Politics of Sex: A Dissent," Ozick defines the terms of her "classical feminism" as: "feminism at its origin, when it saw itself as justice and aspiration made universal, as mankind widened to humankind—rejected anatomy not only as destiny, but as any sort of governing force; it rejected the notion of 'female sensibility' as a slander designed to shut women off from access to the delights, confusions, achievements, darknesses, and complexity of the great world" (288). Ozick concludes, "For writers, there *are* no 'new truths.' There is only one very old [presumably androgynous and universal] truth" (290). Thus in Ozick's terms, the proper role for the progressive woman is to fight to enter male space, without transforming the space. Ozick's approach translates into a Jewish feminism that envisions Jewish women "in the same relation to history and Torah as Jewish men are and have been" ("Notes Toward Finding the Right Question" 26); Ozick thus proposes a polite, non-radical form of cultural appropriation, one that stops short of fully possessing and transforming culture.

The viability of Ozick's mode of feminism is, however, problematized by the conclusion of her golem story; in accordance with the conventional narrative apparatus, the golem impolitely, and radically, goes out of control. While Ozick deviates from the tradition in presenting her golem as explicitly female, the traditional tales themselves gesture to aspects of the feminine in the golem, including the tendency of the monster to transgress rules and regulations. Ozick taps into the implicit fear of the uncontrollable woman in the golem stories, and amplifies it by creating a female monster whose rebellion is figured as female sexuality run amok. As Xanthippe grows, her body and her sexual appetite grow, too, until finally Puttermesser is undone by Xanthippe's insatiable sexual appetite. The golem ravishes every commissioner of Puttermesser's utopian government; succubus-like, she drains them of their powers, immobilizing the administration, leading to the downfall of the earthly paradise that Puttermesser has instated as mayor of New York. Ozick thereby reminds the reader that Puttermesser's is not the first Paradise to be lost because of female appetite. In couching the golem's uncontrollable resistance in sexual terms, and in Edenic terms, Ozick illuminates the anxieties that lie hidden within the folktales; in following the narrative structure of the folktales, Ozick's narrative appears to share the traditional Jewish anxieties toward unbridled female sexuality. The fall from power of Xanthippe and her creator indicates Ozick's ambivalence towards her ambitious protagonist. The closure of Ozick's story traces the collapse of her form of feminism, revealing that in her formulation the feminist project cannot endure. Puttermesser's female dynasty ends with the demise of Xanthippe, as Puttermesser, faithfully re-enacts the male rabbinic ritual, resisting the calls of the previously silent golem to the feminine side of her creator—"'my mother'"—and returns Xanthippe to clay (99). Set within a narrative and cultural context defined and confined by male rabbis, the female creator of the female golem moves toward a re-enactment of female self-destruction, away from the deployment of female power. By the conclusion of the story, Puttermesser is once again marginalized and powerless, dispossessed of Western and Jewish culture, knowledge, and power.

In telling her version of the story, Ozick does manage to seize the kind of power that eludes her protagonist. Exerting her writerly authority as creator of the text, Ozick deploys fantasy and imagination to appropriate narrative power and narrative space, and to present possibilities not available in the actual world. But her Gothic narrative, golem-like (and like Shelley's *Frankenstein*) ultimately resists Ozick's authority. Sarah Blacher Cohen points to the connections between *Frankenstein* and the golem stories to read evocations of *Frankenstein* in "Puttermesser and Xanthippe." Her argument begins with the assertion that "Puttermesser and Xanthippe" (like Shelley's *Frankenstein*) is Ozick's retelling of *Paradise Lost*[12] and that Ozick "mourns the impossibility of making the Messianic ideal a reality in our time" (*Cynthia Ozick's Comic Art* 97). Cohen continues: "Finally the story itself is a monster which Ozick has sired. In a sense, she is like Mary Shelley, who referred to her *Frankenstein* as a 'hideous progeny,' a deformed book she gave birth to in her 'alienated attick workshop of filthy creation'" (97).

In keeping with her non-subversive feminist project, Ozick directly places her tale within the context of the Jewish supernatural story, which is in Jewish culture the realm of male scholars, rabbis who tell tales not for the frivolous purposes of imaginative pleasure but for serious religious and spiritual ends. As David Stern says of the stories that compose his anthology, *Rabbinic Fantasies*, "the [exclusively male] authors of most of the narratives … probably would not have considered their works as being primarily imaginative or fictional" (Stern 4). To consolidate the placement of her text within the tradition of serious rabbinic literature, Ozick suppresses any evocation of the Western supernatural; she works to dissociate her text from the Gothic tradition, with its associations of frivolous emotion and female sensibility. Thus, like George Eliot, admired by both Puttermesser and by her creator, Ozick seeks to distance herself from those texts infamously labeled in George Eliot's essay as "Silly Novels by Lady Novelists" (1856). Yet Ozick's Gothic narrative transgresses the categories constructed by its author, trespassing into other forbidden territory. Against Ozick's will, her narrative slides toward the Western Gothic with its female associations, thus dispossessing the authority of its author, as the golem dispossesses the authority of its creators. Transgressing the boundaries that Ozick sets, "Xanthippe" refuses generic containment within the canon of the rabbinic fantastic, and aligns itself with the Western Female Gothic that Ozick attempts to avoid. It is a critical commonplace to observe that Frankenstein's monster emblematizes the Gothic mode: each bursts out of the containing bounds of category. The textual relationship between "Puttermesser and Xanthippe" and its author re-enacts this process of narrative dispossession. Although Ozick attempts to appropriate an intellectual icon of her male-dominated cultural tradition, pointedly locating her narrative within a supernatural tradition associated with male intellectuality, her text and context undermine her project and dispossess her authority. The story transgressively moves toward the canon of the Western Female Gothic, with its associations of female sensibility and culture. Ultimately Ozick, like Puttermesser, is dispossessed of her creation: the transgressive golem breaches the boundaries between national literatures and gender, dislodging the text from the male rabbinic tradition, and relocating it into the tradition of the Western Female Gothic.

* * *

A survey of golem criticism reveals a persistent association of the golem folktales with Mary Shelley's powerful myth, *Frankenstein* (1818); many critics read the similarity between Shelley's novel and the golem tales as evidence that Shelley appropriated and revised the folktales in constructing her monster.[13] The most assertive claim is Gershon Winkler's; in *The Golem of Prague* he argues:

> Although Mary Shelley lived in England and virtually all the literature concerning golems was written in Germany, she nevertheless had access to German literature. In fact, in one of her letters, she attributes her inspiration for *Frankenstein* to German "ghost tales" she had read.... Indeed, Shelley's Frankenstein [*sic*] is a man-made monster who ultimately turns against its creator, a concept easily traced to the Golem tales prevalent in her time ... circulated by Grimm less than ten years *before* Shelley wrote Frankenstein. It is difficult to imagine that a cultured and erudite literary figure like Mary Shelley should not at some point have come across the numerous Golem tales which abounded in German literature before and during her time. Who is to say whether the German "ghost tales" which inspired her to write *Frankenstein* did not also include Golem tales? [19–20].

As Winkler indicates, there is indeed much internal evidence to support the argument that the golem stories influenced Shelley, or that Shelley appropriated the golem stories. Both the legends and *Frankenstein* manifest similar Gothic tendencies: preoccupation with possession of the body and of the narrative; anxieties of female authority and maternity; the presence of supernatural powers resulting in creatures who are transgressive and destructive; in some versions of the golem story, the golem destroys his creator. Yet Winkler's assumption that Shelley must have been familiar with the golem stories is ultimately speculative and unsatisfying, unless additional external evidence is provided. That evidence does appear to be available. In his essay, "The

Golem and the Robot," Robert Plank cites and translates a text in which Jacob Grimm recorded the legend of the golem in 1808, in a publication called *Zeitung für Einsiedler* (*Papers for Solitaries*)[14]:

> The Polish Jews, after having spoken certain prayers and observed certain fast days, make the figure of a man out of clay or loam which, after they have pronounced the wonder-working *Shem ha-m'phorash* over it, comes to life. It is true this figure cannot speak, but he can to a certain extent understand what one says and commands him to do.... On his forehead the word *Emaeth* (truth:God) is written. But he increases from day to day and can easily become larger and stronger than his house-mates, however small he may have been in the beginning. Being then afraid of him, they rub out the first letter so that nothing remains but *Maeth* (he is dead), whereupon he sinks together and becomes clay again.
>
> But once the owner of a golem carelessly allowed him to grow so tall that he could not reach his forehead. Then in his fear he told this servant of his to draw off his boots, thinking that in so doing he would stoop and that then he could reach his forehead. It happened as he thought it would, and the Jew succeeded in effacing the first letter, but the whole load of clay fell on him and crushed him to death [Plank 22].

Kurt Ranke confirms the significance of the Grimms' publication of the first collection of tales in Germany. He writes in "1812, an act of intellectual discovery had opened a window for the European educated classes into the submerged and despised culture of the peasantry, disclosing undreamt of riches in so outwardly barren an environment" (Foreword *Folktales of Germany* v). In *Mary Shelley's Frankenstein*, Christopher Small argues that Shelley, who by Small's account could not read German, encountered the golem stories through Grimm in *Fantasmagoriana*, an 1812 volume of German stories in French translation. Shelley was to write *Frankenstein* in "the summer of 1816 in the environs of Geneva" (Shelley Preface to *Frankenstein* 2).

There is, then, sufficient internal and external evidence to allow for a textual link between the golem stories and *Frankenstein*.[15] As Western culture is increasingly influenced by film iconography,[16] there is even further cause to connect the two texts. In the introduction to his study *Mary Shelley's Frankenstein: Tracing the Myth*, Christopher Small suggests that Shelley's story (like the golem stories) takes on the form of myth, evolving and growing in the popular imagination, until frozen into the image fixed into permanence by the iconography of Boris Karloff's representation of the creature. Like Small, who observes that the Hollywood film incorporated "elements from the Yiddish tale of *The Golem*" (17), Bonnie Friedman also indicates that in the early film version of *Frankenstein* both James Whale the director, and the actor Boris Karloff were influenced by the imagery used in an earlier German cinematic representation of the golem: *The Golem: How He Came into the World*, directed by Paul Wegener in 1920. Stills from both films clearly indicate that the famous filmic visual image of Shelley's monster derives from the earlier filmic representation of the golem. Wegener explicitly allies himself with the Gothic tradition in the closure of his film: the ghetto is enveloped in flames and the tower of the rabbi, the film's emblem of dark dangerous authority, collapses. Friedman notes that Wegener's film is an instance of cultural misappropriation, useful for promoting proto-Nazi iconography in 1920s Germany. Wegener transformed the Jewish tale so that it devolved into a condemnation of the monstrous, vermin-like Jews, and their monstrous creation. Once again we see a web of Gothic texts in which each text blithely ignores the integrity of the others, blithely borrowing, displacing and dispossessing, all to pursue a serious cultural agenda.

* * *

In *He, She and It* (1991), an American novel that (like *Frankenstein*) is poised between the Gothic and science fiction, Marge Piercy also deploys the transgressive figure of the golem to repossess and to negotiate the distinct traditions that simultaneously influence her and dispossess her as a woman and as a Jew. In her narrative, Piercy explicitly evokes and appropriates both the legends of Jewish tradition, and Shelley's novel,[17] to present an insistently feminist reading of the golem story. Through the convergence of three manifestations of the golem in her text—the medieval golem of Prague, Frankenstein's monster, and the twenty-first-century cyborg-golem of her own creation—Piercy highlights the transformative possibilities of this transgressive figure, as it fluidly evolves in response to changing cultural contexts and anxieties of property and power.

Piercy deploys the conventionally intricate structure of the Gothic, unfolding her golem story through two interwoven narratives. In the primary narrative, set in a post-apocalyptic twenty-first-century world devastated by nuclear war, Shira loses her son to her former husband and returns to Tikva (Hebrew for hope), the beleaguered Jewish free colony on what had been the east coast of the United States. There she is enlisted in acculturating Yod, a cyborg—part human, part robot/computer[18]—who has been created by two scientists (one male, one female—Shira's grandmother) to protect the colony. Embedded and interwoven within Piercy's primary narrative, is the legend of the golem of Prague, created by Rabbi Judah Loew in the sixteenth century; this legend is narrated by Malka, the scientist-grandmother, to Yod. The two narratives are parallel: Piercy provides an updated counterpart for each episode in the golem story. Thus the structure of Piercy's version of the golem legend, like Ozick's, carefully follows the structure of the original folktales. Piercy's golem, Yod, resembles Joseph, Rabbi Loew's golem, in a number of ways. Both golems are created to protect a beleaguered Jewish community: the Jewish community of Prague is threatened by anti-Semitism in the form of the blood libel; the Jews of Piercy's Tikva are threatened by the evil corporate governments, the multis, which rule most of the world. Piercy's golem is named Yod (the tenth letter of the Hebrew alphabet because he is the tenth in a series); the name Yod recalls the name of Rabbi Loew's golem because Yod is also the first Hebrew letter of Yosef, Joseph in Hebrew. Piercy diverges remarkably from the other golem narratives in that her golem does not become a threat to the community; he dies protecting the Jewish colony. However, he too alienates his male creator by becoming too human, thereby transgressing essential boundaries. Thus Piercy revisits the anxieties of creation inherent in the folktale in all of its iterations. In her version, too, the golem's creators are haunted by the ambiguous morality of an act of creation that is overtly illegal and subversive, defying the law of the omniscient and omnipotent multis, as well as appropriating divine powers of creation. Indeed, after the death of Yod, Shira recognizes that reconstructing him would be morally wrong and destroys all the records that would make that recreation possible.

Unlike Ozick's narrative, however, Piercy's revision disrupts the masculinist cultural paradigm that underlies the golem story. Piercy's telling is a radically feminist revision of the golem folktales, a text that Ozick would dismiss as an example of "the Ovarian Theory of Literature" (Ozick "Previsions of the Demise of the Dancing Dog" 266). Piercy's revision, unlike the folktales and unlike Ozick's retelling, relocates creative power in the female characters through the biological channels of sexuality and childbirth. The golem legends work to repress the power of female sexuality and deny the biological power of female creation, so as to valorize the creative power of the male intellect (and the patriarchal God[19]). Ozick does insert the previously absent figure of the mother into the paradigm; however, her description of the process is unchanged, not feminized by the female presence. Piercy's narrative introduces and valorizes the physical component of maternal creation that is repressed by the folktales and by Ozick's retelling. In Piercy's postapocalyptic damaged and male-dominated world, most of the population is infertile; only the inhabitants of free towns like Tikva, flourishing on the "unclaimed margin" (36)[20] outside of the multies, are able to bear children biologically (116). The conception and the birth of Shira's son Ari are remarkable for being achieved as a result of maternal sexuality and biology, without technological intervention. Piercy consolidates her valorization of maternal power in the closure of her novel as she revises the conventionally destructive Gothic closure. At the end of Piercy's novel, only the male characters and male structures—the golem, the male scientist and his records—are destroyed; the female characters and the biological female-centered method of creation that they emblematize prevail.

Through the character of Malka, the scientist-grandmother, Piercy also appropriates and transforms the personae of the golem legends, thereby subverting the patriarchal integrity of the original folktales. In the version of the story that Malka tells to Yod, Malka co-opts the original text by inventing a major female figure who is absent from previous versions of the tale: Chava, the granddaughter of the rabbi. Chava, a midwife, is the prototype of the female scientist, possessing knowledge that is unavailable to men; significantly, she is a woman who controls birth. The name Chava (Hebrew for Eve, meaning life) evokes the female source of all human life and recalls that Eve's transgressive hunger for knowledge has long been associated with the dangers of the subversive female. Malka's insertion of Chava into the original golem tale highlights Piercy's appropriation of the traditional text; Malka like Piercy transforms the original by introducing the figure of the powerful, knowledgeable and sexual woman who counters the male-centered process of golem formation. In addition to re-appropriating knowledge of the old secret powers of biological human creation, long denied to women by the scholarship of the Jewish rabbis and by the techniques of Enlightenment scientists, Piercy also allows her female characters to claim and transform the traditionally male intellectual powers of creation. Ozick places an intelligent, creative woman into a pre-existing, male-constructed paradigm without disturbing the paradigm; Puttermesser creates through methodologies traditionally available only to men, methodologies based on the supernatural powers of a male God. In Piercy's formulation, however, the presence of the female informs the structure of intellectual power and creation. In Piercy's world of the future, the patriarchal powers of God and the rabbis are replaced by the powers of science and biology to which women have access equal to men. The male and female scientist have equal authority in the creation of Yod, who is the most creative and the least destructive—the most human—golem ever created as he is invested with both the male and female principles. In moving her golem narrative out of the inaccessible realm of the mysterious, magical, and gendered world inhabited by the original folktales and by Ozick's narrative, and into the bright open world of science, Piercy redefines the patriarchal paradigms that support those earlier texts.

Piercy further feminizes the context of her tale of unnatural creation in recognizing the influence of the Western Gothic tradition—with its female associations—upon her narrative. Indeed, Piercy's explicit textual acknowledgment of *Frankenstein* as a precursor of *He, She and It* invites an examination of the unexpected similarities between the golem canon and the Gothic canon. Arnold Goldsmith notes the "gothic machinery set in motion" (*The Golem Remembered* 47) in the 1909 golem story published by Yudl Rosenberg. Rosenberg appropriates the Gothic tradition of the discovered manuscript to claim that he has discovered an eyewitness account of Rabbi Judah's sixteenth-century golem. The purportedly recovered narrative contains an episode in which the rabbi prevents a brother from unknowingly marrying his sister—manifesting those Gothic staples, the interrupted wedding and the danger of near-incest. The transgression of the boundaries between the Jewish supernatural tradition and the Western Gothic is also evident in Chaim Bloch's 1919 retelling of the folktale of Rabbi Judah Loew. Bloch borrows many of the conventions of the Gothic: the discovered manuscript; the supernatural; the dark, massive, ruined setting, including the dungeons of the demonized Catholic Church; the struggle between powerless innocence and the potent evil emblematized by the Church. In fact an important link between the Protestant English Gothic canon and the Jewish golem canon is that both fear the Catholic Church, with varying degrees of justification. In this moment of canonic convergence, we see once again how the infinitely fluid and flexible Gothic transforms to accommodate altered anxieties. Although the English fear and the Jewish fear of the Catholic Church stem from different sources, each culture finds in the Gothic space a suitable outlet for its anxieties.

Piercy points to *Frankenstein* in a number of ways. The generic move of her narrative from the Gothic to science fiction recalls the generic fluidity of Shelley's novel that occupies the cusp between supernatural Gothic and science fiction. In her text, Shelley works to provide a quasi-scientific explanation for the supernatural; her creature is animated by "a spark of being" that is derived from "instruments of life" (51). In "The Imperial Moth" Judith Wilt argues that the evolution of the Gothic into science fiction results when anxieties of the suppressed past of history are replaced by fears of the future. Anxieties about the dangers of scientific progress mark both Shelley's and Piercy's texts. Each raises the question that haunts the canon of science fiction and links it to the Gothic project: will unimagined technological wonders result in future good or evil? Piercy also recalls *Frankenstein* through explicit textual borrowings. While Ozick's text represses the presence of Frankenstein's monster (who, nevertheless, hovers beyond the margins), Piercy's text embraces the monster, explicitly comparing Yod to Shelley's creation. The filmmaker son of Yod's male creator, manifesting a sibling rivalry of sorts, jealously teases Yod. He calls himself "'the Son of Frankenstein,'" and explains to the innocent Yod that Frankenstein "'built a monster. Like my father has'"

(148). After Yod reads Shelley's novel, he realizes that he is indeed like the monster, who was also created as a tool for a specific purpose (150). His monstrous association haunts the almost human Yod; Shira, meeting Yod in the Base (a virtual-reality locus) finds herself "on a broad field. Coming toward her was a figure shuffling along. It was Frankenstein's monster, in the form and makeup used by Boris Karloff" (165). In fact it is Yod, taking on the filmic form of Shelley's monster, as Piercy takes on the outline of Shelley's narrative.

Piercy thus transgresses the boundaries between the three monstrous figures that emerge from her multi-layered cultural tradition: the rabbi's golem, her own golem, and Frankenstein's creature. This convergence helps to uncover Gothic anxieties of possession that underlie each narrative: anxieties regarding the limits and dangers of knowledge. In particular, these texts manifest anxieties about the possession of the product of human creation; in each text the creature dispossesses the human creator/parent.[21] The various incarnations of the monster also underline the transgressive resistance of this figure to the boundaries of text and canon based on national literature and genre, and to the authority of the author. The narratives of Piercy and Shelley deploy the Gothic convention of multiple narratives to evidence the typical Gothic concern with narrative possession; oral folktales by their very nature are changeable and implicitly dispute the possibility of narrative authority. The convergence of the three figures in a single text also serves to highlight the distinctions between the three and allows the reader to consider ways in which the medieval figure of the supernatural golem transforms through the centuries as the cultural contexts and anxieties of possession change.

* * *

The anxieties of the medieval Jewish culture that generated the original golem derived from a lack of political and personal power. The Jews of Eastern Europe were surrounded by powerful enemies and so they imagined a monster who would protect them. They were anxious about the maternal power of the female since, as Julia Kristeva notes, their patriarchal theology was based on the repression of the goddess and of the cult of maternity. And so they imagined a birth process from which the maternal was exiled: a birth process re-enacting the first creation by the patriarchal God. Like Adam, the golem is made from clay; animated by linguistic power. Mike Pinsky notes that the golem, in lacking speech, lacks the power to create that is wielded by man and God: "Rabbi Loew's Golem cannot speak for itself, cannot wield power through language and therefore cannot access its own creative potential. The creature can only threaten and destroy" (216). Similarly, the Jews of medieval Europe were denied the power of artistic expression, forbidden by the second commandment from creating graven images, and generally prohibited from arrogantly emulating God's creation. And so the creation they imagine is ultimately dangerous and threatening, representing simultaneously the transgressive act of creating, and the punishment for transgression. "The danger," says Gershom Scholem, "is not that the golem, become autonomous, will develop overwhelming powers; it lies in the tension which the creative process arouses in the creator himself" ("The Idea of the Golem" 191).

Mary Shelley generates her monster in response to a related but re-articulated set of anxieties. Her post–Enlightenment narrative transforms the linguistic supernatural power of God into the equally mysterious and equally dangerous technological power of science. In constructing his creature from dismembered body parts, Victor reconstructs himself as the scientist *cum* criminal. Victor's criminality, like that of the subversive rabbis, is determined by the mores of his own time and place: "Towards the end of the [eighteenth] century body-snatching brought revulsion and popular protest against the medical profession" (L.S. King "Anatomy" 26). Victor, like the rabbis, is punished for the subversive appropriation of knowledge that he does not fully comprehend: like them, he is dispossessed by his creation. Shelley's narrative also transforms the maternal anxieties of possession that are evident in the golem legends; in addition to reflecting the transformed cultural context of *Frankenstein*, the transformations of Shelley's text reflect the feminine perspective of the author. Like the golem legends, *Frankenstein* is a birth myth marked by the Gothic motif of the absent mother. As Barbara Johnson asserts, Shelley's text is marked by the "elimination" (9) of mothers: Victor's mother dies when he is young; Elizabeth, the potential mother of his children, is killed by the monster. While in the golem stories the mother is absent from the birth due to theological rabbinic imperatives, the absence of the woman from Shelley's text is partially a result of contemporary medical tensions: "the practice of obstetrics underwent great change during the eighteenth century as, from around 1720, doctors began to attend more deliveries. This triggered off competition and often acrimonious debate between the midwife, the traditional birth attendant, and her new rival, the obstetrician or 'man-midwife'" (Hilary Marland "Obstertics" 526). Thus the appropriation of the birth process by the male scientist in Shelley's text reflects the diminished role of the woman (as mother and midwife) in the birth process in eighteenth-century England.[22] Yet, although the mother is absent from the birth process enacted by Victor, the female writer of this motherless text does not fully repress the maternal, as the rabbinic creators of the golem stories do. The creative process Victor employs is a re-enactment of birth rather than a suppression: he "labours" for nine months to create a creature composed of flesh, albeit repulsive cadaverous flesh. As critics have noted, it is also possible to see in Shelley's creation myth an expression of her own personal anxieties regarding maternal possession: "It is only recently that critics have begun to see Victor Frankenstein's disgust at the sight of his creation as a study of postpartum depression, as a representation of maternal rejection of a newborn infant, and to relate the entire novel to Mary Shelley's mixed feelings about motherhood" (Barbara Johnson 6). As Johnson further notes, Shelley had an even more specific reason for representing the birth process as resulting in the monstrous: "Her own mother, indeed, had died upon giving her birth" (6).

Shelley's narrative of creation also transforms the anxieties of artistic creation and dispossession that are present in the golem tales. The golem stories emblematize the anxiety of the human male denied artistic expression by God; Shelley's story tells of the woman artist displaced by the male artist, and by the tradition he represents. The portrayal of Victor Frankenstein, working in solitude to create life, is an interrogatory representation of the solitary self-absorbed Romantic poet, whose imagination creates worlds. The monster, as Gilbert and Gubar assert, is the emblem for the dispossessed woman artist, who is deemed monstrous in her deviation from social roles, and who is constructed within Romantic poetics as object rather than subject of poetry. This reading gains broader meaning within the context of Pinsky's observations on the speechlessness of the golem. If Shelley's monster is the emblem of the woman writer, it is important that he possess speech and a degree of narrative authority[23]: the monster's possession of speech allows him to appropriate narrative power from his creator in the name of the repressed and silenced woman whom he represents. The monster's narrative to Victor counters Victor's narrative to Walton; his speech subverts Victor's perspective and locates the responsibility for his monstrous nature onto Victor. "'I was benevolent and good; misery made me a fiend,'" he tells Victor. "'Make me happy, and I shall again be virtuous'" (101).

Piercy's golem, too, is constructed in response to specific cultural and personal contexts of possession; Piercy writes to correct her multiple cultural dispossessions. In appropriating and feminizing an icon that appears in both Jewish and Western culture, Piercy posits an egalitarian paradigm of Jewish culture that includes herself, and locates herself as the inheritor of Mary Shelley's tradition, a female tradition. Like the texts of her precursors, Piercy's golem narrative is also concerned with the question of maternal possession: Shira's child is stolen from her by his father, who is assisted by the multis. As a post-feminist novel of maternal possession, however, *He, She and It* easily alleviates the anxieties it presents. By the end of the novel the mother is in full possession of the child, whom she has biologically produced; the father is conveniently dead, yet another example of the defeated patriarch. The absence of any real tension in the book is exemplified by the "monster" of Piercy's text. Piercy's golem is neither monstrous nor repulsive; indeed, he exerts a strong erotic hold upon Shira. An amalgam of human tissue and computer circuitry, created by male and female scientists, possessed of full powers of speech and able to control the computer technology that produces him, Piercy's golem is a balanced and comforting figure of negotiation,[24] if not of synthesis. Piercy's narrative is ultimately less a reflection of the cultural anxieties and displacements fomented by technology, than a fantasy of consolidation; the mother gains possession of her child; the golem gains possession of himself (and of the mate he fruitlessly seeks in Shelley's version); the Jewish American woman writer gains possession of Jewish culture and of the Western canon.

Thus Piercy ironically deploys a radically transgressive figure in the conservative cause of consolidation. The transgressiveness of the figure of the golem and of the Gothic mode allows Piercy to mediate discordant texts and cultures, and to resolve the problems and tensions manifested by her precursors; ultimately Piercy's golem and the narrative that contains him succeed in erasing all conflict and allaying all anxiety. An example of Piercy's strategy of repressing tension is a maddeningly trite dialogue between Shira and Yod, who says to Shira, "You belong to the earth and I don't" (185). This is, in fact, a telling point, an interesting problem raised by Piercy's construction. The original golem is from the earth, a quality he shares with human creatures, beginning with Adam, the first man created from clay. From the perspective of Jewish cosmology Yod, the cyborg, is truly inhuman and alien. Yet Piercy represses discussions of this complication: Shira blithely explains that both humans and cyborgs are made of the same recycled molecules and Yod is satisfied. In the closure of the novel Piercy provides transcendent solutions to the dilemmas posed by the earlier texts, and to her own problems of dispossession: the accommodating Yod sacrifices himself to save Shira's child; his self-effacement definitively removes the complicated figure of artificial creation in deference to the product of natural and untroubled biology. In this act of self-abnegation, Piercy's golem becomes transcendent, and moves outside of the Jewish tradition; the initial letter of Yod's name, is also the first letter of Yeshua, Jesus in Hebrew, and his Christ-like sacrifice suggests another erasure of boundaries between cultures.

Piercy's easy resolution thus results in a story that lacks the interest of the other more tense and complicated golem narratives, including Ozick's.

Piercy's creation, her narrative, ironically fails as a consequence of the complete power she exerts over her characters and her text. Her narrative and her creature precisely obey her will: the creature obediently promotes her ideology without subverting his creators or the author of the texts. In subduing and sanitizing the golem, removing him from his messy, muddy origins, Piercy diminishes and disempowers him. Piercy's figure is, finally, not a true golem but a mechanical slave; Piercy writes not in the Gothic tradition but in the tradition of those "eighteenth-century mechanics who gave life to the Writer of Neuchâtel and the Chess-playing Turk of Baron von Kempelen" (Umbert Eco "Travels in Hyperreality" 47). Eco compares the inventors of these life-like but lifeless automatons with the creators of Disneyland, the "degenerate utopia" (43),[25] with its fake American Gothic haunted house, and its fake medieval castle. Piercy creates a similar form of utopia or dystopia, reducing a rich and complicated myth to an icon of ideology. In doing so, Piercy unwittingly demonstrates that the continuing source of the power of the golem and of the Gothic lies in its transgressiveness, the ability to generate tension and anxiety. The rabbinic golem is believed to rest to this very day in the attic of the Altneu Synagogue in Prague, awaiting resurrection in another time of need; Shelley's monster continues to stalk his way through the popular imagination. But Piercy's golem, diminished by his creator, pliant and obedient, has been blown to bits and the plans to replicate him have been destroyed.

* * *

The figure of the dybbuk, the dispossessed soul that possesses the body of a living person, is, like the golem, a figure of unnatural appropriation that haunts the tradition of the Jewish folktale. Like the golem, the figure of the dybbuk reveals an alignment with the Gothic tradition in deploying the supernatural to consider real-world issues of property and power. The dybbuk is therefore also available to Jewish American women writers as a mechanism for negotiating their way into Western and Jewish culture. Contemporary transformations of the dybbuk also exemplify the flexibility of the Gothic mode and its ability to respond to the cultural contexts that generate it.

The transgressive figure of the dybbuk (the word means "attachment," as in a soul attaching to the body of another), deriving from the Kabbalistic notion of transmigration of souls, first seized the popular imagination in Jewish Eastern Europe in the sixteenth century. The popular implications of this belief were that any transgressive or deviant behavior, especially on the part of women (Daniel Schifrin "A Play for All Seasons" 35), could be attributed to spiritual possession, the victim thus subject to rabbinical control, including exorcism. The most well-known representation of the dybbuk story is relatively recent: the play *The Dybbuk* (1912–17) by S. Ansky (1863–1920), who set out to recapture the already-disappearing culture of the Jewish *shtetl* (European small town) and who, in the process, reinvented it. In Ansky's version of the folktale, Khonen, betrothed to Leah, dies of a broken heart when she is betrothed to another. He returns as a dybbuk to possess her, and ultimately manages to take full possession through her death. In addition to providing a Gothic-style critique of the patriarchal politics and economics of arranged marriage, Ansky's play invites a consideration of the representation of the dybbuk as the male voice speaking, ventriloquistically, through the possessed female body. Ansky's reading of the folktale reveals that the dybbuk tales, like the golem legends, were a way of expressing and allaying anxiety towards uncontrollable women. The uncontrollable voice that seems to emanate from the woman (the voice that is the emblem of female sexuality in rabbinic culture) is shown in Ansky's play to belong to a figure far less threatening to the patriarchy, the dead male yeshiva student, who is actually expressing his own legitimate patriarchal rights. The woman possessed by the dybbuk who appears to vocalize uncontrollably is, in fact, silent; the powerful voice actually belongs to the possessing male. Ansky's play, then, presents not the wild power of women, but their subjugation.

Tony Kushner's 1998 adaptation of the Ansky play, in which Kushner uncovers a homosexual subtext, indicates a precedent for an association between the figure of the dybbuk and homosexuality. Daniel R. Schifrin writes, "according to Kushner.... Khonon's father and Leah's father, who loved each other as young yeshiva students, promised to consummate their love in the only way the Jewish community would allow—by marrying their children off..." Thus Kushner sees the traditional figure of the dybbuk, as represented in Ansky's play, as "the ultimate image of gender ambiguity and transgression" (Schifrin 35). In their representations of the lesbian dybbuk, Ellen Galford and Judith Katz follow in Ansky's tradition. Like Ansky, they appropriate a figure that implicitly poses questions of sexual ambiguity in Jewish culture; like Ansky, who worked to bring Jewish folktales into the European tradition, they import the figure into the tradition of Anglo/American Gothic literature. As outsiders, they follow the path set by the first English Gothic writer, Horace Walpole, marginalized by his secret homosexual identity. Moreover as Tim Mowl suggests in his biography of Walpole, anxieties of homosexuality lie at the foundation of the outsider Gothic tradition.

As Jewish lesbians more than two centuries later, Galford and Katz are still marginalized by Jewish tradition that has lagged behind the Western world on its wavering path to acceptance of homosexuality. In fact, the situation of the Jewish lesbian has ironically become more complicated in recent times. Although "traditional Jewish legal texts on lesbianism lead to the conclusion that the private sexual behavior of women was viewed as trivial ... now that lesbianism has become public and challenges heterosexuality, the response from traditional circles is anger and revulsion" (Rebecca Albert *Like Bread on a Seder Plate* 33). Responding to the mixed messages of the two cultures that they inhabit, Katz and Galford turn to the supernatural of the Jewish folktale and of the Gothic tradition to find a set of pre-existing tropes available to express the joyous transgressions of the anxious homosexual experience

Ellen Galford's[26] *The Dyke and the Dybbuk* (1993) and Judith Katz's *Running Fiercely Toward a High Thin Sound* (1992) recover and revise the figure of the dybbuk,[27] instating the female line into the patriarchal tradition. Galford and Katz employ the ventriloquistic power of the dybbuk to explore and to counter the traditional silencing of Jewish women, and to seize the authority of female sexuality, emblematized by the forbidden female voice in Jewish culture. In their appropriations of the dybbuk tale, Katz and Galford construct dybbuks who are articulate, female *and* lesbian. These reconstructions reinvent the legends and also work to interrogate the central Jewish texts (the Torah, the Talmud) that originate the patriarchal and heterosexual imperatives of traditional Jewish culture. Katz and Galford remove the veils of shame and secrecy from the figure of the speaking woman. They reconstruct the female speaking subject as unashamedly indecent and lustful, and also as joyful and benign. Like Ozick and Piercy they locate within their subjects the "jouissance" that Cixous finds in the female monster.

Judith Katz's *Running Fiercely Toward a High Thin Sound* presents a dybbuk who is figuratively rather than literally possessed. Nadine is the unhappy, unsocialized, lesbian daughter in a conventional Jewish family. Her seeming mental instability recalls the origin of dybbuk folktales as an explanation for uncontrollable women. Significantly it is Nadine's mother who defines her as a dybbuk; the presence of a mother, and particularly a mother who has the power to define her child's identity, is a radical revision of both the Gothic and the Jewish canons. When Nadine ignites her wild unruly hair (the Jewish hair that so irritates her perfectionist mother) with the family's Sabbath candles, her injuries result in a harsh "monster voice" that inspires her mother to announce: "there's a dybbuk inside her! Just listen!" (18). Katz feminizes Ansky's play in a number of ways. For example, the original play presents a central scene that recurs in Katz's novel. In Ansky's version, an old woman rushes into the synagogue and runs to the Ark of the Torah to pray for her dying daughter. As "she opens the Ark, thrusts her head inside" and begins to chant, the caretaker of the synagogue "gently" asks her if she would like a minyan to pray for her daughter (10–11)—the offer of a minyan suggests that the woman's prayer is inadequate without the presence of the traditional male prayer quorum. Kushner's version of this scene amplifies the cultural misogyny submerged in Ansky's more forgiving text. When Kushner's old woman bursts into the synagogue, the caretaker tells her "'you're not permitted here!'" When she threatens to "'shove my head in the Ark!'" Kushner's caretaker replies "'God forbid'" (18); he offers no support or empathy. Thus in Kushner's not inaccurate rendering of traditional Jewish culture, the penetration of the female into the divine space of the Ark is dangerously transgressive.

Katz's novel also explicates and expands the critique of the politics and economics of marriage, implied in Ansky's play. As in Ansky's play (and in the Gothic tradition), the plot of Katz's narrative centers on the execution of a marriage; in the case of Katz's novel, the marriage of Electa, the sister of Nadine. The ongoing critique of the economics of the institution of heterosexual marriage, introduced by the two lesbian sisters of Electa, and reinforced by Katz's skeptical presentation of a celebration of materialism, redirects the reader's attention to the ambivalence regarding the arranged marriage in Ansky's text. The arranged marriage was a universal in Eastern European *shtetl* life (Mark Zborowski *Life is with People* 42); the commodity of exchange could be male scholarly achievement, as well as worldly goods. Ansky's play, an outgrowth of his ethnographic study of the disappearing world of the *shtetl*, charts the disaster that ensues when Leah's father disregards his daughter's inclination, and betrays an early promise to the friend of his youth, in favor of another, richer suitor. Both texts present a version of a Gothic trope, the interrupted wedding. In the Ansky play, the appearance of the dybbuk and the ultimate death of the bride serve to disrupt the wedding; In Katz's rendering, Nadine performs the narrative function of the disrupting dybbuk. She sneaks into the synagogue before her sister's wedding, and hides in the Ark with the Torah scrolls during the ceremony (a notable transgression on the part of a woman whose access to the Torah is limited by law and practice). The force of Nadine's response to the wedding, mostly sorrow at seeing her "sweet sister" going "down the river … blows [her] out of the Ark" (83): "hair flying every which way, her jeans were covered with mud, her vest was ripped to shreds, she looked really bad, and there she was leaping out of the Ark and running down the aisle" (86). This multi-layered image resonates evocatively: the image recalls the old woman whose presence in front of the ark is barely tolerated by Ansky's romanticized men, and prohibited by Kushner's more realistically drawn misogynists; it recalls the dybbuk's interruption of the wedding in the two plays; it comically literalizes

Nadine's coming out of the closet. Katz accomplishes much in this image: she revises a central Gothic trope; transforms a central figure of the Jewish folk tradition; establishes her narrative power with a clever linguistic image; and thereby makes a place for herself in both traditions.

Indeed, Katz imagines a fantastic unpossessed space that she and her marginalized protagonist may occupy freely. After trying to drown herself, Nadine visits a dream-like place, a fantastic underworld composed of Holocaust images juxtaposed with images of a lesbian utopia. In this space Nadine experiences a wedding that reverses the conventions of the Gothic and *shtetl* weddings: "about a hundred people were marrying each other, and we all were women." This wedding takes place in a synagogue, with a balcony, the section traditionally reserved for women in gender-segregated synagogues, "but no women had to go sit in it." Although there is a rabbi, the women "all took turns" sharing the authority (151). Furthermore, as Rebecca Albert notes, Nadine's difficulty with language evokes Moses, who stuttered, and Elijah, the prophet. She too is a prophet who imagines a new, unpossessed place that might become a utopia: "Her prophetic role is to reclaim the Jewish past as a lesbian and to bring lesbian sensibilities to the stories of Eastern European Jewish life" (160). Thus Nadine, like Katz her creator, and other dispossessed and marginalized writers, explores the expanses of the uncontested Gothic to find a utopia, distant, unknown and fantastic.

In *The Dyke and the Dybbuk,* Ellen Galford also imagines a new and unpossessed territory that she and her marginalized characters may occupy freely, the fantastic underworld inhabited by her witty, wisecracking narrator, the dybbuk Kokos. Unlike most dybbuks, Kokos is not the disembodied voice of a dead person but an independently existing demon; she describes herself as an "unorthodox" (88) demon who uses unconventional approaches in "dybbukry." She is also a rebellious demon, fighting against Mephisto Industries, the demonic conglomerate that has taken over her part of the underworld, and that is trying to phase her out of her job. Kokos' rebellion follows the tradition of Satan (the recurring Gothic figure), who is himself the founder of the underworld in which she works: "I remind myself that this entire industry began with a single act of rebellion against the management Upstairs" (146). Kokos also resists more worldly authority; she battles a dynasty of rabbis over the centuries, as they attempt to free the victims subject to her demonic possession.

Galford deploys her transgressive narrator to inscribe the figure of the vocal woman into Jewish tradition. Kokos narrates the story of Rainbow Rosenbloom, the human whom Kokos possesses as the result of a centuries-old curse. Through the possessing dybbuk, the transgressive Rainbow moves closer to her own tradition. Kokos, secretly bequeathed to Rainbow from her dead mother as a family curse, tells Rainbow a long-buried story of her ancestor Gittel and Anya, her spurned lover. Anya initiated the dybbuk curse upon Gittel's line (96–97). In addition to restoring Rainbow's ancestral history, the suppressed history of her maternal line, Kokos restores her ancestral language. Rainbow's dispossession of the various languages of her tradition—Hebrew, Yiddish, Aramaic—is emblematic of the traditional silence of Jewish women, and of her alienation from her tradition, which has no place for an articulate lesbian. Rainbow's Jewish voice is restored to her by Kokos in her role of ventriloquistic dybbuk. At her family *seder*, Rainbow finds herself, to her surprise, singing the concluding song, *Chad Gadya*, "And in word-perfect Aramaic, too" (33). On an outing with her aunts, Rainbow finds herself regaling them with a Yiddish "rendition of a little amorous [meaning obscene] ditty from a shtetl on the banks of the River Vistula" (162). In these episodes, Galford ironically uses the figure of the dybbuk, a figure of the displaced voice, to restore Rainbow's silent Jewish voice, the emblem of her absence from her tradition.

Despite her tentative stabs at reclaiming her Jewish tradition, which are partially motivated by her infatuation with an Orthodox Jewish woman, Rainbow is a transgressive character, rejoicing particularly, as Kokos the narrator notes, in defying central tenets of Judaism. As a lesbian, she engages in "unspeakable acts that rank right up there with throwing your children into the fire as a sacrifice to Baal." Additionally, she has "flouted that quintessential obligation upon the female Jew to be fruitful and multiply…. As [a] film critic … she's turned her passion for graven images [forbidden by the second commandment] into a vocation" (1–2). On leaving the Passover *seder* at which she has sung, she meets a friend in a Chinese restaurant, where, to counter the overbearing Jewishness of the family *seder*, both women order a smorgasbord of non-kosher delicacies. Kokos says: "That's better. Injunctions maternal and commandments Levitical dissolve into the smoke of sacrilegious burnt offerings" (38). Thus the transgressive lesbian Rainbow, like her haunting rebellious dybbuk Kokos, displays the jouissance advocated by Cixous. In word and deed Rainbow blithely and joyfully challenges the injunctions of the quintessentially patriarchal texts: the Talmud and the Torah.

Yet Rainbow, who finds her voice to sing in Yiddish and Aramaic, does retain her affinity for the traditions of the culture that rejects her; her tense attraction for the tradition is emblematized by her sexual attraction to an Orthodox woman. In her depiction of an Orthodox Jewish community, founded upon the guidelines of the Torah and Talmud, Galford shows the enduring power of the tradition; for as Galford acknowledges, the texts themselves remain resistant to change. Ultimately her appropriation of the dybbuk folktale—rather than her characters' transgressions of the legalisms of the patriarchal texts—allows Galford to offer a positive solution to the problem presented by a tradition of male texts that dispossesses women. In her depiction of the Orthodox community, Galford explicitly locates the place of storytelling as the female domain. While the men study the concretized written texts, legalistically interpreting every question three ways, building "theoretical palaces" (80), the women tell oral stories of poor women and werewolves, of girls who listen to the wind in the trees, of angels and demons (82). In this juxtaposition, Galford counters dry male legalism with the richness of female storytelling. In the realm of storytelling, the place where even the most traditional woman already has a foothold, Galford finds a place for Jewish women to rediscover and re-invent their tradition. Galford posits an imaginative solution for her dybbuk as well: Kokos, unemployed and dispossessed from the underworld at the end of the narrative, also opts for storytelling; she decides to go into filmmaking with her demon friends, pooling their advanced technical skills and their experience with human plots. For Galford, then, as for Piercy, Ozick and Katz, the Judaism of rigid male-dominated legalisms, constructed in the Torah and in the Talmud, may be revised and repossessed through the already flexible and accessible fantastic tales of the tradition, tales of dybbuks and golems that are already part of the Jewish woman's heritage. These American writers appropriate and transform the fanciful stories of their tradition and align them with the supernatural tradition of the Western Gothic, thereby solving their complicated problem of cultural dispossession.

* * *

The recurring Gothic motif of the absent mother emblematizes the erasure of the mother from the Western patriarchy. The folktales of the Jewish tradition display the same literalization of the mother's absence from the patriarchy: the motherless golem birth narrative; the dead mother of Leah in Ansky's The *Dybbuk*. The woman revisionists who re-invent the tales show their sense of cultural displacement in deploying the motif of the absent mother in their texts: the mother of Shira, Piercy's protagonist, is an absent, mysterious figure, although her maternal grandmother is a powerful presence; Ozick's Puttermesser is distanced from her mother as is Katz's Nadine; Rainbow's mother is dead. Yet, the re-enactment of the old Gothic trope in a new Jewish American context reveals new meanings. Galford, whose protagonist's mother is dead, creates her dybbuk to evoke the image of female supernatural power and in doing so evokes the Goddess, the Mother long exiled from Jewish tradition as noted in Adrienne Rich's essay "The Primacy of the Mother," in Kristeva's *Powers of Horror*, and in the collection of essays, *The Absent Mother: Restoring the Goddess to Judaism and Christianity*, by Alix Pirani and Foosiya Miller. Galford's evocation suggests a theological explanation for the motif of the absent mother in the texts of the Jewish canon as well as in the Western Gothic canon: the absence of the mother is emblematic of the abjection of the Goddess by the patriarchal God of the Judeo-Christian tradition. In leading back to the English Gothic, this revision works to suggest another theological explanation for the absence of the mother. As we have seen, the Protestant English Gothic tends to align the Catholic Church with the dark forces of supernatural evil. In exiling the maternal, the English Gothic works to dispossess and disempower Mary, the vestige of the Goddess who maintains a position of power in the Catholic tradition.

Yet, although each of the Jewish writers revisits the trope of the dispossessed mother, each also finds a place for the powerful, active and vocal daughter, suggesting a new future for a reformed tradition. The Gothic text conventionally unfolds in a place that does not actually exist, the unreal Italy of the English Gothic, or Gloria Naylor's Willow Springs, for example. The Jewish American writers appropriate this convention for their purposes; each constructs within her text an unappropriated and unpossessed space, a female utopia in which the female tradition is recreated and restored: Piercy's Tikva; Ozick's New York (under Puttermesser's reign); Katz's New Chelm and dreamworld utopia; and Galford's underworld. In creating these utopias, Piercy, Ozick, Katz and Galford establish a link to another tradition: the tradition of feminist utopias.[28] Ann K. Mellor, who locates Piercy's *Woman on the Edge of Time* in this tradition defines "feminist utopian thinking" as providing "alternative models of sexually egalitarian societies," and remarks that "feminist theory is inherently utopian" ("On Feminist Utopias" 243), in that it imagines worlds that do not yet exist. The fantasy of the feminist utopian vision connects it to the imagination of the Female Gothic that frequently fantasizes interludes of female power. Thus the Gothic utopian fantasy of the four Jewish writers aligns them with the larger feminist project that extends far beyond the boundaries of Jewish culture.

Each of the Jewish utopias in the four novels is a fantastic place, a place structured by the rules of narrative and imagination and not by the rules of tradition and law, a place where fiction counters legalism. Each of these utopias emblematizes the narrative space in which each author creates a foothold within the canon. These stories thus belong to the long tradition of rabbinic (male) Jewish literature called *midrash*, an imagined narrative created in response to a lacuna within a canonical text, a retelling that attempts to explain and embellish the narrative of the canon. The gap that these writers see within the canon is their own absence; their *midrash* fills that gap. This appropriation of culture and narrative space through fantastic enactment indicates important similarities between the projects of the Gothic and the Jewish traditions. As we have seen, the Gothic has long been the space in which the marginal writer may reappropriate narrative ground to imagine the restoration of that which is usurped in the actual world. Jews, long dispossessed, have long told idealized stories of restoration: of the return to the promised land; of the restoration of harmony in Messianic times. Both traditions, then, are haunted by nostalgia for a lost idyllic past and discover possibilities for restoration and repossession in the place of the imagination.

A Multicultural Gothic Quilt: Ozick's The Shawl, Morrison's Beloved, *Erdrich's* The Shawl

Thus Ozick, Piercy, Katz and Galford, like the African American women writers previously discussed—as early as Hannah Crafts and as recently as Natashia Deón, the author of *Grace* (2016)—seize upon the welcoming and flexible Gothic text to find space for themselves as female ethnic writers. In this, the female Gothic writers locate themselves comfortably within the Gothic canon that from its early moments has provided a safe haven for marginalized writers dispossessed by virtue of ethnicity, culture, gender and sexuality. Of course, the various authors take different approaches in adopting the Gothic as a mechanism for appropriating literary space; the variety of the approaches indicates the variety and flexibility of the Gothic canon. In *Linden Hills*, Naylor deploys all the apparatus of the Gothic tradition, excluding the supernatural, to place herself in possession of the narrative; in *Mama Day*, Naylor intertwines the supernatural strains of the Gothic and the African canons to locate herself in both traditions. Ozick, Piercy, Katz and Galford tend to emphasize the supernatural aspect of the Gothic while suppressing some of the other creaky apparatus; their strategy is to interweave the supernatural traditions of the Jewish and the Western Gothic as a way to find a new place in both traditions. These writers also incline toward the Gothic because of its long-term preoccupation with power and property, topics of importance to marginalized writers.

The shared anxieties these various writers articulate within the Gothic invite a serious consideration of the place of Jewish culture and literature in the multicultural paradigm, and a interrogation of the tendency to displace the Jewish text from the multicultural canon because Jews are not typically perceived as being socially, economically, and politically marginalized in American society. The actual place of the Jew in American society is in fact debatable, as indicated by events in the twentieth and twenty-first centuries. Ultimately, that debate is irrelevant to the discussion of the multicultural paradigm. For, Jewish writers[29] are displaced from the cultural center of American culture, writing from within a tradition and a set of cultural influences that are foreign to, and distant from, mainstream American culture; Jewish writers thus represent a contribution to the diversity of American literature. The culturally aware Jew, resisting assimilation into American culture, remains the cultural, and religious, Other.

* * *

The unique history of the Jews also locates them as contributors to diversity, as their story is not the story of the dominant American culture, or of cultural dominance. In fact, just as many African writers are haunted by the history of slavery, turning to the Gothic to reflect its horrors, so do Jewish American writers turn to the Gothic as an appropriate aesthetic for the Holocaust narrative.[30] As the generically transgressive Gothic creates a common space for writers as seemingly disparate as Hannah Crafts, Horace Walpole, Nathaniel Hawthorne and Charles Dickens to come together, in a festival of borrowing, so does common and uncontested Gothic space allow for the convergence of the writers Cynthia Ozick and Toni Morrison, each writing from within her own tradition of historical atrocities ultimately best described within the context of Gothic horror. Cynthia Ozick's novella of 1983, *The Shawl* (comprising the shorter works, "The Shawl" and "Rosa," as well as Toni Morrison's novel *Beloved* (1987) are both extraordinary and powerful books, each standing upon its own merits. Both texts are set during moments of historical trauma: the Holocaust in Europe; slavery in America. Rather than attempt a sweeping story of the millions of people who suffered under both systems, each text personalizes historic tragedy, taking the perspective of a single female victim. The texts, then, take on the power of oral history, delving deeply into the experience of one human being, rather than attempting to provide a panorama of suffering, which ultimately deadens the responses of the reader. Both texts invoke Gothic horror to tell a story that falls well into the Gothic paradigm: the ghostly return of a murdered child; the imprisoned mother; the evil system that nearly destroys them both.

Like their Gothic precursors, Ozick and Morrison find within the Gothic a ready set of tools to describe the experience of their protagonists. Each text, for example, underscores the dehumanization of the individual within the evil systems and the terrifying consequences of such dehumanization. The dehumanization of Rosa is evident at the end of "The Shawl," in Rosa's reaction to the murder of her cherished baby. She stifles her "wolf's screech" (10) by stuffing her mouth with the eponymous shawl that had been used to wrap her child. Sethe is, sadly, dehumanized and demonized by her own sons who, themselves traumatized by the memory of their mother's murder of their sister, tell "die-witch! stories" (205) about their mother. During the course of the uncovered memories that emerge in *Beloved*, we learn that Sethe's master assigned his nephews the task of recording "her human characteristics on the left; her animal ones on the right" (193). These same nephews assaulted Sethe and "'took my milk'" (17), treating her like a farm animal. Remembering her brutal rescue of her children from slavery, she thinks "And no one, nobody on this earth, would list her daughter's characteristics on the animal side of the paper" (251). Which is why Paul D says exactly the wrong words to Sethe when he condemns her action, killing her child to liberate her family from slavery: "'You got two feet, Sethe, not four'" (165). His collusion with the dehumanizing categorization of the white masters drives a wedge between him and Sethe that lasts until the conclusion of the book. Paul D himself experiences the dehumanization of slavery. As a young man he and the other Sweet Home slaves "had taken to calves" (10), because they lack sexual access to women. After he is captured Paul D's captors put "'a bit in my mouth'" (69), and as he passes by the farm rooster, he realizes that in that place the rooster is much more "'free'" and "'better than me. Stronger, tougher'" (72).

Both Ozick and Morrison focus on the particular suffering of women, subject to sexual abuse, and to the wrenching loss of their children (situations that demonstrate the horrible slide of history toward the Gothic). Sethe's mother is repeatedly raped on the Middle Passage, and Sethe is sexually assaulted by the nephews. Rosa is raped by a German, "'I was forced by a German, it's true, and more than once'" (43), although she denies that Magda was the product of a rape. Most significantly, each of the women suffers the violent and brutal death of a deeply cherished baby girl. Nor does either writer spare the reader the horror of the details. We see the death of Magda as she is carried to the electrified fence by a Nazi soldier who hurls her against the fence. And we see Sethe, driven mad by slavery, attempting to kill all of her children to save them from being recaptured, succeeding only in slicing the throat of one daughter, but in doing so, convincing the slave hunters that it would be a bad bargain to take her and her children back into slavery. Both writers emphasize the gendering of suffering—recalling the rhetoric of Harriet Jacobs' *Incidents in the Life of a Slave Girl*—as both protagonists insist on the inability of men to understand their suffering. Sethe sarcastically tells the empathetic Paul D, "'Then you know what it's like to send your children off when your breasts are full'" (16). And Rosa responds to her would-be suitor Persky's attempt at solidarity: "'My Warsaw isn't your Warsaw'" (19). Yet both women are ultimately saved by these decent men, each of whom exorcises the ghost baby and offers the bereaved mother a future.

Both writers also stress the actual inhumanity of the oppressor by showing how such presumed human beings look to their victims. To the childish Beloved, white men are monstrous "men without skin" (210). Rosa sees the murdering camp guard as an inanimate object: "Below the helmet a black body like a domino and a pair of black boots" (9). Both texts use the language of theft and dispossession to articulate the crime imposed upon the victims: Baby Suggs says "Those white things have taken all I had or dreamed" (89). Rosa repeatedly laments that thieves took her life (20, 28). Each writer also deploys the Gothic trope of the rebirth of the dead, the return of the dead, to imagine the ongoing effects of the death of the child. Morrison invokes a non-supernatural form of the trope when she describes Baby Suggs crossing the Ohio River into freedom. Experiencing her own body for the first time as belonging only to herself, "next, she felt a knocking in her chest.... 'My heart's beating,' she said" (141). In this episode Morrison presents a metaphor that is more legal than supernatural. Under slavery the slave was not alive as a separate human being, a legal entity. So, legally, the freed slave came to life from the dead, as reflected in the Baby Suggs' natural experience of feeling her own heart beating. But Morrison moves beyond the natural to the supernatural, presenting the dead baby returned, first as a nebulous ghost: "124 was Spiteful. Full of a baby's venom" (3), and then in more substantial forms. The ghost appears as "a white dress [that] knelt down next to her mother and had its sleeve around her mother's waist" (29), and then as the mysterious young women Beloved, who remembers Sethe's earrings, and who childlike maintains a preference for sweets. When Sethe first sees the returned Beloved, she re-enacts her birth, letting loose a flow of liquid that is more "water breaking from a breaking womb" (51), than the release of a full bladder. But Morrison allows for ambiguity as to Beloved's identity and ghostliness; a number of times we are told that Beloved may be a young women who had been kept as a sexual prisoner in the woods.

The ghost baby in "The Shawl" is more naturalized and psychological than supernatural. The second part of Ozick's novel "Rosa," takes place decades after "The Shawl," thus focusing like *Beloved* on the aftermath and memories of historical horror. In the story, the half-mad Rosa turns to the shawl that covered her dead baby to "restore Magda ... a vivid thwack of restoration like an electric jolt" (62)—recalling the vivifying method of Dr.

Frankenstein. At the end of the novel, when "Magda sprang to life," Rosa puts the shawl over the telephone receiver: "it was like a little doll's head then.... The whole room was full of Magda; she was like a butterfly" (54). The narrator describes a vividly realized Magda seen through Rosa's eyes: "There was Magda, all in flower. She was wearing one of Rosa's dresses from high school.... Magda's hair was still as yellow as buttercups." Magda presents "an explicit face.... She had begun to resemble Rosa's father" (64–65). But Ozick's baby ghost is far more grounded in psychological realism than is Morrison's; Magda is visible only to her mad mother. When the insistent Persky arrives, determined to pull Rosa into the present, "Magda was not there.... Magda was away" (69). Yet, like Morrison's succubus, Beloved, who drains the life from her mother, the imaginary Magda also suggests a subtle threat, a strain that is "ghostly, even dangerous. It is as if the peril hummed out from the filaments of Magda's hair, those narrow bright wires" (66). Magda is dangerous; she recalls her father, Rosa's rapist, and the threat of death and madness that still lurks over the isolated and unhappy Rosa, even though she is no longer imprisoned within actual electrified wires (although she imagines she is on a walk to the beach). These ghost children thus emblematize the inability of the mothers to let go of the past and to return to life.

A number of critics have noted the connections between the "The Shawl" and *Beloved*. Kathleen Brogan discusses both texts in her insightful book, *Cultural Haunting: Ghosts and Ethnicity in Recent American Literature*, although she does not directly compare the two. Adam Zackary Newton considers the convergence of the two texts in *Facing Black and Jew*. In her essay, "Some Thoughts on the Mutual Displacements/Appropriations/Accommodations of Culture in Several Fictions by Toni Morrison, Cynthia Ozick, and Grace Paley," Emily Miller Budick notes some of the parallels between the two texts, but her observations lead her to some problematic conclusions. Budick uses as her starting point Morrison's argument, in "Romancing the Shadow," that much of American literature represses the presence of the enslaved African and the existence of slavery. Budick asserts a similar repression in Western culture of the figure of the Jew, and the historical atrocities inflicted upon Jews. Budick then moves to assert that *Beloved* represents an instance of the kind of repression of cultural experience, in this case that of the Jew. In Budick's harsh assessment, *Beloved*, in its telling of the African tragedy of slavery, draws upon, yet denies, the Jewish Holocaust—a strategy that Budick disparages as appropriation. She asserts: "Morrison's use of Jewish materials [is] less resonant of Jewish history than competitive with it" (388).[31] Yet, Budick's critique of Morrison's possible borrowings from Jewish trauma and Jewish texts is specious, neglectful of Morrison's perspective. *Beloved* need not reference the Jewish Holocaust because it is not about Jews. Budick's cultural narcissism ignores the need for African Americans to tell their own stories, without considering the experience of whites. Moreover, the conventional tendency of Gothic texts to borrow from each other when addressing a variety of social and historical horrors allows Morrison to borrow from Ozick as she likes. That Morrison transgresses the boundaries that divide her text from holocaust iconography, and from Ozick's is, as we have seen, a commonplace of Gothic aesthetics. Certainly, the comparison of Morrison's text to Ozick's amplifies a major aspect of the various borrowings we have examined: each ultimately transforms and revises the earlier works in its own image. In fact, Morrison clearly makes her text her own, in contextualizing it within Christian theology, and in feminizing that theology—taking the novel far beyond Ozick's text.

Morrison's feminist stance alone moves her away from Ozick's influence and ensures that her novel brings some important new insights to the discussion of the female experience of the traumas of history. The temporal focus of each text is an early and significant clue to their divergence. Both texts largely take place in the time after history, and consider the issue of memory in the aftermath of great historical tragedy. The present of *Beloved* is the time after the horrors of history have ended, and the reader learns of Sethe's traumatic experiences under slavery only through her memory—or the powerful version of memory that she calls "rememory"—and from the ongoing conversations that she has with Paul D, who fills in the blanks of her memory, as she fills in the gaps of his. Thus Morrison's story is not so much about living through trauma as about living after trauma, burdened with memories. Of Sethe waking early to bake bread in the restaurant where she works, Morrison writes: "Nothing better than that to start the day's serious work of beating back the past" (73).

The temporality of *The Shawl* is notably different. Ozick's work encompasses two shorter sections: a short story, also entitled "The Shawl," and the novella-length, "Rosa." While "Rosa," like *Beloved*, focuses on the period after trauma, and on the long-term impact of historical trauma, "The Shawl" relates the moment of trauma in brutally vivid and immediate terms, unmediated by the frame of memory. In fact, there is a moment when the story, narrated in the past tense, almost slides to the present. In the final terrible paragraph, when Rosa witnesses Magda's death we hear of "the wolf's screech ascending *now* through the ladder of her skeleton" (10). The differences in the temporal perspectives of the two texts ultimately indicate significant political differences in the feminist stance of each author. The belated temporality of Morrison's text, in addition to the set of conventional Gothic tropes she explicitly invokes, links her novel more visibly to the tradition of the Female Gothic and moves the novel far from the influence of Ozick,[32] whose narrative reveals a stance toward feminism similar to that observed in "Puttermesser and Xanthipe." In "Rosa" Ozick evokes the supernatural to tell her story of female suffering, while pointedly refusing the Gothic tradition, with its female and feminist associations. Admittedly, Ozick briefly invokes an iconic Gothic text—the benevolent Mr. Persky recalls that famous Gothic hero-villain, Mr. Rochester, when he quite casually informs Rosa that his wife is consigned to "'a private hospital, it don't cost me peanuts…. She's in a mental condition'" (27). And Rosa herself recalls Bertha Rochester; in the first lines of "Rosa," we learn that she is a destructive "madwoman." Yet ultimately Ozick's text rejects the Gothic and its female and feminist associations. Ozick's ghost is merely a shawl draped over a telephone, unlike Morrison's fully realized ghost. And while Morrison's text is dominated by a haunted house, 124, whose moods are described at the beginning of each section of the novel, "Rosa" avoids description of any domestic (female) space. One might also argue that the humor of the text—the comic voices of Rosa and Persky—also refuses the lugubrious tradition of the Female Gothic.

In fact, Ozick's distinctive approach to literary tradition is apparent in the generic paradigm that she most strongly references as she refuses the Female Gothic: that most male of literary traditions, the heroic epic. Viewing the texts through this prism, reveals the way in which the Female Gothic opposes the male epic in their divergent constructions of "home." Whereas the Female Gothic, as exemplified by *Beloved*, constructs home as a prison in which the female character is kept from engaging with the world, the male epic figures home as the distant, idealized goal, and refuge from the world. Ozick's construction of home is one of several elements that locates "Rosa" in the tradition of the epic, or its relative, the mock-epic. The structure of Ozick's novella recalls that of Homer's Iliad and Odyssey, the first part taking place during a time of war and death, the second part following the wanderings of a survivor searching for home. Although Homer's hero merely visits the underworld in the second part of the epic, Ozick's protagonist dwells in the land of the dead in the first part of her epic, "The Shawl"; "Rosa" traces Ozick's epic heroine's return to the land of the living. As in the case of Homer's text, Ozick does not fully resolve the question of whether the protagonist actually does re-emerge to the world of life. "Rosa" follows its heroine as she wanders through the wastes of Florida, encountering various adventures while she searches for a missing piece of underwear, also perhaps searching, like Odysseus, for home. It is the thought of her missing underwear, and her certainty that Persky has stolen it, that impel her out into the streets of Miami, into a series of nighttime adventures that also recall that other borrowing from Homer featuring a Jew, Joyce's *Ulysses*. Looking for her underwear, Ozick leaves her apartment, searches the elevator, the lobby and finally the street, where she discovers that "her underpants were not in the road" (45). And thus commences Rosa's nighttime journey, as she wanders from place to place searching: "On the sidewalk in form of the Kollins Kosher Kameo, nothing" (46); after considering where Persky might hide the purloined underwear, she decides that a likely spot would be "under the sand. Rolled up and buried" (47). This thought leads her to a fenced-in gay beach where she is horrified equally by the dual realization that "'you got gays and you got barbed wire'" (51). Of course, this lost underwear, is only a stand-in for Rosa's great loss. When she tells Persky, "'I was looking for something I lost'" (meaning the underwear), and he asks, "'What did you lose,'" her response is "'My life.'" (55). There is a suggestion at the end of the narrative that Rosa, like any great epic hero, does ultimately reach her goal. The readers can hope at least that Rosa will rediscover a life and a home with Persky. In fact, Morrison echoes this ending with the closure of *Beloved*, in which it appears that Sethe will find peace with Paul D, who, like Persky, has exorcised the baby ghost who has kept her mother chained to the past. Thus a close reading of the two texts reveals that both start from a similar position: the bereaved mother, whose daughter has been murdered as a consequence of brutal repression, who is haunted by the ghost of that daughter. Though the books diverge in significant ways, they do find common ground in the Gothic space. While Ozick ultimately abandons this space while Morrison flourishes there, each relates to it, allowing for the conversation before the divergence.

A key divergence is the addition of Christian tropology to Morrison's work. Ozick's story reflects Jewish skepticism regarding the uses of suffering or martyrdom. No benefit comes from Madga's death, which results in Rosa's isolation and estrangement from her only relative, a niece whom she blames for Magda's death. Morrison, however, contextualizes her story within Christian imagery and ideology. In Morrison's novel the innocent child dies to save the rest of her family from slavery and briefly returns from the dead, suggesting a Christological reading of the ghost, and also lending a transcendent meaning to the death of the baby that is absent from Ozick's text: Rosa's family is wiped, out while Sethe's continues through Denver who breaks free of the family trauma. Morrison freely revises Christian theology, feminizing it—and invoking earlier more female-centered myths that influence the Christian tradition, famously the myth of Persephone. In this, Morrison illustrates another great appropriation of the Gothic tradition, the use that Gothic texts frequently make of the Bible, with its surprising offerings of Gothic tropology. Morrison sets the tone for this borrowing in the epigraph of *Beloved* from Romans: "I will call them my people which are not my people; and her beloved which was not beloved" (Romans 9.25). A look at the context of this ancient quote reveals that it also is a borrowing. As much of the Christian Bible, the quote refers to the Hebrew Bible. In fact, Paul explicitly tells his readers that he is drawing from the prophet Hosea. The first words of Romans 9.25, not quoted by Morrison are: "As indeed he says in Hosea." Hosea is the Hebrew Bible prophet who creates an analogy between his disloyal wife and the people of Israel, disloyal to God, punished and ultimately forgiven by God. Certainly, Morrison turns to one other Hebrew Bible text: The Song of Solomon, with its invocations of "my beloved." A number of lines from the biblical text take on greater resonance when read with Morrison's novel: "I am very dark but comely.... Do not gaze at me because I am swarthy.... My mother's sons were angry with me. They made me keeper of the vineyards: but, my own vineyards I have not kept!" (1.5–6). The repetition of variations of "I am my beloved's and my beloved is mine" (2.16; 6.3) are echoed by Morrison's variations. Sethe: "'Beloved, she my daughter. She mine'" (200). Denver: "'Beloved is my sister'" (205). Beloved: "'I am beloved and she [Sethe] is mine'" (210). These repetitions take on added poignancy in the context of slavery in which one could not say with certainty that one's beloved is "mine"—a loved one may, in fact, have been possessed by another. Morrison lends a dignity and gravitas to her simple characters by transgressing the barriers between their narrative and the Bible, and further links her text to the transgressive Gothic tradition.

The image of the sacrificial child and the title of Ozick's story open this web of permeable dispossessed narratives to another text, Louise Erdrich's short story, "The Shawl" (2001). This story too tells of the daughter of a dispossessed people, in this case Native Americans, whose death results in the salvation of her family. The nine year old sister is in a wagon with her mother and baby sister, when a pack of hungry wolves starts to chase them down. The girl realizes that "one person on the wagon has to be offered up, or they all would die ... being who she was, of the old sort of Anishinaabeg, who thinks of the good of the people first, she jumped." While the sacrificed daughter links Erdrich's story to Morrison's, the title suggests an even tighter connection between Erdrich's story and Ozick's. Erdrich calls attention to this connection in the title she gives the story. The titular shawl, as in Ozick's story is all that remains, the only relic of the dead child. To add to the connection, both Ozick's (1980) and Erdrich's (2001) stories were published in the same journal, *The New Yorker*. As in the Ozick story, the supernatural is repressed in Erdrich's "The Shawl," limited to the last image of the story when the nephew of the long-dead girl imagines that "she lifted her shawl and flew." Erdrich's story is set in the non-space of the folktale: "it is told"—similar to the non-existent space of the Gothic text; it is the story of trauma playing out through the generations, of the sins of the father visited on the children.

The convergences of these American novels invite a consideration of the conversation they generate. All the texts of lost daughters and haunted mothers were written between 1980 and 2001. The synchronization of the publication of these texts, with their shared concerns of maternity, raises important questions. Did the death of the Equal Rights Amendment in the early part of the 1980s suggest to women that, despite other advancements, they were, as always, at risk, perilously close to the Gothic situation that had endured for centuries? Do these texts indicate a deep dark recognition that the structures that engendered the Female Gothic remain? That women continue to be besieged by evil patriarchies, unable to prevent their daughters and themselves from being rendered into ghosts? As the decades unfold, the answer continues to be a sad affirmative.

Conclusion
Toward a Fourth Century of American Gothic

The story of American literature is the story of the search for a new American canon—unpossessed by traditions of the past—a search that is paradoxically abetted by the convention-laded Gothic mode. For while the Gothic mode is remarkable for the recurrence of its preoccupations and motifs, it is also notably flexible, evolving to address the concerns of the specific culture that generates it. The American text is itself haunted by the ghost of the English Gothic tradition, the uncanny past form that it wishes to repress. In an attempt to escape this haunting, and as a reflection of unique cultural qualities, the American Gothic revises its English predecessor in myriad ways, responding to uniquely American anxieties of property and power. Subsequent waves of newcomers to America repeat this pattern, addressing their own struggles with the new American world, and with the past of their own cultures.

From its beginnings, American culture has been the site of competing voices, vying for possession of the narrative, in a struggle that is frequently framed as a struggle for more tangible property as well. Judith Fetterley's reading of Washington Irving's "The Legend of Sleepy Hollow" points to the early conflation of struggles for possession of property with struggles for possession of narrative. Fetterley persuasively argues that "Legend" represents a contest for possession of the American canon, emblematized as a struggle for possession of property: "In 'The Legend of Sleepy Hollow,' Irving poses the question of who will be given possession of Sleepy Hollow, that imaginative space which inspires our stories, and who will be driven out. Irving identifies the masculine Brom Bones as the decisive victor, the effeminate Ichabod Crane as the figure to be driven out" ("Not in the Least American" 891). Charles Chesnutt's "Po' Sandy" frames the struggle for narrative control and property, as a racialized contest between former slave and current master; the disempowered Uncle Julius wins the contest for possession of property through his narrative power. Similarly, in Harriet Beecher Stowe's *Uncle Tom's Cabin*, the slave Cassy takes possession of herself by appropriating the Gothic narrative; in materializing Legree's fears, Cassy is able to make her escape and repossess her body from the bonds of chattel slavery. These examples illustrate the uses of the Gothic for the dispossessed and insecure American writer. And the American writer is always newly arrived and dispossessed: belated to the English tradition; or newly arrived and belated to American culture; or displaced from the new cultural traditions of new Americans. In our time of rapid technological change, and an increasingly diverse American identity, all Americans have reason to experience a sense of belatedness or alienation. America is the home country that feels uncannily unhomelike to many of its inhabitants. Nathaniel Hawthorne's Preface to *The House of the Seven Gables* exemplifies the early stage of American belatedness, as American writers struggled to create a tradition in the shadow of England. The Preface also illustrates the use the displaced writer makes of the unclaimed genre of Gothic Romance. In his sense of exclusion and dispossession, Hawthorne echoes his displaced English precursors, men and women writing from the margins, and finding a place in the English Gothic tradition, beginning with the closeted English homosexual Horace Walpole, and culminating (for now) in the displaced and belated American female writers who turn to the Gothic mode from across the spectrum of race, religion and gender identity. These women, like *their* precursors find in the Gothic a narrative space that resists and refuses possession on every level, a sanctuary that welcomes writer excluded by other traditions. Dismissed to the margins of the canon, disdained because of its association with irrational women and other disenfranchised writers, the American Gothic provides free unclaimed space to new claimants. The welcoming and flexible nature of the Gothic mode thus works as a magnet for American writers, allowing them to enter the canon, and to participate in a conversation that has endured for centuries. This narrative of the American Gothic complicates the story that James Watt tells of the English Gothic in *Contesting the Gothic* (1999). Watt considers opposing versions of the English Gothic—Ann Radcliffe's tendency toward terror and suspense, and Matthew Lewis' affinity for gory spectacle and horror. Watt uses his example to argue that the Gothic canon is a site of contestation: "Gothic fiction [is] far less a tradition with a generic identity and significance than a domain which [is] open to contest from the first, constituted or structured by the often antagonistic relations between different writers and works" (*Contesting the Gothic* 6). While the American Gothic canon also presents its share of conflict, as in the case of Morrison and Ozick, the American tradition also offers common ground for textual conversations among diverse writers, as in the case of Hannah Crafts, Gloria Naylor and Marge Piercy. Perhaps another American transformation is the move from contestation to conversation.

Yet, an affinity for the Gothic is not without its confusions and anxieties. The ghost of English literature that loomed for centuries over the Gothic American Gothic text may have been exorcized, but we continue to find sources of anxiety close to home, in our own ever-lengthening past and darkening future. After more than four-hundred years of literature, our early writers, haunted by the English tradition, have evolved from being iconoclasts to becoming icons themselves, haunting the writing of their successors. As American culture becomes more fragmented and diverse, moving from a stable model of centralized cultural authority, the paradigm of cultural possession in America moves closer to the Gothic model of dispossession and multivocality, with attendant anxieties. Paul Lauter's *Canons and Contexts* points to the paradigm of multiple American canons—the comparative literatures of America—a diverse canon that looks remarkably like the individual Gothic text: resisting possession by any one individual; presenting competing viewpoints, while denying any central narrative authority. Lauter's proposed model of multiple American canons is as vast and unknowable, as resistant to possession, as any conventional Gothic space or Gothic narrative. As the Gothic space is unknowable, epistemologically unpossessible, as the Gothic text resists hermeneutic possession, so does the American canon—contested by multiple claimants, speaking in different voices, resistant to possession and definition. As revisions of American history reveal previously repressed horrors, and as more new Americans come to America shouldering the burden of their own cultural and historical pasts, Gothic nostalgia takes on added resonance. Kathleen Brogan reads in "tales of cultural haunting" the deployment of the trope of the ghost as a mechanism for recovery of the past on the part of repressed people whose narrative is too terrible to recall, or whose story is repressed and denied by the dominant narrative of history—a tendency that is visible in texts like Toni Morrison's *Beloved* and Cynthis Ozick's *The Shawl*.

* * *

As the American Gothic unfolds, now entering its fourth century, literary tropes that are now centuries old are taking visible shape. The paradigm of the hungry, greedy American begins with the image of the Puritan settler, Mary Rowlandson, ravenously consuming a raw horse liver, and continues up to Colson Whitehead's voracious zombies. This trope appears in a number of disparate texts—*Edgar Huntly*, "Legend of Sleepy Hollow," *House of the Seven Gables*, *Puddn'head Wilson*, *A Mercy*, among others—illustrating that a long Gothic tradition does indeed make strange bedfellows. Since greed and voracious hunger for objects and human beings continues to taint American culture, the figure of infinite appetite will presumably linger into the future. The invasion trope, amplified in the American Gothic, also dates as far back as the captivity tales of Mary Rowlandson and others, beginning when the secluded and seemingly safe slice of England—transplanted to the new world—is invaded by the demonic "savage" natives. The American invasion trope is thus ironic from its origins—reflecting just as accurately the experience of the displaced Native Americans as that of the displacing English settlers. This trope continues in Brown's *Wieland* as the sanctuary of the young Americans is invaded by the European Carwin, in Poe's "Masque of the Red Death," featuring the invasion of plague, and the disguised "red man" it emblematizes, and in Hawthorne's *House of the Seven Gables* with the double invasion of Phoebe and Holgrave. The trope of invasion continues in Jackson's *We Have Always Lived in the* Castle, with the invasion of the patriarchal Charles, and the rioting villagers, continuing with the invading zombies of *Zone One*. In fact, a consideration of the invasion narratives reveals another timely lesson: although the invading outsider might serve as a catalyst for disaster, often the real threat is to be found already embedded, as a member of the group within the sanctuary, like Brown's Wieland, Jackson's Merricat, and Whitehead's zombies, who all display the dangers that may arise from within the community. With the rising of new media of the twentieth century, and new anxieties of the possibility of invasion from other worlds, invasion narratives transform. Orson Welles' infamous radio broadcast (in 1938) of an adaptation of H. G. Wells' *War of the Worlds* (1897) illustrates the flexibility of the Gothic, as it transforms to adapt to new media, and to confront the political fears of its time. The invasion trope rose to new heights in the invasion films of the 1950s, long presumed to mask and reflect American anxieties about Soviet invasion at the height of the Cold War. A variation of this theme is apparent in the film *I Married a Monster from Outer Space* (1958), which expresses fears of invisible homosexual infiltration of heteronormative post-war American society. The alien invaders in this film are particularly dangerous, as they take possession of the bodies of American family men, passing as "normal" men, and threaten to disrupt the procreation that was imperative during the 1950s. The invisible invader, as in Poe's "Red Death," is a recurring subset of the trope of invasion, The trope of the invisible invader also suggests the fear of the assimilating immigrant, able to "pass" as a "real" American. Like the trope of hunger, the trope of invasion culminates—for the moment—in the invading zombies of Whitehead's novel *Zone One* and its wildly proliferating peers.

* * *

As this book concludes, in the year 2018, it is quite clear that the fictions of the Gothic—and the repressed realities they reflect—are far from over. We are seeing in our time a resurgence of the old tyrannical patriarchy, the return of the American aristocrat; we are witnessing the unveiling of the pervasive depredations of the sexually predatory male. We live in a dark and anxious world; daily, we confront mysterious structures that refuse to reveal their dark secrets, and increasingly realistic fears of an apocalyptic future. In fact, the Gothic mode risks being outpaced by the reality that it reflects. The Gothic writer is in danger of becoming a non-comedic version of Tristram Shandy—the fictional autobiographer of *The Life and Opinions of Tristram Shandy* (1759), written by Laurence Sterne—who finds to his dismay that his narrative lags far behind the actual events of his daily life. The contemporary media provide up-to-the-minute horror that stuns (or freezes, to use Ann Radcliffe's locution) the imagination. Our world could be accurately described by the words of the title of Chapter 42 in Stowe's *Uncle Tom's Cabin*: "An Authentic Ghost Story" (594), or possibly, an authentic horror story. Clearly, something is dreadfully wrong; but the dangers of our world are no longer invisible, requiring the Gothic to unveil hidden legal and social dangers. We no longer need the Gothic text to unmask the frightening American hunger to possess and consume—people, products, and land—that has dogged us since our earlier history. This hunger is now blatantly visible in ways that were unimaginable even in the times of the robber barons: mindless, impersonal, and dangerous hunger, emblematized by zombies, who are certainly the monsters of our time. We no longer require a reminder of the dangers that lie within our American sanctuary, when we can see actual mobs of Americans spewing hatred in the streets. We no longer need to turn to the American Gothic to remind us of the repressed American sins—the abuse of African Americans, Native Americans and other marginal groups—since we are trapped in a time in which the amplification of race hatred roars back from the repression of recent decades. Why then does the creaky old Gothic mode continue to endure, growing in popularity, dominating the artifacts of popular culture, even as its horrors are eclipsed by the actual horrors of the world?

* * *

A closer look at the two dominant figures of horror in the early twenty-first century—the vampire and the zombie—might account for the continuing power of the Gothic. Although these two figures have evolved into distinct forms, they have much in common. Both illustrate the insatiable hunger exhibited by the voracious American through the centuries: they share an appetite for the human body; the vampire requires the blood of human beings to survive. Both fantastic monsters also share the ability to replicate themselves, not through *eros*, but through the death of their victims; both figures are themselves undead, risen from death. The slippage between these two related figures appears in Richard Matheson's novel, *I Am Legend* (1954), which presents a mob of zombie-like vampires who cannibalize humans, but who are also capable of thought. The film version of the novel, made in 2007, moves away from this cusp, toward the model of the contemporary zombie, mindless and devouring. In both versions of *I Am Legend*, we can see in the zombie the vestiges of the vampire: Matheson's zombies are susceptible to sunlight and effect their depredations only in the darkness of night. Both the film and book versions also move the figure of horror from the private realm of the vampire to the public domain of the zombie, capable of causing global apocalypse.

The English and American vampire is a private, almost-invisible monster who was certainly the monster of the moment in the first decade of the twenty-first century, continuing the popularity of the vampire instigated by Anne Rice in *Interview with the Vampire* (1976), and in the books and films that followed. Alluring, seductive and intelligent, the American vampire creates suspenseful terror rather than sheer horror; Rice's vampires present an array of human, though dangerous, qualities. The creature took on cult status with the publication of Stephanie Meyers' wildly popular book series starting with *Twilight* (2005), and followed by an equally popular film series beginning in 2008. Meyers' twenty-first-century American vampire interrogates the link between sexuality and danger, that lurks at the root of the English Gothic, and that emerges in the figure of the English vampire: for example, in Sheridan Le Fanu's *Carmilla* (1871), and Bram Stoker's *Dracula* (1897). Meyers' novels suggest a continuation of Rice's twentieth-century transformation; Meyers presents a vampire who is loving and selfless, instead of predatory and voracious, a vampire who is paradoxically a suitable romantic partner. Yet, Meyers' ultimately reactionary novels actually move backward, reinforcing the link between sex and danger. The hero is only alluring because he is celibate, willing to abstain from sex to protect his partner from the dual (and linked) dangers of sex and vampirism. Thus Meyers actually solidifies the link between the sex and danger forged by her English precursors; in her books, sex would result not only in a fallen woman, but in a fallen female vampire. As in Radcliffe, as in Walpole, sex is a dangerous lure deployed by men to trap women. Meyers' contribution to the paradigm is her depiction of the suitable young man, counter to the tyrannical rapist: her vampire is a sexual man who is nevertheless willing to abstain, an alluring male who places his partner's well-being over his own physical needs. The attractions that such a safe abstaining male holds for a young audience awash in a cultural sea of sexuality are clear. In the sexually-charged twenty-first century, a time when sex did indeed pose dangers to confused young adults, Meyers' audience could take comfort from the linkage Meyer created between abstinence and *eros*. In fact, this linkage gestures to the sentimental novels of the eighteenth and nineteenth centuries, providing young adult readers a secure escape from the actual anxieties and dangers of sex in the twenty-first century.

With the recent explosion of the figure of the zombie as the emblem of horror, the anxiety of sex is replaced by the only anxiety that is even more central to the Gothic: the fear of death. This monster is the reverse of alluring: a dead and decaying body whose invasion of the human body is repulsive and deadly rather than sexy. Additionally, the zombie, lacking all the psychological attraction of the seductive and deceptive vampire, is distinguished by its mindlessness. Rather than desiring the human body—the zombie does not seem capable of even the basic emotion of desire—the mindless zombie operates under some instinctual or visceral compulsion to eat the human body, most particularly the human brain. Perhaps most meaningfully, the zombie moves the locus of horror from the private to the public, from the individual to the masses; it removes horror from the place of darkness and secrecy, and from the experience of the individual, to the spectacular global plane. No longer is horror the story of the encounter of the individual with the dark unknown. Horror is now experienced world-wide and is caused not by a single mysterious figure, but by a world-destroying mob, reflecting the seemingly universal anxiety of our globalized times, as we are all bombarded with the everyday spectacles of horror on a grand scale. A harbinger of global apocalypse, the apocalyptic and existential dangers the zombie engenders derive from the sheer mass of the mob of monsters.

While the term "zombie," comes from Haitian folklore, referring to a reanimated dead body, the contemporary zombie—undead, mindless, voracious, wildly proliferating—invaded the popular imagination through the films of the American filmmaker, George Romero's. The figure of the zombie, a belated monster, was born in film, *The Night of the Living Dead* (1968); it is a truly American monster. Romero's supposedly coincidental casting of an African American actor as the remaining survivor—gunned down at the finale of the film by a local militia—-locates the undercurrent of racial anxiety in the originating text. This theme, an uncanny prediction of the realities of race and power in twenty-first-century American life, is revisited by Colson Whitehead in *Zone One*.

The evolution of the vampire to the zombie in American literature and culture highlights the flexible and enduring power of the Gothic, and the confounding ability of the Gothic to successfully provoke fear through supernatural horror two-hundred years after the time of the Enlightenment. In presaging apocalypse (from the Greek word meaning unveiling or revealing), the zombie advances the Gothic enterprise of demystifying cultural secrets. The new American monster unveils unspoken secrets of American society, and interrogates the few remaining uncontested truths of our culture: the belief in the unlimited possibilities of technology, including the promise of overcoming or extending death; the commitment to the joys of urban life; the faith in the benefits of democracy. The figure of the zombie reveals secret anxieties about these values, anxieties that are typically dismissed by the certainties of American optimism.

While we live in a brave new world of technology, where to question is to reveal oneself as a Luddite, the figure of the zombie reflects concerns about the human future in a technologically-dominated world, expressing the fear that humans will be reduced to mindless automatons, or that humans will be overtaken by the mindless automatons that they create. The heightened power of technology in our increasingly secularized society also impacts upon our relationship to death and the dead body. Whereas in past centuries, the dead body was brought into the home, and presented for viewing, the modern technologies of health care and body disposal work to render the dead and dying as distant and invisible. The repression of the corruption and decay of the corpse is possible in a secular, environmentally-conscious society that increasingly promotes the economic and environmental benefits of cremation. Our society thus succeeds even more that past societies in repressing the unpleasant corporeal realities of death, and the attendant fears of death. The zombie is the exact image of the return of the repressed, repulsively decaying corpse, resisting the sanitizing technologies of death, and mocking the technologies that would extend life beyond the limits of biology. Another cultural American myth countered by the figure of the zombie is the fantasy of urban living. More and more young people are choosing to stay or move to big cities, only to discover that instead of the excitement they sought, they find themselves living in claustrophobic spaces in dirty cities, surrounded by hordes of silent, distant, and seemingly inhuman strangers. As Whitehead shows in *Zone One*, life after the zombie apocalypse is not dissimilar from life before. Both feature mindless crowds aimlessly moving through the blasted urban landscape. Even the possibilities of democracy, the pride of

American culture and history, are brutally challenged by the figure of the zombie masses. The zombie mob and the destruction it engenders is a frightening reflection of the American crowd, the rulers of democracy, who do not always make wise or kind choices. The zombie suggests that the American masses are dead, mindless, retaining only a single, basic human American quality: a voracious, omnivorous hunger.

The zombie, as articulated by Colson Whitehead, also feeds into new versions of that old American anxiety, the fear of not belonging at home, the uncanny sense of *unheimlich*, as defined by Freud. The new American landscape de-familiarized the locus of home for the English settler, so that former Englishmen, like Rip Van Winkle, did not feel at home in the New World. So does the zombie apocalypse transform the familiar landscape into an unfamiliar locus of horror, a major theme of *Zone One*. Americans of the twenty-first century have reason to experience home as unfamiliar: new immigrants may feel unwelcome, or just out of place; long-term Americans may no longer recognize a country that is changing drastically. Many Americans, on both sides of the political divide, sense that they are in a country rendered unrecognizable by the transformations wrought by their own fellow citizens. As after a zombie apocalypse, present-day America seems irrevocably changed, and yet strangely, uncannily, familiar.

Since we are fortunate in not knowing what fresh horrors await America as this century unfolds, we cannot predict the future forms that Gothic horror and terror will take. We can be certain though, that if history and culture continue, presenting new fears of new lurking dangers, the Gothic mode will evolve to reflect, unveil, and even anticipate the threats that lie in store.

Chapter Notes

Introduction

1. Karen A. Weyler expands on these implications in *Intricate Relations: Sexual and Economic Desire in American Fiction: 1789–1814*, asserting the links between sexual and economic possession inform all American literature, not only the Gothic: "Sex and property, broadly construed, constitute in the novel homologous forms of exchange and expenditure.... Both are sites of desire, expenditure and exchange.... At the center of these economic conflicts were the role of the male individual and his economic relationships with other individuals" (2–4). Weyler also notes that "communal, parental, and religious authority waned" (4) thus undermining the patriarchal authority that dominated English life and the English Gothic.

2. We are in Lawrence's formulation "escaped slaves" (4).

3. The possiblity of the occurrence of the Gothic on English soil is generally unthinkable (with the exception of the Brontës). Austen mocks this attitude in a speech made by Henry Tilney to Catherine Moreland as he debunks her discovery of a Gothic series of events in the English countryside: "Remember the country and the age in which we live. Remember that we are English, that we are Christians" (*Northanger Abbey* 172).

4. This denial persists into the twentieth century. Ringe (1982) argues that the major phase of the Gothic ended in 1860 with the writing of Hawthorne's *Marble Faun*. This discussion will reveal that the Gothic mode continues to flourish in American literature.

5. Fiedler adds: "Our fiction ... is, bewilderingly and embarrassingly, a gothic fiction, non-realistic and negative, sadistic and melodramatic—a literature of darkness and the grotesque in a land of light and affirmation" (xxiv).

6. Among the texts that Brogan considers as stories of cultural haunting are Wilson's "The Piano Lesson" (1987), Morrison's *Beloved*, Marshall's *Praisesong for the Widow* (1983), Naylor's *Mama Day*, Kingston's *The Woman Warrior* (1976), Erdrich's *Tracks* (1988) and Ozick's *The Shawl* (1980, 1983). In *Ghostly Matters*, Avery Gordon supports Brogan's reading, writing from a sociological perspective to argue that the figure of the ghost is the manifestation of that which is present but repressed from the constructs of society. Thus, for example, Gordon reads the ghost of *Beloved* (1987) as the emblem of the repressed history of slavery. Gordon's argument builds upon "The Theory of Ghosts" in which Max Horkheimer and Theodor Adorno argue that the presence of the ghost represents the loss of historical perspective and acts to critique a society that reduces individuals to "a mere sequence of instantaneous presents, which leave behind no trace" (Horkheimer and Adorno 178). Significantly, Horkheimer and Adorno see in ghosts the emblem of a disturbed relationship with the past, a dangerous repression of the past that is expressed in "the threateningly well-meaning advice frequently given to emigrants that they should forget the past because it cannot be transplanted" (179). It is likely that this very advice accounts for the prevalence of ghosts in the literature of a nation of immigrants who seek a new history-free world; as we have seen, those who attempt to repress the past are visited by ghosts who attempt to repeat it.

Chapter 1

1. Cited by Fetterley as "Hawthorne's infamous and endlessly quoted jibe" (*Provisions* 3).

2. In "Not in the Least American," Fetterley suggests that women writers were attracted to regional writing for similar reasons: it was considered marginal and not possessed by male writers.

281

3. An interesting exception is to be found in Edith Wharton's "Kerfol" (1916). This story too bears all the trappings of the English Gothic, set in a distance place, Britanny, in a distant time, featuring actual ghosts, the murdered dogs of the long-dead mistress, and the dangerous husband. In this story, the ghost dogs manage to avenge their deaths at the hand of the master, by murdering him. But they cannot protect their beloved mistress. She is accused of murdering her husband, and is confined by her family, as she was during her marriage, dying a madwoman. Once again, the dangerous power of the husband triumphs, imprisoning and effacing his wife even after death.

4. In "'Light of the Home,' Light of the World," Catherine Golden observes that while "Gilman's utopian fiction and theoretical works ... advance her ideas about social motherhood.... Gilman's short stories collectively emphasize the plight of the mother rather than her fantasy" (144). The discrepancy may be accounted for by the commitment of Gilman's short stories to the imperatives of realism; only in her utopian fiction and essays does Gilman allow herself to imagine a world essentially different from the one she inhabits.

5. This protocol recalls that Gothic precursor, Samuel Richardson's *Pamela* (1740–1741), in which the imprisoned woman is denied her writing implements.

6. Who is unnamed until the end of the novel evoking, as Massé notes, the unnamed Mrs. DeWinter of *Rebecca*, among others.

7. In his association with the dead bodies—he is a mortician and lives next to a cemetery—Luther also recalls Victor Frankenstein. In one particularly evocative scene, Luther works on a woman's cadaver: "attention to the smallest details—edges of mouths, curves of wrist—could bring unbelievable life into the body before you. But it was a power not to be abused; it took gentleness and care to turn what was under your hands into a woman" (185).

8. Naylor shares with Walpole a powerful debt to the influence of Shakespeare, as we shall see in Chapter 8.

Chapter 2

1. Quite aptly, this formulation (exhorting the appropriation of the land), was appropriated from another journalist.

2. The distinction between the situations of men and women is made clear by Jill Lepore's *Book of Ages: The Life and Opinions of Jane Franklin* (2013). In contrasting the different destinies of Ben Franklin and his sister Jane, Lepore makes it painfully clear that Ben was able to take advantage of the economic and geographic mobility that was denied to his sister, solely on the basis of gender.

3. These anxieties were more intense in America than in England because the institution of slavery was more pervasive and longer enduring in the United States.

4. An underlying point of Morrison's argument, and a key contention of this book is that "romance ... [is] the head-on encounter with very real, pressing historical forces and the contractions inherent in them" (36).

5. In "William Wilson" Poe deploys another Gothic trope, the trope of the double, to raise questions of self-possession in the context of slavery. In this story, the "evil propensities" of the title character are checked by the double who acts as his moral compass, causing him to feel that he is "the slave of circumstances beyond human control" (272).

6. Both Jacobs and Douglass speak of the situation of the wife of the plantation master who has to helplessly witness her husband betrayal of his marriage vows with the slaves who are his property. Jacobs writes of Mrs. Flint's "anger and wounded pride.... She felt that her marriage vows were desecrated, her dignity insulted" (31), and although Jacobs faults her for having no concern for the young girl who is the object of her husband's depredations, she concludes: "I could not blame her. Slaveholders' wives feel as other women would under similar circumstances" (31). Douglass, too, suggests the frustrated and powerless anger of the slave mistress who is forced to confront the signs of her husband's infidelity in the illegitimate children born to him by his slaves, "a constant offence to their mistress" (2).

7. Leonard Engel reads enclosure as an emblem of death, a withdrawing from the world ("The Role of Enclosure in the English and American Gothic Romance" 64). Within the context of chattel slavery, which was tantamount to civil and social death, Engels' reading is especially powerful.

8. Her English literary antecedents include the bleeding nun, and gory prioress in Matthew Lewis' *The Monk* (1796), as well as the title character in Sheridan LeFanu's *Carmilla* (1872).

9. Douglass thus weaves together the strands of three supernatural traditions that haunt his *Narrative*: the Bible, the Gothic and also the supernatural of African American culture. Both Gladys-Marie Fry and Geraldine Smith-Wright

point to the strong tradition of the supernatural in African folk tradition. Smith-Wright says, "the ghost tale in recent African-American literature has is deepest roots in West African culture" and "is traceable to the era of slavery in the American South" ("In Spite of the Clan"142). Fry points to the roots of the supernatural in "the Black oral tradition [in which] the borderline between human beings and ghosts is often very thin" (*Night Riders in Black Folk History* 73). In fact, Fry notes that the slave owners also appropriated Gothic tropes for their uses: "the oral tradition asserts that fear of the supernatural was a dominant factor employed by whites in controlling the Blacks" (3). The white owners would use the fear of nightly ghosts to frighten their slaves away from escaping, or even gathering at night to stir up insurrection, a fear which Fry asserts is substantiated by the historical record that "seems to indicate that the number [of insurrections] was substantial"—"organized efforts to achieve freedom were neither 'seldom' nor 'rare,' but rather a regular and recurring phenomenon in the life of the South" (39). Fry asserts that "psychological control based on a fear of the supernatural" (45) was an additional way in which slave owners controlled slave minds and bodies. This deployment is an example of the internalization of surveillance and control observed by Michel Foucault in *Discipline and Punish* (1975). Fry states, "the master or his guards could be in only one place at any given time, but a ghost could appear any place at any time in a kind of all-seeing capacity" (59). Fry notes that "some masters undoubtedly did no more than circulate rumors to frighten their slaves," but that other masters initiated "a second step in this control process—masquerading as ghosts" (69), and that the ghostly masks of the enforcing masters evolved to become the costume of the Ku Klux Klan, who appeared "white sheets [that] were by now traditional ghost attire" (122). Fry adds that the Klan also deployed other staples of Gothic terror to strike fear into the hearts of the emancipated African Americans, including: "figures wrapped in sheets and sitting on tombstones.... Ghostly noises ... produced by carrying chains" (143).

10. See my essay on "The Missing Mother."

11. Bodziouck notes that "although it cannot be empirically stated that Douglass—or other writers of slave narratives who used Gothic modes of expression—were familiar with Gothic forms, we do know that Douglass was a voracious reader" (254).

Chapter 3

1. Of course the captivity narrative was not the only genre to anticipate Gothic tropes. The Bible and the plays of Shakespeare, among others, can also claim the origins of many of the tropes that later surface in the Gothic novel.

2. Her name represents a moment of personal dispossession: Mab's own name is unknown. Huntley initially writes, "Some people called her Queen Mab" (197), but later gives himself away as the appropriator of her identity: "Her romantic solitude and mountainous haunts suggested to my fancy the appellation of *Queen Mab*.... Queen Mab soon came into indiscriminate and general use" (200).

3. This word suggests another source of the Gothic uncanny: the Gothic is structured on recurrence, on motifs that incessantly recur within and between texts.

4. Later in the century, Leslie Fiedler picks up on Lawrence's ideas as he anticipates the literary rebirth of the Native American in his 1968 work, *The Return of the Vanishing American* (1968). Fiedler argues that at the end of the twentieth century, the Native American writer has "has begun to reinvent himself—in part out of what remains of his own tribal lore" (12). Fiedler's Introduction, entitled "The Demon of the Continent," is clearly an homage to D.H. Lawrence, and an acknowledgment of Lawrence's foresight in predicting the return of the formerly repressed and invisible figure upon whom Fiedler's work gazes.

5. "Invasion and Contagion: The Spectacle of the Diseased Indian in Poe's 'The Mask of the Red Death.'"

Chapter 4

1. This action recalls the enclosure movement in England, which inspired the preoccupation of the English Gothic with property possession and boundaries, as I discuss in *English Power and Property*.

2. Reminding us of the aphorism inscribed in Goya's etching, "The Sleep of Reason Produces Monsters" (1799).

3. "Tom's docility ... represents adherence to religious values—and this adherence, for Stowe, is strength" (Douglas Introduction *Uncle Tom's Cabin*. 25), an "antidote to the masculine hubris endemic to Western capitalism and imperialism" (27).

4. For example, Lewis' *The Monk*, Charlotte Dacre's *Zofloya*, and Maria Corelli's *Sorrows of Satan*.

5. Far from the unhomeyness of Freud's haunted uncanny.

6. Here as in many of his works, including Moby Dick, Melville reinvents the uncanny American frontier as the uncharted and distant sea.

7. In *The Empire of Necessity*, Greg Gandin writes of the actual events that inspired Melville's narrative: the slave mutiny in 1805, that was witnessed by Amasa Delano when he dropped anchor off the Chilean coast.

Chapter 5

1. Including the murders of the Yates and Beadle families by the fathers of the families. For a detailed discussion of the accounts of these two murders and their influence on *Wieland* see Daniel E. Williams "Writing under the Influence."

2. Reading "Usher" through the prism of the anxieties of slavery expressed in "The Black Cat," the reader may discern in the collapse of the house of Usher and the burial of the last of the Ushers, their immurement, a veiled statement regarding the dangers of slavery. The image of the sister's entombment is an instance of conflation of the situation of the woman and that of the slave; as Leonard Engel points out, Madeleine Usher is the "object of a fanatical love ... [and is] 'possessed' by [Usher]" ("Obsession, Madness and Enclosure" 140). In neglecting to free his sister Usher perpetuates his own slavery to fear—"I dared not speak!" (98). Read thus, the story suggests to the American aristocracy that silence regarding the institution of slavery will result in the destruction of their institutions and of themselves. The description of the house indicates that a single flaw can bring down an entire system: "Perhaps the eye of a scrutinizing observer might have discovered a barely perceptible fissure, which, extending from the roof of the building in front, made its way down the wall in a zigzag direction, until it became lost in the sullen waters of the tarn" (90). Poe worries that the flaw of slavery in the edifice of American democracy will bring the structure down and destroy its inhabitants.

3. Bill Christopherson quotes Paul Fussell to provide a telling explanation for the use of the disembodied voice as an emblem for personal dispossession in *Wieland*: "figuratively speaking, the newly nationalized writer of Brown's era was, like Carwin, a biloquist—a British 'speaker' become American." Thus it is not just the trauma of revolutionary parricide that destabilizes notions of self-possession in post-revolutionary American, but also the trauma of cultural dislocation and displaced identity, as in Rip Van Winkle. The first Americans had to cope with losing their identity as English subjects and being reborn as American citizens.

4. In "Romance and Real Estate," Walter Benn Michaels, highlights the dispossession of the slave, deemed as property within civil law, noting that, as slaves, slaves could not own property, could only *be* property. Michaels thus extrapolates, "the most terrifying spectacle slavery has to offer is the spectacle of *slaves without masters* [italics Benn Michaels'] since the only possible acknowledgement "of the slave as a 'human and immortal creature' is through his master's 'will.' When the master must relinquish ownership either to pay off a debt or because of the death of the master, "the slave's humanity is extinguished also. The slave without a master stands revealed as nothing more than 'a bale of merchandise'" (103). And so, Michaels identifies in the slave population the core fear that Lawrence identifies in the free population: the fear of masterlessness. The previous discussion of Harriet Beecher Stowe's *Uncle Tom's Cabin* suggests otherwise.

5. An observation echoed by Lawrence's "The proper function of a critic is to save the tale from the artist who created it" (2) and appropriated by Bloom in his notion of creative misreading of the text: "Reading ... is a belated and all-but-impossible act, and if strong is always a misreading" (*A Map of Misreading* 3).

6. Fittingly, *The Master* is the title of the biographical novel about James written by Colm Toíbín in 2004.

7. A number of Wharton's other ghost stories also concern themselves with issues of property possession and ghostly dispossession. In "Afterward" (*Ghosts* 1937) a dispossessed ghost takes possession of a corrupt businessman who stole his capital and drove him to suicide. What is notable about "Afterward" is that although the story is set in England, the characters are American, the act of appropriation takes place in America and is set within the contexts of American capitalism. "Kerfol" (*Ghosts* 1937) is set more conventionally in seventeenth-century Europe and posits the conventional Gothic refusal of personal possession through marriage: the brutal and omnipotent husband is undone by the ghosts of his wife's murdered pet dogs. "The Pomegranate Seed" (in *Ghosts* 1937) also present ghostly counters to legal possession through marriage.

8. A recent edition of *Ghosts* appears as *The*

Ghost Stories of Edith Wharton and inexplicably rearranges the order of the stories and omits the Preface.

9. It is only fair to acknowledge that the figure of the usurping servant arises, in fact, in the English Gothic. In *Otranto*, the original usurper of the property is Manfred's grandfather, who was the servant of the proper owner, Alfonso, the Good. The difference is that in Walpole's tale of revolution, the usurping servant is not accorded supernatural powers; his powers of appropriation are limited to his life, although he *does* make a quick return visit when his ghost steps out of his portrait. His power remains human and fallible, unlike that of the supernatural servants of the American tradition. A more powerful servant in the English Gothic appears in the person of Thady Quirk in Maria Edgeworth's *Castle Rackrent* (1800). Thady is the quintessential servile servant who might be more subversive than he appears. After his remarkably neutral account of the fall of the aristocratic dynasty he serves, he reveals that the final owner of Castle Rackrent is his own son, a lawyer, who has risen to claim the vacuum of possession.

Chapter 6

1. Zinn adds: "Horatio Alger stories of 'rags to riches' ... were mostly "a useful myth for control" (255).

2. The name "John" with its bland associations seems to be a name of choice in the American Gothic: the chief male characters in "The Yellow Wallpaper," "Po' Sandy" and "The Diamond as Big as the Ritz" all bear this name. The quality these characters share is that each is conventionally benign and yet the almost inadvertent agent of a brutal patriarchy, suggesting a sort of banality of evil (to borrow from Hannah Arendt) on the part of those who benefit from patriarchal systems. John's unusual surname, "Unger," quite explicitly gestures to the voracious appetite of the young American male that we have noticed earlier.

3. In *House of the Seven Gables*, Nathaniel Hawthorne also equates property possession with sin. As Walter Benn Michaels suggests in "Romance and Real Estate," Hawthorne's novel presents the conflict between two modes of economic activity: the legitimization of property through labor, embodied in Matthew Maule and in the possessors of the Maine lands and the failed aristocratic ambitions of the Pyncheons. Similarly, Hinds locates anxieties about changing terms of acquisition and transmission of property as the source of the dilemma of Brockden Brown's protagonist, Edgar Huntly: "capitalism ... has usurped his property" (53). Thus, although the historic terms of anxiety of property possession are new for each text, there is something old and familiar in the response of Faulkner's American Gothic text to its historical contexts.

4. The title of the novel also evokes that early precursor of the Gothic novel, the Bible. The story of Absalom, David's rebellious son, is replete with those Gothic standbys—incest, family conflict, and questions of lineage and inheritance—that dominate Faulkner's novel and the entire Gothic tradition.

5. Within the context of this reading, Chesnutt's impenetrable dialect and Cable's polyglossia may also be read as American revisions of the conventionally indeterminate and ambiguous Gothic discourse and as symptoms of the ceaseless struggle within American culture to possess the canons of literature and of history.

6. the domestic despot who drains the life from his wife; the usurper who appropriates the family property; the murderer who causes the death of his uncle, "while striving to add more wealth to his only child's inheritance" (*House* 312–313).

7. The title of the novel sets the groundwork for acceptance of this relationship. The biblical story that Faulkner evokes accepts the possibility of marriage between half-sister and brother. In order to forestall rape by Amnon, her half-brother, Tamar, Absalom's sister, suggests a proper marriage instead.

8. The metaphorical representation is so subtle in *House* that Fleischner, for example, misses the allusion and asserts "Hawthorne's customary splitting of politics and art" (99).

9. Jackson solidifies the sense of archaic evil, by evoking the Bible in the words of the doctor, "'You will recall ... the houses described in Leviticus as 'leprous' or ... 'the house of Hades' ... the concept of certain houses as unclean or forbidden ... is as old as the mind of man" (70).

10. Robert Marasco's *Burnt Offerings* (1973) shifts Jackson's themes a bit, following a contemporary woman who eventually sacrifices her family in order to maintain her fleeting possession of a grand patriarchal property.

11. Indeed Morrison's novel features all of the mandated tropes: a fragmented narrative; destabilized identities; the image of the double; a haunted house; dangerous villains; endangered women; and anxious encounters with the Other and the self.

12. Askeland notes that the murder of the child is another moments in which *Beloved* is

influenced (haunted) by *Uncle Tom's Cabin*, which presents a number of wrenching scenes of infanticide by slave mothers.

13. Yet despite the similarities in these central stories—a similarity that may be attributed to the Gothic tendency to revisit key themes both within and between texts—neither *A Mercy* nor *Beloved* is an unnecessary duplicate. Indeed, they are most productively seen as a doubled text, a set of texts that reflect each other, each bringing into focus what is hidden in the other. In *Beloved*, the focus is on the mother Sethe, her motivations and the regretful pain that her decision causes her. *A Mercy* focuses on the daughter who believes that she has been cast off because she is not sufficiently loved by her mother; she never understands her mother's act to be the mercy that it is. When read together, the two novels give us the whole story of the enslaved mother and daughter, just as the separate narratives of *A Mercy* merge to relate a single story. The two novels together also give us the entire picture of the experience of American slavery: as a doubled text they present a diptych, or rather the entire triptych of slavery: the "before" of *A Mercy*, the "after" of *Beloved*, which focuses on the experiences of former slave in 1873, as well as the tortured memories of the "during" that also surface in *Beloved*. The consideration of *A Mercy* and *Beloved* as doubled, or complementary, works of literature reveals another grand pattern in Morrison's work: the pattern of Paradise lost and Paradise found that emerges in the doubling of the two texts. Like fragments of a hologram, that each reveals the image of the whole, both *A Mercy* and *Beloved*, present a number of re-enactments of this grand myth (as do a number of Morrison's other novels, including, of course, *Paradise*). In *Beloved*, the paradise of Sweet Home under the ownership of Mr. Garner, who considered his slaves to be "men," is lost when Mr. Garner dies, and his wife sickens. With the entrance of the schoolmaster, the serpent in the garden, paradise is transformed into a hellish place in which slaves are brutalized and dehumanized. Paradise is temporarily found when Sethe manages to get all of her children across to their grandmother's house, the paradise that holy Baby Suggs has created; this paradise also ends with the entrance of the satanic white men, the four apocalyptic horsemen who ride into the yard, leading to the disintegration of Sethe's family and of her peace. By the end of the novel, with the exorcism of the ghostly Beloved, there is a suggestion that together Sethe, her surviving daughter Denver and Paul D will re-enter a communal Paradise.

14. Cheryl Miller also notes this connection noting that Vaark "hails appropriately enough, from a northern town called Milton" (62).

15. Lori Askeland notes the influence of Stowe's moral, harmonious community of Quakers in Morrisons ideal communities.

16. The "exiled, thrown-away women" (82) inhabit the dark and enclosed Gothic space of the ship's hold. Given the attention that Morrison pays to Edgar Allan Poe's *Voyage of Arthur Gordon Pym* (1838) in her essay, "Romancing the Shadow" (*Playing in the Dark* 1992), the claustrophobic hold in *Pym* might be a source of Morrison's description.

17. Baby Suggs remembers "the heart that started beating the minute she crossed the Ohio River" (147) into freedom.

18. The moral problem with this uplifting narrative is that the happy ending seems to require the death of a child—Morrison's apparent critique of Christian mythology. Possibly Morrison's discomfort with this paradigm finds expression in her feminized revision of the paradigm in *Beloved* and in *A Mercy*. Both books also indicate the deep flaws in a paradise based on child sacrifice.

19. La Vinia Delois Jennings's study provides detailed instances in which historical events that Morrison mentions, are both relevant and accurate. For example, Jennings explains that Morrison validates her vision of an inclusive community by mentioning "'a people's war' of 1676.... Nathaniel Bacon, who incited the 'war' alluded to, amassed 'an army' not defined by race, status, or class" (Jennings "*A Mercy*" 647).

20. In Chapter One of his book, "Peoples," Butler does, however, provide a wealth of information regarding the historical facts that are known, information that may increase the reader's appreciation of the historical context of *A Mercy*, including brief discussions on the slave status of the Native American, and details of the development of the horrifying system of chattel slavery from a loose system of bondage.

21. Jennings provides another explanation for Morrison's concentration on individual voices: "Morrison has said that because the sweep of history is too large ... she concentrates on single characters within the historical moment to convey the specificities of the moment" (Jennings "*A Mercy*" 648).

22. Miller points out harshly, but not inaccurately, that in providing voices for a Native American, a mentally ill slave, two gay men, an African American women, a white women and a penniless orphan "Morrison thus completes a

dramatis personae of contemporary American identity politics"("Mine, Mine, Mine" 62).

23. Cheryl Miller argues that Florens is saved by her writing, purging her past "through the act of writing, through art, and thereby find[ing] herself" (64). Yet this elevating moral does not fully conform to what we know of Florens' situation.

24. Wyatt Masons also sees the significance of the burning of the house by the Native American character, while eliding the Gothic context. In "The Color Money," he writes, "For the daughters of the eagle to truly be free, the white man's house must be burned to the ground."

25. Satan figures in a number of canonical Gothic texts: Matthew Lewis' *The Monk* (1796), Charles Maturin's Melmoth (1820). Of most relevance to this discussion is Charlotte Dacre's *Zofloya* (1806). which features a Moorish slave whose body is possessed by Satan; in the guise of the Moor, Satan seduces the white heroine-villainess.

26. Lori Askelund argues that *Beloved* is influenced by Harriet Beecher Stowe's *Uncle Tom's Cabin* (1852). *A Mercy* also shows traces of this influence. Morrrison's satanic blacksmith echoes Stowe's satanic Simon Legree (785–805).

27. In *The History of Art in the Middle Ages*, Didron recalls "a picture of a devil blowing a bellows into the face of a terrified angel" in a medieval text (2:144).

28. The recurrent Gothic paradigms that appear in *A Mercy* suggest that Morrison's novel is tightly connected to the intertextual tradition of the Gothic, in which meaning is amplified as tropes are repeated from text to text. Much of Gothic textual power derives from the levels of nuanced meaning that develop in the space between the texts, haunting each other through the repetition of iconic themes and variations. Morrison's central assertion that the will to possess leads directly to the downfall of the American aristocrat (the poltroon Vaark) is a recurring Gothic locution. It is also the dictum of Nathaniel Hawthorne's American Gothic, *The House of the Seven Gables* (1851) which casts a long shadow over Morrison's text. Morrison's contention that the corruption of America and Americans begins with the word "Mine" is constantly reiterated in Hawthorne's novel. The naïf, Clifford Pynchon pointedly anticipates Morrison's delineation of Jacob when he says: "A man will commit almost any wrong—he will heap up an immense pile of wickedness as hard as granite ... only to build a great, gloomy, dark chambered mansion for himself to die in" (263). Indeed, there are a number of echoes between *A Mercy* and *The House of the Seven Gables*. In addition to the many connections between the two texts, perhaps Morrison slyly points to this important allusion when Lina sees some runaway slaves, "camped in wintergreen beneath two hawthorns" (64); the clue becomes even more transparent when we remember that Hawthorne's chapter "The Flight of Two Owls" focuses on Clifford and Hepzibah's escape from the House, the Gothic structure that imprisons them. Mason suggests such a connection when he summarizes Morrison's vison of America, the image of Jacob's abandoned house: "Here we have a great big house, built by a white man and now empty, nobody living there. What happened? Greed drove the white man to exploit the land and its peoples, to erect a monument to his own presumption ... by which he—and all those he touched—were undone.... The writing, as it were, is on the walls"(Wyatt Mason 37).

Mason notes that Morrison thereby literalizes the phrase "the writing on the walls" which comes from the Book of Daniel, referring to the prophetic words that God writes upon the walls of a doomed king. Although Mason does not make the connection, this is an exact description of the abandoned House of the Seven Gables at the end of the novel. Yet while indicting possession of property, and while hinting at the kind of "immense pile of wickedness" that a nineteenth-century American might accrue in the pursuit of property, Hawthorne represses any overt indictment of the possession of human flesh from his text; the subject of slavery surfaces only fleetingly and obscurely in the novel. Morrison thus adds another gable to Hawthorne's sinful house: the sin of possessing human beings.

29. For an excellent and comprehensive discussion of this trope, see H.L. Malchow, *Gothic Images of Race in Nineteenth-Century Britain* (Stanford: Stanford University Press, 1996).

30. *A Mercy* also expresses Morrison's powerful and quite moving recognition that suffering and slavery, too, are not linked to race. Each of the characters in Morrison's novel, men and women of a variety of races, suffers exile and enslavement in one form of the other, based on imbalance of power.

Chapter 7

1. The lack of uncertainly of the identity of the writer led to conjectures like that of Celeste-Marie Bernier and Judie Newman who speculate in 2005 that the writer was white, poor, perhaps an Irish immigrant: "In nineteenth-century racist

discourse the Irish and black slaves occupied a close position of identification and opposition" (*The Bondswoman's Narrative* 155). R.J Ellis notes that "in 2004, I proposed" a similar argument (142).

2. As Henry Louis Gates notes, Crafts counters this by being "the subaltern who speaks" (Introduction *Bondswoman's Narrative* xiii).

3. A discussion of the connections between *Jane Eyre* and *Bleak House* may be found in Lisa Jadwin's "'Caricatured, not faithfully rendered': *Bleak House* as a Revision of *Jane Eyre*," *Modern Language Studies* 26, 2–3.

4. Crafts later returns to *Jane Eyre* in an episode that occurs at Lindendale: the wife of the master, after taking "a notion to explore the house in its remotest corners" (184) discovers rooms in which her husband maintains other "wives": slaves, and their children.

5. In fact, she anticipates Toni Morrison's turn to the Bible. For the epigraph of Chapter 1, Craft's quotes from the Song of Solomon: "Look not upon me because I am black; because the sun hath looked upon me" (5). These words, in fact, inform much of Morrison's *Beloved*. For a more developed discussion of Crafts' relationship to biblical texts, see Lawrence Buell's essay, "Bondswoman Unbound" in *In Search of Hannah Crafts*.

6. Hawthorne explicitly links Maule to the African slave with Maule's address to a slave: "Do you think nobody is to look black but yourself?" (188).

7. Hawthorne's explanation accounts for the attraction of the Gothic for American writers seeking to create a new American literature in the nineteenth century. In doing so, American writers, including the marginalized writers of the slave narratives, joined earlier marginalized writers, most notably women and gay men, who carved out an English literature of their own in the Gothic mode that was disdained by more mainstream English writers.

8. Paradoxically, this disclaimer locates her in the grand tradition of novelists who protect themselves from the kind of attack against the novel articulated by Samuel Johnson in *The Rambler* #4. Johnson asserts that because the novel is realistic and is "written chiefly to the young, the ignorant, and the idle" (21), it should serve solely as a model of virtue for its readers. Johnson condemns the kind of novel that presents its readers with models of vice, thereby limiting the possibilities of the novel. More precisely, this disclaimer aligns her with the writers of Gothic Romance who try to achieve credibility for their texts by averring to their historic accuracy. Horace Walpole, for example, documents the veracity of his novel by claiming in his Preface to the first edition of *The Castle of Otranto* (1764), that the text "was found in the library of an ancient catholic family" (5), printed in 1529, and probably written "between 1095 ... and 1243" (5).

9. As Augusta Rohrbach suggests, Crafts also shielded herself from attack by keeping her work out of circulation: she "preserved that freedom by remaining unpublished" ("'A Silent Unobtrusive Way'" 14). This strategy echoes Hawthorne's attempt to remove his work from the attention elicited by mainstream literature in declaring his text a Romance.

10. Crafts yokes Hawthorne's moral even more directly to its biblical source in the epigram to Chapter 4: "[t]he sins of the fathers shall be visited on the children" (44).

11. Both Holgrave and Clifford inveigh against the dangers of inherited property. Holgrave declaims: "The house ought to be purified with fire—purified till only its ashes remain" (184). This evocation of the conventional fate of the Gothic house/castle, suggests the centrality of this notion in the Gothic concept of property. Clifford amplifies: "real estate ... is the broad foundation on which nearly all the guilt of this world rests" (261).

12. Hawthorne develops this metaphor in his Preface to *The Marble Faun* (1859), where he somewhat disingenuously (or is there a subtle irony here?) claims that it is impossible to set a romance in "the broad and simple daylight" of America because America is "a country where there is no shadow, no antiquity, no mystery, no picturesque and gloomy wrong" (vi).

13. Of course, the contrast between light and shadow informs Hawthorne's narrative: in the entrance of the sunny Phoebe into gloomy Seven Gables; in the art of the daguerrotypist, that depends upon the contrast of light and shadow.

14. In her meditation on the re-animating properties of light, Crafts exhibits another strategy that she inherits from her precursor: the deployment of the trope of the picture of the dead as a way to revive the dead while at the same time repressing the notion of the supernatural in the text.

15. Hawthorne uses the same strategy to contain the ghosts of his more overtly Gothic *The Marble Faun*. As Hilda wanders the galleries of Roman palaces, the narrator conjectures about potential ghosts—"Fancy the progenitor of the Dorians thus haunting those heavy halls..."—but these ghosts too are never actualized (247).

16. In "Romance and Real Estate" Walter Benn Michaels demonstrates that, like his predecessors, Hawthorne's Gothic is an anxious response to contemporary problems of property possession. Michaels notes that American laws of property possession, unlike those of the English, disallow the possibility of inalienable property; in America, all property can be sold and bequeathed, lost and stolen. Michaels further indicates that the year 1850, when Hawthorne was writing, saw the beginning of one of the peak periods in nineteenth-century American land speculation, when excited people borrowed huge amounts for investments.

17. Moreover, as Michael North indicates in "Authorship and Authography," the photograph and its predecessor, the daguerreotype, are media that disrupt the notion of authority, in this case creative authority. Indeed, "Daguerre offered his device to the French republic on the understanding that such an invention could never be protected by patent or copyright" (North 1382). This invention can never be owned because it is a form of "autography," created by the sun, one piece of real estate that is truly unpossessible.

18. The conclusion of *Wieland* provides an odd variation of this theme: the new territory in which the new dynasty is to be established is Europe.

19. Ian Watt teases out the significance of past and present in the Gothic and suggests that in the American Gothic text the biblical admonition regarding the "sins of the fathers..." is recast as Freudian paradigm: "Freudian theory can itself be seen as a Gothic myth" in presenting "the individual, much as Gothic does, as essentially imprisoned by the tyranny of an omnipotent but unseen past" (167). Watt is quite right in framing the Gothic masterplot as a retelling of the Freudian myth of origins. What he ignores, however, is that the Freudian model of anxious successor and tyrannical progenitor is to be found not only *within* the Gothic text, but *between* Gothic texts as well. This model is particularly visible in the response of the anxious American Gothic to the political and cultural tyranny of its past: *The House of the Seven Gables* exemplifies the American attempt to cast off bonds of cultural and historic tyranny and to seize possession of a new American literature.

20. A similar image occurs in Charles Maturin's *Melmoth the Wanderer*: "the portraits of their high descended ancestry seemed starting from their gorgeous frames to converse, as the tale of their virtues and their valours was told in their presence" (457).

21. John Stauffer notes the utility of the trope of the portrait as an indicator of the discrepancy between "surface of things" and "hidden and haunted depths" ("The Problem of Freedom" 56). An example of this is to be found in the portrait of Hannah's master that under Hannah's scrutiny changes "from its usually kind and placid expression to one of wrath and gloom... wrinkled with passion, the lips turgid with malevolence" (17).

22. Russ Castronovo notes the connection and recognizes that Sir Clifford's family undergoes "the trial of family separation suffered by slave families" ("The Art of Ghost-Writing" 202), while also pointing to a key distinction: "the white family's images and not its bodies are subjected to sale" (202).

23. Another way of looking at this: Crafts uncovers the subtext of Hawthorne's consideration. In Hawthorne's scene of revelation, Holgrave reminds us that the attempt to recover the deed "cost the beautiful Alice Pyncheon her happiness and life" (316), indeed her freedom.

24. Crafts' deployment of the trope of the portrait that links her to a number of precursors, including Hawthorne and to the Gothic tradition, has attracted the attention of a number of scholars. Lawrence Buell reads the scene in the portrait gallery as evoking "Radcliffean gothic novels and gothic tales à la Edgar Allan Poe" (20). In noting the connection of Craft's portraits to Hawthorne's, John Stauffer also notes the significance of the trope of the portrait in the Gothic tradition, citing examples from Poe and Melville as well as Walpole and Hawthorne.

25. In *Slavery and the Romantic Imagination*, Debbie Lee notes the convergence, explaining: "slavery was the great moral question of the age and Romanticisim the great aesthetic development" (1). Lee points to the transatlantic nature of this convergence, which was not limited to American Gothic or Romanticism. Lee argues that "writers forged the Romantic imagination, in large part, because of their continued attempts to write creatively about the complex and glaringly unequal relationships between Africans and Britons" (3–4). Lee builds on Malchow's *Gothic Images of Race in Nineteenth-Century Britain 1996*, which was an early attempt to identify race, often encoded, in English Gothic Literature. In the collection *In Search of Hannah Crafts*, the essays by Russ Castronovo and Patricia Wald touch on the use that Crafts makes of the Gothic tradition of horror.

26. Drawing on the recurrent image of the tragic mother that underscores the message of *Uncle Tom's Cabin*, Crafts embeds a number of

narratives that recall Stowe: one mother "jump[s] into the river when she found that her child was irretrievably gone"; "another mother looking for her sold child [is] torn apart by bloodhounds" (108). In the narrative of the Cosgroves, also at Lindendale, we learn of a master who plans to callously sell his children and their mother driving the mother to stab "the infant" and throw "it with one toss into the arms of its father" (183), before killing herself.

27. Implicit in this argument is the assumption that both Crafts and Hawthorne's novels relate to the Gothic tradition. For, although defining either novel narrowly as a "Gothic novel" would be limiting, each does draw freely upon the famous tropes of the Gothic: the haunted house; dysfunctional family; contested property; and repressed past wrongs, including the horrifying wrongs of history.

28. A comparison of the two scenes of family portraiture is significant because it reveals Crafts' response not only to Hawthorne but to the traditional representation of women in the canon of the Gothic, a tradition to which Hawthorne faithfully adheres. In "The Missing Mother," I argue that English and American Gothic texts tend to repress the figures of the wife and of the mother, rendering them silent and invisible. Although I do not include Hawthorne in this discussion, *Seven Gables* clearly exemplifies this tendency. *Seven Gables* also illustrates the tendency of eighteenth- and nineteenth-century American literature to repress the figure of the father, as representative of the cultural patrimony of England that American were attempting to elude.

29. Bernier and Newman see a reference to Harriet Jacobs' slave narrative in the story of Hannah's flight, "In her choice of name, 'Jacob'; the reference to a faithful slave brother preoccupied with protecting his sister; and the point of origin, South Carolina" (158).

Chapter 8

1. It is worth noting that in *Mama Day* as in *The House of the Seven Gables* and *Edgar Huntly*, the missing document is a legal document of possession rather than a narrative manuscript. In *The House of the Seven Gables* the location of the half remembered deed to the vast lands in Maine, long sought by the Pyncheons, is revealed in the concluding chapter by Holgrave whose discovery restores his property and his identity. The deed to the Maine lands, though legible, is worthless like the belated deed in Naylor's novel: time has invalidated their legal power to convey propriety. Hawthorne and Naylor appear to suggest that the central secret of the American narrative is that the ownership of property and of persons is invalid.

2. This recalls D.A. Miller's contention in *The Novel and the Police* that despite various layers of narrative in Collins' *The Woman in White*, the absence of contradictions between the narratives yields a monolithic undisrupted telling.

3. Naylor also alludes to her other books, including *Linden Hills* and *Bailey's Café*, by mentioning central characters from those books in a peripheral way. Similarly, the character of Mama Day makes a cameo appearance in *Linden Hills*.

4. When George arrives at Willow springs, he thinks it is even better than "paradise" (175).

5. George takes Cocoa to see Bailey's Café (BC) where he was born. Naylor further develops the myth of George as Jesus and his mother as Mary in the novel *Bailey's Café* (1992), which, following the Gothic tradition, connect to the intertextual web of Naylor's novels.

6. The dream is echoed twice by dreams that Cocoa has. Soon after George's dream, Cocoa dreams that George is "swimming in the Sound" (189) but without any assistance of Mama Day, and without any echoes of Jesus. Cocoa has the same dream later in the novel when she is sick: "I was having that terrible dream again with you nearly drowning in The Sound" (252).

Chapter 9

1. In *The Madwoman in the Attic*, for example, Sandra M.Gilbert and Susan Gubar identify the nineteenth century as the moment when English women writers experienced "anxiety of authorship."

2. In the context of this discussion it is significant that Gilbert and Gubar locate the emblem of anxiety of authorship within monsters created by nineteenth-century English women writers.

3. "Any strong literary work creatively misreads and therefore misinterprets a precursor text or texts" (Bloom *The Western Canon* 8).

4. Gershom Scholem suggests that the folktales themselves are generically transgressive: in the golem stories, "we have a strange convergence of legend and ritual" ("The Idea of the Golem" 173). The same statement might also be applied to the dybbuk folktales, in which the demon is exorcized through the application of rabbinic ritual.

5. These are not the only instances of late

twentieth and early twenty-first-century revisions of and returns to the Golem story. There has been an outpouring of recent representations of the Golem including: Pete Hamill's *Snow in August* (1997); the short story "The Monster," a telling of the golem story from the point of view of Shylock, found in Alan Isler's collection of stories, *The Bacon Fancier* (1997); the novel *The Golems of Gotham* (2002) by Thane Rosenbaum; Michael Chabon's *Kavalier & Clay* (2000); Frances Sherwood's *The Book of Splendor* (2002). "Briah," a play by the Israel playwright Yossefa Even-Shoshan, that tells of a female golem who falls in love with her creator invites comparison with the myth of Pygmalian and Galatea. And most memorably, *The Forward* of September 15, 2000, records that at a meeting of Jewish educators, "a small team of participants" sculpted golems out of clay as they attended a workshop on "How to Make a Golem" (18).

6. Judith Halberstam argues that the monster exists as the "infinitely interpretable" (*Skin Shows* 20) emblem of horror in response to the Other. In "The Laugh of the Medusa," Hélène Cixous locates the monstrous Other as the female Other, inhabiting a dark mysterious continent. In *The Madwoman in the Attic*, Sandra M. Gilbert and Susan Gubar argue that nineteenth-century English women writers displaced their own anxieties of authorship and authority onto the figure of the monster. Other critics locate fears of the maternal at the center of tales of monsters. In *Powers of Horror*, Julia Kristeva argues that the figure of the mother is a source of horror because it represents a threat to constructed cultural categories. Yet other critics suggest that it is the female ability to create life that results in anxieties of maternal power. In *Monstrous Imagination* Marie Hélène Huet discovers the enduring Renaissance belief that the disorder of the maternal imagination was responsible for monstrous progeny at the root of accounts of attempts to create life without maternal influence; she includes discussions of *Frankenstein* and the golem legends in her argument. Dennis Todd examines an instance of a monstrous birth hoax in 1826 and argues that even in the Enlightened eighteenth century when the imagination had dwindled in power, the assertion that a mother's imagination could misshape a fetus was accepted by common people and by medical experts (*Imagining Monsters* 60–63).

7. Adler goes on to argue for an "analogy between their [the rabbi's] own experience of marginality and stigma in an often-hostile empire, and women's vulnerability and powerlessness under patriarchal institutions" (103).

8. The mayor's name is a linguistic joke. Malachy Mavett is a play on the Hebrew "malach hamavett," the Angel of Death. The alternate name, Matt Mavett, recalls the Hebrew letters inscribed on the golem's forehead: "met" means dead; "mavet" death.

9. Deut. 16.20. Significantly this verse ends with the promise that just action will result in inheritance of the land.

10. Feminist critics have long noted the need of intellectually creative women for a tradition of women, the need to discover female precursors within the cultural tradition. In *A Room of One's Own*, Virginia Woolf argues for the necessity of female precursors and a female tradition to female artists. This necessity drives later works like Ellen Moers' *Literary Women* and Elaine Showalter's *A Literature of Their Own*. Readers note that the absence of a female tradition is inscribed in literature by an absence of mothers from literary texts. Adrienne Rich, for example, in writing of Jane Eyre's motherlessness, cites Chesler's comment: "'women are motherless children in a patriarchal society'" (Rich "Temptations" 91).

11. Ozick's complicated, ironically skeptical stance toward feminism can be seen in her characterization of Puttermesser's feminism: "she was careful never too speak of 'man's' nature. She always said 'humankind' instead of 'mankind.' She always wrote 'he or she' instead of just 'he'" (24). The name Ozick gives her feminist protagonist can also be construed as an ironically ambivalent commentary on her politics: the name Puttermesser means "butter knife," a sly Freudian dig, perhaps, at her attempts to co-opt male power.

12. Bonnie Friedman assumes that because Shelley "devoured German ghost stories, she was no doubt herself influenced by versions of the golem legend" ("A Wandering Jew"11). David Ketterer (somewhat disrespectfully) states: "Mary [sic] may have had some familiarity with other legends involving the animation of inert figures; for example, stories associated with the Golem, a huge clay statue periodically animated by a rabbi supposedly in the cause of Jewish vengeance. In some versions of the legend, the golem, like Frankenstein's monster, turns on its master" (*Frankenstein's Creation* 20); Norma Rowen and Samuel Holmes Vasbinder also observe this connection. Albert J. Lavalley, writing about "The Stage and Film Children of Frankenstein," speculates, "Mary Shelley may have been familiar with the medieval legends of the artificial man who becomes both a protector to the Jews and a possible scourge" (252). Radu

Florescu also notes the similarities between the two stories without verifying any textual relationship (*In Search of Frankenstein* 225).

13. The German text may be found in Völker 7.

14. An argument may also be made for a relation of mutual influence between the golem stories and the Western Gothic. As Goldsmith indicates (47) both Bloch and his precursor Yudl Rosenberg make extensive use of Gothic conventions in their twentieth-century golem narratives. This relationship is considered below within the discussion of Piercy's *He, She and It*.

15. In an echo of the nineteenth-century response to photography that Nancy Armstrong observes in *Fiction in the Age of Photography*.

16. Echoing Sandra M. Gilbert and Susan Gubar's reading of *Frankenstein*.

17. Barbara Johnson's observation ("My Monster / My Critic") on *Frankenstein* may also be applied to Piercy's work: "the realization that the very technological advances that make it possible to change the structure of parenthood also threaten to extinguish earthly life altogether. But it is startling to note that this seemingly contemporary pairing of the question of parenthood with a love-hate relation to technology is already at work in Mary Shelley's novel, where the spectacular scientific discovery of the secrets of animation produces a terrifyingly vengeful creature who attributes his evil impulses to his inability to find or to become a parent" (6). Piercy's novel also evokes Shelley's own post-apocalyptic science fiction novel, *The Last Man* (1826): both speculate about the ultimate possession of a future fragmented world.

18. Piercy is not the first Jewish writer to associate the power of the golem, a technological wonder of its time, with the power of the computer. In "The Golem of Prague and the Golem of Rehovot," a speech dedicating a new computer in Israel in 1964, Gershom Scholem, the scholar of Jewish mysticism and Kabbalah, argues for similarities between the two creations and named the newly built computer Golem Aleph (Golem A).

19. The repression of the maternal in the creation of Adam prefigures the subversive reenactment of creation by the golem makers and by Victor Frankenstein.

20. This description of Tikvah reminds us that Piercy, like the other displaced Gothic writers we have examined, stakes out unclaimed canonical territory to make a narrative place for herself.

21. In some golem versions and in *He, She and It*, the figure is directly responsible for the death of the creator; in *Frankenstein*, the creature destroys all that its creator loves.

22. The absence of the midwife from the technologies of birth since the eighteenth century amplifies the significance of Piercy's invention of Chana, the midwife of her embedded golem narrative.

23. In contrast to the golem who as the code for a woman in an insistently patriarchal culture is completely speechless.

24. There is a precedent for deployment of the mediating possibilities of the figure of the golem. In "The Cosmic Adam," Susan Niditch, reading the rabbinic representations of Adam (the precursor of all golems, denoted a "golem," an unformed creature, in the rabbinic literature), sees a figure that negotiates the tensions between polarities constructed by rabbinic culture: male and female; spiritual and physical.

25. Alberto Eco borrows this term and idea from Louis Marin's essay on Disneyland.

26. Although Galford lives and writes in England, she is American by birth, training and sensibility.

27. The dybbuk, like the golem, has experienced an explosive revival of interest. Romain Gary's *The Dance of Genghis Cohn* (1968) features a dybbuk-haunted Nazi; Chayefsky's play, *The Tenth Man* (1959), is a retelling of this folktale; Tony Kushner recently revised Ansky's *The Dybbuk*. Women artists who revive the dybbuk for their purposes include Francine Prose in *Hungry Hearts* (1981) and Pearl Lang, the dancer-choreographer whose dance "The Possessed" (1975) is documented on film. Eleanor Reissa, with Zalman Mlotek, has written "Zise Khaloymes" a recent play in which the dead immigrant mother of an assimilated Jewish woman returns as a dybbuk; despite the daughter's attempt to exorcise her mother's dybbuk, she is influenced by her and returns to her Jewish identity. A recent film of interest is the Polish/Israeli *Demon* (2016) which updates the figure of the dybbuk and returns it to Poland.

28. It is possible to imagine the benevolent orders of nuns in Radcliffe as early precursors of these female utopias.

29. Or, to be more precise, those Jewish writers who engage with the cultural contexts of their own tradition. The pool of such writers continues to grow, very probably in response to the possibilities offered by the multicultural paradigm.

30. Judith Halberstam discussed the iconographic convergence of the Gothic and the imagery of Nazism in *Skin Shows*.

31. Possibly Budick's best evidence for this

argument is her invocation of the dedication of Morrison's novel: "60 Million and more." Budick argues, that this number evokes and attempts to outdo, the 6 million of the Holocaust.

32. In her essay "Maternal Narratives" in the collection *Reading Black/Reading Feminist*, edited by Henry Louis Gates, Marianne Hirsch articulates the feminist aspect of *Beloved*, arguing that Morrison's novel restores the figure of the mother as an inherently valuable subject. As Helene Moglen suggests in her essay, "Redeeming History," Morrison thus counters the cultural tendency to abject the mother that is noted by Julia Kristeva in *Powers of Horror*, and that appears as a recurring trope in the Gothic text.

Works Cited

Adler, Rachel. "The Virgin in the Brothel and Other Anomalies: Character and Context in the Legend of Beruriah." *Tikkun* 3 (1988): 28–32, 102–105.

Albert, Rebecca. *Like Bread on the Seder Plate: Jewish Lesbians and the Transformation of Tradition*. New York: Columbia University Press, 1997.

Alcott, Louisa May. "The Abbot's Ghost." *Louisa May Alcott Unmasked: Collected Thrillers*. Ed. Madeleine Stern. Boston: Northeastern University Press, 1995. 539–582.

_____. "Behind the Mask." *Louisa May Alcott Unmasked: Collected Thrillers*. Ed. Madeleine Stern. Boston: Northeastern University Press, 1995. 361–429.

_____. *A Long Fatal Love Chase*. New York: Dell, 1995.

_____. "A Nurse's Story." *Louisa May Alcott Unmasked: Collected Thrillers*. Ed. Madeleine Stern. Boston: Northeastern University Press, 1995.

Alexie, Sherman. *Indian Killer*. New York: Grove Press, 2008.

Anderson, Sherwood. "Hands." *Winesburg, Ohio*. New York: Penguin, 1987.

Andrews, William. "Hannah Crafts's Sense of an Ending." *In Search of Hannah Crafts*. Ed. Henry Louis Gates, Jr., and Hollis Robbins. New York: Perseus, 2004.

Andrews, William L., ed. Introduction *Classic American Autobiographies*. New York: Signet (Penguin), 2003.

Anolik, Ruth Bienstock. "Invasion and Contagion: The Spectacle of the Diseased Indian in Poe's 'The Mask of the Red Death.'" *Demons of the Body and Mind*. Jefferson, NC: McFarland, 2010.

_____. "The Missing Mother: The Meanings of Maternal Absence in the Gothic Mode." *Modern Language Studies* 33, 1/2 (Spring–Autumn 2003): 24–43.

_____. *Property and Power in English Gothic Literature*. Jefferson, NC: McFarland, 2016.

Ansky, S. *A Dybbuk and Other Tales of the Supernatural*. Adapt. Tony Kushner. Trans. Joachim Neugroschel. New York: Theatre Communications Group, 1998.

_____. *The Dybbuk and Other Writings*. Trans. Golda Werman. New York: Schocken, 1992.

Armstrong, Nancy. *Desire and Domestic Fiction: A Political History of the Novel*. New York: Oxford University Press, 1987.

_____. *Fiction in the Age of Photography: The Legacy of British Realism*. Cambridge: Harvard University Press, 1999.

Armstrong, Nancy, and Leonard Tennenhouse. *The Imaginary Puritan: Literature, Intellectual Labor, and the Origins of Personal Life*. Berkeley: University of California Press, 1992

Askeland, Lori. "Remodeling the Model Home in *Uncle Tom's Cabin* and *Beloved*." *American Literature* 64.4 (December 1992).

Atwood, Margaret. *The Handmaid's Tale*. New York: Anchor, 1985.

Austen, Jane. *Northanger Abbey*. London: Penguin, 1995.

Baldick, Chris. Introduction. *Melmoth the Wanderer*. By Charles Maturin. New York: Oxford University Press, 1989. vii-xix.

Ballinger, Gill, Tim Lustig, and Dale Townshend. "Missing Intertexts: Hannah Crafts's *The Bondswoman's Narrative* and African American Literary History." *Journal of American Studies* 39.2 (2005): 207–237.

Bergland, Renée L. "Diseased Minds, Public Minds: Native American Ghosts in Early National Literature." *The Gothic Other*.

Eds. Ruth Bienstock Anolik and Douglas L. Howard. Jefferson, NC: NC: McFarland, 2003.

———. *The National Uncanny: Indian Ghosts and American Subjects*. Hanover: University Press of New England, 2000.

Berlin, Ira. "Time, Space, and the Evolution of Afro-American Society on British Mainland North America." *The American Historical Review* 85.1 (February 1980): 44–78.

Bernier, Celeste-Marie, and Judie Newman. "*The Bondwoman's* Narrative: Text, Paratext, Intertext and Hypertext." *Journal of American Studies* 39.2 (2005): 147–165.

Blackstone, William. *Commentaries on the Laws of England*. 5 vols. Philadelphia: Rees Welsh, 1897.

Bloch, Chayim. *Golem: Legends of the Ghetto of Prague*. Whitefish, MT: Kessinger, 1997.

Bloom, Harold. *The Anxiety of Influence*. New York: Oxford University Press, 1975.

———. *A Map of Misreading*. New York: Oxford University Press, 1975.

———. *The Western Canon: The Books and School of the Ages*. New York: Harcourt Brace, 1994.

Bodichon, Barbara Leigh Smith. "A Brief Summary, in Plain Language, of the Most Important Laws Concerning Women: Together with a Few Observations Thereon." 1854. *Mistress of the House: Women of Property in the Victorian Novel*. By Tim Dolin. Aldershot: Ashgate, 1997.

Bodziock, Joseph. "The Cage of Obscene Birds: The Myth of the Southern Garden in Frederick Douglass's *My Bondage* and *My Freedom*." *The Gothic Other: Racial and Social Constructions in the Literary Imagination*. Eds. Ruth Bienstock Anolik and Douglas Howard. Jefferson, NC: McFarland, 2004.

Borges, Jorge Luis. "Kafka and His Precursors." *Labyrinths: Selected Stories and Other Writings*. New York: New Directions, 1964.

Brogan, Kathleen. "American Stories of Cultural Haunting: Tales of Heirs and Ethnographers." *College English* 57 (1995): 149–165.

———. *Cultural Haunting: Ghosts and Ethnicity in Recent American Literature*. Charlottesville: University Press of Virginia, 1998.

Brontë, Anne. *The Tenant of Wildfell Hall*. New York: Penguin, 1979.

Brontë, Charlotte. *Jane Eyre*. Ed. Q.D. Leavis. New York: Penguin, 1985.

———. *Jane Eyre*. New York: Norton, 1987.

Brontë, Emily. *Wuthering Heights*. Norton Critical Edition. Eds. William M. Sale and Richard J. Dunn. New York: Norton, 1990.

Brown, Charles Brockden. *Edgar Huntly*. New York: Penguin, 1988.

———. *Wieland*. Oxford: Oxford University Press, 1994.

Brown, Gillian. "Hawthorne, Inheritance, and Women's Property." *Studies in the Novel* 23 (1991): 107–118.

Budick, Emily Miller. "Some Thoughts on the Mutual Displacements/Appropriations/Accomodations of Culture in Several Fictions by Toni Morrison, Cynthia Ozick, and Grace Paley." *Prospects* 20 (1995): 387–404.

Buell, Lawrence. "Bondwoman Unbound: Hannah Crafts's Art and Nineteenth-Century U.S. Literary Practice." *In Search of Hannah Crafts*. Eds. Henry Louis Gates, Jr., and Hollis Robbins. New York: Perseus, 2004.

Burke, Edmund. *A Philosophical Enquiry into the Origin of Our Ideas of the Sublime and the Beautiful*. New York: Oxford University Press, 1990.

Butler, Jon. *Becoming America: The Revolution Before 1776*. Cambridge: Harvard University Press, 2000.

Caminero-Santangelo, Marta. *The Madwoman Can't Speak: Or Why Insanity Is Not Subversive*. Ithaca: Cornell University Press, 1998.

Castronovo, Russ. "The Art of Ghost-Writing." *In Search of Hannah Crafts*. New York: Perseus, 2004.

Chayefsky, Paddy. *The Tenth Man*. New York: Random House, 1961.

Chesler, Phyllis. *Women and Madness*. Garden City, NY: Doubleday, 1972.

Chesnutt, Charles. "Po Sandy." *Conjure Woman and Other Conjure Tales*. Durham: Duke University Press, 1993.

Christian, Barbara. "Gloria Naylor's Geography: Community, Class and Patriarchy in *The Women of Brewster Place* and *Linden Hills*." *Reading Black, Reading Feminist: A Critical Anthology*. Ed. Henry Louis Gates, Jr. New York: Penguin, 1990. 348–373.

Christophersen, Bill. *The Apparition in the Glass: Charles Brockden Brown's American Gothic.* Athens: University of Georgia Press, 1993.

Cixous, Hélène. "The Laugh of the Medusa." *Signs* 11 (1976): 875–893.

Cohen, Sarah Blacher. *Cynthia Ozick's Comic Art: From Levity to Liturgy.* Bloomington: Indiana University Press, 1994.

Corelli, Marie. *The Sorrows of Satan.* New York: Oxford University Press, 1996.

Crafts, Hannah. *The Bondswoman's Narrative.* Ed. Henry Louis Gates, Jr., and Hollis Robbins. New York: Warner Books, 2002.

Cramer, Kathryn. "Possession and 'The Jolly Corner.'" *The New York Review of Science Fiction* (January 1994): 19–22.

Dacre, Charlotte. *Zofloya, or the Moor.* New York: Oxford University Press, 1997.

DeLamotte, Eugenia C. *The Perils of the Night: A Feminist Study of Nineteenth-Century Gothic.* New York: Oxford University Press, 1990.

Deón, Natasha. *Grace.* Berkeley: Counterpoint, 2016.

Dickens, Charles. *Bleak House.* New York: Penguin, 1985.

Dickenson, Donna. *Property, Women and Politics: Subjects or Objects?* New Brunswick: Rutgers University Press, 1997.

Didron, Adolphe Napoléon. *The History of Art in the Middle Ages.* Trans. Margaret Stokes. 2 vols. London: George Bell, 1886.

Dolin, Tim. *Mistress of the House: Women of Property in the Victorian Novel.* Aldershot: Ashgate, 1997.

Douglass, Frederick. *Narrative of the Life of Frederick Douglass, an American Slave.* New York: Dover, 1995.

Edgeworth, Maria. *Castle Rackrent.* New York: Oxford University Press, 1964.

Edmundson, Mark. *Nightmare on Main Street: Angels, Sadomasochism, and the Culture of the Gothic.* Cambridge: Harvard University Press, 1997.

Elbert, Monica, and Bridget M. Marshall. *Transnational Gothic: Literary and Social Exchanges in the Long Nineteenth Century.* Burlington, VT: Ashgate, 2013.

Ellis, R. J. "'So amiable and good': Hannah Crafts and *The Bondswoman's Narrative*," its Lineages." *Mississippi Quarterly* 62, 1–2 (Winter 2009): 137–162.

Engel, Leonard. "Obsession, Madness and Enclosure in Poe's 'Ligeia' and 'Morella.'" *College Literature* 9 (1982): 140–145.

———. "The Role of the Enclosure in the English and American Gothic Romance." *Essays in Arts and Sciences* 11 (September 1982): 59–68.

Erdrich, Louise. "The Shawl." *New Yorker*, March 5 2001.

———. *Tracks.* New York: Harper & Row, 1989.

Erickson, Amy Louise. *Women and Property in Early Modern England.* New York: Routledge, 1993.

Eyries, J.B.B. *Fantasmagoriana ou Recueil: Histoires, D'Apparitions de Spectres, Revenans, Fantômes, etc.* 2 vols. Paris: Schoell, 1812.

Faulkner, William. *Absalom, Absalom!* New York: Vintage, 1990.

Felman, Shoshana. "Turning the Screw of Interpretation." *Literature and Psychoanalysis: The Question of Reading Otherwise* 55–56 (1977): 94–207.

Fetterley, Judith. Introduction. *Provisions: A Reader from Nineteenth Century American Women.* Ed. Fetterley. Bloomington: Indiana University Press, 1985.

———. "'Not in the Least American': Nineteenth-Century Regionalism." *College English* 56 (1994): 877–894.

———. *The Resisting Reader.* Bloomington: Indiana University Press, 1978.

Fiedler, Leslie A. *The Return of the Vanishing American.* New York: Stein and Day, 1968.

Finkelstein, Norman. *The Ritual of New Creation: Jewish Tradition and Contemporary Literature.* Albany: State University of New York Press, 1992.

Fitzgerald, F. Scott. "The Diamond as Big as the Ritz." *The Short Stories of F. Scott Fitzgerald.* New York: Scribner's, 1995. 182–216.

Fleischner, Jennifer. "Hawthorne and the Politics of Slavery." *Studies in the Novel* 23 (1991): 96–106.

Florescu, Radu. *In Search of Frankenstein.* Boston: New York Graphic Society, 1975.

Foucault, Michel. *The Archaeology of Knowledge.* Trans. A.M. Sheridan Smith. New York: Pantheon, 1972.

———. *Discipline and Punish: The Birth of the Prison.* Trans. Alan Sheridan. New York: Vintage, 1979.

———. *The Order of Things: An Archaeology*

of the Human Sciences. New York: Vintage, 1973.

Franklin, Benjamin. *The Autobiography of Benjamin Franklin*. New York: Signet, 210.

Franklin, Ruth *Shirley Jackson: A Rather Haunted Life*. New York: Liveright, 2016.

Freud, Sigmund. "The Uncanny." First published in *Imago*, Bd. V. 1919. Reprinted in Sammlung, Fünfte Folge. Translated by Alix Strachey.

_____. "The 'Uncanny.'" *Writings on Art and Literature*. Stanford: Stanford University Press, 1997. 193–233.

Fry, Gladys-Marie. *Night Riders in Black Folk History*. Knoxville: University of Tennessee Press, 1975.

Fussell, Paul. "*Wieland*: A Literary and Historical Reading." *Early American Literature* 18 (1983): 171–186.

Galford, Ellen. *The Dyke and the Dybbuk*. Seattle: Seal Press, 1993.

Gates, Henry Louis, Jr., and Hollis Robbins, eds. *In Search of Hannah Crafts*. New York: Perseus, 2004.

Gates, Henry Louis Gates, Jr. *The Signifying Monkey: A Theory of African-American Literary Criticism*. New York: Oxford University Press, 1988.

Gilbert, Sandra M., and Susan Gubar. *The Madwoman in the Attic: The Woman Writer and the Nineteenth-Century Literary Imagination*. New Haven: Yale University Press, 1979.

Gilman, Charlotte Perkins. "The Giant Wistaria." *Frontier Gothic: Terror and Wonder at the Frontier in American Literature*. Ed. David Mogen, Scott P. Sanders and JoAnne Karpinski. Rutherford: Fairleigh Dickinson University Press, 1993. 165–173.

_____. "The Yellow Wallpaper." *Herland and Selected Stories*. New York: Signet, 1992. 165–180.

Ginsberg, Lesley. "Slavery and the Gothic Horror of Poe's 'The Black Cat.'" *American Gothic: New Interventions in a National Narrative*. Eds. Robert K. Martin and Eric Savoy. Iowa City: University of Iowa Press, 1998. 99–128.

Goddu, Teresa. *Gothic America: Narrative, History and Nation*. New York: Columbia University Press, 1997.

Golden, Catherine. "'Light of the Home,' Light of the World: The Presentation of Motherhood in Gilman's Short Fiction." *Modern Language Studies* 26 (Spring/Summer 1996): 136–147.

Goldsmith, Arnold. *The Golem Remembered, 1909–1980: Variations of a Jewish Legend*. Detroit: Wayne State University Press, 1981.

Gomez, Jewelle. "Naylor's Inferno." *Women's Review of Books* 2.2 (August 1985): 7–8.

Goodman, Allegra. "Sarah." *The Family Markowitz*. New York: Farrar, Straus and Giroux, 1996.

Grabo, Norman S, ed. Introduction. *Edgar Huntly: Or, Memoirs of a Sleep Walker*. By Charles Brockden Brown. New York: Penguin, 1988.

Granqvist, Raoul. *Imitation as Resistance: Appropriations of English Literature in Nineteenth-Century America*. Madison: Fairleigh Dickinson University Press, 1995.

Grimm, Jacob. "Entstehung der Verlagspoesie." *Zeitung für Einsiedler* 7 (1808): 56. *Kleinere Schriften*. Vol. 4. Berlin, 1869. 22.

Grossberg, Michael. *Governing the Hearth: Law and Family in Nineteenth-Century America*. Chapel Hill: University of North Carolina Press, 1985.

Halberstam, Judith. *Skin Shows: Gothic Horror and the Technology of Monsters*. Durham: Duke University Press, 1995.

Halttunen, Karen. "Gothic Imagination and Social Reform: The Haunted House of Lyman Beecher, Henry Ward Beecher and Harriet Beecher Stowe." *New Essays on Uncle Tom's Cabin*. Cambridge: Cambridge University Press, 1986. 107–134.

Hamill, Pete. *Snow in August*. New York: Warner, 1997.

Hartman, James D. *Providence Tales and the Birth of American Literature*. Baltimore: The Johns Hopkins University Press, 1999.

Hawthorne, Nathaniel. *The House of the Seven Gables*. New York: Penguin, 1986.

_____. *The Marble Faun*. New York: New American Library, 1987.

Hedges, William L., ed. Introduction. *The Legend of Sleepy Hollow and Other Stories [The Sketch Book of Geoffrey Crayon, Gent.]*. By Washington Irving. New York: Penguin, 1988.

Higonnet, Patrice. *Attendant Cruelties: Nation and Nationalism in American History* New York: Other Press, 2007.

Hinds, Elizabeth Jane Wall. "Charles Brockden Brown's Revenge Tragedy: *Edgar Huntly* and the Uses of Property." *Early American Literature* 30 (1995): 51–70.

Hirsch, Marianne "Maternal Narratives." *Reading Black/Reading Feminist.* Ed. Henry Louis Gates, Jr. New York: Plume, 1990.

———. "Maternity and Rememory: Toni Morrison's *Beloved.*" *Representations of Motherhood.* Eds. Donna Bassin, Margaret Honey and Meryle Mahrer Kaplan. New Haven: Yale University Press, 1994. 92–110.

Horkheimer, Max, and Theodor W. Adorno. "The Theory of Ghosts." *Dialectic of Enlightenment.* Trans. Edmund Jephcott. Stanford: Stanford University Press, 2002. 178–179.

Huet, Marie Hélène. *Monstrous Imagination.* Cambridge: Harvard University Press, 1993.

Idel, Moshe. *Golem: Jewish Magical and Mystical Traditions on the Artificial Anthropod.* Albany: State University of New York Press, 1990.

Irving, Washington. *The Legend of Sleepy Hollow and Other Stories [The Sketch Book of Geoffrey Crayon, Gent.].* New York: Penguin, 1988.

———. "Traits of Indian Character." *The Legend of Sleepy Hollow and Other Stories [The Sketch Book of Geoffrey Crayon, Gent.].* New York: Penguin, 1988.

Jackson, Shirley. *The Haunting of Hill House.* New York: Penguin, 1984.

———. *We Have Always Lived in the Castle.* New York: Penguin, 1962.

Jacobs, Harriet. *Incidents in the Life of a Slave Girl.* New York: Dover, 2001.

Jadwin, Lisa. "'Caricatured, not faithfully rendered': *Bleak House* as a Revision of *Jane Eyre.*" *Modern Language Studies* 26, 2–3.

James, Henry. Preface. *Portrait of a Lady.* New York: Bantam, 1987. v-xviii.

———. Preface. *The Tragic Muse. The Art of the Novel: Critical Prefaces.* New York: Scribner's, 1946. 79–97.

———. "The Turn of the Screw." *American Gothic Literature.* Ed. Charles L. Crowe. Malden, MA: Blackwood, 1999. 276–338.

Jennings, La Vinia Delois. "*A Mercy*: Toni Morrison Plots the Formation of Racial Slavery in Seventeenth-Century America." *Callaloo* 32.2 (2009): 645–649.

Jillson, Cal. *Pursuing the American Dream: Opportunity and Exclusion over Four Centuries.* Lawrence: University of Kansas Press, 2004.

John, Richard R. "Robber Barons Redux: Antimonopoly Reconsidered." *Enterprise and Society* 13 (March 2012): 1–38.

Johnson, Barbara. "My Monster/My Self." *Diacritics* 12 (1982): 2–10.

Katz, Judith. *Running Fiercely Toward a High Thin Sound.* Ithaca: Firebrand Books, 1992.

Keller, Delores. "Toni Morrison's Sermon on Manhood: God in the Hands of Nine Angry Sinners." *The Midwest Quarterly* 51.1 (Autumn 2009): 45–56.

Kerber, Linda K. *No Constitutional Right to Be Ladies: Women and the Obligations of Citizenship.* New York: Hill and Wang, 1998.

Ketterer, David. *Frankenstein's Creation: The Book, the Monster, and the Human Reality.* Victoria, British Columbia: University of Victoria Press, 1979.

Kiely, Robert. *The Romantic Novel in England.* Cambridge: Harvard University Press, 1972.

King, L. S. "Anatomy." *The Penguin Dictionary of Eighteenth-Century History.* Eds. Jeremy Black and Roy Porter. London: Penguin, 1996.

Kolodny, Annette. *The Lay of the Land: Metaphor as Experience and History in American Life and Letters.* Chapel Hill: University of North Carolina, 1975.

Kopec, Andrew. "Irving, Ruin, and Risk." *Early American Literature* 48.3: 709–735.

Krausse, Sydney J. "Penn's Elm and *Edgar Huntly*: Dark 'Instruction to the Heart.'" *American Literature* 66.3 (September 1994): 463–485.

Kristeva, Julia. *Powers of Horror: An Essay on Abjection.* Trans. Leon S. Roudiez. New York: Columbia University Press, 1982.

Krupat, Arnold. "Review: Red Matters." *College English* 63 (May): 655–661.

———. *The Voice in the Margin: Native American Literature and the Canon.* Berkeley: University of California Press, 1989.

Langley, Winston E., and Vivian C. Fox, eds. *Women's Rights in the United States: A Documentary History.* Westport: Praeger, 1994.

Lauter, Paul. *Canons and Contexts.* New York: Oxford University Press, 1991.

Lawrence, D. H. *Studies in Classic American Literature.* Viking Compass Edition. New York: Viking Press, 1964.

Le Bon, Gustave. *The Crowd: A Study of the Popular Mind*. Dunwoody: Norman S. Berg, 1968.

Lee, Debbie. *Slavery and the Romantic Imagination*. Philadelphia: University of Pennsylvania Press, 2002.

Lefebvre, Henri. *The Production of Space*. Trans. Donald Nicholson-Smith. Oxford: Blackwell, 1974.

Levine, Robert S. "Trappe(d): Race and Genealogical Haunting in *The Bondswoman's Narrative*." *In Search of Hannah Crafts*. Eds. Henry Louis Gates, Jr., and Hollis Robbins. New York: Perseus, 2004.

Lewis, Matthew. *Journal of a West India Proprietor, 1815-17*. Boston: Houghton Mifflin, 1929.

———. *The Monk*. Oxford: Oxford University Press, 1995.

Lloyd, Tom. *Crises of Realism: Representing Experience in the British Novel, 1816-1910*. Lewisburg: Bucknell University Press, 1997.

Locke, John. "Of Property." *Second Treatise: An Essay Concerning the True End of Civil Government*. 1689. *On Moral Business: Classical and Contemporary Resources for Ethics in Economic Life*. Eds. Max L. Stackhouse et al. Grand Rapids: Eerdmans, 1995. 203-207.

Maddox, Lucy. *Removals: Nineteenth Century American Literature and the Politics of Indian Affairs*. New York: Oxford University Press, 1991.

Malchow, H.L. *Gothic Images of Race in Nineteenth-Century Britain*. Stanford: Stanford University Press, 1996.

Manning, Susan, ed. Introduction. *The Sketch-Book of Geoffrey Crayon, Gent*. Oxford: Oxford University Press, 1996.

Marland, Hilary. "Obstetrics." *The Penguin Dictionary of Eighteenth-Century History*. Eds. Jeremy Black and Roy Porter. London: Penguin, 1996.

Marshall, Bridget M. *The Transatlantic Gothic Novel and the Law, 1790-1860*. Burlington, VT: Ashgate, 2011.

Mason, Wyatt. "The Color Money." *The New York Review of Books*, March 12, 2009. 37.

Massé, Michelle. *In the Name of Love: Women, Masochism and the Gothic*. Ithaca: Cornell University Press, 1992.

Maturin, Charles. *Melmoth the Wanderer*. New York: Oxford University Press, 1968.

Mellor, Anne K. "On Feminist Utopias." *Women's Studies* 9 (1982): 241-262.

Melville, Herman. "Hawthorne and His Mosses." *Heath Anthology of American Literature*. 2nd ed. Eds. Paul Lauter et al. Vol. 1. Lexington, MA: Heath, 1994. 2613-2625.

Michaels, Walter Benn. Introduction. *The Gold Standard and the Logic of Naturalism: American Literature at the Turn of the Century*. Berkeley: University of California Press, 1987. 3-28.

———. "Romance and Real Estate." *The Gold Standard and the Logic of Naturalism: American Literature at the Turn of the Century*. Berkeley: University of California Press, 1987. 85-112.

Miller, Cheryl. "Mine, Mine, Mine." *Commentary* 127.3 (March 2009): 62-64.

Minkin, Jacob S. "Golem." *The Universal Jewish Encyclopedia*. Ed. Isaac Landman. 10 vols. New York: The Universal Jewish Encyclopedia, 1941.

Moers, Ellen. *Literary Women: The Great Writers*. New York: Doubleday, 1976

Mogen, David, Scott P. Sanders, and JoAnne Karpinski, eds. Introduction. *Frontier Gothic: Terror and Wonder at the Frontier in American Literature*. Rutherford: Fairleigh Dickinson University Press, 1993.

Moglen, Helene. "Redeeming History: Toni Morrison's 'Beloved.'" *Cultural Critique* 24 (1993): 17-40.

Moreland, Richard C. "Faulkner and Modernism." *The Cambridge Companion to William Faulkner*. Ed. Philip M. Weinstein. New York: Cambridge University Press, 1995. 17-30.

Morrison, Toni. *Beloved*. New York: New American Library, 1988.

———. *A Mercy*. New York: Knopf, 2009.

———. "Romancing the Shadow." *Playing in the Dark: Whiteness and the Literary Imagination*. New York: Vintage, 1993. 31-59.

Mowl, Tim. *Horace Walpole: The Great Outsider*. London: Murray, 1996.

Naylor, Gloria. *Linden Hills*. New York: Penguin, 1986.

———. *Mama Day*. New York: Vintage, 1989.

———. *The Women of Brewster Place*. New York: Penguin, 1983.

Neary, Lynn. "Toni Morrison Discusses *A Mercy* with Lynn Neary." National Public Radio Book Tour. October 27, 2008. Quoted in La Vinia Delois Jennings. "A

Mercy: Toni Morrison Plots the Formation of Racial Slavery in Seventeenth-Century America." *Callaloo* 32.2 (2009): 645–703.

Newton, Adam Zachary. *Facing Black and Jew: Literature as Public Space in Twentieth-Century America*. Cambridge: Cambridge University Press, 1999.

Niditch, Susan. "The Cosmic Adam." *Journal of Jewish Studies* 34 (1983): 137–46.

North, Michael. "Authorship and Authography." *PMLA* 116 (2001): 1377–1385.

Ozick, Cynthia. "Literature and the Politics of Sex: A Dissent." *Art and Ardor: Essays*. New York: Dutton, 1984. 284–290.

———. "Notes Toward Finding the Right Question." *Lilith* 6 (1979): 19–29.

———. "On Living in the Gentile World." *Modern Jewish Thought*. Ed. Nahum N. Glazer. New York: Schocken, 1977. 167–74.

———. "Previsions of the Demise of the Dancing Dog." *Art and Ardor: Essays*. New York: Dutton, 1984. 263–284.

———. *The Puttermesser Papers*. New York: Knopf, 1997.

———. *The Shawl*. New York: Vintage, 1990.

Piercy, Marge. *He, She and It*. New York: Fawcett Crest, 1991.

Pinsker, Sanford "No Seats for Jews on the Multicultural Bandwagon." *Forward* (16 March 2001): 12.

Pinsky, Mike. "The Mistaken Mistake: Permutations of the Golem Legend." *Journal of the Fantastic in the Arts* 7 (1996): 215–227.

Pirani, Alix, and Foosiya Miller. *The Absent Mother: Restoring the Goddess to Judaism and Christianity*. New York: HarperCollins, 1991.

Plank, Robert. "The Golem and the Robot." *Literature and Psychology* 15.1 (Winter 1965): 12–28.

Poe, Edgar Allan. "The Black Cat." *The Short Fiction of Edgar Allan Poe*. Eds. Stuart Levine and Susan Levine. Urbana: University of Illinois Press, 1990. 254–259.

———. "The Fall of the House of Usher." *The Short Fiction of Edgar Allan Poe*. Eds. Stuart Levine and Susan Levine. Urbana: University of Illinois Press, 1990. 88–98.

———. "The Masque of the Red Death." *The Short Fiction of Edgar Allan Poe*. Eds. Stuart Levine and Susan Levine. Urbana: University of Illinois Press, 1990.

———. "William Wilson." *The Short Fiction of Edgar Allan Poe*. Eds. Stuart Levine and Susan Levine. Urbana: University of Illinois Press, 1990. 271–283.

Pointer, Richard. "From Imitating Language to a Language of Imitation: Puritan-Indian Discourse in Early New England." *Puritanism and Its Discontents*. Eds. Laura Lunger Knoppers. Newark: University of Delaware Press, 2003.

Post, Charles. "Agrarian Class Structure and Economic Development in Colonial British North America: The Place of the American Revolution in the Origins of US Capitalism." *Journal of Agrarian Change* 9.4 (October 2009): 453–483.

Radcliffe, Ann. *The Italian*. New York: Oxford University Press, 1968.

———. *The Mysteries of Udolpho*. New York: Dutton, 1973.

———. *A Sicilian Romance*. New York: Oxford University Press, 1993.

Ranke, Kurt, ed. Foreword. *Folktales of Germany*. Chicago: University of Chicago Press, 1966.

Reséndez, Andrés *The Other Slavery*. Boston: Houghton Mifflin Harcourt, 2016.

Rich, Adrienne. "The Primacy of the Mother." *Of Woman Born: Motherhood as Experience and Institution*. New York: Norton, 1986. 84–109.

———. "The Temptations of a Motherless Woman." 1973. *On Lies, Secrets, and Silence: Selected Prose 1966-1978*. New York: Norton, 1979. 89–106.

Ringe, Donald A. *American Gothic: Imagination and Reason in Nineteenth Century Fiction*. Lexington: University of Kentucky Press, 1982.

Robbins, Hollis. "Blackening *Bleak House*: Hannah Craft's The Bondswoman's Narrative." *In Search of Hannah Crafts*. Eds. Henry Louis Gates, Jr., and Hollis Robbins. New York: Perseus, 2004.

Roberts, Siân Silyn. "A Transnational Perspective on American Gothic Criticism." *Transnational Gothic: Literary and Social Exchanges in the Long Nineteenth Century*. Eds. Monica Elbert and Bridget M. Marshall. Burlington, VT: Ashgate, 2013.

Rohrbach, Augusta. "'A Silent Unobtrusive Way.'" *In Search of Hannah Crafts*. Eds. Henry Louis Gates, Jr., and Hollis Robbins. New York, Perseus, 2004.

Rowen, Norma. "The Making of Frankenstein's Monster. Post-Golem Pre-Robot." *The State of the Fantastic: Studies in the Theory and Practice of Fantastic Literature and Film: Selected Essays from the Eleventh International Conference on the Fantastic in the Arts*. Ed. Nicholas Ruddick. Westport: Greenwood, 1992. 169–177.

Rowlandson, Mary. *A True History of the Captivity and Restoration of Mrs. Mary Rowlandson*. Classic American Autobiographies. New York: Signet, 2003.

Rudich, Norman. "Faulkner and the Sin of Private Property." *The Minnesota Review* 17 (1981): 55–57.

Sade, Marquis de. "Reflections on the Novel." 1800. *The 120 Days of Sodom and Other Writings*. Eds. and trans. Austryn Wainhouse and Richard Seaver. New York: Grove Weidenfeld, 1996. 97–116.

Sánchez-Eppler, Karen. "Gothic Liberties and Fugitive Novels: *The Bondswoman's Narrative* and the Fiction of Race." *In Search of Hannah Crafts*. Eds. Henry Louis Gates, Jr., and Hollis Robbins. New York: Perseus, 2004.

Schifrin, Daniel R. "A Play for all Seasons." *Hadassah Magazine* 78 (May 1997): 32–35.

Scholem, Gershom. "The Golem of Prague and the Golem of Rehovot." *The Messianic Idea in Judaism and Other Essays on Jewish Spirituality*. New York: Schocken, 1995.

_____. "The Idea of the Golem." *On the Kabbalah and Its Symbolism*. Trans. Ralph Manheim. New York: Schocken, 1965. 158–204.

Segal, Charles M., and David C. Stineback. *Puritans, Indians, and Manifest Destiny*. Foreword Sacvan Bercovitch. New York: Putnam, 1977.

Shelley, Mary W. *Frankenstein*. New York: Dutton, 1973.

Sinche, Byran. "Appendix C: John Hill Wheeler's Library Catalogue." *Hannah Crafts. Bondswoman's. Narrative*. Ed. Henry Louis Gates, Jr. New York: Warner, 2002.

Small, Christopher. *Mary Shelley's Frankenstein: Tracing the Myth*. Pittsburgh: University of Pittsburgh Press, 1973.

Smith-Wright, Geraldine. "In Spite of the Klan: Ghosts in the Fiction of Black Women Writers." *Haunting the House of Fiction: Feminist Perspectives on Ghost Stories by American Women*. Eds. Lynette Carpenter and Wendy K. Kolmar. Knoxville: University of Tennessee Press, 1991.

Stauffer, John. "The Problem of Freedom in *The Bondswoman's Narrative*." *In Search of Hannah Crafts*. Ed. Henry Louis Gates, Jr., and Hollis Robbins. New York: Perseus, 2004.

Stern, David. Introduction. *Rabbinic Fantasies: Imaginative Narratives from Classical Hebrew Literature*. Eds. David Stern and Mark Jay Mirsky. New Haven: Yale University Press, 1998.

Stoddard, Elizabeth Drew. "Lemorne *versus* Huell." *Heath Anthology of American Literature*. 2nd ed. Eds. Paul Lauter et al. Vol. 1. Lexington, MA: Heath, 1994. 2660–2672.

_____. *The Morgesons*. New York: Penguin, 1984.

Stowe, Harriet Beecher. *Uncle Tom's Cabin*. New York: Penguin, 1981.

Teukolsky, Rachel. "Pictures in Bleak Houses; Slavery and the Aesthetics of Transatlantic Reform." *ELH* 76 (2009): 491–522.

Thomas, Ronald R. "Double Exposures: Arresting Images in *Bleak House* and *The House of the Seven Gables*." *NOVEL: A Forum on Fiction* 31.1 (1997): 87–113.

Todd, Dennis. *Imagining Monsters: Miscegenations of the Self in Eighteenth-Century England*. Chicago: University of Chicago Press, 1995.

Vaughan, Alden T., and Edward W. Clark. *Puritans Among the Indians: Accounts of Captivity and Redemption 1676–1724*. Cambridge: Harvard University Press, 1981.

Verhoeven, W.M. "Gothic Logic: Charles Brocken Brown and the Science of Sensationalism." *EJAC* 20.2: 91–99.

Völker, Klaus, comp. *Künstliche Menschen: Dichtungen und Dokumente über Golems, Homunculi, Androiden unde liebende Statuen*. Munich: Hanser, 1971.

Wald, Patricia. "Hannah Crafts." *In Search of Hannah Crafts*. Eds. Henry Louis Gates, Jr., and Hollis Robbins. New York: Perseus, 2004.

Walpole, Horace. *The Castle of Otranto*. New York: Oxford University Press, 1964.

Ward, John C. "The Virtues of the Mothers: Powerful Women in *Bleak House*." *Dickens Studies Newsletter* 14.2 (June 1, 1983): 37–42.

Watt, James. *Contesting the Gothic: Fiction, Genre and Cultural Conflict, 1764–1832*. Cambridge: Cambridge, 1999.

———. "Time and Family in the Gothic Novel: *The Castle of Otranto.*" *Eighteenth Century Life* 10 (October 1986): 159–170.

Weisbuch, Robert. *Atlantic Double-Cross: American Literature and British Influence in the Age of Emerson.* Chicago: University of Chicago Press, 1989.

Weyler, Karen A. *Intricate Relations: Sexual and Economic Desire in American Fiction: 1789–1814.* Iowa City: University of Iowa Press, 2004.

Wharton, Edith. *The Ghost Stories of Edith Wharton.* New York: Scribner's, 1973.

Whitehead, Colson. *Sag Harbor.* New York: Anchor, 2010.

———. *The Underground Railroad.* New York: Doubleday, 2016.

———. *Zone One.* New York: Anchor, 2012.

Williams, Daniel E. "Writing Under the Influence: An Examination of *Wieland*'s 'Well Authenticated Facts' and the Depiction of Murderous Fathers in Post-Revolutionary Print Culture." *Eighteenth Century Fiction* 15.3–4 (April–July 2003): 643–668.

Wilson, Jean. "Toni Morrison: Re-Visionary Words with Power." *Frye and the Word: Religious Contexts in the Writings of Northrop Frye.* Eds. Jeffery Donaldson and Alan Mendelson. Toronto: University of Toronto Press, 2004.

Wilt, Judith. "The Imperial Mouth: Imperialism, the Gothic and Science Fiction." *Journal of Popular Culture* 14 (1981): 618–628.

Winkler, Gershon. "Frankenstein and the Golem." *The Golem of Prague.* New York: Judaica Press, 1980. 19–20.

Winston, Hannah. "Professor's 10-Year Quest Identifies Novelist Who Fled Slavery" [Interview with Gregg Hecimovich]. *The Chronicle of Higher Education* (September 20, 2013): A22.

Yellin, Jean Fagan. Introduction. *Incidents in the Life of a Slave Girl.* By Harriet A. Jacobs. Cambridge: Harvard University Press, 1987.

Zinn, Howard. *A People's History of the United States.* New York: Harper Perennial, 1980.

Zitkala-Ša (Gertrude Bonnin). "Four Autobiographical Narratives (1900–1902)." *Classic American Autobiographies.* New York: Signet, 2014.

Index

African American writers 14; see also Chesnutt, Charles; Crafts, Hannah; Douglass, Frederick; Morrison, Toni; Naylor, Gloria; Whitehead, Colson
African Americans see African American writers; race; slavery
Alcott, Louisa May: "A Nurse's Story" 25–27; "Perilous Play" 129–133
Alexie, Sherman: Indian Killer 69–74
American identity 57, 64–65, 71–72, 78, 81–82, 106; see also Twain, Mark, Pudd'nhead Wilson
the American writer, struggle for identity and authority 13, 43–44, 84–85, 97, 119–120, 125–127, 178, 272; see also Crafts, Hannah; Irving, Washington; women writers and writing
aristocrats and aristocracy see patriarchs and patriarchy
Armstrong, Nancy: The Imaginary Puritan 1
Austen, Jane: Northanger Abbey 135, 281n3
authorial anxiety see narrative control

Bible, influence on Gothic literature 181, 206, 227–233, 239, 268–269, 285n4, 285n7, 285n9, 287n28, 288n5, 290n5, 291n9; Abraham and Isaac 116–117; Hell, the Devil, Satan 27–32, 42, 56–58, 86, 89, 146–148, 166–167, 171–175, 197, 257, 287n25; paradise and paradise lost 167, 173–174, 286n13; "The sins of the fathers shall be visited upon the children" 25, 188, 198, 205–206, 288n10, 289n19; see also female utopias
Bloom, Harold: The Anxiety of Influence 193; A Map of Misreading 284n5; The Western Canon 12–13, 235, 290n3
Brogan, Kathleen: "American Stories of Cultural Haunting" 13; Cultural Haunting 13–14, 281n6
Brontë, Charlotte: Jane Eyre 46, 134, 180–181, 267, 288n3, 288n4, 291n10
burial, premature see immurement
Brown, Charles Brockden 1, 107; Edgar Huntly 3, 12, 56, 60–66, 108–114; transformations of American literature 180; Wieland 5, 114–120, 289n18

castles see houses and castles
Catholics in Gothic literature 9, 90–91
Chesnutt, Charles: "Po' Sandy" 38–40, 271
children, loss and death 22, 28, 30–31, 45, 139, 229–230, 245, 286n18, 289–290n26; see also Erdrich, Louise, "The Shawl"; Morrison, Toni, Beloved; Ozick, Cynthia, The Shawl
claustrophobia of the Gothic 32, 43–44, 54
comedy, Gothic 8, 49, 102, 118–121, 124–127, 163, 240, 256–257
confinement 1, 23, 28, 43, 45, 58, 183; see also claustrophobia of the Gothic; immurement
coverture see law and legal systems
Crafts, Hannah: The Bondswoman's Narrative. 178–220
crowd see mob
curse 193, 195, 197, 217, 257–258

Dickens, Charles: Bleak House 183–184, 192–196, 215–216
disguise see masquerade and disguise
diversity, American 14, 178–270
the double 22, 30, 82, 95–97, 111, 118, 128, 183, 199, 240, 282n5; see also Twain, Mark, Pudd'nhead Wilson
Douglass, Frederick: Narrative of the Life of Frederick Douglass 40–44
the dybbuk 236, 253–259
dynasty see patriarchs and patriarchy; property

enclosure see claustrophobia of the Gothic; confinement; immurement
Erdrich, Louise: "The Shawl" 269–270; Tracks 74–76
ethnic writers see diversity, American

Faulkner, William: Absalom! Absalom! 150–156
Felman, Shoshana: "Turning the Screw of Interpretation" 135–137
female Gothic see women writers and writing
female utopias 257, 260–261, 292n28,
Fiedler, Leslie: Love and Death in the American Novel 10, 12, 281n5, 283n4

303

Fitzgerald, F. Scott: "The Diamond as Big as the Ritz" 145–150
Franklin, Benjamin 106–107
freedom, anxieties of 104–142
French Revolution 5, 48, 80, 117
Freud, Sigmund 67, 135–137; "The Uncanny" 10, 11, 12, 50, 82; *see also* the double

Galford, Ellen: *The Dyke and the Dybbuk* 255, 257–259
Gates, Henry Louis: *In Search of Hannah Crafts see* Crafts, Hannah, *The Bondswoman's Narrative*
ghosts *see* supernatural
Gilman, Charlotte Perkins: "The Yellow Wallpaper" 21–24
Goddu, Teresa: *Gothic America* 6, 14, 85, 209
the golem 236–253, 290–1n5; *see also* Shelley, Mary *Frankenstein*
Gothic tropes 25, 44, 46, 248, 285n11, 290n27; *see also* confinement; immurement; invasion; portrait; supernatural

Hawthorne, Nathaniel: *The House of the Seven Gables* 8, 35, 184–203, 205–209, 212–214, 220, 272–273; *The Marble Faun* 11, 288n12, 288n15; on women writers 20, 281n1; *see also* hunger and voraciousness, American greed
hero-villain *see* Alcott, Louisa May, "A Nurse's Story"; Stoddard, Elizabeth, "Lemorne Versus Huell"
homosociality and homosexuality 30, 209–210, 254–259
houses and castles (of the patriarchy) 22; abandonment 161, 202, 221; burning 28, 37, 48, 52, 61, 153, 167, 172, 287n24, 288n11; destruction 129, 149–150; *see also* Jackson, Shirley, *The Haunting of Hill House*
humor in the Gothic *see* comedy, Gothic
hunger and voraciousness, American greed 8, 35, 49, 53–54, 57, 64, 95–96, 120–121, 147, 150, 158, 175, 196, 206, 273, 275–279, 285n2

immurement 35–37, 39, 64, 150, 284n2
incest *see* Faulkner, William, *Absalom! Absalom!*
Indians *see* Native Americans
inheritance *see* property
insanity and other altered states 3, 22–25, 36, 113, 118, 130–132, 162–163, 197, 265; *see also* scientists and science
intertextual connections and appropriations 54, 178–220; American Gothic 178–270, 287n28; American influence on English literature 1, 192–194; American revisions and transformations of English literature 23–24; Anglo-American 2–4, 11, 193; English influence on American Gothic literature 10, 13, 21, 23–32, 48, 99, 102, 134, 148, 151, 179, 187, 199, 271–273; repressions of English influ-

ence on American literature 11, 12, 14, 63–64, 82; *see also* Austen, Jane, *Northanger Abbey*; Brontë, Charlotte, *Jane Eyre*; Crafts, Hannah, *The Bondwsoman's Narrative*; Dickens, Charles, *Bleak House*; Hawthorne, Nathaniel; James, Henry, *The Turn of the Screw*; Radcliffe, Ann; Walpole, Horace; Wharton, Edith
intoxication and drug use *see* insanity and other altered states
invasion trope in American literature 5, 50, 274; *see also* Brown, Charles Brockden, *Wieland*; Poe, Edgar Allan, "The Masque of the Red Death"
Irving, Washington: "The Legend of Sleepy Hollow" 11, 12, 80, 120–126, 271; "Rip Van Winkle" 80–82; "The Spectre Bridegroom" 126–127; "Traits of Indian Character" 60

Jackson, Shirley: *The Haunting of Hill House* 156–164; *We Have Always Lived in the Castle* 48
Jacobs, Harriet: *Incidents in the Life of a Slave Girl* 44–46, 182, 290n29
James, Henry: *The Turn of the Screw* 133–139
Jewish American writers 234–270; *see also* the dybbuk; the golem
judges *see* lawyers and judges

Katz, Judith: *Running Fiercely Toward a High Thin Sound* 255–257

land and landscape 9, 12, 58, 64, 83–84, 85; *see also* the sea
law and legal systems 3–5, 23, 43, 92; *coverture* 5, 19, 21, 24; English common law 5, 18, 19; primogeniture 28, 31, 33; *see also* marriage; property; slavery
Lawrence, D. H.: *Studies in Classic American Literature* 6–8, 66–69, 73–74, 104–105, 283n4
lawyers and judges *see* Crafts, Harriet, *The Bondswoman's Narrative*; Dickens, Charles, *Bleak House*; Hawthorne, Nathaniel, *The House of the Seven Gables*; Irving, Washington, "The Legend of Sleepy Hollow"; Stoddard, Elizabeth, "Lemorne Versus Huell"
Le Bon, Gustave: *The Crowd see* mob
Lewis, Matthew Lewis: *The Monk* 1, 48

madness *see* insanity and other altered states
Manifest Destiny 34
marriage 21–26, 256; demystification of 27; dynastic *see* Faulkner, William *Absalom! Absalom!*; Naylor, Gloria *Linden Hills*; *see also* patriarchs and patriarchy; wife
masculinity *see* patriarchs and patriarchy
masquerade and disguise: transgender and transrace 96–97, 219–220; *see also* Poe, Edgar Allan, "Masque of the Red Death"
matriarchy 48; *see also* Naylor, Gloria, *Mama Day*

Index

Melville, Herman: *Benito Cereno* 89–94; "Hawthorne and His Mosses" 20
men, young: in the patriarchy 7, 8, 9, 29–30; without patriarchs 104–133
Michaels, Walter Benn: "Romance and Real Estate" 88, 284*n*4, 285*n*3, 289*n*16
mob 46–54, 60, 68–70, 275–279
monsters *see* supernatural
Morrison, Toni: *Beloved* 46–47, 262–270, 286*n*13, 288*n*5; *A Mercy* 164–175, 286*n*13; "Romancing the Shadow" 6, 34–35, 105, 265, 282*n*4
mother: absent and restored 43, 45, 182–184, 187, 197, 213, 250, 259–260, 290*n*28, 293*n*32; power of maternity 246; renunciation of role 216; slave mother (*see* Jacobs, Harriet *Incidents in the Life of a Slave Girl*); *see also* matriarchy
multiculturalism *see* diversity, American
murder, interfamily 148; parricide (*see* Revolution [American]); *see also* Brown, Charles Brockden, *Wieland*; Poe, Edgar Allan, "The Black Cat"

narrative authority and control (and subversion of) 4, 39–40, 135–137, 151, 169, 210–212; *see also* Naylor, Gloria, *Mama Day*
Native American writers *see* Erdrich, Louise; Sherman, Alexie
Native Americans 2–4, 6, 9, 19, 55–76, 84, 167, 175, 200; Indian Removal 9, 57, 59, 80; *see also* Lawrence, D.H.
Naylor, Gloria: *Linden Hills* 27–32; *Mama Day* 231–233

Ozick, Cynthia 236, 246; *The Shawl* 261–270; "Xanthippe and Puttermesser" 238–243

patriarchs and patriarchy 3, 5, 7, 9, 18 21–32, 41, 44–45, 67–69, 139–142, 143–175, 195–203, 212, 221; absent, failed 7–9, 78–142, 152, 157–158, 247, 258–259; American 123–124, 143–175, 191–192, 213–215, 275, 284*n*1; racial darkness 174; *see also* hero-villain; man young, in the patriarchy; robber barons; slaves and slavery
Piercy, Marge 236; *He She and It* 245–253
Poe, Edgar Allan 35–36; "The Black Cat" 36; "The Fall of the House of Usher" 127–129; "The Masque of the Red Death" 67–68
portrait, Gothic trope 184, 189–192, 194, 206–209, 212–213, 288*n*14, 289*n*20, 289*n*21, 289*n*24, 290*n*28
primogeniture *see* law and legal systems
property 3, 9, 19, 38, 44, 61–63, 79–80, 100, 108–109, 114, 139–142, 148, 153, 170, 172, 195–206, 216–219, 223, 281*n*1, 289*n*16; intellectual 111–113; *see also* land and landscape; slavery
Puritan ideology and literature 1, 2, 6, 10, 55–57, 106; *see also* Rowlandson, Mary, *A True History of the Captivity and Restoration of Mrs. Mary Rowlandson*

race and racial anxiety 28–29, 31–32, 49–50, 149, 154–156, 175, 176, 277, 287*n*29, 289*n*25
Radcliffe, Ann 1, 20–21, 27–30, 33, 136.
rape and sexual abuse 41, 43, 44–45, 95, 263, 265
realism of American (women) writers 20–27, 187, 282*n*4; *see also* supernatural, realistic, "explained"
rebirth *see* return from the dead
return from the dead 42, 65–66, 75–76, 126–127, 183, 264, 286*n*17
Revolution (American) 2, 7, 18, 32, 78–81, 114, 118, 138, 202; *see also* freedom, anxieties of
robber barons 143–150, 160; *see also* patriarchs and patriarchy
Rowlandson, Mary: *A True History of the Captivity and Restoration of Mrs. Mary Rowlandson* 2, 56–57

scientists and science 22, 25, 100–101, 130, 157–158, 163, 245, 247–248
the sea 130–132; *see also* Melville, Herman, *Benito Cereno*
servants and subalterns 25–27, 30, 93, 98, 133–142, 205, 217, 285*ch*5*n*9, 288*n*2
Shakespeare, William 225–227
Shelley, Mary: *Frankenstein* 239, 242–245, 248–253, 282*n*7, 291*n*12, 292*n*17, 292*n*19
slave narratives 36, 38, 40–46, 186, 209; *see also* Douglass, Frederick; Jacobs, Harriet
slaves and slavery 2, 25, 21, 34–48, 51–53, 57, 85–101, 147–150, 286*n*20; *see also* Crafts, Hannah, *The Bondswoman's Narrative*; Morrison, Toni, *Beloved, A Mercy*; Naylor, Gloria, *Mama Day*; servants and subalterns; slave narratives; Whitehead, Colson, *Underground Railroad*
Stoddard, Elizabeth: "Lemorne Versus Huell" 24–25
Stowe, Harriet Beecher: *Uncle Tom's Cabin* 86–89, 182, 287*n*26, 289*n*26
subaltern *see* servants and subalterns
supernatural 1–3, 14; ghosts 46, 67, 383*n*9; ghosts as social repression 281*n*6, 291*n*6; realistic, "explained" 20–27, 38, 40, 42, 75–76, 123, 127, 171, 191, 195, 207; repressed ghosts 19, 83–84; zombies 49–54, 275–279; *see also* Freud, Sigmund, "The Uncanny"; Lawrence, D.H.; Poe, Edgar Allan, "The Masque of the Red Death; Sherman, Alexie, *Indian Killer*

Tennenhouse, Leonard: *The Imaginary Puritan* 1
transatlantic connections *see* intertextual connections and appropriations
tree images 122, 185–6, 194
Twain, Mark: *Puddn'head Wilson* 94–103
tyrant *see* patriarchs and patriarchy

vampires 275–277

Walpole, Horace 209–210, 254; *The Castle of Otranto* 28–31, 152–153, 196–203, 288*n*8
Wharton, Edith 284*ch5n*7, 284*ch5n*8; "Mr. Jones" 139–142, 282*n*3
Whitehead, Colson: *Sag Harbor* 49–50; *Underground Railroad* 51–54; *Zone One* 5, 49–51, 53, 275–279
wife: abjection 37, 141, 144–145, 148, 214, 282*n*3, 282*n*6, 290*n*28; death, murder 36, 160, 214; *see also* marriage; matriarchy; mother; women
women 5, 18–32; abjection 162; and magic 38; 231–233; *see also* marriage; mother; rape and sexual abuse; wife
women writers and writing 14, 19–22, 179, 183

zombies *see* supernatural

www.ingramcontent.com/pod-product-compliance
Lightning Source LLC
Chambersburg PA
CBHW051209300426
44116CB00006B/489